Violence in Defeat

In the final year of the Second World War, as bitter defensive fighting moved to German soil, a wave of intra-ethnic violence engulfed the country. Bastiaan Willems offers the first study into the impact and behaviour of the Wehrmacht on its own territory, focusing on the German units fighting in East Prussia and its capital Königsberg. He shows that the Wehrmacht's retreat into Germany, after three years of brutal fighting on the Eastern Front, contributed significantly to the spike of violence which occurred throughout the country immediately prior to defeat. Soldiers arriving with an ingrained barbarised mindset, developed on the Eastern Front, shaped the immediate environment of the area of operations, and of Nazi Germany as a whole. Willems establishes how the norms of the Wehrmacht as a retreating army impacted behavioural patterns on the home front, arguing that its presence increased the propensity to carry out violence in Germany.

Bastiaan Willems is a Research Fellow in Modern European History at University College London.

Cambridge Military Histories

Edited by

JENNIFER D. KEENE, Chapman University

HEW STRACHAN, Professor of International Relations, University of St Andrews and Emeritus Fellow of All Souls College, Oxford

GEOFFREY WAWRO, Professor of Military History, and Director of the Military History Center, University of North Texas

The aim of this series is to publish outstanding works of research on warfare throughout the ages and throughout the world. Books in the series take a broad approach to military history, examining war in all its military, strategic, political and economic aspects. The series complements *Studies in the Social and Cultural History of Modern Warfare* by focusing on the 'hard' military history of armies, tactics, strategy and warfare. Books in the series consist mainly of single author works – academically rigorous and groundbreaking – which are accessible to both academics and the interested general reader.

A full list of titles in the series can be found at:

www.cambridge.org/militaryhistories

Violence in Defeat

The Wehrmacht on German Soil, 1944–1945

Bastiaan Willems

University College London

CAMBRIDGE
UNIVERSITY PRESS

Shaftesbury Road, Cambridge CB2 8EA, United Kingdom

One Liberty Plaza, 20th Floor, New York, NY 10006, USA

477 Williamstown Road, Port Melbourne, VIC 3207, Australia

314–321, 3rd Floor, Plot 3, Splendor Forum, Jasola District Centre, New Delhi – 110025, India

103 Penang Road, #05–06/07, Visioncrest Commercial, Singapore 238467

Cambridge University Press is part of Cambridge University Press & Assessment, a department of the University of Cambridge.

We share the University's mission to contribute to society through the pursuit of education, learning and research at the highest international levels of excellence.

www.cambridge.org
Information on this title: www.cambridge.org/9781108790642

DOI: 10.1017/9781108856270

First published 2021
First paperback edition 2024

A catalogue record for this publication is available from the British Library

ISBN   978-1-108-47972-1   Hardback
ISBN   978-1-108-79064-2   Paperback

Contents

Figures

Maps

Tables

Acknowledgements

This book has been over a decade in the making, and if it wasn't for the help of dozens of encouraging individuals, it would not exist. The work is a remodelled version of my PhD thesis, which, in turn, was born out of my Bachelor's and Master's theses, both of which examined the different aspects of the Red Army's siege of Königsberg. My first thanks should therefore go to my supervisors on these projects, Ad van Kempen at the Fontys University of Applied Science in Tilburg, and Iain Lauchlan and Pertti Ahonen at the University of Edinburgh. It was Pertti who gave me the confidence to continue with this topic and pursue a PhD. At its earliest stage, Valery Galtsov and Viktor Apryshchenko invited me to develop my argument at their universities in Kaliningrad and Rostov respectively, where, despite the location, my argument moved away from the role the Red Army played in the final year of the war. At the halfway mark of my research, Dr Ahonen left for Finland to take up a professorship, and I was fortunate enough for Stephan Malinowski to take over the role as primary supervisor, a development that suited the new direction of the dissertation particularly well. Eventually, in the final year of the PhD, the Soviet element was dropped completely, and Iain stepped down from the project in favour of Tim Buchen. Stephan and Tim have been instrumental in carrying that project to the finish line. Life as a PhD student would not have been possible without the funding of the German Historical Institute, the Erasmus traineeship schemes, the University of Edinburgh School of History, Classics, and Archaeology McMillan Award, and the SPIN Foundation.

The next step was fostered by my two examiners, Jeremy Crang and Sönke Neitzel, who not only offered feedback on the work in front of them but also gave me concrete advice on how to turn a stilted thesis into a readable publication. This process was a very humbling one, as I found I could turn to many pioneers of the field of Second World War studies. Bernhard Gotto, Johannes Hürter, the late Jürgen Zarusky, David Motadel, Peter-Lutz Kalmbach, Jeff Rutherford, Peter Lieb, Andreas Kossert, Adrian Wettstein, David Glantz, Ilya Dementsev, and particularly Ben Shepherd, all took time to provide constructive criticism to a young academic. Being able to hold the fruit of my labour is thanks to Michael Watson and Emily Sharp at Cambridge University Press who patiently guided me through the final editing process.

I also wish to thank the staffs of the Institut für Zeitgeschichte, the Bundesarchiv Berlin-Lichtenfelde, the Bundesarchiv Lastensausgleich in Bayreuth, and the Bundesarchiv Militärarchiv in Freiburg, as well as those of the National Archives in Kew, the Yad Vashem Archives in Jerusalem, and the Archiwum Museum Stutthof in Sztutowo. I have particularly warm feelings towards the staff of the different regional archives: the Gosudartvenniy Arkhiv Kaliningradskoi Oblasti in Kaliningrad, the Ostpreußisches Landesmuseum in Lüneburg, the Kulturzentrum Ostpreußen in Ellingen, and the former Archiv Stadt Königsberg in Duisburg. Lastly, the staffs of the Imperial War Museum, the University of Edinburgh Library, the National Library of Scotland, the National Library of Latvia, the Deutsche Nationalbibliothek in Frankfurt am Main and the Staatsbibliothek in Munich were all incredibly helpful.

Innumerable friends, including Ben Holzhauser, Joe Schuldt, Sergey Nikitin, Joe Curran, Michał Palacz, Christoph Heurich, Victor Cazares Lira, Katherine Rossi, Rick Tazelaar, Max Stocker, Alberto Esu, and Kirsty Bailey – who left us much too soon – helped me along the way, providing moral support and offering academic rigour in their advice. Among these friends, however, I without doubt owe the greatest depth of gratitude to Vince Colthurst, who combined his sincere efforts to further my argument with his humour and hospitality. Along this arduous journey, I was lucky enough to encounter Alison John who, as my partner, has been a constant source of love and support, and whose daily use of words like Wehrmacht and Gauleiter has increased more than she ever anticipated.

Lastly, I would like to thank my family, particularly my parents, Bart and Jenny. Their patience and encouragement have been the bedrock of my own confidence in the project, and allowed me to pursue my passion.

Chronology of Events

1914–1944

1 August 1914	Start of the First World War
26–30 August 1914	Battle of Tannenberg
September 1914	One-third of East Prussia's population flees in anticipation of its invasion by Russian forces
7–22 February 1915	Winter Battle of the Masurian Lakes
August 1916–1918	High Command under Hindenburg and Ludendorff assumes control of the war effort
11 November 1918	German army signs armistice
28 June 1919	Versailles Treaty cuts off East Prussia from the rest of Germany
24 February 1920	Declaration of Party programme of the NSDAP
January 1924	Klaipeda Revolt
3 September 1928	Erich Koch becomes Gauleiter of East Prussia
30 January 1933	*Machtergreifung* (Nazi seizure of power)
16 March 1935	Hitler openly breaks with the military restrictions imposed by the Versailles Treaty
9 November 1938	Königsberg's Neue Synagoge destroyed during the Kristallnacht
1 September 1939	German invasion of Poland
22 June 1941	Operation Barbarossa commences
16 July 1941	Koch becomes *Reichskommissar für die Ukraine*
14 February 1943	Führerbefehl 4 turns scorched earth practices into official military policy
18 February 1943	Goebbels proclaims Total War
8 March 1944	Führer Directive 53 orders the establishment of fortress cities
22 June 1944	Start of Operation Bagration, the Soviet summer offensive
20 July 1944	Plot to kill Hitler in his East Prussian headquarters, the Wolfssschanze
18 October 1944	Formation of the Volkssturm

East Prussian Operations

October 1944	Evacuation of the border regions of East Prussia; one-quarter of province's population displaced
9 October 1944	First Baltic Front reaches the Baltic at Heydekrug, south of Memel
16 October 1944	Third Belorussian Front commences the Gumbinnen Operation
21 October 1944	Nemmersdorf captured by Red Army
23 October 1944	Nemmersdorf recaptured by Wehrmacht
27 October 1944	Start of Nemmersdorf propaganda
12 January 1945	Second Belorussian Front starts operations by breaking out of the Rozan bridgehead on the Narew, north of Warsaw
13 January 1945	Third Belorussian Front starts East Prussian offensive between Ebenrode and Schlossberg
21 January 1945	Koch orders the families of Gauleitung employees to be evacuated by a special train
27 January 1945	Memel abandoned by German troops
27 January 1945	Koch announces the general evacuation of Königsberg
27 January 1945	Lasch appointed as Fortress Commander of Königsberg
30 January 1945	Königsberg encircled
15 February 1945	Reich Justice Minister Thierack announces the establishment of summary courts in areas that were immediately threatened
19 February 1945	Operation Westwind commences, Metgethen recaptured
25 February 1945	Start of Metgethen propaganda
27 February 1945	Large scale evacuation from Königsberg starts
10 March 1945	Evacuation 'postponed until further notice' due to 'technical issues'
13–29 March 1945	Destruction of the Fourth Army in the Heiligenbeil Pocket
6 April 1945	Final storming of Königsberg
9 April 1945	Surrender talks commence
10 April 1945	Surrender signed
13 April 1945	Final offensive towards Pillau commences
27 April 1945	Pillau captured
7 May 1945	Surrender of the German Wehrmacht, remnants of Armee Ostpreußen surrender in Hela

Abbreviations

AKO	Archiv Kulturzentrum Ostpreußen
ARLZ	Auflockerung, Räumung, Lähmung und Zerstörung – Breaking-down, Evacuation, Paralysing, and Destruction
BArch	Bundesarchiv
BDM	Bund Deutscher Mädel – League of German Girls
BDO	Bund Deutscher Offiziere – League of German Officers
GAKO	Gosudarstvennyi Arkhiv Kaliningradskoi Oblasti
Hiwi	Hilfswillige – Auxiliary volunteer
HJ	Hitlerjugend – Hitler Youth
IfZArch	Institut für Zeitgeschichte archive
KPD	Kommunistische Partei Deutschlands – Communist Party of Germany
NKFD	Nationalkomittee Freies Deutschland – National Committee for a Free Germany
NKVD	Narodnyi Komissariat Vnutrennikh Del – People's Commissariat for Internal Affairs
NSDAP	Nationalsozialistische Deutsche Arbeiterpartei – National Socialist German Workers' Party
NSF	Nationalsozialistische Frauenschaft – National Socialist Women's League
NSFO	Nationalsozialistischer Führungsoffizier – National Socialist Leadership Officer
NSV	Nationalsozialistische Volkswohlfahrt – National Socialist People's Welfare
OKH	Oberkommando des Heeres – Supreme High Command of the German Army
OKW	Oberkommando der Wehrmacht – Supreme Command of the Armed Forces
OL	Ostpreußisches Landesmuseum
OT	Organisation Todt
RAF	Royal Air Force

RVK	Reichsverteidigungskommissar – Reich Defence Commissioner
SA	Sturmabteilung
SD	Sicherheitsdienst
SS	Schutzstaffel
TNA	The National Archives
WPrO	Wehrmacht Propaganda Offizier – Wehrmacht propaganda officer

Introduction

Historiography and Purpose of the Study

War and conflict often force men and women to take decisions they had never considered during peacetime. In his 1845 novel *Twenty Years After* – a sequel to *The Three Musketeers* – Alexandre Dumas describes a scene in which one of the book's main antagonists, a man known as Mordaunt, reports to Sir Oliver Cromwell after a battle with the guard regiment of King Charles I, which resulted in the King's capture:

> 'The Colonel of the regiment which served as the escort of the king – I mean Charles – was slain, I believe?' said Cromwell, looking straight at Mordaunt.
> 'Yes sir.'
> 'By whom?'
> 'By me.'
> 'What was his name?'
> 'Lord de Winter.'
> 'Your uncle?' exclaimed Cromwell.
> 'My uncle! Traitors to England are no relatives of mine.'
> Cromwell continued thoughtful a moment, looking at the young man; then with that deep melancholy which Shakespeare describes so well, he said, 'Mordaunt, you are a dreadful servant.'
> 'When the Lord commands, one must not trifle with orders. Abraham raised the knife over Isaac; and Isaac was his son.'
> 'Yes,' said Cromwell; but the Lord did not allow the sacrifice to be accomplished.'
> 'I looked around me,' said Mordaunt; 'and I saw neither goat or kid caught in the thickets of the plain.'
> Cromwell bowed.
> 'You are strong among the strong, Mordaunt,' said he ...[1]

---

[1] Alexandre Dumas, *Twenty Years After* (Oxford: Oxford University Press, 2008), p. 512.

Although this fictitious story takes place about three hundred years before the events discussed in this work, the interaction between Cromwell and Mordaunt still manages to address many of the themes that will be examined here. It shows how individuals redefine others within changing situations: Charles is no longer Cromwell's king, Lord de Winter no longer Mordaunt's uncle. These changes have repercussions for the actors' attitudes towards them yet it remains vague what these precisely are. Secondly, the orders Cromwell gave to Mordaunt were evidently ambiguous enough to be interpreted differently to how they were meant, a recurrent issue in warfare. Mordaunt had to make a 'judgement under uncertainty', and, as sociologists have long demonstrated, it is likely that he considered his actions to be 'representative' of the situation, and as the only workable alternative available to him at the time. What to outsiders might appear 'irrational' nevertheless developed from prior ways that actors, such as Mordaunt, had approached and solved their problems and informed their decisions.[2] Cromwell acknowledges this by professing both shock and approval, as such showing the ambivalence and duality in his understanding of Mordaunt's actions. Ultimately, Cromwell's reaction is rooted in pragmatism and utilitarianism: the mission, after all, is accomplished. Finally, it shows war's inherent hardening nature: it takes mere seconds for the traumatic and onerous issue to be put to rest.

Nazi Germany's death knell came exactly one hundred years after Dumas's examination of the different strata in military thought and the way these informed soldiers' actions and concerns. For most Germans, the first months of 1945 became synonymous with unparalleled destruction, seemingly arbitrary death from without and within, and unequivocal and total military defeat.[3] How these three notions related to each other is much less known, if only because '1945' was almost immediately appropriated. In post-war West Germany the notion of a *Stunde Null*, or 'zero hour', was introduced to represent May 1945, highlighting the break with Germany's totalitarian past. Adhering to this concept meant that all misery that had befallen the country had to be traced back to Nazism, which was readily done.[4] At the same time, East German scholars presented the violence in 1945 as proof of widespread disagreement with a regime that had pursued the 'imperialist interest of German

---

[2] Amos Tversky and Daniel Kahneman, 'Judgment under Uncertainty: Heuristics and Biases', *Science* (185) 1974, pp. 1124–31.

[3] Richard Bessel, *Germany 1945, From War to Peace* (New York: Pocket Books, 2010), pp. 4–7.

[4] Manfred Görtemaker, *Geschichte der Bundesrepublik Deutschland, Von der Gründung bis zur Gegenwart* (Munich: C.H. Beck, 1999), pp. 159–60. See for example: *Stunde Null und danach – Schicksale 1945–1949*. Ten volumes (Leer: Verlag Gerhard Rautenberg, 1983–7).

monopoly capital', while also playing up the role of the anti-Fascist resistance.[5] Moreover, virtually from the moment Allied troops entered their communities, Germans throughout their country drew on the terror and fear they felt in 1945 to present themselves as victims of National Socialism.[6] This study proposes a new approach towards the perception of late-war violence. Above all, it seeks to restore agency to the German armed forces, the Wehrmacht, and examines the mark it left on the German wartime community.

Both the sheer scale and the diversity of violence were unparalleled in German history, and to untangle the various strands of responsibility, culpability, and involvement, this study will restrict itself to an analysis of the events in East Prussia and its capital, Königsberg. We will return to further underlying reasons for this decision below, but first address the general narrative. In 1945, the omnipresent violence throughout Germany led to a sense of 'general hopelessness' among its population, as Allied bombardments reduced city after city to rubble, while revenge-driven Soviet troops molested tens of thousands of women in Eastern Germany.[7] The final months of the war also saw a massive increase in German-versus-German violence, or intra-ethnic violence, mainly in the form of decentralised summary courts. Since this type of violence took place against the background of the widespread racist violence that has come to define the National Socialist regime, it is generally – but inaccurately – grouped together with it. During the previous years, the Nazi regime had persecuted racial minorities and social outsiders, but within its own borders had at least sought to keep repression and mass murder from the public eye.[8] In the final months of the war the violence

---

[5] Hajo Dröll, 'Die Zusammenbruchskrise des faschistischen Systems in Deutschland', in Niethammer, Borsdorf, and Brandt (eds.), *Arbeiterinitiative 1945*, p. 173; Gerhard Förster and Richard Lakowski, *1945: Das Jahr der endgultigen Niederlage der faschistischen Wehrmacht* (Berlin: Deutscher Militärverlag, 1985); Wolfgang Schumann and Olaf Groehler (eds), *Deutschland im Zweiten Weltkrieg 6: Die Zerschlagung des Hitlerfaschismus und die Befreiung des deutschen Volkes (Juni 1944 bis zum 8. Mai 1945)* (Berlin: Akademie-Verlag, 1985).

[6] For example: Jürgen Thorwald, *Es begann an der Weichsel. Flucht und Vertreibung der Deutschen aus dem Osten* (Stuttgart: Steingrüben 1949); Jürgen Thorwald, *Das Ende an der Elbe. Die letzten Monate des Zweiten Weltkriegs im Osten* (Stuttgart: Steingrüben 1950). See also: Saul Padover, *Lügendetektor: Vernehmungen im besiegten Deutschland 1944/45* (Frankfurt a.M.: Eichborn Verlag, 1999); Bill Niven (ed.), *Germans As Victims: Remembering the Past in Contemporary Germany* (Basingstoke: Palgrave Macmillan, 2006); Atina Grossmann, *Jews, Germans, and Allies: Close Encounters in Occupied Germany* (Princeton, NJ: Princeton University Press, 2007), ch. 1: 'Poor Germany'.

[7] Heinz Boberach (ed.), *Meldungen aus dem Reich: Die geheimen Lageberichte des Sicherheitsdienstes der SS 1938–1945, Band 17* (Herrsching: Pawlak Verlag, 1984), p. 6734.

[8] David Bankier, *The Germans and the Final Solution: Public Opinion under Nazism* (Oxford: Blackwell, 1992), chs. 4 and 7; Michael Burleigh, *The Third Reich: a New History* (London: MacMillan, 2000), pp. 631–2; Robert Gellately and Nathan Stoltzfus (eds.),

against these groups escalated and increasingly took place out in the open. These so-called *Endphaseverbrechen* – 'Crimes of the final phase' – have been the focus of in-depth research. During the first decade of the twenty-first century, these crimes were examined within the framework of their respective organisations such as the Gestapo, the Hitler Youth, the prison system, and the concentration camp system. Scholars convincingly demonstrated that there was not a single Nazi institution that did not resort to radical measures during the final months of the war.[9]

Further research followed shortly afterwards and placed these crimes within the context of the crumbling German community. Scholars like Sven Keller stressed that despite the Nazi regime's failure to meet most of its promises, which was clear to most Germans by the summer of 1944, it was still able to mobilise the German population for the defence of their country by means of increasingly radical laws and orders.[10] The radicalised Party official as the linchpin in the violence towards the German population was fairly readily accepted, since National Socialism and violence are inextricably linked.[11] 'Looking at the ruinous landscape left behind by National Socialism – a landscape shaped by war, racism, exclusion and murder, violence seems to be the common denominator,' Richard Bessel rightly observed, further noting that when the Third Reich broke down in 1945, violence itself was the only aspect of National Socialist system to sustain.[12]

Yet one of the biggest differences in the violence in 1945 and the violence during the years earlier was that it focused on 'regular' German Volksgenossen as well, rather than merely on the different minority groups. In rapid succession, the regime established summary courts

Social Outsiders in Nazi Germany (Princeton, NJ: Princeton University Press, 2001); Saul Friedlander, *The Years of Extermination: Nazi Germany and the Jews 1939–1945* (London: Weidenfeld & Nicolson, 2007), pp. 92–3.

[9] Daniel Blatman, *The Death Marches, the Final Phase of Nazi Genocide* (London: Belknap Press of Harvard University Press, 2011); Nikolaus Wachsmann, *Hitler's Prisons, Legal Terror in Nazi Germany* (London: Yale University Press, 2004), pp. 319–31; Michael Kater, *Hitler Youth* (Cambridge, MA: Harvard University Press, 2004), pp. 215–30; Gerhard Paul, ' 'Diese Erschießungen haben mich innerlich gar nicht mehr berührt': Die Kriegsendphasenverbrechen der Gestapo 1944/45', in Paul and Mallmann (eds.) *Die Gestapo im Zweiten Weltkrieg*, pp. 543–68.

[10] Sven Keller, *Volksgemeinschaft am Ende: Gesellschaft und Gewalt 1944/45* (Munich: Oldenbourg Verlag, 2013), pp. 419–26; Cord Arendes, Edgar Wolfrun, and Jörg Zedler (eds.), *Terror nach Innen: Verbrechen am Ende des Zweiten Weltkrieges,* (Göttingen: Wallstein Verlag, 2006).

[11] On Party behaviour in Eastern Germany, see: Alastair Noble, *Nazi Rule and the Soviet Offensive in Eastern Germany, 1944–1945: the Darkest Hour* (Eastbourne: Sussex Academic Press, 2010).

[12] Richard Bessel, 'Eine "Volksgemeinschaft" der Gewalt', in Schmiechen-Ackermann (ed.), p. 359.

(15 February and 9 March), implemented the 'Nero Decree' (19 March), which called for the destruction of the German infrastructure, and the 'flag order' (3 April), which for all German men made hoisting a white flag punishable by death. These orders shared the communality that they were meant to affect the larger German public. Instigated by the Nazi elite and steeped in Nazi rhetoric, they have been considered 'the last gasp of the regime', willing to drag all Germans along with them into destruction.[13] The decentralised and disparate nature of the violence, which, moreover, seemed to flare up with little warning or rationale, further allowed scholars to draw parallels between earlier Nazi political violence, such as in 1932–3, and the violence in 1945.[14] However, the fractured state of Germany by 1945 made it significantly harder for policy decisions taken in Berlin to be implemented 'on the ground'. By confining the research to one province, this study examines how the central decision-making processes translated into intra-ethnic violence on a local level.

Within the historiography of '1945', sustained attention has also been devoted to the violence committed by Soviet troops against German refugees. The persistent narrative is that of a failing Party bureaucracy that prevented, and often forbade, the population of threatened areas from preparing for evacuation, thereby leaving them at the mercy of the Soviets.[15] This study addresses the events in the months prior to and during the East Prussian offensive, the Soviet offensive which started on 12/13 January 1945 as part of a larger strategic effort to destroy German forces east of the Oder river – the final natural barrier before Berlin. Covering the period between July 1944 and May 1945, it will focus sustained attention on the considerations that underpinned the different evacuation measures in East Prussia, expanding on the research of Heinrich Schwendemann who examined the motivations behind strategic and tactical decisions taken by Wehrmacht commanders during the final months of the war.[16] It will closely link it to the research of David Yelton, who examined the establishment and deployment of the Volkssturm

---

[13] Manfred Zeidler, 'Der Zusammenbruch des NS-Staates', in Ralph Giordano (ed.), *Kriegsende in Deutschland*, pp. 42–9.

[14] Sven Keller, 'Volksgemeinschaft and Violence: Some Reflections on Interdependencies', in Steber and Gotto (eds.), *Visions of Community in Nazi Germany*, pp. 226–39.

[15] Theodor Schieder (ed.), *Dokumentation der Vertreibung der Deutschen aus Ost-Mitteleuropa, Die Vertreibung der deutschen Bevölkerung aus den Gebieten östlich der Oder-Neisse, Band I*, (Munich: Deutschen Taschenbuch Verlag, 1984). Popular history works addressing this theme are: Cornelius Ryan, *The Last Battle* (New York: Simon & Schuster, 1966); Antony Beevor, *The Fall of Berlin* (New York: Penguin, 2002).

[16] See: Heinrich Schwendemann, 'Der deutsche Zusammenbruch im Osten 1944/45', in Rusinek (ed.), *Kriegsende 1945*, pp. 125–50.

militia during the final year of the war.[17] The two scholars both established that the military was much more closely involved in decisions that directly impacted the German civilian population.

The continuing focus on Party behaviour meant that the largest and most violent player present in Germany in 1945 – the German Wehrmacht – has remained underappreciated as an actor. Although the Wehrmacht's role in the defeat of the Third Reich has been examined, the intra-ethnic violence that took place during the final fighting in Germany is rarely traced back to it.[18] Research into the motivations behind the violent behaviour among the ranks of the Wehrmacht goes back to Bartov's 1985 standard work 'The Eastern Front, 1941–45: German Troops and the Barbarisation of Warfare', which not only addressed the violent interaction its members had with an environment they perceived as hostile but also provided an insight into the ideological indoctrination explaining the troops' motivations.[19] In the decades that followed, Wehrmacht behaviour on the Eastern Front remained the focus of in-depth studies. The crimes committed by the Wehrmacht during the German occupation of the Soviet Union are central in these works, and numerous scholars convincingly demonstrated that the Wehrmacht was actively involved in the Holocaust, while also participating in countless acts of genocide against local populations. The focus on the policies in the Soviet Union however also means that the examination 'stops' at the German border: the summer of 1944 is generally the end-point of these studies.[20] Whereas numerous studies address the violent behavioural patterns of the Wehrmacht in the occupied cities in Eastern Europe, so far no research exists that asks critical questions about the relation between the Wehrmacht and its own

---

[17] David Yelton, *Hitler's Volkssturm: the Nazi Militia and the Fall of Germany 1944–1945* (Lawrence: University Press of Kansas, 2002).

[18] Andreas Kunz, *Wehrmacht und Niederlage: Die bewaffnete Macht in der Endphase der nationalsozialistischen Herrschaft 1944 bis 1945* (Munich: R. Oldenbourg Verlag, 2005)

[19] Omer Bartov, *The Eastern Front 1941–45: German Troops and the Barbarisation of Warfare* (Houndmills: Palgrave, 2001).

[20] See for example: Timothy Patrick Mulligan, *The Politics of Illusion and Empire: German Occupation Policy in the Soviet Union, 1942–1943* (New York: Praeger, 1988); Theo Schulte, *The German Army and Nazi Policies in Occupied Russia* (Oxford: Berg, 1989); Christopher Browning, *Ordinary Men: Reserve Police Battalion 101 and the Final Solution in Poland* (New York: HarperPerennial, 1998); Hamburg Institute for Social Research, *Crimes of the German Wehrmacht: Dimensions of a War of Annihilation 1941–1944. An Outline of the Exhibition* (Hamburg: Hamburger Edition, 2004); Dieter Pohl, *Die Herrschaft der Wehrmacht: Deutsche Militärbesatzung und einheimische Bevölkerung in der Sowjetunion 1941–1944* (Munich: R. Oldenbourg Verlag, 2008); Jeff Rutherford, *Combat and Genocide on the Eastern Front: the German Infantry's War, 1941–1944* (Cambridge: Cambridge University Press, 2014).

population.[21] This study addresses this gap by applying the findings regarding Wehrmacht behavioural patterns on the Eastern Front to Germany itself by examining in detail conditions in Königsberg during the final months of the Second World War.

There is certainly scope for this avenue of research: although the breadth of the violence on the Eastern Front has been fairly well examined, the magnitude of the horror ensured that it is too often viewed as being perpetuated by inertia. Its principal actors, it sometimes appears, 'underwent' the violence, whether they were victims, bystanders, or perpetrators. It is not hard to trace back where this notion originates from. Within the scholarship into military behaviour on the Eastern Front, the first occupation years (1941–2) are examined most extensively, since during this period a string of deadly, racially motivated 'criminal orders' were implemented which were subsequently discussed in the field and elaborated on in war diaries.[22] Moreover, the unfamiliarity with the area, and the very human incapability to grasp the size of the Western Soviet Union – a thousand miles separated Leningrad from Stalingrad, over six hundred miles lie between Brest and the outskirts of Moscow – makes us glance over the fact that 'the Eastern Front' is a collective name for what was in reality hundreds of separate battlefields that all impacted their participants in different ways. The learning curve of the ordinary German soldier, the Landser, was determined by the different experiences they underwent, and these would shape their adaptability and responsiveness to the battles that lay ahead. This 'interplay between military developments and the behaviour of the combatants' was first examined by Christian Hartmann, who found that different military circumstances prompted different acts of violence.[23] By the end of 1941 most genocidal orders were in place, and we thus tend to consider the winter of 1941 as something of a 'baseline' in regard to soldiers' brutality. That troops

---

[21] Stephan Lehnstaedt, *Okkupation im Osten: Besatzeralltag in Warschau und Minsk 1939–1944* (Munich: Oldenbourg, 2010).

[22] Christian Hartmann, Johannes Hürter, and Ulrike Jureit (eds.), *Verbrechen der Wehrmacht: Bilanz einer Debatte* (Munich: C.H. Beck, 2005); Alex Kay, Jeff Rutherford, and David Stahel (eds.), *Nazi Policy on the Eastern Front, 1941: Total War, Genocide, and Radicalisation* (Rochester, NY: University of Rochester Press, 2012). See further: Christian Gerlach, *Kalkulierte Morde: Die deutsche Wirtschafts- und Vernichtungspolitik in Weißrußland 1941 bis 1944* (Hamburg: Hamburger Edition, 1999); Christian Streit, *Keine Kameraden: Die Wehrmacht und die sowjetischen Kriegsgefangenen 1941–1945* (Stuttgart: Deutsche Verlags-Anstalt, 1978); Felix Römer, '"Im alten Deutschland wäre solcher Befehl nicht möglich gewesen": Rezeption, Adaption und Umsetzung des Kriegsgerichtsbarkeitserlass im Ostheer 1941/42', *VfZ* (56) 2008, pp. 53–99.

[23] Christian Hartmann, *Wehrmacht im Ostkrieg: Front und militärisches Hinterland 1941/42* (Munich: R. Oldenbourg Verlag, 2009), pp. 245, 243–423.

continued to radicalise through interaction with their environment is easily overlooked, and especially during times of military defeat the mental and physical strain led to a sharp increase in violence.[24] As soldiers kept interacting with their environment in reaction to the different wartime developments, 'barbarisation', and thus the nature of violence, evolved continuously. It seems therefore unlikely that after four years on the Eastern Front – either as occupiers or as fighters – German troops could simply leave behind their violent mindset as they crossed back into Germany.[25] Breaking the cycle of violence would, moreover, be a near-impossible task, especially for the army's veteran core groups. As the British military historian Basil Lidell-Hart asserted on the eve of the fighting in East Prussia: 'The only thing harder than getting a new idea into a military mind is to get an old idea out.'[26] Put more bluntly, 'terrorising' had become part of the Wehrmacht's arsenal: it had terrorised foreign civilians and terrorised its own men on a scale unequalled in military history.[27] The move towards the violent maltreatment of their own civilians might therefore be more unassuming to the Landser than we would care to admit.

The rationale behind radical Wehrmacht behaviour has long been sought in the ideological indoctrination of the troops, but although this is undoubtedly important, it meant that other explanations were left largely ignored.[28] Vejas Liulevicius drew attention to the German military's stay in Russia during the First World War, showing that a radicalised Nazi mindset was not at all a prerequisite for a harsh occupation and brutal behaviour towards populations.[29] Similarly, Peter Lieb examined German conduct on the Eastern Front during the First World War and its aftermath, concluding that the events that manifested themselves could not be considered precursors to the war of annihilation 25 years later.[30] Other factors, such the strain of war, are still largely left

---

[24] Rutherford, *Combat and Genocide on the Eastern Front*; Jürgen Kilian, 'Wehrmacht, Partisanenkrieg und Rückzugsverbrechen an der nördlichen Ostfront im Herbst und Winter 1943', *VfZ* (61) 2013, pp. 173–99.

[25] The experiences of war prompted a 'new normal', a development which, of course, was not at all limited to soldiers. See for example: Ian Buruma, *Year Zero: a History of 1945* (London: Atlantic Books, 2013), p. 7.

[26] Aimeé Fox, *Learning to Fight: Military Innovation and Change in the British Army, 1914–1918* (Cambridge: Cambridge University Press, 2018), p. 1.

[27] Robert Citino, *The German Way of War: From the Thirty Years' War to the Third Reich* (Lawrence: University Press of Kansas 2005), p. 273.

[28] Omer Bartov, *Hitler's Army: Soldiers, Nazis, and War in the Third Reich* (Oxford: Oxford University Press, 1992), ch. 4, 'The Distortion of Reality'.

[29] Vejas Liulevicius, *War Land on the Eastern Front: Culture, National Identity, and German Occupation in World War I* (Cambridge: Cambridge University Press, 2001).

[30] Peter Lieb, 'Der deutsche Krieg im Osten von 1914 bis 1919: Ein Vorläufer des Vernichtungskriegs?', *VfZ* (65) 2017, pp. 465–506.

unexplored. Whereas war neurosis (what is today called 'post-traumatic stress disorder') is examined in depth when it concerns the other belligerents during the Second World War, an examination of the mental state of German troops is still absent.[31] Nazi medicine itself lay at the core of this underappreciation, since troops' mental illnesses did not fit into the idea of a healthy fighting *Volk*. As German soldiers' mental traumas were equated to cowardice, or even considered as treasonous, they remained unaddressed during the National Socialist era, while also in post-war Germany the general advice was to 'trivialise, tone down, consciously forget and suppress' traumatic experiences.[32] The traumas of German soldiers and civilians alike have received little attention in the existing literature, although the topic is gaining in prominence.[33]

Only recently has a group of German scholars, led by the historian Sönke Neitzel and the social psychologist Harald Welzer, set out to assess the 'military–sociological and social–psychological' motivations of German soldiers. With war as a frame of reference, the authors found the views of German troops on 'fighting, killing and dying' to be rather similar when compared to modern-day soldiers.[34] This group also included Felix Römer, who published the landmark work 'Kameraden', using the bugged conversations of German prisoners of war recorded at Fort Hunt, Virginia. Also for Römer, the National Socialist indoctrination is merely one of the dimensions to explain the behaviour of Wehrmacht soldiers. For Römer, the 'actual combat and the dynamics of violence, the historical–cultural framework of the respective society and its military, the culture within the actual unit, and finally also the individual disposition of each combatant' were the main driving forces behind military conduct.[35] The troops' attitude towards their fellow countrymen, however, could not be included in the work, since the time of capture of the examined German POWs mostly predated the allied

---

[31] See for example: Edgar Jones and Simon Wessely, *Shell Shock to PTSD: Military Psychiatry from 1900 to the Gulf War* (Hove: Psychology Press, 2005).

[32] Geoffrey Cocks, *Psychotherapy in the Third Reich: the Göring Institute* (New Brunswick: Transaction, 1997), p. 82; Hilke Lorenz, *Kriegskinder: Das Schicksal einer Generation* (Munich: List, 2003), p. 19.

[33] Svenja Goltermann, *Die Gesellschaft der Überlebenden: Deutsche Kriegsheimkehrer und ihre Gewalterfahrungen im Zweiten Weltkrieg* (Munich: Deutsche Verlagsanstalt, 2009); Jörg Echternkamp, *Soldaten im Nachkrieg: Historische Deutungskonflikte und westdeutsche Demokratisierung 1945–1955* (Munich: Oldenbourg, 2014).

[34] Sönke Neitzel and Harald Welzer, *Soldaten, On Fighting, Killing and Dying: the Secret World War II Transcripts of German POWs* (New York: Alfred A. Knopf, 2012); Christian Gudehus, Sönke Neitzel, and Harald Welzer (eds.), *'Der Führer war wieder viel zu human, viel zu gefühlvoll': Der Zweite Weltkrieg aus der Sicht deutscher und italienischer Soldaten* (Frankfurt a.M: Fischer Taschenbuch Verlag, 2011); Harald Welzer, *Täter: Wie aus ganz normale Menschen Massenmörder werden* (Frankfurt a.M., Fischer Verlag, 2005).

[35] Felix Römer, *Kameraden, Die Wehrmacht von innen* (Munich: Piper, 2012), p. 468.

advance into Germany. It is nevertheless noteworthy that among these men the concern for and the treatment of the German population was apparently hardly worthy of sustained conversation. The research into the role of the German armed forces during times of violent transition is currently experiencing a revival, with German military involvement increasingly sought – and found – at the centre of intense domestic violence; this study fits into this new current.[36]

We now turn to the main questions this study addresses. It argues that the violence against German civilians during the defence of their country can only be understood by restoring agency to the soldiers of retreating Wehrmacht units as active participants, thus looking beyond the traditionally viewed actors. To what extent could the arrival of military units in Germany help to explain the spike in violence in Germany in 1945? Was this violence deliberate, or was it a by-product of the fighting; was it ordered, or was it spontaneous? What explains the difference in behaviour between these units and those German troops that were already garrisoned throughout the country? Every possible answer, in turn, only prompts more questions. What could be gained by exercising violence, and who gained from it? Most importantly, why would German troops and Party officials decide to resort to violence against their fellow countrymen, and how did they justify this to themselves? Finally, this study seeks to distinguish continuities and discontinuities in military behaviour as troops returned from fighting abroad to fight on the home front. Thus, its purpose is to determine to what extent the violence in 1945 can be separated from its totalitarian context. By presenting a microhistory of East Prussia and Königsberg, it presents a new view on the role of the Wehrmacht within German society. Research has so far mainly addressed the extent to which National Socialism impacted the Wehrmacht, yet it hardly examined what mark the Wehrmacht left on the German wartime community. Examining the interplay between Party and Wehrmacht bodies, this study seeks to clarify how the two actors shaped late-war German society.

Methodology and Outline

Examining events that occurred in Germany in 1945 means wading through a dense historiography. The secondary literature is virtually infinite, and some of the most highly regarded historians have recently

---

[36] See particularly: Mark Jones, *Founding Weimar: Violence and the German Revolution of 1918–1919* (Cambridge: Cambridge University Press, 2016).

written about it.[37] It seems a near impossible task to take a fresh look at the way events transpired, especially when it concerns a loaded topic such as violence. Therefore, rather than examining Germany as a whole, this study will examine the events in Germany's easternmost province, East Prussia, from the autumn of 1944 onwards, with a particular focus on its capital, Königsberg. Soviet troops reached the province's borders in the late summer of 1944 which led to a series of defensive measures being taken. That autumn Königsberg was declared a *Festung* (fortress), and was besieged by Soviet troops between late January and April 1945, after Soviet troops had overrun much of the rest of East Prussia. The German city Königsberg no longer exists; today it is known as Kaliningrad, the capital of the Russian *Oblast* with the same name, an often-overlooked exclave wedged in between Poland and Lithuania. As the area fits awkwardly in the story of (West- and East) Germany, its recent history has long been ignored by historians.[38] This means at the same time that many generalisations still dominate our current perception of the area, and the lack of scholarship means that, in some extreme cases, established scholars have had to resort to citing amateur historians.[39]

The first obstacle in researching East Prussia is the highly fractured source base. Parts of Königsberg's archives were evacuated in late 1944, and due to Germany's turbulent post-war era, archival sources concerning the city are still on the move. Sources that specifically focus on East

---

[37] See: Stephen Fritz, *Endkampf, Soldiers, Civilians, and the Death of the Third Reich* (Lexington: University Press of Kentucky, 2004); Michael Geyer, 'Endkampf 1918 and 1945: German Nationalism, Annihilation, and Self-Destruction', in Lüdtke and Weisbrod (eds.), *No Man's Land of Violence*, pp. 35–68; Rolf-Dieter Müller (ed.) *Das Deutsche Reich und der Zweiten Weltkrieg Teil 10/1 Der Zusammenbruch des Deutschen Reiches 1945: Die militärische Niederwerfung der Wehrmacht* (Munich: Deutsche Verlags-Anstalt, 2007); Bessel, *Germany 1945*; Ian Kershaw, *The End, Hitler's Germany, 1944–45* (London: Allen Lane 2011); Ulrich Herbert, *Geschichte Deutschlands im 20. Jahrhundert* (Munich: C.H. Beck, 2014), ch. 10, 'Untergang'; Nicholas Stargardt, *The German War: a Nation under Arms, 1939–1945* (London: Bodley Head, 2015), Part 6, 'Total Defeat'.

[38] This point was most convincingly stressed in 2002 and remains relevant today. See: Manfred Kittel, 'Preußens Osten in der Zeitgeschichte. Mehr als nur eine landeshistorische Forschungslücke', *VfZ* (50) 2002, pp. 435–64. Concerning East Prussia, Andreas Kossert is an honourable exception. See: Andreas Kossert, *Ostpreußen, Geschichte und Mythos* (Munich: Siedler, 2005); Andreas Kossert, *Damals in Ostpreußen, Der Untergang einer deutschen Provinz* (Munich: Pantheon Verlag, 2008). See further: Hermann Pölking, *Ostpreußen: Biographie einer Provinz* (Berlin: be.bra Verlag, 2011). The plight of East Prussians in 1944–5 does, however, fit in the story of 'Germans', and played an important role in the *Historikerstreit*. See: Andreas Hillgruber, *Zweierlei Untergang. Die Zerschlagung des Deutschen Reiches und das Ende des europäischen Judentums* (Berlin: Siedler, 1986); Collection of essays by multiple authors, *Historikerstreit: Die Dokumentation der Kontroverse um die Einzigartigkeit der nationalsozialistischen Judenvernichtung* (Munich: Piper, 1991).

[39] For example, Kershaw, in *The End*, uses the work of Isabel Denny, *The Fall of Hitler's Fortress City: the Battle for Königsberg 1945* (London: Greenhill Books, 2007).

Prussia and Königsberg were found in the Archiv Stadt Königsberg in Duisburg, the archive of the Ostpreußisches Landesmuseum in Lüneburg and the Gosudarstvennyi Arkhiv Kaliningradskoi Oblasti in Kaliningrad, although none of these can boast of (as they indeed do not) a coherent or organised collection of primary source material focusing on the era. In 1952, Duisburg, out of a 'general patriotic sense of obligation,' took upon itself the task to become Königsberg's Patenstadt (sister-city, or, more literally: adoptive city), and Duisburg's mayor, Oberbürgermeister August Seeling, immediately encouraged former inhabitants to submit memorabilia, images, files, native literature and the like to serve as a basis for a museum or archive.[40] That these people would be less than eager to provide charged and frowned upon materials from the National Socialist era (which might even be incriminating) requires little explanation. The sources reflect this: a mere six folders contained materials pertaining to the Nazi years, with a strong focus on the last months of the war – the period of East Prussian victimhood. By 1952, some 6,000 East Prussians were living in Duisburg, 1,000 of them from Königsberg, but by 2014 this group had shrunk to a size that no longer warranted the museum and archive. In 2014 they closed their doors and the archival holdings were divided over two museums whose current mission is to preserve the East Prussian cultural heritage, and which are both institutionally funded by the German Bundesregierung. The Ostpreußisches Landesmuseum in Lüneburg in Lower Saxony can boast the longest tradition of the two institutions, having been founded in 1958 as a cultural hub for the tens of thousands of East Prussian refugees that settled in the area after the war. The establishment of the Kulturzentrum Ostpreußen in Ellingen in Bavaria is more recent and dates to 1981, following Bavaria's 1978 appointment as Patenland (adoptive state) of East Prussia. In Kaliningrad itself very few sources dealing with 1944–5 have remained. Many of the holdings of Königsberg's archives were evacuated in 1944 (and are now part of the Geheimes Staatsarchiv – Preußischer Kulturbesitz in Berlin), and therefore the documents that can be found there do not deal with the last year of the war. Innumerable records were destroyed during the siege, and the little that remains in the city can be found in the GAKO.

The broader German context has allowed itself to be reconstructed with considerably more ease, with sources found in the larger archives of the Bundesarchiv Berlin-Lichtenfelde, Bundesarchiv-Lastenausgleich in Bayreuth, and the Bundesarchiv-Militärachiv in Freiburg, archives which

---

[40] August Seeling, 'Duisburg übernimmt Patenschaft für Königsberg', Ostpreussen-Warte, January 1952, p. 7.

all pose their own challenges. These challenges, however, are better established among researchers. In Berlin, documents from the Party and state are often deliberately couched in language that obscures their real purpose, or, at the other end of the spectrum, tell particularly little and merely serve to profess loyalty to the regime. The materials in the Lastenausgleichsarchiv in Bayreuth also reveal a double agenda, albeit a completely different one. In 1952, the West German government enacted the Lastenausgleichsgesetz ('Equalization of Burdens Act'), which sought to financially compensate Germans who had particularly suffered from the war and its aftermath. This financial incentive, however, caused an Opferkonkurrenz: a competition between different victim groups. This, in turn, led to a crude victim narrative that placed the traumatic events of 1945 front and centre, since this was the most straightforward way to ensure compensation.[41] As a result, the sources at the Lastenausgleichsarchiv are filled with heart-wringing stories, but we should keep in mind that this was also the emotion they consistently sought to invoke.

Lastly, the military files held at the Militärarchiv in Freiburg also have their biases, gaps, and oversights. Not only were many military documents destroyed at the end of the war, by then many war diaries were no longer kept at all either. Moreover, seeing that war diarists would often deliberately omit the mention of atrocities in efforts to keep their unit's reputation unsullied, it stands to reason that they had similar reservations mentioning the occasions in which they neglected and mistreated their own civilians.[42] Occasionally, the holdings in these archives could be compared to those at the National Archives in Kew, the Yad Vashem Archives in Jerusalem, and the archives of the Institut für Zeitgeschichte in Munich. The wide range of sources encountered during this Europe-wide search encouraged the reconsideration of the variables at play during the defence of East Prussia. Yet important regional studies, such as that of Jill Stephenson, who analysed Württemberg during the National Socialist era, drew attention to the differences existing between the German provinces, urging future historians not to draw sweeping conclusions.[43]

---

[41] Bastiaan Willems and Joe Schuldt, 'The "European Boundaries" of the East Prussian Expellees in West-Germany, 1948–1955', *Novoe Proshloe/The New Past* (3) 2018, pp. 32–3; Pertti Ahonen, 'Domestic Constraints on West German Ostpolitik: the Role of the Expellee Organizations in the Adenauer Era', *Central European History* (31) 1998, pp. 31–63.

[42] Wolfram Wette, *Die Wehrmacht: Feindbilde, Vernichtungskrieg, Legende* (Frankfurt a.M.: S. Fischer Verlag, 2002), 119–24; Hannes Heer, *Vom Verschwinden der Täter: der Vernichtungskrieg fand statt, aber keiner war dabei* (Berlin: Aufbau-Verlag 2004), ch. 2.

[43] Jill Stephenson, *Hitler's Home Front, Württemberg under the Nazis* (London: Hambledon Continuum, 2006); Jill Stephenson, 'The Volksgemeinschaft and the Problems of Permeability: the Persistence of Traditional Attitudes in Württemberg Villages', *German History* (34) 2016, pp. 49–69.

If East Prussia is to serve as a case study for the violence in late-war Germany, appreciating the province's unique factors, while at the same time providing a framework that allows us to better understand the larger context of this violence, is the most challenging task of this study. After Soviet forces had cut through East Prussia in January 1945, Königsberg became one of the clearest examples of what is referred to as the late-war *Verinselung*, or 'islandisation', of Germany: the fragmentation of the regime that allowed local authorities to assume a more active role.[44] Between late January 1945 and early April 1945 the city was besieged, limiting its contact with the outside world. As such it might be considered a 'microcosm', whose unicity should be examined before continuing to the main questions this study seeks to answer.[45] At the same time, the inclination to generalise always lures, if only because Nazi propaganda was determined to present a view of an egalitarian society.[46] Moreover, due to years of practice, by 1945 most high-ranking Nazi officials were extremely skilled in presenting their message. As a result, using their decrees can indeed seem more appealing to historians than using the stiff, telegram-style orders of commanders, who had little reason – and even less time – to devote energy to style or sentence structure. The risk of following National Socialist principles as a base for understanding German behaviour becomes particularly apparent in a diary entry of Reich Propaganda Minister Joseph Goebbels, dated 27 March 1945:

I express my astonishment [to my subordinate] that in the west not one symbol of resistance has manifested itself, as it has in the east, like in Breslau or Königsberg. He asserts that the population in the west is beaten senseless by the months and years of enemy bombing, and that they prefer a horrible end over an endless horror. I believe it has also to do with the fact that the people in the west are by nature not as tough as those in the east. The people in the west are closer to France, that over-civilized country, while the people in the east are closer to Poland and Russia, the more primitive countries of Europe.[47]

This simplified explanation, routed in the pseudo-scientific Social Darwinist theories held so dear by the Nazis, is logically not at all sufficient as an answer. At the same time, Goebbels's statement highlights that

[44] Wolfgang Franz Werner, *'Bleib übrig!': Deutsche Arbeiter in der nationalsozialistischen Kriegswirtschaft* (Düsseldorf: Schwann, 1983), p. 329. Andreas Kunz refers to this process in the military context as 'atomisation'. See: Kunz, *Wehrmacht und Niederlage*, p. 96.

[45] The term 'microcosm' is borrowed from Norman Davies and Roger Moorhouse, *Microcosm: a Portrait of a Central European City* (London: Pimlico, 2003).

[46] Richard Bessel, 'The War to End All Wars: the Shock of Violence in 1945 and its Aftermath in Germany', in Lüdtke and Weisbord (eds.), *No Man's Land of Violence*, p. 85.

[47] Joseph Goebbels, *Tagebücher 1945: Die letzten Aufzeichnungen* (Hamburg: Hoffmann und Campe, 1977), pp. 391–2.

after twelve years of National Socialist propaganda, there were still local differences that needed to be observed. Despite continuous efforts of different East Prussian expellee organisations, who after the war sought to present the strong local culture as a kind of hurdle that prevented any significant change, it is nevertheless clear that National Socialism reached deep in East Prussia. By retracing its appeal and reach in the province, we can determine what East Prussians identified with as the war reached the borders of their province in the summer of 1944. Borrowing from the field of nationalism studies, we find that most of its scholars 'share the understanding that identities are something opposed to [self-] interests', and, therefore, establishing which actors challenged those interests during the final stage of the war gives us the best indication of the balance of power in Königsberg.[48]

The assessment of these different factors forms a substantial 'preamble' to what is the main aim of this study – examining the role of the German Wehrmacht in the intra-ethnic violence in Germany in 1944–5. Establishing who benefited from the violence is an important aspect of this study, but a Germany-wide approach can lead to a singling out of sources that fit the presumptions of the researcher. By limiting this study to East Prussia, the cross section will seek to uncover actors that have previously been underappreciated. This will be achieved though juxtaposing Party and Wehrmacht orders to a wide variety of situation reports, journals, diaries, questionnaires, and private recollections. These sources allow us to retrace the decisions of victims and perpetrators as well as the motives that lay behind them, and might help us to better understand why Germany's defeat was so total. Above all, it illuminates the priorities of those in charge in the final months of the war.

To do so, this study is divided into six chapters. The first two chapters discuss the actors prior to their interactions with each other and define the core concepts as they will be used throughout this work. Chapter 1 starts with an analysis of the role of the East Prussian community within the Total War Germany was waging, as such defining the mental and physical position that its native population occupied, since, within the scope of this study, these people became the main victims of late-war violence. Subsequently, we will determine what impact the Party and the Wehrmacht had on this position, using the construction of the Ostwall and the establishment of the Volkssturm as 'stress-tests'. The chapter closes with an examination of East Prussians' perception of their province in the light of the ever-nearing front line, and how this shaped their attitude

---

[48] Siniša Malešević, *Identity as Ideology: Understanding Ethnicity and Nationalism* (Basingstoke: Palgrave MacMillan, 2006), pp. 17–18.

towards the wider German community. Chapter 2 then retraces the path of the German Landser as they fought their way back to German soil. During its stay on the Eastern Front, the German Wehrmacht had shown an unparalleled disregard for human life, and it is therefore worthwhile to examine to what extent the mindset that was born out of experiences in the East could transfer back into Germany. In this way, it will help to explain why German soldiers continued to fight – and encouraged others to do the same – long after they themselves felt that the war had been lost.

The two following chapters address the late-war environment and the role the different actors played in it. Chapter 3 examines how the direct environment shaped actors' behavioural patterns. The fighting in Germany predominantly took place in urbanised areas yet the character-istics of the urban battlefield have so far not been considered in the examination of late-war violence. From March 1944 onwards, as part of Germany's 'fortress-strategy', more and more cities were designated as fortresses, or Festungen, a decision that was meant to bolster their defensibility. Field commanders immediately lamented the strategy's outdated nature which forced garrisons to become surrounded, while Party members feared that an increased military presence in these 'fort-resses' would undermine their authority. These criticisms shaped the relations between the two and would eventually also determine how civilians would undergo the war's final months. During Königsberg's siege, however, Party and Wehrmacht tried to find some common ground, and Chapter 4 explores how this uneasy balance of power mani-fested itself. It does so by analysing how propaganda in the city presented the different events that took place on a local, national, and international level. An assessment of the themes explored in local media will help to reveal how, in a fractured Germany, local authorities presented their message and how they sought to link it to the larger picture.

Finally, the last two chapters examine how intra-ethnic violence tran-spired during the final months of the war. Chapter 5 examines in depth the evacuation in East Prussia, where we will consider the collaboration between the Party and the Wehrmacht. It will help to establish their authorities, as well as the radicalising nature of their proximity. Nowadays 'evacuation' is understood as the transporting of civilians, and it is this view that perseveres about the provinces in Eastern Germany as well. Analysing the evacuation measures, and moreover retracing what their exact purposes were can help us to understand the relationship between the Party and the Wehrmacht on one hand, and the civilian population on the other. Lastly, Chapter 6 will continue to explore the consequences of the German troops' proximity to the German population. It focuses on two elements: the introduction of the radicalised mindset of the German troops in East Prussia, and the adherence to military law in German society. How did these two elements shape the behaviour in Königsberg? The origins of radicalised legislation as it was implemented in Germany are traced back to pre-existing military law, once again highlighting that this law did not take the need of civilians into account.

This work serves to increase our understanding of behavioural patterns during the final year of the war and brings to light new aspects of Germany's transition from war to peace. Most importantly, it stresses that the idea of the Wehrmacht as an obstacle for the radicalisation of the German late-war society should be revisited, and expounds how the dynamics observed between the different actors in East Prussia could be interpreted to reconstruct a more complete view of violence in defeat.

1 Regionality and Total War in East Prussia

Introduction

In late January 1945, the East Prussian capital of Königsberg was threatened with encirclement. The city was still packed with civilians, and many of them, such as Wilhelm Strüvy, a prominent and well-respected member of the East Prussian community, had a small window of time to flee Königsberg and leave East Prussia. Despite his age – Strüvy was 58 – he repeatedly turned the opportunity down, choosing instead to take part in the defence of the city, feeling that '[i]f the province falls, I can fall as well!'[1] During those same days, a woman explained her motivation to stay in Königsberg to her doctor, assuring him that the city would hold out: 'Our Führer will not let us be captured by the Russian, he'd rather gas us'.[2] These radical statements reveal a willingness of German contemporaries to closely connect personal well-being to their immediate environment – an environment that, with few exceptions, had been completely transformed during the previous years of 'Total War'. Germans' perception of war had – due to the lack of alternative news sources – primarily been shaped by their own propaganda and their personal experiences. Therefore, although these fanatical sentiments reveal the permeability of the regime's language, they hardly reveal which legislation and which bodies shaped daily life in East Prussia.

To fully understand the behavioural patterns of East Prussia's civilians in 1945, this chapter examines the interplay between actor and environment in the province throughout the war years. Contemporaries and historians alike have so far examined late-war violence in Germany along two main strands. As a rule, the violence is mainly treated as a

[1] 'Wilhelm Strüvy siebzig Jahre', *Das Ostpreußenblatt*, 10 March 1956, p. 3.
[2] Hans Graf von Lehndorff, *Ostpreußisches Tagebuch: Aufzeichnungen eines Arztes aus den Jahren 1945–1947* (Munich: dtv, 1961), pp. 18–19. Note the mention of 'The Russian' as a single entity, rather than 'the Russians' (plural) as identifiable human beings. This phrasing was part of continuous efforts to dehumanise the Soviets.

continuation of radicalised domestic Nazi policy, while further excesses are explained through the age-old adage 'war is war': since war is inherently violent in nature, the barbarity it engenders is a logical result.[3] This sentiment has allowed both the Wehrmacht as well as the German civilian population to be portrayed as passive actors, swept up in the maelstrom of war, subject to this radicalisation, but hardly contributing to it. By focusing on East Prussia, we will be able to trace back the motivations of the bodies involved, the language that was used in the decision-making process, and the friction the implementation of different policies caused in German society. Moreover, restoring agency to the different actors on a local level will help us separate thought-through deliberations from decisions prompted by circumstances, providing us with a more nuanced view of what led to the radicalisation of German wartime society.

East Prussia's Path to 1945

The violent behavioural patterns that emerged in 1945 had many fathers. It is tempting to explain the violence of 1945 as a product of a society shaped by National Socialism, if only because propagandists at the time consistently portrayed Germany as a Nazified state, which they encapsulated in the word *Volksgemeinschaft*, or 'people's community'. On 24 February 1945, Königsberg's *Preußische Zeitung*, like most other Party outlets, celebrated the twenty-fifth anniversary of the declaration of the National Socialist Party programme, which had presented twenty-five points to achieve the Nazi vision for Germany. According to the editors of the *Preußische Zeitung*, the existence of a Volksgemeinschaft had emboldened the German people: 'Then a crippled nation, today a people fighting with extreme fanaticism. Then a survivor of a disintegrated social order, today a developing, unwavering Volksgemeinschaft'.[4] Progress within German society was consistently traced back to the added value of institutions and policies introduced by the Nazis, thereby downplaying the continuities with the pre-Nazi era. Yet every adult had a frame of reference that extended beyond the twelve years of the Nazi dictatorship, and both the social changes that took place prior to the National Socialist

---

[3] Sven Keller, 'Volksgemeinschaft and Violence: Some Reflections on Interdependencies', in Steber and Gotto (eds.), *Visions of Community in Nazi Germany*, pp. 226–39: Kershaw, *The End*, esp. ch. 6, 'Terror Comes Home'. See for example: Brooks D. Simpson and Jean V. Berlin (eds.) *Sherman's Civil War: Selected Correspondence of William T. Sherman, 1860–1865* (Chapel Hill, NC: University of North Carolina Press, 1999), p. 697: William T. Sherman, September 1864: 'If the people raise a howl against my barbarity and cruelty, I will answer that war is war, and not popularity-seeking'.

[4] 'Ich prophezeie den Sieg des Deutschen Reiches!', *Preußische Zeitung*, 25 February 1945.

era and those happening during it would shape events in East Prussia during the last year of the war.

Psychological studies tell us that behavioural patterns of both individuals and groups can largely be determined by evaluating the perception of past experiences, and it seems therefore sensible to start the examination of East Prussia at the beginning of the population's living memory, in the late nineteenth century.[5] During this period, the heyday of the Second Reich, German nationalism, actively fuelled by the monarchy and *völkisch* movements, reached previously unknown heights. Sustained energy was devoted to the question of what it meant to be German, resulting in debates about where the borders of 'Germandom' lay, how these had come about historically, and how they corresponded with the current situation. In the age of Empire, the predictable conclusion was that Germany needed to expand, a notion that it shared with virtually every other European state. Although during the previous centuries the East Prussians had actually maintained fairly good relations with the East, within the German debates, the county's eastern borderlands were presented as points of friction between the Germans and the Slavs.[6] East Prussia, Germany's easternmost province, played a prominent role in these debates, as it was both the province that embodied Germany's aspirations for a colonial empire that would expand eastwards, as well as the province where the angst for an invasion by barbaric Slavic neighbours took its clearest shape.[7]

East Prussians saw their primordial fears confirmed in late 1914, during the first months of the First World War, when three major battles and numerous smaller border disputes were fought out between German defenders and the Russian armies that had entered East Prussia. Although the battles ended in clear German victories, the material and personal damage had been enormous. More than a third of the population fled in August and September 1914, while of those who stayed behind some 1,500 died at the hands of the Russian troops. Besides vast material damage to the province, some 13,000 of its civilians were deported to Russia, of whom well over a third would not return. The fighting for the province reached every front page in

---

[5] Donald Dietrich, 'National Renewal, Anti-Semitism, and Political Continuity: a Psychological Assessment', *Political Psychology* (9) 1988, pp. 385–411.

[6] The best analysis of East Prussia's relation with its neighbours can be found in Jürgen Manthey, *Königsberg, Geschichte einer Weltbürgerrepublik* (Munich: Carl Hanser Verlag, 2005).

[7] Gregor Thum, 'Megalomania and Angst: the Nineteenth-Century Mythization of Germany's Eastern Borderlands', in Bartov and Weitz (eds.), *Shatterzones of Empire*, pp. 23–41; Roderick Stackelberg, *Idealism Debased: From Völkisch Ideology to National Socialism* (Kent, OH: Kent State University Press, 1981), pp. 1–18.

Figure 1.1 A postcard from the Ostpreussenhilfe series depicting East Prussian
refugees during the First World War. *Source:* Author's collection

Germany with the German victory at Tannenberg in August 1914 and
ended in late February 1915 with a victory at the Winter Battle of the
Masurian Lakes. As such, East Prussia held a unique position in
Germany's First World War experience, being the only German province to have experienced actual combat.[8]

During the interwar period, few East Prussians are likely to have
changed their attitude towards their neighbours. The 1919 Treaty of
Versailles had given birth to the 'Polish Corridor', which granted the
newly formed state of Poland access to the sea, thereby cutting off East
Prussia from the rest of Germany. It was a 'thorn in the flesh' that most
Germans – East Prussians in particular – wanted extracted. Much of the
fear they felt stemmed from the realisation that the German armed forces,
the *Reichswehr* (with a strength of a mere 100,000 men as a result of the
restrictions of Versailles), would be unable to provide any real opposition
to the Polish army, which possessed some 300,000 troops.[9] As Poland
waged a number of wars with neighbouring states – most importantly with
Lithuania and the Soviet Union – war remained on East Prussia's door-
step (primarily in the east and south), adding to the feelings of unease and

[8] Alexander Watson, *Ring of Steel: Germany and Austria–Hungary at War, 1914–1918*
(London: Allen Lane, 2014), pp. 160–81.
[9] Richard Bessel, *Nazism and War* (New York: Modern Library, 2006), p. 21.

insecurity. Shortly after the First World War, the western part of the Neidenburg district, which included the city of Soldau, had to be handed over to Poland. A final humiliation came in 1924, when as a result of the 'Klaipeda Revolt' the area north of the river Memel was separated from the province and incorporated into Lithuania. Moreover, there were clear signs that in the region of the corridor the German population was increasingly being persecuted, and even ethnically cleansed.[10] On all sides East Prussia was compromised, becoming the embodiment of what throughout Germany was referred to as 'the bleeding frontier'.[11]

During this period, the fate of East Prussia continued to be placed within a history of a centuries-long battle with the East: the victories at Tannenberg in 1914 were widely publicised as a revenge for the battle lost by the Teutonic Knights in 1410 in that 'same' location. Numerous books were published along this line, most famously *Schlachtfelder in Ostpreußen*, a work written by officers from the province which addressed all the battles that took place between the Middle Ages and 1918.[12] The *Tannenberg-Denkmal*, of which construction started in 1924, also embraced this medieval memory culture, its layout deliberately reminiscent of a Teutonic castle.[13]

The feeling of being beleaguered by 'the East' had a tangible impact on East Prussia, and resulted in the construction and strengthening of fortification works throughout the province. Moreover, paramilitary organisations spawned in the region, arising from the fear that the small *Reichswehr* would be unable to defend East Prussia in the event of a Polish incursion. Even prior to the National Socialist dictatorship, the *Reichswehr* actively tapped into this fear, and when members of the armed wing of the NSDAP – the *Sturmabteilung* (SA) – proved willing to assist in the country's defence, the army offered military training to these men, and these efforts were particularly successful in East Prussia.[14]

---

[10] Roger Moorhouse, '"The Sore That Would Never Heal": the Genesis of the Polish Corridor', in Fisher and Sharp (eds.), *After the Versailles Treaty*, p. 193.

[11] Kossert, *Ostpreußen*, pp. 217–32; Richard Bessel, *Political Violence and the Rise of Nazism: the Storm Troopers in Eastern Germany 1925–1934* (New Haven, CT: Yale University Press, 1984), p. 6.

[12] Wehrkreiskommando I, *Schlachtfelder in Ostpreußen* (Königsberg: Königsberger Allgemeine Zeitung Volz & Co., 1932).

[13] Stefan Goebel, *The Great War and Medieval Memory: War, Remembrance and Medievalism in Britain and Germany, 1914–1940* (Cambridge: Cambridge University Press, 2007), pp. 36–8, 127–34.

[14] Richard Lakowski, *Ostpreußen 1944/45: Krieg im Nordosten des Deutschen Reiches* (Paderborn: Ferdinand Schöningh, 2016), pp. 60–3; Kurt Dieckert and Horst Großman, *Der Kampf um Ostpreussen. Der umfassende Dokumentarbericht* (Stuttgart: Motorbuch Verlag, 1998), pp. 16–20; Bessel, *Nazism and War*, p. 22; Christian Tilitzki, *Alltag in Ostpreußen 1940–45. Die geheimen Lageberichte der Königsberger Justiz* (Würzburg: Flechsig, 2003), p. 10.

More widely, Germany, which in the early 1920s was seriously politically divided, also had to overcome major domestic crises. On numerous
occasions unrest turned violent as different factions and parties made
grabs for power.[15] This led to the rise of a yearning to be part of a stable
country, unified behind a set of core values, which had last been the case
during the first weeks of the First World War when a 'manufactured
image' of euphoric nationalism had taken hold of the country.[16] Many
parties and organisations therefore stressed the importance of creating a
Gemeinschaft, – a community – which they considered far superior to the
traditional *Gesellschaft*, or society. The National Socialists also believed in
the added value of a *Gemeinschaft* which they, in line with widely held
attitudes, structured around the *Volk*, the 'healthy, undefiled members of
the community, whose devotion to the national good had not been
corrupted by selfish materialism'.[17] They connected to this idea of a
Volksgemeinschaft the 'promise of normality', both in the private and
public sphere, a 'goal that ordinary Germans had been longing for since at
least 1915, after hopes of a quick victory in the First World War had been
dashed'.[18] They saw the Volksgemeinschaft as a promise for a better
future, and to achieve this community it required the constant participation of the people. As such, the Volksgemeinschaft was meant as a
dynamic process rather than a clearly defined final objective.[19] Central
to the National Socialist *Volk*-thinking was the emphasis on Germany as a
self-sufficient state (an autarky), which meant that East Prussia, as an
agricultural province, would continue to receive considerable economic
benefits.[20] The traumatic experience of the First World War, when the
British 'hunger-blockade' brought Germany to the brink of famine,

[15] Jones, *Founding Weimar*.

[16] Peter Fritzsche, *Life and Death in the Third Reich* (Cambridge, MA: Belknap Press of
Harvard University Press, 2008), pp. 38–9. Interesting within the scope of this study is
Fritzsche's use of the word 'fortress'. He asserts that 'the people's community was also
always a statement of collective strength. It expressed "the peace of the fortress" that
enabled Germans to mobilise against their external enemies in World War I'.

[17] Stackelberg, *Idealism Debased*, pp. 4–5. Under Nazism, *Volk* was defined as a 'community
of blood'. See: Ingo Haar, 'German *Ostforschung* and Anti-Semitism', in Fahlbusch and
Haar (eds.), *German Scholars and Ethnic Cleansing, 1919–1945*, p. 2.

[18] Andreas Wirsching, '*Volksgemeinschaft* and the Illusion of "Normality" from the 1920s to
the 1940s', in Steber and Gotto (eds.), *Visions of Community in Nazi Germany*, p. 150.

[19] Michael Wildt, '*Volksgemeinschaft*: a Modern Perspective on National Socialist Society',
in Steber and Gotto (eds.), *Visions of Community in Nazi Germany*, p. 43.

[20] Dieter Hertz-Eichenrode, *Politik und Landwirtschaft in Ostpreußen 1919–1930:
Untersuchung eines Strukturproblems in der Weimarer Republik* (Cologne: Westdeutscher
Verlag, 1969), p. 2; Magnus von Braun, *Weg durch vier Zeitepochen: Vom ostpreußischen
Gutsleben der Väter bis zur Weltraumforschung des Sohnes* (Limburg a.d. Lahn: C.A. Starke
Verlag, 1965), pp. 198–205, 210–25; Wolfgang Schivelbusch, *Three New Deals:
Reflections on Roosevelt's America, Mussolini's Italy, and Hitler's Germany, 1933–1939*
(New York: Picador, 2007), pp. 224–5.

significantly contributed to this desire.[21] This agriculturally autarkic vision resonated particularly well among the majority of the East Prussian population, especially its rural Protestant inhabitants, and during the March 1933 elections – the last elections before Hitler established a dictatorship – East Prussia was the province with the highest percentage of NSDAP voters, an absolute majority of 56.5 per cent.[22] Much of this support should be traced back to the tireless efforts of Erich Koch, who in 1928 came to the province to head the newly created Nazi 'Gau Ostpreußen' as its provincial leader, or *Gauleiter*.[23] Most Gauleiter – Koch included – had stood by Hitler during the Party's early years, in which it was fighting for political power, a period known as the *Kampfzeit* or 'time of struggle'. Having proven their loyalty long before Hitler could repay them, these Party members from the first hour – *Alter Kämpfer* – could count on the dictator's unconditional trust and backing. They therefore yielded massive informal powers as well, which allowed them to assert increasing control over every aspect of their provinces.[24]

What certainly struck a chord locally during the Nazi rule were the efforts to incorporate East Prussia's martial heritage into the regime's official line, placing it, like before, into the perceived centuries-long struggle with 'the East'.[25] The Nazi regime took over care for the Tannenberg-Denkmal, which up to then was privately funded, rechristening it *Reichsehrenmal Tannenberg*.[26] Parallels were also drawn between the war Nazi Germany was to wage and the battles of the Teutonic Order in the Thirteenth century against the pagan Pruzzi; its Grand Master, Hermann von Salza (1165–1239), for example, had an SS Panzer battalion named after him, which in July and August 1944, in an event dripping with symbolism, even defended the 'Tannenberg Line' in Estonia.[27] Gauleiter Koch further adhered to the martial narrative: 'The history of East Prussia', he wrote in a guide about the province, 'is one of struggle.

---

[21] Watson, *Ring of Steel*, pp. 330–74.

[22] Martin Broszat, *The Hitler State: the Foundation and Development of the Internal Structure of the Third Reich* (London: Longman, 1981), p. xvii; Richard Hamilton, *Who Voted for Hitler?* (Princeton, NJ: Princeton University Press, 1982), pp. 361–71, 485.

[23] Karl Höffkes, *Hitler's politische Generale: Die Gauleiter des Dritten Reiches. Ein Biographisches Nachschlagwerk* (Tübingen: Grabert-Verlag, 1997), pp. 185–6.

[24] Jochen von Lang, *Bormann: the Man Who Manipulated Hitler* (London: Book Club Associates, 1979), pp. 241–3; Bessel, *Germany 1945*, p. 59.

[25] See for example: 'Vorbild Ostpreußen: Ein leuchtendes Beispiel der Tatbereitschaft aller', *Völkischer Beobachter*, 7 August 1944, quoted in Franz Seidler, *'Deutscher Volkssturm', Das letzte Aufgebot 1944/45* (Munich: Herbig, 1989), p. 31. 'As a result of being under a centuries-long threat of the East, East Prussia is a land of soldiers.'

[26] Goebel, *The Great War and Medieval Memory*, pp. 36–8.

[27] Holger Thor Nielsen and Richard Landwehr, *Nordic Warriors: SS-Panzergrenadier-Regiment 24 Danmark, Eastern Front, 1943–45* (Coventry: Shelf Books, 1999), p. 111.

Figure 1.2 The Tannenberg-Denkmal as a prominent tourist sight, ca. 1939.
Source: Author's collection

Struggle shaped the East Prussian people, it created their spiritual attitude'.[28] Meanwhile, the resonance of National Socialist principles and prejudices among large swathes of the East Prussian nobility shows that the Nazis achieved considerable success in fashioning their movement as a worthy standard bearer of Prussian militarism.[29]

In line with both the recent nationalist traditional way of thinking about the province and the National Socialist line, Gauleiter Koch saw East Prussia as 'a vanguard, path-breaking outpost for the German people on their way from the west to the east'.[30] A contribution in the official 'Europa Handbook' of the German Foreign Office also suggested that the German cities in the East, 'founded and settled by the knights of the German Order and citizens of the old tribes, became the centres of higher culture, and were able to radiate their formative power far beyond the borders of the German people ... upon the Slavic hinterland'.[31]

---

[28] Kossert, *Damals in Ostpreußen*, p. 104.
[29] Stephan Malinowski, *Von König zum Führer: Sozialer Niedergang und politische Radikalisierung im deutschen Adel zwischen Kaiserreich und NS-Staat* (Berlin: Akademie Verlag, 2003), pp. 73–89, 476–82; Christopher Clark, *Iron Kingdom: the Rise and Downfall of Prussia 1600–1947* (London: Penguin, 2007), pp. 151–3, 655–65.
[30] Schivelbusch, *Three New Deals*, pp. 224–5.
[31] Deutsches Institut für Außenpolitische Forschung, *Europa, Handbuch der politischen, wirtschaftlichen und kulturellen Entwicklung des neuen Europa* (Leipzig: Helingsche Verlagsanstalt, 1943), p. 138.

According to a widely published speech of *Reichswirtschaftsminister* Walther Funk at the opening of the October 1941 *Ostmesse* – Königsberg's biannual fair to promote Eastern goods – East Prussia was to serve as a 'transit highway' between the rest of Europe and the *Ostraum*.[32] The province's agricultural heritage was harnessed to this imperialist martial reading in the form of the '*Blut und Boden*' (blood and soil) rhetoric. Slogans like 'The German sword has liberated the east. Now the farmer follows with the plough' met the agreement of most East Prussians.[33] In 1939, that German sword corrected the 'injustices' done to the province's borders. Memel 'returned to the Reich' in March 1939 following German threats to Lithuania to invade the area, while the Polish regions of Zichenau (Ciechanów) and Sudauen (Suwalki) were also added to the territory of East Prussia following Germany's occupation of the country.[34]

As a border region, or *Grenzland*, East Prussia was strongly affected by Lithuanian and Polish influences. Large parts of the province, especially its south-eastern part, the *Masuren*, consisted of people who spoke either Polish or their own distinct language, known as *Masurisch*. These people, mainly Protestant farmers, considered themselves Germans, which they convincingly showed in 1920 when in the plebiscite for self-determination of the region, an overwhelming 98 per cent of them voted to stay part of Germany. Thirteen years later, a majority of them also voted for the NSDAP.[35] This cultural and ethnical diversity had long been celebrated as a positive, but in the 1920s it was increasingly seen as a threat to *Volk* unity, prompting a fervent Germanisation drive of different newly established *Heimat- und Deutschtumsverbände*.[36] Yet despite their fervent nationalism, these organisations nevertheless managed to irk the National Socialist authorities. Their objective with *Heimat*, or home soil, was to give credence to the diverse cultural content of Germany's different regions, as such providing the building blocks for the German

---

[32] Bundesarchiv (hereafter BArch) R 55/317, pp. 49–58. Rede des Reichswirtschaftsminister und Reichsbankpräsident Walther Funk anlässlich der Eröffnung der Deutschen Ostmesse in Königsberg Pr. am 12. Oktober; Our Special Correspondent, 'German Plans for Russia', *The Times*, 14 October 1941, p. 3.

[33] Heinz Schreckenberg, *Ideologie und Alltag im Dritten Reich* (Frankfurt a.M.: Peter Lang, 2003), p. 117–29.

[34] Wolf Gruner and Jörg Osterloh (eds.), *Das 'Großdeutsche Reich' und die Juden. Nationalsozialistische Verfolgung in den 'angegliederten' Gebieten* (Frankfurt a.M.: Campus Verlag, 2010), chs. 'Memelgebiet' and 'Regierungsbezirk Zichenau'.

[35] Michael Burleigh, *Germany Turns Eastwards: a Study of Ostforschung in the Third Reich* (London: Pan Books, 2001), pp. 185–7.

[36] Andreas Kossert, '"Grenzlandpolitik" und Ostforschung an der Peripherie des Reiches. Das ostpreußische Masuren 1919–1945', *VfZ* (51) 2003, p. 127.

Map 1.1 East Prussia during the Second World War

nation. This 'regionalism' stood in the way of a united *Grossdeutschland*, and after the Nazi takeover these associations were disbanded or incorporated (*Gleichgeschaltet*) into the National Socialist *Bund Deutscher Osten*. This organisation stepped up the nationalist efforts and soon many East Prussian place names were Germanised; in some areas of the *Masuren* up to 70 per cent of the place names were changed.[37] Nevertheless, it took until 1939 – when it was explicitly forbidden – for churches in the region to stop conducting services in Polish.[38]

The change in the appreciation of the multi-ethnic nature of the province and the challenges this posed can best be observed in Königsberg's academic culture. Scholars from Königsberg's Albertus University, a *Grenzland* university, had been at the forefront of *Ostforschung*, the

---

[37] Celia Applegate, *A Nation of Provincials: the German Idea of Heimat* (Berkeley: University of California Press, 1990), pp. 12–14, 197–227; Kossert, 'Grenzlandpolitik', pp. 136–8.
[38] Kossert, 'Grenzlandpolitik', pp. 136–8.

research on Eastern Europe and the region's relation to the German people. As Nazi officials saw the potential of these efforts for their racial agenda, they redirected funding to different research projects, which increasingly served to provide a pseudo-scientific foundation for German issues about ethnicity, resettlement, or population control.[39] These scholars were truly 'hardened warriors' on issues of Germandom, eager to align their scholarship to political priorities. Many of these 'experts' were subsequently deployed in the occupied East, posing increasingly radical solutions to race matters, and so actively giving shape to Germany's war of annihilation.[40] In these ways, East Prussia was far from untouched by National Socialism, as the regime's racism permeated important parts of its community, rallying both members of East Prussia's smaller communities as well as its academia.

Gauleiter Koch, who in the early 1930s had still occupied the socialist left wing of the Nazi Party, eventually became one of the regime's most notorious racist hardliners.[41] In the second half of the decade, he adopted, internalised, and eventually propagated, the regime's discriminatory dogmas in East Prussia. On 16 July 1941, in extension to his duties in East Prussia, Hitler appointed him as 'Reichskommissar für die Ukraine' (Reich commissar for Ukraine), which he would govern with an iron fist.[42] Koch brought many of his East Prussian subordinates with him and left little doubt as to what was expected of them: 'I will draw the very last out of this country. I did not come to spread bliss. I have come to help the Führer. The population must work, work, and work again', he told a Party meeting in Kiev. 'We definitely did not come here to give out manna. We have come here to create the basis for victory'.[43] Although the province's close ties to National Socialism were unmistakable, there were also large parts of East Prussia, especially its countryside, where the Volksgemeinschaft was less influential. There are two main reasons for this. Firstly, East Prussia was sparsely populated.

[39] Haar, 'German *Ostforschung* and Anti-Semitism', pp. 1–16; Kossert, 'Grenzlandpolitik'.
[40] Burleigh, *Germany Turns Eastwards*, pp. 54–5, 138, 169, 212–13.
[41] Manthey, *Königsberg*, pp. 647–8.   [42] Kershaw, *Hitler 1936–1945*, p. 406.
[43] Wendy Lower, *Nazi Empire-Building and the Holocaust in Ukraine* (Chapel Hill: University of North Carolina Press, 2005), pp. 106–10; Ralf Meindl, *Ostpreußens Gauleiter Erich Koch: eine politische Biographie* (Osnabrück: Fibre Verlag, 2007), pp. 385–7; Internationaler Militär Gerichtshof Nürnberg, *Der Prozess gegen die Hauptkriegsverbrecher vor dem Internationalen Militärgerichtshof Nürnberg 14. November 1945–1. Oktober 1946, Band XI, Amtlicher Text in deutscher Sprache Verhandlungsniederschriften 8. April 1946–17. April 1946* (Nürnberg: Reichenbach Verlag/ Obersten Kontrollrat, 1947), pp. 595–6.

Table 1.1 *Inhabitants of East Prussian cities by early 1939*

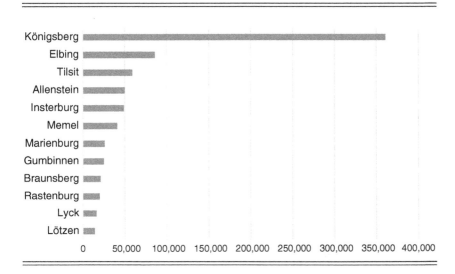

Königsberg was the only sizeable city of the province, counting some 361,000 inhabitants by 1939. Elbing, in the province's far west, held 86,000, with Tilsit (59,000) and Allenstein (50,000) completing the rather small list of East Prussian cities with over 50,000 inhabitants.[44] The province's limited population density, a mere 66.3 inhabitants per square kilometre, or 170 inhabitants per square mile, did not justify the presence of different National Socialist offices.[45] Moreover, on average only one in twenty-five people in the countryside possessed a radio set, and as there were also hardly any cinemas in these less populated areas, the regime struggled to get its message across.[46] Secondly, most farmers were content with their rural lifestyle which meant that few of them used the institutions of the Volksgemeinschaft to challenge their sociocultural

---

[44] The city of Elbing was only part of East Prussia between November 1920 (when as a result of the Versailles Treaty the province of West Prussia was dissolved) and November 1939 (when it once again became part of Reichsgau Westpreußen, which would soon become Reichsgau Danzig-Westpreußen).

[45] For the impact of these offices on local communities, see: Wildt, *Hitler's Volksgemeinschaft*, pp. 142–3; Stephenson, *Hitler's Home Front*, p. 168.

[46] Richard Grunberger, *A Social History of the Third Reich* (London: Weidenfeld and Nicolson, 1971), p. 152; Stephenson, 'Problems of Permeability', pp. 59–60.

position.[47] For most people in the East Prussian countryside – as noted in a report from Königsberg's Gestapo in July 1935 – the Volksgemeinschaft remained an abstract idea that few of them subscribed to of their own accord.[48]

In September 1939 Germany went to war, which brought a new, yet not completely unfamiliar, set of challenges for the East Prussian population. Immediately prior to the start of the war, rationing was introduced throughout Germany for many major consumer goods.[49] In conjunction with this, laws were passed to counter the illicit slaughter of animals, although the practice nonetheless grew throughout the course of the war. Sentences were particularly harsh in East Prussia, and even included death penalties, causing outrage among the rural population.[50] Nevertheless, the strict laws remained in place because the regime was determined to avoid a collapse of the home front as a result of undernourished urban populations. These measures could not prevent some people from feeling disadvantaged by the new situation which led to a polarisation between townspeople and farmers, echoing themes from 1914–18, laying bare the differences which traditionally existed between townspeople and the rural population.[51]

A further strain on the province's economy was the army's requisitioning of horses which it stepped up as the war broke out. East Prussia had a proud horse-breeding tradition, and since the army's contingent of horses – for which it demanded high standards and adhered to strict rules – had to go from 120,000 to 590,000 almost overnight, the remaining horses were of lesser quality. Although some horses were considered indispensable, the constant procurement of the province's best horses certainly impacted its agricultural output.[52]

In East Prussia, mobilisation for war significantly changed the community structure. East Prussia ranked among the provinces with the lowest number of indispensable (so-called *uk-gestellt*) workers, which meant that a large proportion of men could be taken out of the workforce to serve in

---

[47] John Connelly, 'The Uses of Volksgemeinschaft: Letters to the NSDAP Kreisleitung Eisenach, 1939–1940', in Fitzpatrick and Gellately (eds.), *Accusatory Practices*, p. 155–7.

[48] Wildt, *Hitler's Volksgemeinschaft*, p. 156.

[49] Stephenson, *Hitler's Home Front*, p. 168; Jeremy Noakes (ed.), *Nazism 1919–1945, Volume 4. The German Home Front in World War II* (Exeter: Exeter University Press, 1998), p. 511.

[50] Tilitzki, *Alltag in Ostpreußen*, pp. 52–4.

[51] Stephenson, *Hitler's Home Front*, pp. 172–3; Stephenson, 'Problems of Permeability', p. 58.

[52] Patricia Clough, *In Langer Reihe über das Haff: Die Flucht der Trakehner aus Ostpreußen* (Munich: Deutsche Verlags-Anstalt, 2005), p. 16; Burkhart Müller-Hillebrand, *Horses in the German Army (1941–1945)* (Washington DC: Historical Division, 1952), pp. 15, 88–91; R. L. DiNardo and Austin Bay, 'Horse-Drawn Transport in the German Army', *Journal of Contemporary History* (23) 1988, p. 130.

Figure 1.3 A 'Total War-horse' of inferior quality on the East Prussian home front.
One of its eyes has been surgically removed. *Source:* Author's collection

the armed forces. For example, in terms of percentage, East Prussian industries provided the highest numbers of industrial workers to the army.[53] Since former farmers constituted the largest segment of the German army, the men of Wehrkreis I, the East Prussian military district, were disproportionately represented among its ranks from early on. As a result, entire school classes were sent to the countryside to perform 'harvest service' during extended summer holidays to make good their absence.[54] Concurrently, the regime's wartime measures to conscript women into the workforce encountered less indignation in East Prussia than in Germany's urbanised provinces; since agricultural enterprises traditionally depended on female labour, this measure was not seen as an excessive one.[55]

---

[53] Rüdiger Overmans, *Deutsche militärische Verluste im Zweiten Weltkrieg* (Munich: R. Oldenburg Verlag, 1999), p. 316; Richard Overy, *War and Economy in the Third Reich* (Oxford: Clarendon Press, 1994), p. 296; Richard Overy, *Historical Atlas of the Third Reich* (Harmondsworth: Penguin, 1996), p. 99.

[54] Helga Gerhardi, *Helga: the True Story of a Young Woman's Flight As a Refugee and How She Re-united Her War-Scattered Family* (Aylesbury: Virona Publishing, 1994), p. 61.

[55] Noakes (ed.), *Nazism 1919–1945, Volume 4*, pp. 316–24; Grunberger, *A Social History of the Third Reich*, pp. 354–5.

The community structure was also affected by evacuation from bombed areas. As Germany's easternmost province, which, moreover, possessed little heavy industry, East Prussia was bombed significantly less than the western parts of the country and few East Prussians could therefore relate to the plight of their bombed-out compatriots.[56] Memel and Königsberg were bombed in late June 1941 by the Soviet Air Force immediately after the commencement of Operation Barbarossa, the German invasion of the Soviet Union, but these attacks were considered as little more than 'little fleabites' back in Berlin.[57] As a result of the limited bombing of the province, East Prussia from mid-1943 onwards became a reception area for almost 200,000 *Luftkriegsevakuierte*, air war evacuees, mainly from Berlin. Their reception required some adjustment, and the personal sacrifices the province's population had to make whilst billeting these people caused some friction. Population levels in the province had never been so high which resulted in a stricter rationing of food, gas, and electricity.[58] Furthermore, many former city dwellers, mainly Berliners, had trouble adjusting to the unfamiliar food and conditions of East Prussia's countryside, and according to Dr Max Draeger, the president of Königsberg's Higher Regional Court, '"complained" far more than the quiet, reserved East Prussians'.[59] In turn, when relatively well-fed Königsbergers were evacuated to Saxony after their city was bombed in August 1944, the young Sigrun Pluske was placed with a 'kind' family, which nevertheless 'really did not want us, because they said "You had so much food during the years of war, while we had all the bombing and very little food. Now you come and eat our little food", so there was a little hate on account of that'.[60] The war forced the German population to confront deep-routed local differences that had long existed between the provinces but as these remarks show, little headway was made in bridging the divide.

During the war, East Prussia again played its traditional role as bridge-head, and was used twice as a springboard for military campaigns – in the autumn of 1939, in the period leading up to the invasion of Poland, and in

---

[56] Ian Kershaw, *The 'Hitler Myth': Image and Reality in the Third Reich* (Oxford: Oxford University Press, 2001), pp. 201–7; Overy, *Historical Atlas of the Third Reich*, p. 102.

[57] Alastair Noble, 'A Most Distant Target: the Bombing of Königsberg, August 1944', *War & Society* (25) 2006, p. 58.

[58] Meindl, *Ostpreußens Gauleiter*, p. 401; Tilitzki, *Alltag in Ostpreußen*, p. 59.

[59] Marlis Steinert, *Hitler's War and the Germans: Public Mood and Attitude During the Second World War* (Athens, OH: Ohio University Press, 1984), p. 263.

[60] Imperial War Museum Sound Archive, Catalogue No. 12287, Sigrun Johanna Wilhelmiene Strooband, Reel 2. See also: Dorothea Bjelfvenstam, *Man nannte uns Hitlermädchen: Kinderlandverschickung von Königsberg nach Sachsen* (Föritz: Amicus-Verlag, 2012), pp. 7–8.

Figure 1.4 Nurses and troops in Insterburg, June 1941.
Source: Author's collection

the spring of 1941, in preparation for Operation Barbarossa. Numerous reports from the *Sicherheitsdienst* (SD) show that it was common among East Prussians to pride themselves on their close proximity to the troops, as they were able to hear soldiers' stories before the rest of the population, an extra source of first-hand information at a time when this was scarce.[61] The province was to remain a bridge between the rest of Germany and the northern and central sector of the Eastern Front throughout the war, and trainloads of supplies passed through the province constantly, while wounded soldiers were brought back to the province's many army hospitals.[62]

Although these factors firmly tied East Prussians to a war that was portrayed as being waged for the benefit of the Volksgemeinschaft, at the same time its institutions such as the *Ortsgruppe* and the *Kreisleitung*

[61] Heinz Boberach, *Meldungen aus dem Reich: Die geheimen Lageberichte des Sicherheitsdienstes der SS 1938–1945, Band 7* (Hersching: Pawlak Verlag, 1984), pp. 2273, 2275, 2463.
[62] Kossert, *Damals in Ostpreußen*, p. 128; Joachim Hensel, *Medizin in und aus Ostpreußen, Nachdrucke aus den Rundbriefen der 'Ostpreußischen Arztfamilie' 1945–1995* (Starnberg: Druckerei Josef Jägerhuber, 1996), pp. 375–9.

devoted less and less attention to the concerns of civilians, instead increasingly adopting auxiliary military roles.[63] This development meant that these local Party offices lost their relevance; rather than being manifestations of a society based on reciprocity between the state and its citizens, they represented a one-sided arrangement where the population gave and the regime took, and the offices' decreased interaction with the local community encouraged the East Prussian population to return to more traditional loyalties.

It is considerably harder to determine how well the Nazi racial agenda resonated within the province. The conquest of vast territories in Eastern Europe opened up new opportunities for the regime to pursue its genocidal policies which meant that it had to divert resources away from more easily relatable domestic issues, as such putting a strain on the promise of the Volksgemeinschaft. The regime's attention to the different minority groups considered racially inferior revealed the disparity between the concerns of the regime and those of the German public. By early 1944, over 200,000 foreign labourers worked in East Prussia, a number that increased to 237,000 by September 1944 and comprised one-tenth of the province's population.[64] Polish forced labourers had been the first to arrive in East Prussia in larger numbers, mainly as farm hands. With most German men at the front this led – despite a strict ban – to many unauthorised contacts between German women and Polish men, an unremarkable development given the significant Polish influence in the province's history. Nevertheless, penalties for those caught were notoriously harsh. The court of Königsberg, its judges felt, had to be exemplary in its convictions, since the inhabitants of East Prussia – the German province closest to the East – were more likely to succumb to the temptations of racial impurity.[65] This approach revealed the tensions between the requirements of war and achieving a racially pure Volksgemeinschaft. Pursuing one goal inevitably meant compromising the other, a balancing act with which the German leadership remained uneasy till the end.

Moreover, while most Germans had still hardly internalised the regime's anti-Semitic line and did not share its sense of urgency, in East Prussia, as

---

[63] Carl-Wilhelm Reibel, *Das Fundament der Diktatur: Die NSDAP-Ortsgruppen 1932–1945* (Paderborn: Ferdinand Schöningh, 2002), 351–9; Michael Kater, *The Nazi Party: a Social Profile of Members and Leaders, 1919–1945* (Oxford: Blackwell, 1983), pp. 221–8.

[64] BArch R 59/65, p. 52: Die ausländische und die protektoratsangehörigen Arbeiter und Angestellten im Großdeutschen Reich nach den wichtigeren Staatsangehörigkeiten in den Gauarbeitsamtsbezirken am 15. Februar 1944; Gosudarstvennyi Arkhiv Kaliningradskoi Oblasti (hereafter GAKO), 'Nemetski Fondi', Fond H-21, No. 46, Opis 1, Delo, 2,1, p. 59: Liste der im Gaugebiet Ostpr. Eingesetzten ausländ. Arbeitskräfte (Stichtag 30.9.1944).

[65] Kossert, *Ostpreußen*, p. 303.

elsewhere, the execution of the Holocaust could count on the 'tacit support' of the majority of the population.[66] As early as 1929 Jewish gatherings had been disrupted in East Prussia by armed Nazi gangs, and in 1935 police reports mention near lynchings in the province. During the *Kristallnacht*, on 9 November 1938, Königsberg's Neue Synagoge went up in flames, and from January 1939 onwards the city's Jews were increasingly forced into special 'Jew-houses'.[67] In June 1942 most of East Prussia's Jewish population were deported and killed in the Maly Trostenets extermination camp on the outskirts of Minsk, and in August of that year a last large group of elderly Jews was deported to Theresienstadt.[68] Meanwhile, East Prussia's Roma and Sinti Gypsy communities were persecuted. Initially they were herded into a purpose-built camp in Königsberg and used as forced labourers in an adjacent factory, but in March 1943 the camp was closed down after which its inhabitants were deported to Auschwitz.[69] By then, the killing conducted by the Einsatzgruppen, the SS paramilitary death squads, would have been widely known across Germany, although a 'conscious decision' was made to 'turn a deaf ear' to it.[70] This stemmed from two uneasy realisations: they had defined themselves opportunistically in the light of their changing environment, and their perverted consciousness had, as a result, enabled the province to actively facilitate the racial war of extermination.[71]

---

[66] Robert Gellately and Nathan Stolzfus, 'Social Outsiders and the Construction of the Community of the People', in Gellately and Stolzfus (eds.) *Social Outsiders in Nazi Germany*, pp. 3–5, 10; Kershaw, *The 'Hitler Myth'*, pp. 229–30.

[67] Kossert, *Ostpreußen*, 286–92; Fritz Gause, *Die Geschichte der Stadt Königsberg in Preußen*, *III. Band, Vom Ersten Weltkrieg bis zum Untergang Königsbergs* (Cologne: Böhlau, 1971), pp. 146–9. Scholars have repeatedly pointed out that most of these events were orchestrated by the local Party leadership. See: Stephenson, 'Problems of Permeability', pp. 52–3.

[68] 'Hitlerites Invade Jewish Gathering at Koenigsberg', *Jewish Telegraph Agency*, 26 February 1929; Alfred Gottwaldt, 'Die Deportation der Juden aus Ostpreußen 1942/ 43', in Neumärker and Kossert (eds.), *'Das war mal unsere Heimat ... '*, pp. 125–35. Two large transports left from Königsberg, one to Maly Trostenets outside Minsk on 24 June 1942 and one on 25 August 1942 to Theresienstadt. A number of smaller transports followed. By mid-1943 only around 30 Jews remained. For a general outline on the exclusion and extermination of Königsberg's Jews, see: Stefanie Schüler-Springorum, *Die jüdische Minderheit in Königsberg, Preussen: 1871–1945* (Göttingen: Vandenhoeck & Ruprecht, 1996), esp. ch. IV, 'Im Dritten Reich'. On the deployment of Jews in Königsberg's industries, see: Michael Wieck, *Königsberg, Zeugnis vom Untergang einer Stadt* (Augsburg: Bechtermünz Verlag, 1998), pp. 116–84.

[69] Guenter Lewy, *The Nazi Persecution of the Gypsies* (Oxford: Oxford University Press, 2000), p. 93.

[70] Bankier, *The Germans and the Final Solution*, pp. 145–6. Einsatzgruppe A assembled near Gumbinnen on 21–2 June 1941 in preparation for their operations. See: Andrej Angrick and Peter Klein, *The 'Final Solution' in Riga: Exploration and Annihilation, 1941–1944* (Oxford: Berghahn Books, 2012), pp. 49–50.

[71] Fritzsche, *Life and Death in the Third Reich*, pp. 264–8, 285.

The remote and recent past placed East Prussians in a situation where on the one hand they could rationalise their actions in terms of their own history while on the other they were fully satisfying the demands of the National Socialist regime. Thus, while the regime encouraged the persistence of local ideas and traditions, it would also champion its central message which revolved around the creation of a national Volksgemeinschaft. The lack of consistency between the two currents of thought did not seem to bother the regime unduly as long as the population acquiesced to the direction it took. The absence of the Party institutions in large parts of East Prussia, and the lack of their appeal, meant that the Nazi efforts to recast life on a local level were unsuccessful in the province. War only increased the gap between East Prussians and the larger German society as the insecurity of the war meant that they became less and less inclined to concern themselves with events outside those of their immediate situation. It seems therefore unlikely that the population's behaviour during the last year of the war can be traced back to the permeability of the Nazi ideology. At the same time, it is likely that most East Prussians felt that they, along with the majority of the German population, had 'burned their bridges' and had no option but to tie their fate to the outcome of the war.[72] The East Prussians' commitment to the war efforts should not be judged along the lines of agreement with the regime. Instead, their compliance was largely rooted in the lack of viable alternatives. As the war went on, the regime's demands towards its population continued to increase, culminating in the proclamation of Total War. The effects of this development will be discussed in the next section.

Total War in East Prussia

What encompasses 'Total War' has proven hard to determine.[73] East Prussia's diarists, when describing the increasingly radical measures that were being taken on the home front, do not use the word 'Total' in their description of the war. Instead, they point to personal changes in their lives without necessarily linking them to a larger picture. Total War has long been considered a monolithic concept and has consequently been painted in broad brush strokes.[74] Even General Erich von Ludendorff,

---

[72] Ibid., p. 266.

[73] See particularly the discussion in the fifth and final volume of a series examining this concept: Roger Chickering and Stig Förster, 'Are We There Yet? World War II and the Theory of Total War', in Chickering, Förster, and Greiner (eds.), *A World at Total War.*

[74] See for example: Jochen Hellbeck, 'Battles for Morale: an Entangled History of Total War in Europe', in Geyer and Tooze (eds.), *The Cambridge History of the Second World War, Volume III.*

Germany's most prolific advocate of Total War during the interwar years, felt hesitant about theorising it, feeling that 'war is reality, the gravest reality of a people'. What he could determine, however, was that 'the nature of Total War requires that it can only be waged when a whole people is truly threatened in its way of life, and is determined to commit itself to it'.[75] This sense of commitment, as we will see, was interpreted differently among the principal actors, and depended on their experiences.

This section reconstructs the considerations that underpinned Germany's Total War efforts. It first examines what the concept meant within German military thought in the years prior to the war. It then considers the impact of Total War among the ranks of the Wehrmacht and on the German home front during the war itself, after which it stresses the importance of analysing Total War on a local level. Finally, it will move toward a discussion of two case studies, the construction of the *Ostwall* around the borders of East Prussia and the formation of the East Prussian *Volkssturm*. This section argues that for war to be total, it requires both a physical and a mental component. The physical component is illustrated by the increasing use of men and materiel; the mental component concerns the internalisation of a sense of urgency and direct threat. These components were present in East Prussia and among East Prussians by the time Soviet forces reached the province's borders.

When on 18 February 1943 propaganda minister Joseph Goebbels asked an ecstatic hand-picked crowd in the Berlin *Sportpalast* whether they wanted Total War, 'a war more total and radical than anything that we can even imagine today', he asked a question charged with two decades of German trauma. Germans' experience and perception of the First World War ensured that the following war would inevitably be total. That war had turned from a spectacle to which young boys flocked with hopes of glory and validation into an industrial war of attrition that involved the entire nation. Between 1914 and 1918 men and women hundreds of miles behind the front lines had to work round the clock to produce weaponry, but also suffered horribly from the British hunger-blockade, which caused severe food scarcities throughout the country leading to riots, looting, inflation, and countless deaths.[76] This type of absolute warfare, which Ludendorff coined as 'Total War', was 'not only aimed against the armed forces, but also directly against the people'.[77] As such, the survival of a nation no longer merely required that the opposing state and its army be subdued, it demanded the total destruction of the enemy nation.[78]

[75] Erich von Ludendorff, *Der Totale Krieg* (Munich: Ludendorff Verlag, 1935), pp. 3, 6.
[76] Watson, *Ring of Steel*, pp. 330–74.   [77] Ludendorff, *Der Totale Krieg*, p. 6.
[78] Jan Willem Honig, 'The Idea of Total War: From Clausewitz to Ludendorff', in National Institute for Defence Studies (ed.), *The Pacific War as Total War*, pp. 34–7.

Long before Hitler assumed the dictatorship in 1933 he had subscribed to these ideas.[79] Yet, the Second World War did not start as a total war for Germany, since in the years leading up to the conflict the concept had not been part of its military mainstream. Instead, German military and political leaders often pointed to measures they felt needed to be 'total': 'total armament', 'total mobilisation', 'total administration', 'total control', and 'total command of operations'.[80] These terms were neither mutually exclusive nor were they ever meant to provide a complete picture of the war effort, but perhaps the most outstanding observation about 'Total War' is the small role the army seems to have played in it. Looking at these concepts, we see that only 'command of operations' belongs on the battlefield itself. During the interwar period the military expressed little interest in exploring the concept in depth. Only in 1937 did Generalleutnant (later Field Marshal) Wilhelm Keitel seek to clarify it, stating that Total War 'demands the marching in step of the Wehrmacht and the civil administration', an assertion that immediately introduces the four major groups of actors involved in this work: the Wehrmacht, Party and state bodies, and civilians.[81] Initially 'Total War' was thus about providing the Wehrmacht with the means to continue the fight rather than about the fight itself.

A major reason that German policymakers in the 1930s steered away from the idea that Germany set out to fight a total war was a mental one. While the Nazi leadership was at no turn opposed to putting the population through another war, there was always a lingering fear of a repetition of '1918', namely a collapse of the home front. It was painful to remember that, when put to the test, the German population had been incapable of shouldering the burdens of war.[82] In the years preceding the Second World War, Nazi officials nevertheless had been prepared to take far-reaching measures, and the period leading up to 1939 saw a drop in living standards and a significant decline of consumer goods.[83] Although during this period the efforts to subordinate the German economy to the impending war were hampered by a failure to set out a clear and unified agenda, by the time the conflict broke out the regime had successfully channelled most available resources to the war effort.[84] However, there

---

[79] Jürgen Förster, 'From "Blitzkrieg" to "Total War", Germany's War in Europe', in Chickering, Förster, and Greiner (eds.), *A World at Total War*, pp. 90–1.

[80] Ibid.   [81] Ibid.

[82] Eleanor Hancock, *The National Socialist Leadership and Total War, 1941–5* (New York: St Martin's Press, 1991), pp. 11–15; Hellbeck, 'Battles for Morale: an Entangled History of Total War in Europe', p. 360.

[83] Hancock, *The National Socialist Leadership and Total War*, pp. 17–19.

[84] Adam Tooze, *The Wages of Destruction: the Making and Breaking of the Nazi Economy* (London: Allen Lane, 2006), ch. 7.

were war measures, such as the stopping of overtime payments, that met with opposition from the population, and as token compromises the regime decided to reverse some of them. In line with National Socialist ideology, it also continued to hold off full-scale deployment of women in the workforce while – recalling the discontent caused by food shortages during the First World War – it showed reluctance to impose too strict rations.[85]

Throughout the second half of the 1930s the population was nevertheless gradually prepared for war. Yet, the tensions that resulted from the conquests of the Rhineland in 1936, the Sudetenland in 1938, the Memel area in 1939, and the occupation and division of the rest of Czechoslovakia later that year had all been eased by international appeasement. Hitler, however, saw an open conflict with Britain and France as inevitable on Germany's path towards continental hegemony, and from the spring of 1939 onwards actively sought to provoke them. He focused his energies on Danzig, an area where long-standing animosities between Germans and Poles could be exploited. This would serve as a sufficient pretext to go to war with Poland. Fear and resentment were stoked in Danzig throughout the summer, allowing German propaganda to pitch the Poles as an immediate threat to German national security. The regime deployed similar language as used twenty-five years earlier, presenting the conflict on the horizon as yet another 'war of national defence'. The military did not oppose the conflict – it was the most obvious theatre to showcase Germany's re-found military might – but in the months leading up to the conflict the population proved to be less easily convinced of its necessity. When war came, a resigned wait-and-see attitude dominated. There were no outbursts of spontaneous patriotism, yet there were also no protests either; the war did not come as a big surprise.[86] The first German tanks that rolled into Poland in the early hours of 1 September 1939 had been designed, manufactured, and financed by measures that clearly steered towards total war, yet for the time being the regime still stopped short of proclaiming that Germany was waging one.

Once the war commenced, a certain military arrogance, rooted in the dismissal of their enemies' strength, continued to prevent German leaders from entertaining the concept in earnest, and the successes of the *Blitzkrieg*, first in Poland, but most notably in France in June 1940, seemed to confirm these ideas.[87] Moreover, admitting that a 'total war' had to be waged meant admitting that an inferior enemy could not be

---

[85] Hancock, *The National Socialist Leadership and Total War*, pp. 21–4.
[86] Stargardt, *The German War*, pp. 23–7, 37–9. [87] Bessel, *Nazism and War*, p. 107.

effortlessly overcome, and thus conflicted with the official line of Germany's racial superiority. For the average German, Total War never seemed further away than when the *Wochenschau* showed the tight, seemingly endless Wehrmacht formations marching along Paris's Avenue Foch after the defeat of France, whose army was widely considered to be the only one capable of curbing Germany's continental ambitions.[88]

By that time, however, Hitler was already contemplating his next move – a war with the Soviet Union. That war was to be fought completely differently than those before. Seeing 'Judeo-Bolshevism' and Slavism as existential threats to Germandom, his views on warfare against the Soviet Union had always included the decimation and suppression of its populations as well. In late March 1941, he informed his military leadership that the coming war in the East would be a war of annihilation, a *Vernichtungskrieg*. Defeating the Red Army would remain one of the core tasks of the Wehrmacht, but brutal ideological and economic targets were also included in the German war aims in 1941, ensuring that the war would be total from the onset (see Chapter 2). The vastness of the Soviet Union, whose resources and population were there for the taking, invited German planners to pursue an uncompromising agenda. The war aims that the German high command set in order to control these were by all means 'total'.

The attack on the Soviet Union, 'Operation Barbarossa', commenced on 22 June 1941, as some 3.5 million German troops crossed its border. From the onset German soldiers were tasked with implementing a set of 'criminal orders', forcing them to jettison notions of restraint, morality, and civility, all the while showing an increasing disregard for the humanity of their opponent.[89] As a result, many of these men also started to realise that the magnitude of the total war they were waging could have repercussions. 'If you had seen what we saw you'd know we mustn't lose the war', a soldier on leave confided to his audience, thereby implicitly subscribing to the idea that a nation's desire to win war at all costs would always encourage its escalation, and, in the absence of any inhibiting factor, would inevitably become total.[90] The Soviet people, spurred on by their leadership and confronted with German aggression, had little choice but to fight a Total War. Red Army units made widespread use of scorched earth policies (even if this meant that their own population would suffer), thousands of partisan detachments were set up to harass and destroy German supply lines, civilians were ruthlessly deployed in the

---

[88] Newsreel 'Eine Parade über die Avenue Foch beschliesst diese Stunde der Ehrung', *Die Deutsche Wochenschau – OKW-Monatsbildbericht*, June 1940.
[89] Chickering and Förster, 'Are We There Yet?', p. 2.
[90] Grunberger, *A Social History of the Third Reich*, p. 41.

defence of their cities, the country's economic might was completely subordinated to the war effort, while the NKVD (the Soviet secret police) oversaw mass arrests, deportations, and thousands of executions of those accused of disloyalty to the regime.[91] Confronted with this dogged Soviet determination, be it voluntary or by coercion, the German soldier on the Eastern Front soon learned that he was fighting a Total War in which only one ideology – either National Socialism or communism – could survive.

The German home front, meanwhile, experienced the war differently, but the war there also moved in a 'total' direction from 1941 onwards. Somewhat paradoxically, the total ruthlessness of the war waged in the Soviet Union ensured that there were no reservations to exploit occupied territory to the fullest, which, in stark contrast to the First World War, meant that resources and foodstuffs kept arriving in Germany in large numbers, easing the burdens of its population.[92] Those on the German home front nevertheless soon learned what Total War entailed as they were on its receiving end. Lacking much of the agency that Wehrmacht soldiers had, German civilians, unsurprisingly, held different views on the scope of the war. By the autumn of 1941 the Allies had decided to launch an all-out bombing campaign against German urban centres. Unable to establish a foothold on the continent, their ethical restraints eroded as a result of the *Blitz*, and acknowledging that their instruments were too imprecise to hit specific targets, they opted to wage Total War directly against the German people as a whole, commencing a policy known as 'morale bombing'.[93] Although German morale never broke as a result, the bombing put an enormous strain on the Volksgemeinschaft and clearly laid bare its limitations. In the west of Germany, air raid alarms determined the rhythm of life, and living in air raid shelters became a daily reality of ordinary Germans' war experience.[94] Looting in the wake of bombing became so common that punishments eventually even included the death penalty.[95] In bombed-out communities the desire for revenge was so deeply felt that their inhabitants disregarded the Church's condemnation of vengeance as un-Christian, instead openly hankering for the arrival of *Vergeltungswaffen* (vengeance weapons).[96] As in every society that experiences shortages, the

---

[91] John Barber and Mark Harrison, *The Soviet Home Front: a Social and Economic History of the USSR in World War II* (London: Longman, 1991), ch. 4; David Stone (ed.), *The Soviet Union at War, 1941–1945* (Barnsley: Pen & Sword, 2010), chs. 1 and 6.

[92] Chickering and Förster, 'Are We There Yet?', p. 8.

[93] Richard Overy, *The Bombing War: Europe 1939–1945* (London: Penguin Books, 2014), pp. 245, 258–65.

[94] Neill Gregor, 'A Schicksalsgemeinschaft? Allied Bombing, Civilian Morale, and Social Dissolution in Nuremberg, 1942–1945', *Historical Journal* (43) 2000, pp. 1051–70.

[95] Süß, *Tod aus der Luft*, pp. 152–68.

[96] Grunberger, *A Social History of the Third Reich*, p. 34.

black market flourished, and the alternative economic networks that emerged – which in their very essence demanded its members place their trust in each other rather than official bodies – further eroded the grip of authorities on their people.[97]

The *seelische Geschlossenheit*, or 'psychological unity' that Total War demanded crumbled as the war went on.[98] Shopkeepers and public officials noticed a decline of the use of the 'Heil Hitler' greeting, while the Party badge was worn less and less in public.[99] Those factory workers who by the second half of the war still had not been drafted into the army, aware of how indispensable they were, knew that even when they refused to comply with work standards, threats from superiors were entirely hollow.[100] Cracks in the regime's propaganda message were observed almost as soon as the war broke out. When a teacher gave her class a homework assignment, 'What do people say about the war?' (aimed to map the views of the kids' parents and relatives), she found that

[t]he themes which recur are food shortages, war-weariness and the question of who was to blame. On the last, the children stated that some people said the Jews wanted war but others did not hesitate to blame Hitler.[101]

As most fathers were sent to the front, the lack of parental supervision meant that juvenile delinquency increased. The police observed an over-all 'moral decline' of the youth, with some girls even 'descending into prostitution'.[102] Among teenagers, the Hitler Youth, which many saw as an antechamber to military life, lost its appeal. Especially in Western Germany, dissenting youths, such as the *Edelweiss*-pirates or *Navajos*, formed their own subcultures with their own styles and customs, which the Nazi leadership found hard to suppress.[103]

As 1942 rolled by without a final victory for Germany, immediately followed by the devastating defeat of the Sixth Army at Stalingrad in February 1943, the regime decided to drop all pretence. In the 18 February *Sportpalast* speech, Goebbels presented the concept of 'Total War' for the first time to the German population and framed the decision to involve them as a positive development. For this war to be over as soon as possible (a notion embodied by the slogan: 'Total War – Shortest

---

[97] Malte Zierenberg, *Berlin's Black Market: 1939–1950* (Basingstoke: Palgrave MacMillan, 2015), p. 47–50.
[98] Honig, 'The Idea of Total War: From Clausewitz to Ludendorff', pp. 36, 39.
[99] Noakes (ed.), *Nazism 1919–1945, Volume 4*, p. 117.
[100] Werner, *'Bleib übrig!'*, p. 321
[101] Bankier, *The Germans and the Final Solution*, p. 143
[102] Tilitzki, *Alltag in Ostpreußen*, pp. 59–61.
[103] Noakes (ed.), *Nazism 1919–1945, Volume 4*, pp. 447–56; Kater, *Hitler Youth*, pp. 115–66.

War!'), Germans had to focus on the swift and violent removal of Jews and other *Untermenschen* (sub-humans), and the subjection of those nations that allowed international Jewry to thrive.[104] Goebbels admitted that defeat at the hands of Mongol hordes, which would reduce Germany to 'Bolshevik-Jewish slavery', was a real possibility and thus literally named a key marker of Total War – its sense of urgency and direct threat. Germany's nationhood lay in the balance; it was 'a struggle for self-defence and survival of a threatened and beleaguered racial community'.[105] From then on, every German knew that their nation was fighting a total war even when they did not personally experience its direct consequences.

To those with more intimate knowledge of the German war effort, the speech was received with mixed feelings. General Ludwig Crüwell, an *Afrikakorps* veteran who even during his time as a prisoner of war in British captivity remained a staunch supporter of the regime, merely considered it 'a rabble-rousing speech (*Aufputschrede*), which on the whole only deals with measures that are already underway'.[106] Indeed, despite the bravado of the speech, there was very little that could be done immediately to further the war effort.[107] Early in 1942 orders had already been passed down directing German industry to curtail resources for post-war planning, culminating in a blanket ban a year later.[108] Tank and aircraft production certainly increased significantly in 1943, but this was the result of planning and streamlining efforts that were long underway rather than the result of radical intervention from the administration.[109]

One of the most tangible results of Total War was that Gauleiter were given considerably more powers. As part of this Total War effort, Gauleiter were tasked with closing down factories and shops, and they were also placed in charge of implementing decrees that sought to secure manpower for the armed forces.[110] Yet, although Gauleiter felt little need to circumvent these orders, it was mainly left to company directors to

---

[104] Randall Bytwerk (ed.), *Landmark Speeches of National Socialism* (College Station: Texas A&M University Press: 2008), pp. 112–39.
[105] Christopher Browning, 'The Holocaust: Basis and Objective of the Volksgemeinschaft?', in Steber and Gotto (eds.), *Visions of Community in Nazi Germany*, p. 223. See also: Förster, 'From "Blitzkrieg" to "Total War"', p. 103.
[106] Sönke Neitzel, *Abgehört: Deutsche Generäle in britischer Kriegsgefangenschaft 1942–1945* (Berlin: Propyläen, 2005), p. 95.
[107] Richard Evans, *The Third Reich at War: How the Nazis Led Germany from Conquest to Disaster* (London: Penguin, 2009), pp. 423–7; Steinert, *Hitler's War and the Germans*, p. 263; Grunberger, *A Social History of the Third Reich*, p. 152.
[108] Martin Kitchen, *Nazi Germany at War* (London: Longman, 1995), pp. 48–9.
[109] Tooze, *Wages of Destruction*, ch. 18.
[110] Hancock, *The National Socialist Leadership and Total War*, pp. 147–50; Nathan Stoltzfus, *Hitler's Compromises: Coercion and Consensus in Nazi Germany* (New Haven, CT: Yale University Press, 2016), p. 7; Noakes, *Nazism 1919–145, Volume 4*, pp. 74–6.

establish how many of their firm's workers could be given up or replaced by foreign labourers.[111] Depending on the Gauleiter, the scope of Total War could even be decided on a local level, and its driving forces were thus undeniably centrifugal in nature, contributing to a 'dissolution of coherent government'.[112] Moreover, this decentralisation accelerated a process which Reichsleiter Martin Bormann referred to as *Gebietsegoismus*, or 'regional egoism': as central oversight subsided, local officials tended to favour their own *Gaue* in regard to foodstuffs and other products, and efforts to curb the practice yielded only limited results.[113] The hardships imposed by the regime and the sacrifices it demanded differed from province to province. As such, Total War counteracted the egalitarian principles of the Volksgemeinschaft, making it difficult for Germans to adhere to its mission as the war continued.

By early 1944 the possibility of an invasion of German territory became a pressing issue and discussions of the topic could no longer merely be regarded as defeatist. From the first days of the war, the organisation of domestic military affairs had been increasingly left to provincial authorities, with the final authority being placed with the province's Gauleiter in his capacity as *Reichsverteidigungskommissar* (Reich Defence Commissioner, or RVK). Contrary to the First World War, Germany was not placed under martial law and the civilian administration was not subordinated to military oversight. Instead, it was the RVKs who were to control the civil defence of the *Reich* and oversee all administrative branches within the *Wehrkreis* (military district) that they administered. The purpose of the RVK was to 'align the measures concerning the civil defence and the concerns of the armed forces in closest possible cooperation with the appropriate army departments in the *Wehrkreise*'.[114] Since all regulations the military wanted to implement at a provincial level had to be put in front of RVKs (and their staff), the Wehrmacht's ability to interfere in internal politics was limited, which was something Hitler consistently sought to ensure.[115]

The Wehrmacht and the Party thus had to work closely together, building on the framework that had been put in place both on a national level and by the RVK staff. The first detailed circular concerning a

---

[111] Hancock, *The National Socialist Leadership and Total War*, pp. 156, 163.

[112] Hans Mommsen, 'The Dissolution of the Third Reich', in Biess, Roseman, and Schissler (eds.), *Conflict, Catastrophe and Continuity*, p. 104; Steinert, *Hitler's War and the Germans*, p. 190.

[113] Werner, *'Bleib übrig!'*, p. 330.

[114] Reichsgesetzblatt Teil I, Nr. 158, 2 September 1939. 'Verordnung über die Bestellung von Reichsverteidigungskommissaren', p. 1565.

[115] Jürgen Förster, *Die Wehrmacht im NS-Staat: Eine Strukturgeschichtliche Analyse* (Munich: R. Oldenbourg Verlag, 2007), p. 34; Hüttenberger, *Die Gauleiter*, p. 155.

combined agenda regarding Germany's defence, dated 31 May 1944, was distributed by the Party chancellery. It showed a constructive attitude towards the army and a seemingly sincere intention to cooperate: 'In the smooth interaction of all German defensive forces lies the guarantee for quick and effective action and thus for success.'[116] Two further decrees concerning the 'cooperation between Party and army in an area of operations within the Reich' were distributed on 13 July 1944 and 20 September 1944.[117] The area of operations (the *Operationsgebiet*) was not merely a term that indicated the deployment of troops and materiel; it was also a juridical concept which within the military legal system indicated that the area would be subject to martial law.[118] Local Party officials, unsurprisingly, looked at the establishment of areas of operation on home soil with scepticism and suspicion as they feared being sidelined by the army in their own province. To alleviate these concerns, the day after the September decree Field Marshal Gerd von Rundstedt distributed an upbeat memorandum to highlight the opportunities of collaboration, asking the Gauleiter 'to act towards the population in a way that makes them aware of the necessity of this struggle and every single budding consequence', and expressing his confidence in the co-operation, given that he already knew 'with what tireless devotion the Gauleiter and all of their subordinated Party departments commit themselves to Führer and Fatherland'.[119] The memorandum's language showed that the army was trying to reach out, although it did not necessarily reveal any true sentiment on von Rundstedt's behalf, especially as the relationship between the Party and the army at the time was particularly strained. That summer, on 20 July, Hitler barely survived a bomb placed by *Oberst* Claus von Stauffenberg, while the army's simultaneous coup to take over the government – Operation Valkyrie – was only just thwarted.[120] It meant that Hitler lost his last shred of trust in his generals.[121]

Unsurprisingly, the decrees – which curtailed military operational freedom on German territory – have repeatedly been mentioned in the same breath as the assassination attempt, but looking at the dates of the two decrees suggests the measures were unlikely to have been implemented out of anger towards the military. The first of the two decrees was issued a

---

[116] Percy Schramm, *Kriegstagebuch des OKW, Band IV: 1. Januar 1944–22. Mai 1945* (Frankfurt a.M.: Bernard & Graefe, 1961), pp. 1565–8.

[117] Detailed orders (Befehl des Chefs OKW betr. Vorbereitungen für die Verteidigung des Reiches) can be found in: Schramm, *Kriegstagebuch des OKW, Band IV*, pp. 1569–72.

[118] See Chapter 6.

[119] BArch NS 6/ 348, p. 25: Anlage zum Rundschreiben 255/44 vom 21.9.1944.

[120] Kater, *The Nazi Party*, pp. 226–9; Hancock, *The National Socialist Leadership and Total War*, pp. 127–46; Evans, *The Third Reich at War*, pp. 492–4.

[121] Ian Kershaw, *Hitler 1936–45: Nemesis* (London: Penguin, 2001), p. 687.

week before the assassination attempt, the second decree a full two months afterwards, which left enough time for the ensuing storm to calm down before it was introduced. Moreover, in the case of an attack on home soil a country's army and its civil bodies simply *had* to collaborate, making – in the case of Nazi Germany – a Party involvement in defensive measures unavoidable. It is neither a hallmark of a totalitarian regime nor a sign of brutalisation. When a German invasion of Britain beckoned in 1940, the British government assumed a martial role that was rather similar to Germany's in 1944; it monitored civilians' reactions to the war, established a Home Guard, organised evacuation, and built defences.[122]

The first effort in which the Party assumed a prominent role was the construction of the *Ostwall* (East wall) defences along the eastern borders of Germany.[123] The idea of erecting defensive positions at the rear of the front was not a new one and was put forward by the army from the moment the tide of the war turned against Germany. Commanders started pushing for the creation of a defensive position along the older German and Russian frontier fortifications. Its main purpose would be to assure 'temporary inactivity' in the east in order to evict the western allies who were expected to conduct a large-scale cross-channel operation that spring.[124] This line of thought reflected that of the German high command, which also operated on the assumption that, once a first Allied cross-channel operation had been fought off, a potential second Allied operation would then be at least two years in the making. During this period, the forces that had so far defended Western Europe could be transferred to the East where they would once again confront and defeat the Red Army, thereby bringing the Allied alliance to its knees.[125] The idea, moreover, was hardly a new one: in a sense it echoed the hopes connected to the peace negotiations with Russia's new government in Brest-Litovsk between late 1917 and early 1918. By obtaining peace in the East, the German high command envisioned at the time that it would

---

[122] Peter Fleming, *Invasion 1940: an Account of the German Preparations and the British Counter-measures* (London: Rupert Hart-Davis, 1957), pp. 84–99.

[123] Noble, 'The Phantom Barrier', pp. 442, 466; Noble, *Nazi Rule and the Soviet Offensive*, pp. 26–8; Kershaw, *The End*, pp. 101–5. The singular term 'Ostwall' is deceptive since the Ostwall actually consisted of a series of defensive lines.

[124] See for example: Heinz Guderian, *Panzer Leader* (London: Penguin, 2009), p. 326. Karl-Heinz Frieser likened Germany's broader European defensive strategy for 1944 to a room with two doors: the door to the East was to be barricaded, while the Western door could be opened with the goal of throwing the invaders out. See: Karl-Heinz Frieser 'Irrtümer und Illusionen: Die Fehleinschätzungen der deutschen Führung', in Frieser (ed.), *Das Deutsche Reich und der Zweiten Weltkrieg 8*, p. 522.

[125] Gerhard Weinberg, *Germany, Hitler, and World War II* (Cambridge: Cambridge University Press, 1995), p. 282; Steinert, *Hitler's War and the Germans*, p. 258.

be able to free up dozens of divisions to deal a decisive blow on the Western Front – thus forcing the *entente* to the negotiating table.[126] Although ultimately German troops from the East arrived in much smaller numbers and, moreover, too late to turn the tide of the war, it did show that even in a war's eleventh hour nothing was decided yet. This time around the situation on the Eastern and Western Fronts was reversed, but the premise remained largely the same. As such, the strategy even 'revenged' the defeat of 1918 and thus ticked many of the boxes of the National Socialist warfare.

Therefore, on the Eastern Front, German soldiers were to simply stay put. Reichsführer-SS Heinrich Himmler, shortly after his appointment as Commander-in-Chief of the Reserve Army, told an audience of officers on 25 July that '[t]he time for intelligent operational methods is past. In the east, the enemy is on our borders. The only type of operation available here is to advance or to stand still'.[127] Both the Chief of Staff of the OKH (Oberkommando des Heeres, the High Command of the Army), Generaloberst Heinz Guderian, and the Chief of the OKW (Oberkommando der Wehrmacht, the High Command of the Armed Forces) Field Marshal Wilhelm Keitel passed down orders to commence the construction of fortifications in Eastern Germany.[128] The involvement of both the OKH and the OKW, the German military's highest planning and executive bodies, shows the importance the German High Command immediately attached to the construction of the positions. Meanwhile, based on the assertion that 'an impassioned appeal of the Führer to the idealism and patriotism of the entire people would be sufficient to call hundreds of thousands of volunteers to the colours within a few days so as to erect a dam in the east', on 13 July Gauleiter Koch ordered all German males between the ages of fifteen and sixty-five from East Prussia's border districts to construct defensive positions.[129] East Prussia would be shielded by the so-called Ostpreussen-Schutzstellung, the section of the Ostwall that was built twelve miles in front of East Prussia's border and roughly followed the river Memel in the province's north and the Narev in the east and south.[130]

The construction of this Ostwall was accompanied by a massive propaganda campaign which stressed the link between Front and Heimat. The

[126] David Stephenson, *1914 – 1918: the History of the First World War* (London: Allen Lane, 2004), pp. 392–3.

[127] Peter Longerich, *Heinrich Himmler* (Oxford: Oxford University Press, 2012), p. 717.

[128] Noble, 'The Phantom Barrier', p. 445.

[129] Ibid., pp. 446–7; BArch R 55/616, p. 105: Betrifft: Errichtung eines Grenzschutzes im Osten, 13 July 1944.

[130] Noble, *Nazi Rule and the Soviet Offensive in Eastern Germany*, pp. 102, 107.

effort was widely portrayed as a popular movement, yet the regime left no doubt that participation in the construction was compulsory.[131] Although a sincere sense of patriotism combined with a deep-seated fear of the Soviets was common among the workers (a theme to which we will return in Chapter 4), far-reaching means of coercion were nevertheless used to ensure participation as well. These measures included prison sentences and death penalties according to martial law, immediately revealing the army's impact on the province.[132] Irrespective of its military use, the digging was a means of pacifying the province's population as media outlets diverted attention from the looming Soviet threat, transforming the construction of the Ostwall into an expected manifestation of the province's resolve.[133] The Wehrmacht did not oppose this total mobilisation of the East Prussian civilian population: in a fight for what it rightly viewed as the very survival of not only itself, but the German state, the German High Command had long encouraged units to make full use of their direct environment. During the Wehrmacht's stay on the Eastern Front, this emboldened most troops to fully exploit all available resources at their disposal, so much so that the army had come to rely on the forced assistance of civilians in the construction of defensive works and many other auxiliary tasks.[134] Troops had grown desensitised to the vast use of forced labour which had been explained as vital to the war effort, thereby directly linking the suppression of populations to traditional concepts of obedience, honour, and patriotism.[135]

Gauleiter Koch received repeated praise from different army commanders for his assistance in the construction of the Ostpreussen-Schutzstellung.[136] Although they might have felt that they were press-ganged into expressing their gratitude, what Koch could achieve in East Prussia was exactly what the military could not – rallying large numbers of people and materials for the defence of the province.[137] The Soviet summer offensive of 1944, Operation Bagration, had been disastrous for the Wehrmacht, and afterwards the German army

---

[131] Noble, 'The Phantom Barrier', p. 449.

[132] Noble, *Nazi Rule and the Soviet Offensive in Eastern Germany*, p. 101.

[133] To justify the use of civilian populations during times of great peril, Nazi leaders found a precedent in the French *levée en masse* in the wake of France's defeat at Sedan in 1793. See: Wolfgang Schivelbusch, *The Culture of Defeat: On National Trauma, Mourning, and Recovery* (London: Granta, 2003), p. 9.

[134] See Chapter 2.

[135] Omer Bartov 'Trauma and Absence: France and Germany, 1914–1945', in Addison and Calder (eds.), *Time to Kill*, p. 354.

[136] Noble, 'The Phantom Barrier', pp. 450–1.

[137] Noble, *Nazi Rule and the Soviet Offensive*, p. 106.

Figure 1.5 A highly symbolic depiction of soldiers manning a trench in East
Prussia while the men who dug it can be seen leaving in the background,
November 1944. *Source:* Berliner Illustrierte Zeitung, 9 November 1944

completely lacked the resources to oversee these efforts themselves.
In his war diary, Generaloberst Erhard Raus, the commander of the
Third Panzer Army, noted that 'everywhere people could be seen
digging', and praised the resourcefulness of the workers.[138] Over
300,000 East Prussians were called up, while an additional 200,000
forced labourers, mainly from Lithuania and Poland, and 25,000
men of the Reichsarbeitsdienst (RAD) also took part in the
construction.[139] Meanwhile, Koch repeatedly played up his role,
claiming that 'without the Party there is no *Frontgau* East Prussia',
and maintained that 'only the Party can take up the responsibility to
guide the masses'.[140] Even though this bragging caused scorn among
the ranks of the military, the recognition the Party sought for its role
in the province's defence was certainly deserved.

[138] Erhard Raus and Steven Newton, *Panzer Operations* (London: Da Capo Press, 2003), p.
305–6.
[139] BArch Ost-Dok. 8/593, pp. 4–7: Magunia.
[140] BArch Ost-Dok. 8/510, p. 6: Dieckert.

Over the autumn, Soviet troops were halted at the borders of the province and a period of calm set in during which the Wehrmacht assumed ultimate authority over the defensive efforts in the province. An extensive evaluation report, dated 6 February 1945, even went as far as to refer to the Ostwall positions as 'OKH-Stellungen' (positions of the OKH), continuing that 'under the long-term leadership of the General Staff, by the call up [and] use of a large number of people, a multi-layered defensive position system has emerged between August 1944 and the beginning of the Russian offensive'.[141] Since the digging took place close behind the front line, army pioneers were often present to guide the efforts as well.[142] Despite the army's increasing authority in these matters, the Party remained actively involved throughout the process. On 11 January 1945, the Party chancellery reported that 65,000 people were still involved in the digging of defensive positions in East Prussia, and over 700,000 in total throughout Eastern Germany. The same report indicated that Gau East Prussia had agreed to transfer 15,000 civilians previously under its own supervision to Army Group Centre – the army group tasked with the defence of the province – to assist in the construction of its positions.[143]

Despite the efforts to work closely together, there were certainly conflicts between Gauleiter Koch and the OKH, most infamously regarding the construction of defences around Königsberg. In November 1944 the army ordered the construction of the 55 mile-long 'Frischung-Kanal-position', which would protect Königsberg and the Samland area. Koch disagreed with this choice and would continue to divert manpower to build out the 120 mile-long 'Heilsberg-Deime-position', which would enclose a wider area. He disregarded the army's protestations that there would be no troops available to defend the position – an argument that could be deflected by accusing the army of defeatism.[144] The working relationship between the Party and army in East Prussia during this period was aptly described by Heinrich Lindner, a high-ranking official in Koch's staff, as 'bearable'.[145] In addition, conflicts not only emerged

[141] BArch RH 2/332, p. 57: Generalstab des Heeres Abt. Landesbefestigung Nr. 2145/45 geh. 6. Februar 45. Gedanken zum Stellungsbau auf Grund der Winterschlacht. 'unter Einsatz eines zahlenmässig grossen Volksaufgebotes'.
[142] BArch Ost-Dok. 8/584, p. 3: Wenzel; BArch Ost-Dok. 8/593, 7: Magunia. For concrete orders of pioneers to local Party officials, see: BArch RH 2/316, p. 133: Oberkommando des Heeres Gen St d H/ Gen d. Pi u. Fest/ Gen z.b.V. – Staffel ZNr. 11400/44 geh. H. Qu.OKH., 10.11.44.
[143] BArch RH 2/331b, p. 95: Op Abt/Abt Lds Bef. 11.1.45 Vortragsnotiz.
[144] BArch RH 2/331b, p. 93: Fernschreiben gez. Guderian OKH/GenStdH/Op Abt/Abt. Lds Bef Nr. 445/45 g.Kdos. 12.1.45; BArch RH 2/332, p. 58: Generalstab des Heeres Abt. Landesbefestigung Nr. 2145/45 geh. 6. Februar 45. Gedanken zum Stellungsbau auf Grund der Winterschlacht.
[145] BArch Ost-Dok. 8/561, p. 3: Lindner.

between the Party and the army but also among different commanders. Generaloberst Guderian had to interfere in a conflict between Generalmajor Hans Mikosch and the frustrated commander of the 'Inster-Angerapp-position', Generalmajor Ewald Kraeber, since Mikosch had passed down incorrect orders to prevent the strengthening of this position. Guderian sent a telegram to reverse Mikosch's orders stressing that they had been 'inaccurate'.[146] Guderian's interference nevertheless did not alleviate the conflict between the two men, since just over a week later Generalmajor Kraeber was transferred to Army Group South, where he was put in charge of the construction of similar positions.[147]

By the time the Red Army commenced the East Prussian offensive, the majority of positions were not yet completed, and after the war army commanders repeatedly blamed this on conflicts with the Party.[148] However, there should be no doubt that the Wehrmacht held the final authority in the command of operations in the province. Oberregierungsrat Otto Wenzel, one of Gauleiter Koch's advisors, recalled in that regard the construction of the Ostwall, 'The Wehrmacht basically both set out the greater lines as well as the wishes for its implementation.'[149] The increased army influence is also indicated by two internal propaganda reports on the digging, both from early November 1944, which do not mention the Party at all but simply refer to the 'Schanzwerk der Bevölkerung' (entrenchment work of the population), or as 'Grenzbefestigungen' (frontier fortifications).[150] Countless army orders dating from the autumn still exist that talk in depth about the construction of defensive positions. Party orders are considerably scarcer.[151] In the summer of 1944 East Prussia's population got its first

---

[146] BArch RH 2/316, p. 108: Fernschreiben gez. Guderian Chef GenStdH Nr. 4071/44 g. Kdos 12 Nov 1944.

[147] BArch R H2/316, p. 85: Fernschreiben gez. v. Bonin OKH/ GenStdH/ Op Abt (Fest) Nr. 14869/44 geh 21.11.44.

[148] Otto Lasch, *So fiel Königsberg: Kampf und Untergang von Ostpreußens Hauptstadt* (Munich: Gräfe und Unzer Verlag, 1958), p. 26–32.

[149] BArch Ost-Dok.8/584, p. 3: Wenzel.

[150] BArch R 55/608, p. 30: Der Chef des Propagandastabes Berlin, den 8.11.1944. Vertraulich! Mundpropagandaparole Nr. 5 Betr. Bedeutung der Grenzbefestigungen; BArch R 55/602, p. 103: material ueber den volkskrieg in ostpreussen. 13 November 1944.

[151] See for example: BArch RH 2/316, pp. 108–10: Fernschreiben gez. Guderian Chef GenStdH Nr. 4071/44 g.Kdos 12. Nov 1944. BArch RH 2/316, pp. 112–14: Der Chef des Generalstabes des Heeres Op Abt (Fest) Nr. 11 886/44 g.K. H.Qu., 11.11.44 Anweisung für den Ausbau und die Verteidigung ständiger Festungen; BArch RH 2/ 317, p. 70: Oberkommando des Heeres GenStdH/Op.Abt./Org.Abt. Nr II/47289/44k. Kdos H.Qu, den 8. Dezember 1944 'Unterstellungsverhältnis der Abschnitts- und Festungs-Kdten im Osten'. On Party orders dated between 11 July and 9 September,

sense of what it was like to be part of a Total War, as large parts of the province were mobilised to assist in the construction of the Ostwall defences. Farmers lamented their deployment during the harvest time, and many positions were dug through fields which significantly diminished the crop yields for the years ahead.[152] Work on the Ostwall continued until the start of the East Prussian offensive in January 1945. Extensive indoctrination through Party outlets assured that civilians interpreted the efforts as Party-led, which, since the army's involvement was simultaneously downplayed, cemented the Party's status as the most prominent proponent of Total War. However, the Wehrmacht's limited presence in the national media should not be confused with an unwillingness on its part to deploy civilians, which becomes particularly clear when analysing the Volkssturm.

The Volkssturm, Nazi Germany's last-ditch militia, has been subjected to more comprehensive research than the Ostwall.[153] We will therefore divide our examination of the Volkssturm into two parts: this section will examine the period from its establishment in late September 1944 until the initial defence of Festung Königsberg in late January 1945, in order to determine how the Party–Wehrmacht relations shaped the militia. In Chapter 6 we will return to the Volkssturm and analyse its deployment during Königsberg's siege (late January 1945 – early April 1945). As with the Ostwall, the Volkssturm is traditionally presented as a brainchild of the Party, but again it was the Wehrmacht that spearheaded its creation. Measures to include elements of the German home front in the defence of Germany date back as early as 1941.[154] By August 1943 all men born after 1884 (i.e. fifty-nine years or younger at the time) were registered by orders of Field Marshal Keitel, although they were not yet to be called up.[155] The Party, on the other hand, initially opposed the creation of a militia, mainly driven by the notion that its creation would negatively impact home-front morale.[156] However, while in August and early September 1944 Guderian gave shape to the new militia, by mid-September the final responsibility was definitively shifted to the Party.

---

see: Institut für Zeitgeschichte (hereafter IfZArch) MA 736/ NSDAP Hauptarchiv Gau Ostpreussen, Königsberg Pr., den 2 Dezember 1944. Aufstellung A. Ostwallbau.

[152] Dieckert and Großman, *Der Kampf um Ostpreussen*, p. 31.

[153] Yelton, *Hitler's Volkssturm*; Franz Seidler, *'Deutscher Volkssturm'*, *Das letzte Aufgebot 1944/45* (Munich: Herbig, 1989); Hans Kissel, *Der Deutsche Volkssturm 1944/1945: Eine territoriale Miliz im Rahmen der Landesverteidigung* (Berlin: Verlag E.S. Mittler, 1962).

[154] Yelton, *Hitler's Volkssturm*, pp. 7–12.

[155] Rudolf Absolon, *Die Wehrmacht im Dritten Reich: 19. Dezember 1941 bis 9. Mai 1945* (Boppard am Rhein: Boldt Verlag, 1995), p. 287.

[156] Yelton, *Hitler's Volkssturm*, p. 18.

The Party came to oversee the Volkssturm in this circuitous way largely because of Hitler's lack of confidence in the military after 20 July, as we have seen above.[157]

On 25 September 1944 Hitler issued the 'Führer decree concerning the formation of the German Volkssturm' to his Gauleiter.[158] The scope of the Volkssturm was to be all-embracing: on 18 October a national call-up made clear that it was to include 'all able-bodied men from 16 to 60 years'.[159] The higher age groups, the East Prussian propaganda office maintained, would provide steel to the force: 'The soldier of the First World War can weather a storm ('ist Sturmerprobt'), is steadfast and he does not lose his nerves.'[160] Nevertheless, the age of the recruits became the focal point of widespread scorn: 'It is a stew, consisting of young vegetables and old bones!'[161] Since participation was compulsory, mocking the Volkssturm was perhaps the most effective way to express disagreement with the course the regime was now taking, as well as a way to channel some of the anxieties that arose as a result of the call-up. In East Prussia, where the Volkssturm was mustered with great zeal and almost immediately deployed, ridicule was rife, and as a result was closely monitored and reported on.[162]

It was again the Party that took the initial lead in East Prussia. Gauleiter Koch even outdid his Führer and ordered the creation of the East Prussian Volkssturm two days before the rest of Germany.[163] According to Oberregierungsrat Wenzel, the idea for the Volkssturm originated here from the experiences of the mobilisation for the Ostwall, and it is not hard to see why he thought so.[164] While explaining the validity of the Party's role in the establishment of the Volkssturm to his direct subordinates – his *Kreisleiter* – in early October, Koch recalled '[h]ow in a few hours [after the call for the construction of the Ostwall] the first ground was moved, and how from these humble beginnings already in eighty-two days a gigantic defensive work has risen. At the time, I only relied on ourselves and on the force of our province'.[165] Koch noted that the Ostwall had been dug in a National Socialist spirit, and now it was time to man it as

[157] Ibid., pp. 12–13, 19–31.
[158] Martin Moll (ed.), *Führer-Erlasse 1939–1945* (Hamburg: Nikol Verlag, 2011), 460. *EdF über die Bildung des Deustchen Volkssturm*, 25 September 1944.
[159] Yelton, *Hitler's Volkssturm*, p. 13.
[160] BArch R 55/602, pp. 103–5. Sondermann, 13 November 1944.
[161] Werner Haupt, *Königsberg – Breslau – Wien – Berlin: Der Bildbericht vom Ende der Ostfront* (Friedberg: Podzun-Pallas Verlag, 1978), p. 33.
[162] See for example: Paul Ronge, *Im Namen der Gerechtigkeit, Erinnerungen eines Strafverteidigers* (Munich: Mindler Verlag, 1963), p. 307.
[163] Dieckert and Großmann, *Der Kampf um Ostpreussen*, pp. 63–4.
[164] BArch Ost-Dok.8/584, p. 6: Wenzel.   [165] Seidler, 'Deutscher Volkssturm', p. 297.

such. It was also apparent that the raising of the Volkssturm again allowed him to take his spot in the limelight in the Party's Total War efforts.[166]

By the time the East Prussian Volkssturm was decreed, two Soviet Fronts (the equivalents of army groups) were already threatening East Prussia. One of them, the First Baltic Front headed by Army General Ivan Bagramyan, stood in central Lithuania, within 100 miles from the East Prussian borders. On 5 October it started its push to the Baltic Sea with the port city of Memel – the northernmost East Prussian city – as its strategic goal. Just four days later, on 9 October, it had reached the Baltic at Heydekrug, south of Memel, thereby cutting off the city. Memel's Volkssturm men – completely unprepared – were immediately deployed in its defence and suffered heavy casualties.[167] The neighbouring Third Belorussian Front under Army General Ivan Chernyakhovsky launched an operation towards the heart of East Prussia on 16 October, known in German historiography as the 'Gumbinnen Operation'.[168] Volkssturm units were again deployed and, together with the divisions of the Third Panzer Army, they halted the thrust before Gumbinnen, a city in the East of the province, after which the Soviet troops were pushed back. By the end of the month the offensive had been repelled and the Volkssturm, according to the East Prussian propaganda office, could proudly look back on its baptism by fire. Moreover, 'except for isolated and unimportant misunderstandings the cooperation [with the Wehrmacht] is outstanding'.[169] Privately however, Gauleiter Koch took another line, and on 25 October he sent a telegram to Reichsleiter Bormann to highlight the performance of the Volkssturm during the last days, while simultaneously accusing the army leadership of poor performance.[170]

Nevertheless, during the final months of 1944 the Party and the Wehrmacht in East Prussia attempted to improve relations. Although Gauleiter Koch continued to oppose these efforts, most Kreisleiter – who in many cases headed the Volkssturm battalions – were open to closer collaboration.[171] Initially, the Wehrmacht used the Volkssturm to perform a string of semi-military tasks, such as organising the evacuation of goods and civilians and digging defensive positions. Yet by

[166] Ibid., pp. 55–6, 297–9; Alastair Noble, 'The People's Levy: the Volkssturm and Popular Mobilisation in Eastern Germany 1944–45', *Journal of Strategic Studies* (24) 2001, p. 172.

[167] Noble, *Nazi Rule and the Soviet Offensive*, p. 132. Heinz Schön, *Die letzten Kriegstage: Ostseehäfen 1945* (Stuttgart: Motorbuch Verlag, 1995), p. 44.

[168] Dieckert and Großmann, *Der Kampf um Ostpreussen*, pp. 16–17.

[169] BArch R 55/602, p. 104: Sondermann, 7 November 1944.

[170] Seidler, '*Deutscher Volkssturm*', pp. 326–7.

[171] Yelton, *Hitler's Volkssturm*, pp. 120–1; BArch Ost-Dok. 8/536, p. 7: Hoffmann.

Figure 1.6 A propaganda picture of two Volkssturm recruits, one young, one old, being trained by a non-commissioned officer of the Panzergrenadier-Division Grossdeutschland, October 1944. *Source:* Bundesarchiv Bild 183–J30793, Schwahn

December, army commanders treated the Volkssturm virtually the same as other units. In the north of East Prussia, near Tilsit, for example, six Volkssturm battalions (mostly mustered in nearby Ragnit and Tilsit and numbering around 240 on average, barely half of the regular battalion strength) were to man positions close behind the front line in anticipation of the East Prussian offensive.[172] By the end of 1944, Volkssturm units were fully incorporated into the military chain of command, with army and corps commanders possessing 'full tactical and logistical control over every Volkssturm battalion engaged in Eastern security occupations'.[173]

---

[172] BArch RH 24–9/138, p. 63: Bezug: FS Pz.AOK 3 v.10.12.44 Betr.: Volkssturm.: BArch RH 24–9/138, p. 134: Bezug: FS Pz.AOK 3 Ia Nr. 12493/44 geh. v. 20.12.44; BArch RH 24–9/137, pp. 106–7: Generalkommando IX. Armeekorps K.Gef.Stand, den 11.11.1944 Ia Nr. 4006/44 geh. For further details on the appreciation and collaboration, see: BArch RH 24–9/137, pp. 108–9: Generalkommando IX. Armeekorps K.Gef. Stand, den 11.11.1944, Ia Nr. 4029/44 geh.

[173] Yelton, *Hitler's Volkssturm*, p. 119.

When the East Prussian offensive finally commenced in January 1945, Volkssturm battalions were fully deployed in its defence, often with little regard to their fighting value. In some cases, such as during counter-attacks on the town of Schlossberg near the province's eastern border, a Volkssturm battalion was wiped out due to a lack of cooperation with the nearby 1st Infanterie-Division.[174] Yet closer cooperation with the army did not necessarily lead to a better chance of survival for Volkssturm units. At the village of Nautzken, near Königsberg, the commander of the 286th Sicherungs-Division dismissed the concerns of the commander of a Volkssturm Standbattaillon (a type of unit meant for work further behind the front) that his men would be completely useless in battle. The battalion was ordered to defend positions against the mainstay of the Soviet Forty-third Army, with predictably devastating results.[175] It should be noted, however, that there were certainly instances when the Volkssturm performed well beyond expectation, and that they were not mere cannon fodder.[176] During the initial fighting for the city in late January 1945, some 10,000 Volkssturm men defended Königsberg, many of whom had earlier defended their own towns and villages closer to the East Prussian border, and who in some cases had thus been fighting for over two weeks. Especially in the northern and eastern sectors of Königsberg they were able to fight off sustained Soviet attacks, initially virtually on their own and later with the help of newly arrived regular units.[177]

Germany's geopolitical position by mid-1944, with the allies poised to invade from both the east and the west, forced Party and Wehrmacht to work closely together. By analysing Total War on a provincial level, this section has managed to move away from the persistent focus on a select Nazi elite and instead refocused on the impact of the war on the lives of civilians. In East Prussia, the construction of the Ostwall and the establishment of the Volkssturm involved a previously unknown, virtually total scale of mobilisation. The two efforts share important similarities: they were openly championed by the Party, who took up the propagandist lead

---

[174] Werner Richter, *Die 1. (ostpreussische) Infanterie-Division* (Munich: Schildbuchdienst-Vertrieb, 1975), p. 144; Vasili Boiko, *S dumoj o Rodine* [With a thought of the motherland] (Moscow: Voenizdat, 1982), p. 237.

[175] Helmut Borkowski, *Die Kämpfe um Ostpreußen und das Samland 1944–1945* (Lengerich: Self-published, 1994), pp. 41–2.

[176] Yelton, *Hitler's Volkssturm*, p. 120.

[177] Bastiaan Willems, 'Defiant Breakwaters or Desperate Blunders? A Revision of the German Late-War Fortress Strategy', *The Journal of Slavic Military Studies* (28) 2015, pp. 362–3, 371; Yelton, *Hitler's Volkssturm*, p. 122. On the continuous defensive operations of a Volkssturm battalion during the first two weeks of the Soviet offensive, starting in the border town of Goldap and ending in Königsberg, see: Bruno Just, Wolfgang Rothe and Horst Rehagen, *Hitler's Last Levy in East Prussia: Volkssturm Einsatz Bataillon Goldap (25/235)* (Solihull: Helion, 2015).

as well, even though it had been the army that initially conceived these measures and had pushed for them. German propaganda consistently highlighted the close cooperation between the army and the Party, particularly focusing on the latter's role in these projects. This aimed to sustain morale, as too large an emphasis on the army would have increased the anxiety of the German population that the battle front was approaching their homes. The army nevertheless assumed command of operations by organising the digging efforts and gradually taking control over the deployment of Volkssturm units. The resulting friction should largely be traced back to the unwillingness of men like Koch to relinquish power in their provinces to the army. Nevertheless, with the Wehrmacht on German territory these inroads were inevitable. The final section will therefore examine how the East Prussian population perceived these changes in their province and how the presence of these actors shaped the mentality in East Prussia.

Visions of the East Prussian Community in Late 1944

By the summer of 1944, East Prussians were slowly turning away from the National Socialist regime, which, up to that point, had been beneficial to them. Propaganda had long cemented the relationship between East Prussians and the regime, but as the tide of war turned, they proved able to detach themselves from some of its core messages. It would, however, be a simplification merely to portray this as opportunism. From its conception, the NSDAP had put itself forward as the 'guardian of the Volksgemeinschaft', but by mid-1944 – with even troops themselves increasingly fearing that they 'could not do justice to the traditional role as protector of wife and child' – the population now believed that it had to look after – and even defend – itself.[178] This in turn would have far-reaching consequences. National Socialist propaganda had always presented the German people as the 'victims of the tide of events' that transpired from 1914 onwards, which had been a powerful narrative to explain Germany's path to war, since war was championed as the only way to undo this injustice.[179] A victim narrative was now likely to re-emerge, but with the glaring difference that Germans could present themselves as victims of the National Socialist regime since it was the

---

[178] Library of Congress, 'Die NSDAP sichert die Volksgemeinschaft: Volksgenossen braucht Ihr Rat und Hilfe so wendet Euch an die Ortsgruppe', www.loc.gov/pictures/item/2004680176/ ; Echternkamp, *Soldaten im Nachkrieg*, p. 71.

[179] Wirsching, '*Volksgemeinschaft* and the Illusion of "Normality" from the 1920s to the 1940s', p. 151.

Nazis that had exposed them to the dangers of war. How this shift in attitude resonated in East Prussia will be examined in this section.

For East Prussians, August 1944 became the watershed month of the war, a month in which East Prussia turned from a province where 'the plight of the time could be forgotten' into a war zone.[180] The month started festively with a four-day-long string of recitals, concerts, and torchlight processions as the Albertus University celebrated its four-hundred-year anniversary.[181] Rectors from across the country were invited to attend the festivities, a commemorative stamp was presented, and the university inaugurated no less than eight new chairs. It could all be mistaken, a doctor noted, for a peacetime event.[182] During the summer the weather had been particularly agreeable, adding to a false sense of safety.[183]

Yet by that time anxiety was already creeping up on the East Prussian population. As a result of the Soviet summer offensive, Operation Bagration, which commenced on 22 June 1944, Army Group Centre was pushed out of the Soviet Union. Some thirty of its divisions were wiped out and 300,000 German troops were killed, wounded, or taken prisoner in the process – a devastating loss that even eclipsed the casualties at Stalingrad.[184] 'These days our people look with concern to the Eastern Front', an East Prussian official bluntly wrote to his colleague in mid-July. 'The break-through of the Bolsheviks near Wilna (Vilnius) is gradually recognized in all its severity by the entire German people.'[185] By the end of the month, the front line had reached Białystok, a mere 50 miles from the East Prussian border, which meant that within five weeks it had been pushed westwards over 300 miles.[186] The biggest blow to the morale of East Prussians, however, came in the last week of August, when two RAF bomber raids destroyed much of the city centre of Königsberg, turning it into a flaming inferno that left 4,200 dead and 150,000 people homeless.[187]

---

[180] Karl Springenschmid, *Raus aus Königsberg! Wie 420 ostpreußische Jungen 1945 aus Kampf und Einsatz gerettet wurden* (Kiel: Arndt, 1993), p. 20.

[181] IfZArch MA 736/NSDAP Hauptarchiv Gau Ostpreussen: Semesterbericht der Studentenführung Ostpreußen für die Monate Juli, August und September.

[182] Gause, *Die Geschichte der Stadt Königsberg*, p. 158; von Lehndorff, *Ostpreußisches Tagebuch*, p. 47.

[183] Hans-Werner Rautenberg, 'Der Zusammenbruch der deutschen Stellung im Osten und das Ende Königsbergs. Flucht und Vertreibung als Europäisches Problem', in Jähnig and Spieler (eds.) *Das Königsberger Gebiet im Schnittpunkt deutscher Geschichte*, p. 115.

[184] Ben Shepherd, *Hitler's Soldiers: the German Army in the Third Reich* (London: Yale University Press, 2017), pp. 444–50.

[185] BArch R 55/616, p. 105: Errichtung eines Grenzschutzes, 13 July 1944.

[186] Karl-Heinz Frieser, 'Der Zusammenbruch der Heeresgruppe Mitte im Sommer 1944', in Frieser (ed.), *Das Deutsche Reich und der Zweite Weltkrieg 8*, pp. 568, 582.

[187] Noble, *Nazi Rule and the Soviet Offensive*, pp. 165–9.

In late July, the front line came to a standstill along the borders of East Prussia and stayed there until mid-October, which meant that the military presence in the province increased. If the bombing had not already rid East Prussians of the illusion that their province was out of reach of the war's horrors, the army's arrival left no doubt that war was, in fact, very close. The province's population lost much of its agency since the military situation dictated virtually every aspect of life in the province. About a quarter of the East Prussian population was evacuated from vulnerable areas from July onwards, but at the same time orders were passed down to prevent people from leaving the province.[188] Criticism of these evacuation measures increased in the wake of the so-called 'Gumbinnen Operation' of October 1944. On 16 October, Soviet troops started this offensive and within a few days overran most of the evacuated areas, after which areas yet to be evacuated were captured as well. In his diary even Goebbels expressed criticism towards Gauleiter Koch's evacuation measures, as he felt that Koch had overestimated the strength of the Wehrmacht and had relied on it too much in his decision only to evacuate the far east of East Prussia.[189]

Public anxieties were further stoked by the events in and around Nemmersdorf, an East Prussian village that was captured by Soviet troops on the morning of 21 October 1944. Two days later, in the early morning of 23 October 1944, German troops recaptured it. At least twenty-six German civilians, most of them women, children, and elderly, were said to have been found killed in Nemmersdorf, and by 26 October this information had reached Goebbels.[190] 'These atrocities are terrible indeed', he wrote in his journal. 'I will use them as an opportunity for a big press release, so that among the German people even the last guileless waverers will be clear about what awaits the German people if Bolshevism actually takes hold of the Reich.'[191] Goebbels's thinking was influenced by what he called a 'strength-through-fear' approach. Its main aim was for the German people to 'remain convinced – as indeed the facts warrant – that this war strikes at their very lives and their national possibilities of

---

[188] See Chapter 5. Schieder, *Dokumentation der Vertreibung der Deutschen aus Ost-Mitteleuropa I, Band 1*, pp. 15E, 65; BArch R 55/616, p. 59, pm 9.7.44 15.45 an das rpa ostpreussen z.hd.d.Leiter koenigsberg; BArch R 55/616, pp. 86–9, Betrifft: Einführung von Reisebeschränkungen auf Grund der militärisch-politischen Lage, 10 July 1944; BArch R 55/616, p. 93: Sondermann, 10 July 1944.

[189] Elke Fröhlich (ed.), *Die Tagebücher von Joseph Goebbels, Teil II Diktate 1941–1945, Band 14: Oktober bis Dezember 1944* (Munich: K.G. Saur, 1996), p. 100 (entry of 25 October 1944).

[190] Berhard Fisch, *Nemmersdorf, Oktober 1944: Was in Ostpreußen tatsächlich geschah* (Berlin: edition ost, 1997), pp. 9, 119–20, 146–7.

[191] Frohlich (ed.), *Die Tagebücher von Joseph Goebbels, Band 14*, p. 110 (entry of 26 October).

development, and they must fight it with their entire strength'.[192] On 27 October the Party daily, the *Völkischer Beobachter*, opened with a massive front-page article: 'Terrible crimes in Nemmersdorf' and in the following days the coverage continued, with the casualty number being inflated to sixty-one.[193] But the campaign backfired. Not only were many Germans surprised to find out that Nemmersdorf had not been evacuated, but the reported atrocities also significantly intensified the fear of the Soviets among East Prussians.[194] By early November, East Prussian propaganda reports showed increasing reluctance to publicise such Soviet actions: 'The question of the atrocities committed by the Bolshevists in the areas of East Prussia occupied by them is not to be gone into at present, so as to avoid any atmosphere of panic among the population.'[195] Yet much of the damage that was done as a result of the over-eager news coverage would never be overcome. 'Nemmersdorf' indisputably and definitively demonstrated to the province's population that they could not rely on the regime to ensure their safety anymore.[196]

The mistrust in the authorities, however, did not mean that civilians changed their behaviour, if only because they had little else to base an informed decision on. Authorities kept claiming that the situation was under control. Even the recent Soviet incursion could be 'explained away', since, as a correspondent of the *Völkischer Beobachter* assured its readers, 'as long as the Soviets vainly assault this bastion, their whole front, down to the Carpathians, will remain paralyzed'.[197] Although assurances that the front would hold were often considered empty, in 1944 evacuation was nevertheless seen as an unpopular prospect. German wartime propaganda contributed to this notion: ever since the chaotic 'exodus' of French civilians in the summer of 1940, it had railed against evacuation as 'disorderly and cowardly flight', which it juxtaposed to the stoic 'German' attitude of standing fast in the face of grave

[192] Leonard Doob, 'Goebbels' Principles of Propaganda', *The Public Opinion Quarterly* (14) 1950, pp. 433, 438–9.

[193] Furchtbare Verbrechen in Nemmersdorf, *Völkischer Beobachter*, 27 October 1944; Fisch, *Nemmersdorf, Oktober 1944*, p. 146.

[194] Bernhard Fisch 'Nemmersdorf 1944: ein bisher unbekanntes zeitnahes Zeugnis', *Zeitschrift für Ostmitteleuropa-Forschung* (56) 2007, pp. 105–6; Peter Longerich, *Goebbels: a Biography* (London: Bodley Head, 2015), pp. 660–1.

[195] The National Archives (hereafter TNA) HW 1/3301A: West Europe, 31 October 1944. General: Time of dispatch: 1pm 26.10.44, Directive, No. 22 of 26/10, From SS Main Office, Signed Unterstuf Holst.

[196] BArch R 55/608, p. 29: Der Chef des Propagandastabes, Berlin, den 7.11.1944. Vertraulich! Mundpropagandaparole Nr. 4 Betr.: Nemmersdorf; Kossert, *Damals in Ostpreußen*, pp. 144–5.

[197] Von unserem Berichterstatter, 'Feindoffensive ohne Entscheidung', *Völkischer Beobachter*, 7 November 1944, p. 2.

situations.[198] Charlotte Gottschalk made up her mind on New Year's Day, 1945. 'We discussed for the first time whether I should evacuate with the children. I had no desire at all to do this, because neither my parents nor my husband could come with me. What was I supposed to do alone and among strangers, while it was [still] so comfortable at home?'[199] When some 800 East Prussians were brought to Demmin (in the western part of Pomerania) in early January 1945, but could not be housed in the city itself, they claimed that had they known that earlier, 'they would just have stayed with the Russians'.[200] Such statements fit into a largely forgotten undercurrent in wartime German society, namely that at the time there were already some Germans who believed 'that the Russians are not that bad'.[201] After many years of war, some East Prussians simply wanted it to be over as soon as possible, and, owning up to the emerging geopolitical situation, even considered a life under (temporary) Soviet rule.

The vocalisation of these sentiments, the observance of regionalism, and the mistrust in the authorities, attest to the East Prussians' desire to use their attachment to their province both as a validation of their identity and as a way to claim a certain disconnect with the regime and wider German society. At the same time, however, adhering to this version of East Prussian regionalism meant staying put in the province, thereby accepting that they would be among the first to face the might of the expected Soviet offensive. It left many East Prussians feeling 'stuck between a rock and a hard place', which severely affected their mood. 'The population of East Prussia's capital celebrated Christmas and New Year's Day in a lethargic calm, with one eye on what probably lay ahead', a doctor remembered, 'but – since an immediate threat did not yet exist – there were festive banquets everywhere, it was like a dance on a volcano'.[202] This behaviour allowed East Prussians to frame the paralysing resignation that was taking hold of them as a continuity of their local customs. The willingness of East Prussians to connect their fate to that of the province, as we will see in the coming chapters, was recognised and

---

[198] Julia Torrie, 'For Their Own Good': Civilian Evacuations in Germany and France, 1939–1945 (London: Berghahn Books, 2010), p. 32.

[199] Charlotte Gottschalk, email message to author, November 2009.

[200] BArch R 55/616, p. 31, untitled document, 15 January 1945. Demmin would become notorious a few months later as one of the towns with the largest number of suicides (around 1,000). Refugees' stories contributed to the widespread fear of the Soviets. See: Beate Lakotta, 'Tief vergraben, nicht dran rühren', Spiegel Special, 2/2005, pp. 218–21; Florian Huber, Kind, versprich mir, dass du dich erschießt: Der Untergang der kleinen Leute 1945 (Berlin: Berlin Verlag, 2015).

[201] Deichelmann, Ich sah Königsberg sterben, p. 7.

[202] IfZArch ZS/A-2/ 02–96: Bericht von Herrn Dr. Gerhardt.

appreciated by local authorities and would be fully exploited during the province's defence.

Conclusion

East Prussians, like most Germans, felt a strong attachment to their Heimat – their home soil – and Germany's short history as a unified nation encouraged that, by the time Soviet forces reached East Prussia's borders, regionalism still played an important role in its population's self-assertion. The province's location in the far east of Germany and the absence of natural resources meant that it had not developed a thriving industry or the (liberal) habits connected to the urbanisation that tend to accompany it. Many East Prussians felt a certain disconnect with the modern times they were living in and considered themselves to be traditional; other Germans, less forgivingly, often viewed them as a little backward. National Socialist propaganda, however, actually celebrated the province's perceived 'backward' characteristics as building blocks for the new Volksgemeinschaft. Both its role as 'provider' for the German nation and the province's 'centuries-long struggle' with 'the East' were placed front and centre in propagandist efforts, warming East Prussians to the Nazi regime. Rather than the changes it envisioned, National Socialism appealed to East Prussians due to its promise of continuity. The Nazis' convincing 1933 election victory in East Prussia showed that its inhabitants – to a greater extent than their compatriots – gave Hitler the mandate to materialise his vision.

In the years between 1933 and 1939 the new regime delivered on many of its promises. East Prussian agriculture was revived and unemployment fell drastically. Germany seemed to have rid itself of its earlier constraints and the regime could count on the trust of the vast majority of its population. When war came in September 1939 few people were anxious or concerned, although given the fate East Prussia suffered in 1914, it was certainly not met with the same kind of patriotic enthusiasm as 25 years earlier. Daily life in the province changed little during the first war years, although many of its farmers were called up to serve in the Wehrmacht. Yet since women had traditionally already played an important role in the province's agriculture, few considered this a real burden. What *did* change the community structure, however, was the simultaneous destruction of its Jewish population and the vast influx of foreign labourers. Since East Prussia was the first German stopover to and from the Eastern Front, its population was likely to overhear soldiers' unfiltered stories of annihilation and genocide. Neither the awareness that the war in the East was a racially fuelled war of extermination, nor the realisation that their province was running on slave labour, led to open protest among East Prussians, although some nevertheless sought to mentally distance themselves from the regime. The coming of 'Total War' sped up this process of detachment as it reinforced the perceived importance of regionality. Since most Total War measures were organised on the provincial rather than national level, the pull from 'Berlin' diminished, while Gauleiter were allocated more powers. This centrifugal tendency also assured that the Volksgemeinschaft came to be increasingly defined on a local level, while wartime circumstances themselves – notably the availability of food and the frequency of bombing raids – contributed to the further retreat of local populations from the German community at large. This allowed local factors and actors to assume greater importance which meant that Total War could have distinct regional and temporal differences.

For East Prussians, the impact of Total War was only really felt when they were called up to construct the Ostwall during the summer of 1944. The army, which had taken up positions around the East Prussian border, oversaw most of the efforts, showing that despite the constraints that were imposed at a national level it still managed to exert significant influence at a local level. A similar tendency was seen with the East Prussian Volkssturm. By the end of 1944, army and corps commanders had gained full control over the militia's deployment even though the Party was technically in charge. Meanwhile, up to the autumn of 1944, the Wehrmacht had largely been absent from Germans' Total War experience, yet as the number of troops that moved into Germany increased, so did the Wehrmacht's influence over everyday life. As the Wehrmacht moved into East Prussia, parts of the population started to explore opportunities to leave the province. Most of them nevertheless decided against it, even as they realised that such a decision might expose them to the dangers of war. Their motivation to remain represented the sentiment of most East Prussians, which was rooted in a strong sense of regional identity on the one hand and the diminishing trust in the Volksgemeinschaft on the other. East Prussians' eventual role in the province's defence was thus not merely the result of decisions taken by a fanatical Party-elite in Berlin, but this did not mean that their experiences during the last half year of the war were in any way less brutal than in areas where the regime's line was more closely observed. Because of their decision to stay, East Prussians were introduced to the behavioural patterns of their own military, unaware how these had changed during the previous years of brutalised fighting. How the change of mindset among the members of the Wehrmacht impacted military behaviour in East Prussia will therefore be the focus of the next chapter.

2 Eastern Front Battles on German Soil

Introduction

'Nearly four years of Asiatic war have given the front-line soldier a different face', Generaloberst Ferdinand Schörner wrote in an order of the day in late February 1945, 'they hardened and fanaticized him in the fight against the Bolsheviks'.[1] In order to understand why Germany had to go down in flames before the Wehrmacht laid down its weapons, the motives and recent experiences of the ordinary German soldier – the Landser – must be considered. Hardliners such as Schörner found strength in the regime's message, but most soldiers did not. The vast majority nevertheless continued to fight to the very end, adhering to many of the same principles they had adhered to before. The consequences of this 'inertia' were clearly visible in East Prussia. Just as, in the wake of the First World War, 'the continuation of wartime attitudes into peace furthered a certain brutalisation of politics' and encouraged 'a heightened indifference to human life',[2] the arrival of the Wehrmacht in East Prussia from mid-1944 onwards likewise left a considerable societal imprint on the province. Experiences on the Eastern Front had shaped the behaviour of the soldier, and those patterns of behaviour could not simply be left behind; on the Eastern Front, the German soldier had been swept up in an 'expanding torrent of destruction',[3] and many of those ingrained behavioural patterns continued to manifest themselves after the soldiers had returned to Germany. This observation is not intended as a moral judgement; the German soldier, like any other, 'is not, indeed, a machine that can just be turned off, and it would be inhumanely righteous not to

---

[1] Streit, *Keine Kameraden*, p. 244.
[2] George Mosse, *Fallen Soldiers: Reshaping the Memory of the World Wars* (Oxford: Oxford University Press, 1990), p. 159.
[3] Michael Geyer, 'German Strategy in the Age of Machine Warfare, 1914–1945', in Paret (ed.), *Makers of Modern Strategy*, p. 593.

look with sympathy on his plight'.[4] It *is* important to emphasise, however, that the Wehrmacht was not a *Radikalisierungshinderniss* – an obstacle for radicalization – in German society late in the war. This chapter shows how military conduct during times of defeat and retreat reshaped the soldiers' perception of their immediate environment. By drawing a direct parallel between the obedient execution of genocidal orders on the Eastern Front and the subsequent execution of fanatical *Durchhaltebefehle* (hold-out-orders) during the last months of the war, this chapter argues that much of the intra-ethnic violence of this final period of fighting can be traced back to a mindset of radicalisation systemic throughout the Wehrmacht.

The 'Heart Rate' of the Eastern Front Soldier

At the 1948 Nuremberg High Command Trial, the defence of former generals centred on their military oath, which gave them little room to divert from 'superior orders'.[5] In the years that followed, when more generals started to publish their memoirs, a slightly different line was pursued. These men would claim that when the opportunity presented itself they had tried to circumvent or even counteract these orders.[6] The crux of both arguments was that their involvement in Germany's war of annihilation did not mean that they necessarily agreed with its underlying motivations. Orders serve to transform the thought of a superior into the actions of a subordinate, but the German military tradition had long stressed the importance of independent thinking.[7] The rigour with which German military orders were carried out certainly varied depending on the time and the location, but this should not be attributed merely to the extent of individual agreement or disagreement with the regime. The implementation of orders largely depended on officers' 'horizon of expectations'; upbringing, background, education, political experience, and personal beliefs all shaped the way these men interpreted the orders

---

[4] Michael Walzer, *Just and Unjust Wars: a Moral Argument with Historical Illustrations* (New York: Basic Books, 2000), p. 307.

[5] Valerie Hébert, *Hitler's Generals on Trial: the Last War Crimes Tribunal at Nuremberg* (Lawrence: University Press of Kansas, 2010), ch. 4, 'The Soldiers' Defence'; Fritz, *Endkampf*, p. 147.

[6] Guderian, *Panzer Leader*, esp. ch. 11, 'Chief of the General Staff'; Regarding East Prussia see: Lasch, *So fiel Königsberg*, p. 23; Dieckert and Großmann, *Der Kampf um Ostpreussen*, pp. 88–9, 110–18; Friedrich Hoßbach, *Die Schlacht um Ostpreußen: Aus den Kämpfen der deutschen 4. Armee um Ostpreussen in der Zeit vom 19.7.1944–30.1.1945* (Überlingen: Otto Dikreiter Verlag, 1951), pp. 57–70.

[7] Römer, *Kameraden*, ch. VII, 'Truppenführer'.

they received.[8] It is therefore hardly surprising that, although genocidal orders were carried out between 1941 and 1944, there were many instances in which they were questioned. On occasion the moral undercurrents of individual soldiers surfaced, even when voicing objections was not without personal risk.[9]

However, little attention has been paid to how these racially motivated orders affected the soldiers' broader mindset. The processes of implementation and subsequent reflection had a deep impact on the soldiers' frame of reference. After all, the mental adjustment of those millions of soldiers who fought a Total War on the Eastern Front did not appear in a vacuum. Just as a sportsman's intense practice for competitions lowers his resting heart rate, the increasingly radical nature of the war also lowered the level of the troops' ability to consider non-military norms as part of their behavioural patterns. This newly emerging outlook on everyday life, the 'lowered resting heart rate of the Wehrmacht soldier', came to define military conduct, and crucially it continued to shape the actions of troops as they retreated onto German soil. Compared to their earlier behaviour on the Eastern Front, their conduct on home territory might have been more humane, but nevertheless these soldiers were, often by their own admission, changed men – and that change had been for the worse. This section reconstructs the wider consequences of Eastern Front soldiers' altered perception of the way in which they perceived and carried out orders. These men 'imported' a radicalised mindset from the Soviet Union into Germany, without necessarily adhering to the underlying motivations, but seem to have been completely unaware of the mental baggage they carried along.

When Germany went to war in 1939, the National Socialist regime had been in power for six years. During these six years it had made great strides in imposing its world views, but – as we also saw in Chapter 1 – it certainly did not permeate every walk of society. In the military, dissenting voices had been steadily silenced throughout the 1930s so that by the time the war started the German army was marching in step with the regime.[10] Yet, the millions of men who joined the ranks of the Wehrmacht can hardly be considered to have had a shared outlook on matters of life and morality. In the months leading up to the war with the Soviet Union, Hitler styled it as the 'decisive battle of races and world views', and although it was clear which world view had to be defeated – 'Judeo-Bolshevism' – large swaths of

[8] Robert Holub, 'Reception Theory: School of Constance', in Selden (ed.), *The Cambridge History of Literary Criticism, Vol. 8*, ch. 11.
[9] Thomas Kühne, *Kameradschaft: Die Soldaten des nationalsozialistischen Krieges und das 20. Jahrhundert* (Göttingen: Vanderhoeck & Ruprecht, 2006), pp. 113–17.
[10] Wette, *Die Wehrmacht*, ch. 6; Bessel, *Nazism at War*, ch. 2.

the German military had not yet internalised the world view of the National Socialist regime.[11] Many soldiers realised that the Nazi project was far from complete by the time the war began, but a significant proportion of them also felt that what the regime *had* achieved in the 1930s was 'just enough' to convince them that the war which they were fighting would help to shape Germany's future. The notion that they were effecting change gave soldiers a sense of agency in the midst of a chaotic and frightening environment and could assume great currency. Germany's future was worth fighting for, and, as one soldier tellingly noted, 'I will undergo its spiritual struggle to the end.'[12] Nevertheless, politics and political leaning mattered relatively little in the soldier's decision to continue fighting. Although patriotism, regime-loyalty, and military *habitus* were closely linked, soldiers often styled themselves simply as 'good Germans', which inherently included the quality of being an exemplary fighter. Since this label transcended traditional political divisions, being a good soldier could be achieved without necessarily being a committed National Socialist, and by and large most troops considered themselves to be indifferent to politics and ideology.[13] A lack of ideological commitment among the troops was the rule rather than the exception, and throughout the war the Nazi leadership complained bitterly about the failure to create a truly 'political soldier'.[14]

Rather than a National Socialist spirit, an atmosphere of *Kameradschaft* (camaraderie) prevailed in the German army, which was built around small atomised units and highly ritualised behaviours. It encouraged a certain idea of masculine conduct, which in real terms meant debauchery, drinking bouts, minor theft, and sexual escapades – all practices that were strongly condemned back in Germany, but, encouraged by the notion that comrades 'got each other's back', widely accepted in the army. Being part of an in-crowd of comrades offered solace away from home and soldiers regularly styled themselves as being part of a family, calling each other 'brothers', their commander 'father', and referring to a good cook as the 'mother' of a group. However, the clichéd images which Kameradschaft perpetuated also ensured that soldiers had little room to diverge from the mores of their units. Soldiers constantly felt watched and judged by their comrades; hardness was the norm and

[11] Johannes Hürter, *Hitlers Heerführer: Die deutschen Oberbefehlshaber im Krieg gegen die Sowjetunion 1941/42* (Munich: R. Oldenbourg Verlag, 2006), p. 257.

[12] Stephen Fritz, *Frontsoldaten: the German Soldier in World War II* (Lexington: University Press of Kentucky, 1995), pp. 159–63, 208–14 (p. 214).

[13] Felix Römer, 'Volksgemeinschaft in der Wehrmacht? Milieus, Mentalitäten und militärische Moral in den Streitkräften des NS-Staates', in Welzer, Neitzel, and Gudehus (eds.), '*Der Führer war viel zu human, viel zu gefühlvoll*', pp. 74–6.

[14] Hancock, *The National Socialist Leadership and Total War*, p. 128.

Figure 2.1 Muddy and tired, but together: Kameradschaft in East Prussia, early 1945. *Source:* Author's collection

showing signs of softness was frowned upon. It meant that many outsiders and loners, who as a result of the increasingly comprehensive draft were present in virtually every unit, were often excluded, mocked, or even physically threatened. On the other hand, being labelled a good *Kamerad* was one of the highest accolades a soldier could receive. Kameradschaft was the glue that held a unit together and was not perceived negatively since it helped to maintain its staying power.[15] A 'good soldier', and a good Kamerad, shared the experience of his peers, especially in darker times. Yet, serving in the Wehrmacht on the Eastern Front did not merely mean facing the intense cold and defending a hopeless position together; it also meant that when comrades were tasked to carry out genocidal orders, most soldiers would seek to overcome any personal objections and carry them out as well. As such, the expectations of Kameradschaft in the East fundamentally lowered soldiers' 'heart rate', even though they might not have recognised it themselves.

On the Eastern Front, more than on any other theatre of war, troops were tasked to carry out the regime's genocidal orders which they, not that long before, would have condemned strongly. Although some men decided to join the army as a way to escape the regime's oppressive

---

[15] Kühne, *Kameradschaft*, pp. 113–71.

domestic rule, serving in the Wehrmacht almost without exception led to a mental paradigm shift. Even when the Landser considered the sustained propaganda as crude, or those who used National Socialist language as careerist fanatics, he less frequently questioned whether or not National Socialism was correct (a conversation that might have been held at home), but rather examined how and why its declarations about race, nation, and space should be understood.[16] Shortly before the surrender of the Sixth Army at Stalingrad, one soldier from the encircled cauldron wrote home that

The Führer has promised to get us out of here. . . . I still believe it today, because I simply must believe in something. If it isn't true, what is there left for me to believe in? . . . If what we were promised is not true, then Germany will be lost, for no other promises can be kept after that.[17]

Soldiers were imprinted with the idea that the war in the Soviet Union was a Total War, a war in which only one of two diametrically opposed world views could survive, and the only way to safeguard the existence of one was to utterly annihilate the other. This line of thought gave rise to a narrative in which the institutional ruthlessness of the Wehrmacht was considered legitimate, while the violence committed by troops was regarded as a necessary evil prompted by the threat of Bolshevism. Especially on the Eastern Front, the military was the sharp end of the National Socialist vision and although most generals only had a superficial understanding of it, they understood that its racial dimension would have to be realised.[18] The commander of the Seventeenth Army, Generaloberst Hermann Hoth, for example, stressed to his men that rooting out the 'same Jewish class of people which has done so much harm to our Fatherland' was a matter of a 'law of self-preservation'.[19] But although this cause was consistently portrayed as legitimate, it still sig- nalled a departure from previous military conduct to which troops had to adjust. The 'criminal orders' that the Wehrmacht visited on the Soviet Union eventually ensured the death of millions of Soviet citizens, but they certainly also left their mark on those who were tasked to execute them. The orders proposed a significant hardening of military conduct, not only on a macro-level, at which, for example, entire divisions were deployed to comb an area for partisans in cooperation with Einsatzgruppen, but also

---

[16] Fritz, *Frontsoldaten*, ch. 8, 'Trying to Change the World'; Omer Bartov, 'The Missing Years: German Workers, German Soldiers', *German History* (8) 1990, pp. 50–7, 62–5.
[17] Bartov, 'The Missing Years', p. 60.
[18] Johannes Hürter, 'The Military Elite and the *Volksgemeinschaft*', in Steber and Gotto (eds.), *Visions of Community in Nazi Germany*, pp. 266–7.
[19] Hébert, *Hitler's Generals on Trial*, p. 121.

at a micro-level, where the individual soldier was forced to negotiate his personal morality.

The point of departure for this process of self-reflection were the questions of what the role of a soldier ought to entail, and of what might fall outside that role. *Soldatentum* – being a soldier – had been part of the fabric of German society for generations, and the ability to order themselves to fight war had for centuries been at the centre of German national pride. Propaganda portrayed German soldiers as brave and determined fighters, but, unsurprisingly, not as agents of genocide. When the topic of Jewry was addressed in the field, the troops' reaction was often one of annoyance and boredom.[20] As recruits, these men were taught to fight and kill enemy combatants, and to see combat as their job, and although they were also indoctrinated with racist ideas, they were kept in the dark about their anticipated role in the implementation of the regime's 'vision'. As a result, most German soldiers arriving on the Eastern Front were unprepared for many of the tasks that lay ahead, as their expectations had been deliberately misdirected. The vast majority styled themselves as soldiers of the world's most advanced military and neglected to consider the gravity of their genocidal behaviour.[21] The aim of creating this self-image certainly was not to evade their responsibilities; rather, it reflected the ideals and aspirations connected to the profession. Once in the Soviet Union, regular combat and mundane military tasks comprised much of the daily experiences of soldiers, while many Wehrmacht soldiers could also look back on accomplishments of which they *could* be proud, be it the capture of a fortified position or the steadfast defence in the face of a Soviet assault. Unaware of the centrality of genocide in the mission of their regime, they had little reason to consider themselves as anything other than 'ordinary men'.

Most of them also understood that they were part of a machinery which would, by its very nature, cause considerable damage. Yet, as philosophers since the medieval period have argued, as long as its ultimate intention is just, the unavoidable 'spillage' of war – such as the death of civilians or the destruction of crops – ought not to be condemned. Armies therefore have a moral obligation to ensure that military conduct focuses on the core task of defeating the enemy, for they otherwise violate the laws of war.[22] Hitler's racial agenda for the East, however, ensured that, on the Eastern Front, the 'spillage of war' was an integral and intended aspect of

---

[20] Sven Oliver Müller, *Deutsche Soldaten und ihre Feinde, Nationalismus an Front und Heimatfront im Zweiten Weltkrieg* (Frankfurt a.M., S.Fischer, 2007), pp. 90–4.

[21] Neitzel and Welzer, *Soldaten*, pp. 334–43.

[22] Nicholas Fotion, *War and Ethics: a New Just War Theory* (London: Continuum, 2007), pp. 20–3.

the army's operational procedures, and it immediately became part of the military conduct of the Wehrmacht.[23] In attempting to defeat the Red Army, Hitler sought to annihilate as much of the Soviet population as possible. This Vernichtungskrieg thus marked a departure from the ways in which wars had previously been waged, and the desire to resort to the intensity of violence envisioned by Hitler had to be conveyed to the troops. The war diary of Generaloberst Franz Halder, the OKH chief of staff, shows that from the outset the High Command sought to do so by linking the regime's genocidal visions to military necessity. 'The troops must fight back with the methods with which they are attacked', Halder wrote on 30 March 1941 after a meeting with Hitler. 'This need not mean that the troops should get out of hand. Rather, the commander must give orders which express the common feelings of his men. This war will be very different from the war in the West. In the East, harshness today means lenience in the future.'[24] In just a few sentences, Halder had managed to turn Hitler's genocidal plans into an 'answer' to assumed provocative Soviet conduct, and as a military necessity that was ultimately rooted in benevolence.

To the military planners at Hitler's High Command, however, it was clear from the very start that German troops, who had until then fought a comparatively clean war, would inevitably struggle with the new demands placed upon them during Operation Barbarossa. The Total War proposed by Hitler would irredeemably commit the German military to tasks which strained the very limits of their profession. The slew of 'criminal orders' might have been couched in language that stressed their military necessity but the fact that these orders jettisoned notions of humanity and proportionality would not be without its consequences. During the drafting process, commanders noted that whereas soldiers might to some extent be able to review individual orders and take an informed position on them, these orders would cumulatively cause an irreversible barbarisation (Verwilderung) among the troops.[25] During the execution of these orders, Wehrmacht soldiers would find themselves at the tip of the spear of the National Socialist ideology. National Socialism might not necessarily have helped these men make sense of their daily life at the front but it certainly helped them to make sense of killing. Self-evidently, there was little hesitation among the top ranks of the army to place men in positions in which they had to commit mass murder. More

---

[23] Kay, Rutherford, and Stahel (eds.), *Nazi Policy on the Eastern Front*.
[24] Franz Halder, *War Journal of Franz Halder* (Fort Leavensworth, KS: Archives Section, 1950), p. 43.
[25] Helmut Krausnick, 'Kommissarbefehl und "Gerichtsbarkeitserlaß Barbarossa" in neuer Sicht', *VfZ* (25) 1977, pp. 708–9.

important, however, was the role ideology played during the moment the soldier adopted his role as killer and the place ideology subsequently occupied in his self-image.

Among the men the need to kill enemy soldiers was readily recognised, but depriving women and children of life was a part of Total War few of them understood. Propagandists were aware of this, and therefore did not seek to explain *how* this should be done, but instead focused on the very fact that it ought to be done. They similarly realised that ideological indoctrination alone was insufficient to turn individuals into killers, but since they also knew that the cruelty which they demanded was social in origin, they did not require all soldiers to believe in the regime's mission and methods. Instead, military propaganda time and again tied the German presence in the Soviet Union to the need to counter the threat posed by Judeo-Bolshevism, a task that would have to be performed by the units of the Wehrmacht.[26] The groundwork had been laid by national media outlets, which consistently presented Germany's enemies as racially inferior and dehumanised 'others', revealing their conspiratorial and destructive agendas and urging a 'purification' from society of those elements harbouring these beliefs. When the situation demanded it, propagandists were able – through the perpetuation of racial stereotypes, myths about Jewish bloodlust, constant sloganeering, and strong symbolism – to ramp up this fear and paranoia to a fever pitch.[27] Rounding out this process were the unit commanders, whom the men looked up to, who had been taught that they should consider it 'a given that every officer, in every situation, acts according to the ideology of the Third Reich, even when such ideologies are not explicitly expressed'.[28] Famously, in the hours leading up to the execution of hundreds of Jews in Józefów, the men of Reserve Police Battalion 101 were told that 'in Germany the bombs were falling on women and children' while 'the Jews had instigated the American boycott that had damaged Germany' and were involved in partisan activity.[29] As such, a narrative emerged in which it was clear that the home front would be grateful for the actions of the German units, although they might not understand the extremities of the methods used in the field. Nevertheless, for many men, especially those who styled themselves as 'decent' or morally superior, being faced with an order to kill (or actively prevent living) meant having to confront an acute personal

[26] Jaques Semelin, *Purify and Destroy: the Political Uses of Massacre and Genocide* (London: Hurst, 2007), p. 238–9.

[27] Ibid., pp. 17–51, 247–8.

[28] Bryce Sait, *The Indoctrination of the Wehrmacht: Nazi Ideology and the War Crimes of the German Military* (Oxford: Berghahn, 2019), p. 85.

[29] Browning, *Ordinary Men*, p. 2.

crisis. It was a descent into horror during which they had to search for some flicker of security and permanency, which they found in their units' shared identity. By subscribing to the perceived norms of the unit, they established themselves within familiar frameworks which in turn, being defined by the radical 'us-versus-them' mentality, eased the transition into violence. Every soldier did this at his own pace and the underlying motivations differed from person to person, but the perpetuation of his unit's shared and accepted social framework helped him in the execution of these orders. By styling himself as part of a military unit rather than as an individual, and by presenting the unit as an agent of the regime's vision, the lone Landser was able to absolve much of his personal responsibility. More so, his regime, through the assurance that what he did was necessary for Germany's survival, benevolently promised to assume the responsibility itself.[30] Soldiers emerging from these atrocities thus styled themselves as resolute and uncompromising vanguards of Germany, an idea strengthened and reasserted every time they subsequently carried out a criminal order or a radical measure.

Famously, the May 1941 Barbarossa Decree effectively turned the Eastern Front into a lawless region.[31] It encouraged deadly action against alleged partisans and collective reprisals against entire villages that were suspected of harbouring them. At the same time, the decree overhauled military law as it suspended the prosecution of soldiers who committed criminal acts against the local population.[32] Between the lines, the decree gave German troops almost unrestricted scope to behave as they wished whilst in the Soviet Union. The German soldier was to make his presence felt. The terrorising nature of this conduct was fully appreciated but could be explained as being part of a German way of war that emerged during the prior century. Already in 1877, in the popular journal *Deutsche Rundschau*, the German General Julius von Hartmann expanded on the military necessity of this type of behaviour: 'If individuals are hit hard, as warning examples to others, that is certainly deeply regrettable, but this harshness is a healthy and preserving good deed for the whole. Where

---

[30] Semelin, *Purify and Destroy*, 238–65.

[31] The 'Decree on the Jurisdiction of Martial Law and on Special Measures of the Troops', more commonly known as the 'Barbarossa Decree' was designed to actively encourage brutalisation. It removed 'offences committed by enemy civilians' from military jurisdiction. Instead, suspects brought in front of a German officer were to be summarily judged (often a euphemism for execution). At the same time, the decree called for 'collective violent measures' as a way to deter communities from harbouring suspected criminal elements. See: Felix Römer, 'The Wehrmacht in the War of Ideologies: the Army and Hitler's Criminal Orders on the Eastern Front', in Kay, Rutherford and Stahel (eds.), *Nazi Policy on the Eastern Front, 1941*, p. 75.

[32] Römer, 'Im alten Deutschland wäre solcher Befehl nicht möglich gewesen', pp. 53–99.

there is popular uprising, terrorism becomes a necessary military principle.'[33] This approach to warfare was taken to heart during the preparation for Operation Barbarossa, especially since military planners operated on the racist presumption that Slavic and Asiatic peoples would understand the use of the whip better than that of the carrot. Despite the presentation of the Barbarossa Decree as militarily necessary, many commanders nonetheless realised that conducting this large number of terroristic and extra-legal measures could have adverse long-term effects on the troops' mental state.[34] Although some commanders might have used these objections as a means of conveying their moral objections to the decree, by addressing the mental burden which was being placed upon their troops they were among the first to recognise that the habits and coping mechanisms developed while adjusting to the new realities of the war would be hard to get rid of in the long term.

These men came to realise that the situation in the field was often incompatible with the regime's genocidal demands, and practical needs could therefore win out over ideology. Being on the Eastern Front meant interacting with the people there, which inevitably shaped soldiers' outlook. Many of the policies were unfamiliar to the troops and lay outside the expected duties, but their implementation soon became an unavoidable part of soldiers' daily life.[35] Repression, exploitation, and enslavement were recurrent features in Germany's war of annihilation, yet few men realised how important the component *Vernichtung* was within the war they were waging.[36] In the Soviet Union, warfare and genocide complemented each other, and since these men saw combat as their main job, it allowed them to examine their behaviour through the prism of military professionalism. The long-standing military doctrine of *Auftragstaktik* – or 'mission tactics' – helped the average field commander to rationalise his actions and view them as necessary. Auftragstaktik encouraged higher headquarters to present junior officers with their mission and to give them leeway to conduct it using their own judgement 'on the ground'.[37] Although the system of command had become much

[33] Isabel Hull, *Absolute Destruction: Military Culture and the Practices of War in Imperial Germany* (Ithaca, NY: Cornell University Press, 2004), pp. 122–6.

[34] Johannes Hürter and Felix Römer, 'Alte und neue Geschichtsbilder von Widerstand und Ostkrieg', *VfZ* (54) 2006, pp. 315–16.

[35] Rutherford, *Combat and Genocide*, pp. 3–4.

[36] Christoph Rass, 'Verbrecheriche Kriegsführung an der Front: Eine Infanteriedivision und ihre Soldaten', in Hartmann, Hürter, and Jureit (eds.), *Verbrechen der Wehrmacht*, p. 89.

[37] Marco Sigg, *Der Unterführer als Feldherr im Taschenformat: Theorie und Praxis der Auftragstaktik im deutschen Heer 1869 bis 1945* (Paderborn: Schöningh, 2014); Martin van Crefeld, *Command in War* (Cambridge, MA: Harvard University Press, 1985), p. 270. Citino, *The German Way of War*, pp. 152–3, 302–8.

stricter during the war, its spirit continued to 'live on' among the many field commanders who had been trained in previous years. Thus, even amidst a war of annihilation, the mission and its men were often central concerns of their commanders, who actively took into consideration what Halder called the 'common feelings' of their subordinates. Efforts to reflect on the plight of the Soviet population were therefore neither born out of a sense of compassion towards them nor were they strictly the end result of a cynical deflection of responsibility. The regime's emphasis on morale encouraged commanders to manage the expectations of their men, which meant that once they were confronted with orders pertaining to genocide they needed to be able to explain how these orders were beneficial to the success of their mission. Among many soldiers, the brutality of the war prompted a 'loss of orientation, confusion, and fear', and the criminality of the orders often pushed soldiers yet one step further. Despite commanders' assurance that the orders were legitimate and proportionate, soldiers were often still deeply shaken, and the surest way to overcome this shock was to venture on a path that allowed them to 'rationalise' their conduct.[38]

The idea that actions in the field were proportionate within the costs and benefits of war largely determined whether soldiers considered themselves to be ethically correct.[39] This meant that despite the regime's sustained efforts there was often a discrepancy between what a German soldier was prepared to do and what he ethically agreed with. Therefore, what a soldier considered 'militarily necessary' itself reflected a certain moral undercurrent. The reception of the June 1941 'commissar order', which demanded the execution of Jews and Red Army commissars upon capture, highlights how troops inserted their moralities into the war they were waging and juxtaposed these to the regime's genocidal demands and notions of military necessity. Initially, the implementation of the order – the genocidal and extra-legal nature of which was recognised from its inception – was rationalised by the idea that the removal of the commissar as the ideological backbone of the Red Army would hasten its collapse.[40] Protests against the order however steadily increased. Some soldiers struggled with the guilt of having to carry it out and divisional chaplains were regularly sent to these men in an effort to sooth their conscience.[41] Although some commanders questioned the order's ethical

---

[38] Hannes Heer, 'How Amorality Became Normality: Reflections on the Mentality of German Soldiers on the Eastern Front', in Heer and Naumann (eds), *War of Extermination*, pp. 331–3.

[39] Fotion, *War & Ethics*, pp. 10–20.

[40] Rutherford, *Combat and Genocide*, pp. 212–13.

[41] Shepherd, *Hitler's Soldiers*, pp. 142–3.

foundations, most protests did not focus on the practice itself but on its adverse side-effects; since the order discouraged commissars (and consequently their units) from surrendering, it therefore prolonged battles. Eventually, in May 1942 the order was revoked in order to 'strengthen the inclination of encircled Russian forces to desert and surrender'.[42] It was a rare compromise on behalf of Hitler who, aware that his insistence on enforcing it might alienate his field commanders, seems to have recognised that the army's inevitable acts of genocide had to be reconciled with ideas of 'military necessity'.

The triadic relationship between genocide, brutalisation, and military necessity also manifested itself during the siege of Leningrad. During its siege, many civilians tried to filter through the lines to escape hunger. As a reduced civilian population would increase the city's defensibility, the commander of Army Group North, Field Marshal Wilhelm Ritter von Leeb, ordered his artillery 'to prevent any such attempts at the greatest possible distance from our lines by opening fire as early as possible, so that the infantry is spared ... shooting at civilians'. Although the order technically lay within military law in the strictest sense, German commanders recognised its genocidal implications.[43] Yet again their protests were not concerned with the population of Leningrad but with the German troops. In mid-November 1941, an entry in Army Group North's war diary noted that commanders feared a 'loss of inner balance' among the troops that would leave them 'no longer ... scared of committing such acts even after the war was over'.[44] The siege of Leningrad involved a completely different method of war than the German troops expected. Instead of active movement, the wartime experience of the units at Leningrad until mid-1943 was characterised predominantly by trench warfare. This demodernisation became the plight of most Eastern Front soldiers; tanks were destroyed more quickly than they could be replaced and became an increasingly rare sight, while as a result of the infamous biannual Russian rainy season (the *Rasputitsa*), roads turned to mud, hindering the supply of new materiel. Finally, the soldiers' distorted sense of proportionality and racist attitudes towards the local population ensured that during the unforgiving winter they felt little hesitation in stealing items of clothing or in evicting people from their homes.[45]

---

[42] Johannes Hürter, 'Auf dem Weg zur Militäropposition. Tresckow, Gersdorff, der Vernichtungskrieg und der Judenmord. Neue Dokumente über das Verhältnis der Heeresgruppe Mitte zur Einsatzgruppe B im Jahr 1941', *VfZ* (52) 2004, pp. 527–62; Christian Hartmann, *Operation Barbarossa: Nazi Germany's War in the East, 1941–1945* (Oxford: Oxford University Press, 2013), p. 91.
[43] Walzer, *Just and Unjust Wars*, pp. 161, 166–7.   [44] Stargard, *The German War*, p. 186.
[45] Bartov, *Hitler's Army*, pp. 12–28.

It is in instances such as these that we witness the lowering of the 'heart rate' of the Wehrmacht soldier. Unwilling or altogether unable to reflect on the unparalleled nature of their criminal behaviour, soldiers reasoned themselves into a line of thought which acknowledged this institutional ruthlessness but considered it to be an unavoidable part of their method of war. The 'criminal orders' which Wehrmacht troops were to adhere to while in the Soviet Union conditioned them to abandon their former principles, making any subsequent return to civilian norms increasingly difficult. In most cases, it took mere weeks for soldiers to describe themselves as becoming 'hard' and 'indifferent' to the practices which resulted from those orders. As long as there was the faintest pretext to portray the wave of indiscriminate, racially motivated violence as militarily rational, few men had problems adjusting to the new realities of the war in the East.[46] Moreover, the seeming ease with which troops internalised the new 'law of the land' was often also part of a necessary coping mechanism. A soldier who had come with the intention of fighting a regular war nevertheless found himself caught in the crossfire of a Vernichtungskrieg, if only because of the virtual absence of alternatives. While fighting abroad, desertion was not a realistic option, because punishments when caught by their own police units were extremely severe, and because partisans were active behind the front and would show little mercy after capturing a German soldier.[47] By contrast, the rationale to stay part of the Wehrmacht's destructive machinery was clear. 'As long as a retreat is orderly and the structure of the component units of an army is maintained', a psychological report of German prisoners of war attested, 'strategic difficulties do not break up the army'.[48] The vast majority of Wehrmacht soldiers supported the military course of the regime, if only because the information which reached them was fragmentary and highly distorted.[49] Finally, their role as occupiers was not necessarily considered extraordinary or unique to the Nazi experiment; during the First World War the German military had occupied and exploited large parts of Russia (known as *Ober-Ost*, an area comprising of the current-day Baltic states and northern Belarus), and ruled its population with an iron fist.[50]

---

[46] Heer, 'How Amorality Became Normality', p. 332; Shepherd, *War in the Wild East*, pp. 229–34.

[47] Shepherd, *War in the Wild East*, pp. 223–4. On punishment, see Chapter 6.

[48] Edward Shils and Morris Janowitz, 'Cohesion and Disintegration in the Wehrmacht in World War II', *The Public Opinion Quarterly* (12) 1948, p. 289.

[49] Ibid., 289, 300–1; Echternkamp, *Soldaten im Nachkrieg*, pp. 69–79.

[50] Watson, *Ring of Steel*, pp. 398–415.

The years of occupation, which roughly covered the period between 1942 and early 1944, further forced commanders to reflect on the practicalities of the regime's genocidal demands. Some units could occupy and defend parts of the front while simultaneously overseeing the destruction of its local populations, but often there would be friction between these tasks and on many occasions the two were even completely incompatible. Although some commanders carried out their orders out of sheer careerism and in full agreement with the regime, many others instead styled themselves as pragmatists in order to justify the extraordinary harshness with which they dealt with the situations which faced them.[51] This was not an effort to divorce or distance themselves from the regime but rather an acknowledgement of the fact that the Total War and the war of annihilation could not be waged simultaneously. A nation's ability to fight a Total War, as we saw in Chapter 1, depends in large part on its capacity to mobilise civilians, and on the Eastern Front this task fell largely on the army. This often meant that, simply put, a sizeable portion of Soviet civilians had to be kept alive; it was soon realised that an overly harsh approach would drive civilians into the hands of the partisans, thus endangering supply lines in the army's hinterland, while local civilians could also serve as a readily available source of forced labour.[52] Keeping these people alive and complacent also meant that German military authorities would have to reflect on an increasing number of civil and civic questions, such as the establishment of schools or the setting up of semi-autonomous local governments of 'friendly peoples'.[53] Rather than as a faceless horde, it often made more military sense to appreciate the population's diversity. This is well illustrated by German approaches towards Islamic communities in the south of the Soviet Union, in the Caucasus and the Crimea. Here, German authorities adopted an accommodating policy towards different Muslim minorities. After a two decades-long communist ban, they were once again allowed to practice their religion, as such ensuring the pacification of the newly conquered areas and at the same time bolstering recruitment from these groups.[54]

The clearest manifestation of the fact that in 'the East' the regime's racial agenda was often pursued with at least one eye on military necessity was the army's increased use of Soviet auxiliary 'volunteers', known as *Hilfswillige*, or *Hiwis*. Realising that even the call-up of older reservists was absolutely insufficient to administer the vast area that had fallen into German hands,

[51] Shepherd, *War in the Wild East*, pp. 232–3.
[52] See: Johannes Due Enstad, *Soviet Russians under Nazi Occupation: Fragile Loyalties in World War II* (Cambridge: Cambridge University Press, 2019).
[53] Mulligan, *The Politics of Illusion and Empire*, p. 127.
[54] David Motadel, 'Islam and Germany's War in the Soviet Borderlands, 1941–5', *Journal of Contemporary History* (48), 2013, pp. 784–820.

Figure 2.2 A very young Hilfswillige serving with a German unit in East Prussia, late 1944. *Source:* Author's collection

army units started deploying semi-voluntary assistants, mostly either drafted from local populations or taken from the enormous pool of Soviet prisoners of war. These people, who were often more than willing to help in order to escape hunger and persecution, became vital parts of many German units. Initially they were tasked with odd jobs, such as laundry, cooking, and driving, but they were also trusted to do repairs, would help interpret, did guiding and scouting, and even gave advice on local issues. Gradually the German army started arming these people, and used them as sentries or as part of anti-partisan actions. Hundreds of thousands of them served in different capacities – sometimes even as part of frontline combat units – in the German army, but, reflecting the awareness that racial issues were contested, the scope of their deployment was kept from Hitler until mid-1942.[55]

The procurement of labour also inevitably meant that Wehrmacht soldiers came into direct contact with the Soviet population which added unforeseen complexity to the relationship between the two groups.

[55] J. Lee Ready, *The Forgotten Axis: Germany's Partners and Foreign Volunteers in World War II* (London: McFarland, 1987), pp. 156–7, 193–4.

German soldiers came to know the desperation of Soviet villagers' plight, and especially at places where the front line was fairly static, fraternisation was unavoidable. For example, liaisons between young Soviet girls and Wehrmacht men, sometimes forced, sometimes voluntary, became a fairly common sight. Moreover, in villages where German soldiers were billeted, they sometimes tried to recreate somewhat of a *Heimatgefühl*, a 'feeling of home', and frequently shared their rations with young children and elderly inhabitants so as to create an illusion of normality. Soon propaganda started warning against 'misplaced acts of charity' since these 'cost the home front food', but many soldiers felt that this was inevitable for the population to stay on their side.[56] Again, military necessity trumped the strict adherence to the genocidal war of annihilation.

In defeat 'military necessity' changed in nature, and the military situation during the final year of the German occupation of the Soviet Union significantly contributed to the idea that German soldiers were military professionals largely unaffected by the demands of the Nazi regime. Starting in the summer of 1943, and reaching its peak in 1944 – which became known as the year of Stalin's Ten Blows (named in honour of the Soviet Union's wartime leader Joseph Stalin, who as Supreme Commander of the Red Army had overseen ten successful strategic offensives along the entire Eastern Front) – Soviet forces increasingly succeeded in imposing their will on the Wehrmacht, drawing German forces into hundreds of major and minor battles.[57] The 286th Sicherungs-Division, for example, whose task between 1941 and 1943 had been to 'pacify' the Army Group North Rear Area, was made available to the Fourth Army at the turn of 1944 and eventually deployed in combat in East Prussia.[58] Since the majority of soldiers were now being deployed in or near battle rather than kept at the rear, it also meant that criminal orders were increasingly carried out closer to the front line in the area of operations. Compounding the tendency to resort to brutal means was that the more a unit was pushed to the edge, the more it felt compelled to pursue a hard line in order to survive. Thus, the proximity to the front line gave soldiers a sense of urgency, which more readily allowed them to consider the different brutal measures as militarily necessary. Finally, the constant bludgeoning of 1943 and 1944 left little time to reflect on the consequences of their behaviour: chaos, trauma, destruction, insecurity, death – all these matters consumed the average Landser

---

[56] Rutherford, *Combat and Genocide*, pp. 177–80, 186, 289–93.
[57] Alexander Hill, *The Red Army and the Second World War* (Cambridge: Cambridge University Press, 2017), ch. 21.
[58] Shepherd, *War in the Wild East*, pp. 48, 72, 84–107; Tessin, *Verbände und Truppen der deutschen Wehrmacht*, vol. 9, s.v. '286'.

much more than questions of justness and injustice during the costly retreat from the Soviet Union.[59]

The relentless combat, the brutality of war, and the resulting high casualty rates altered the Landser's self-image, the way he viewed his surroundings, and his view of those near. Whereas the average time between recruitment and death of a Wehrmacht recruit drafted in 1939 was four years, by early 1945 this had plummeted to a month.[60] This was not only the result of external factors such as the improved Soviet operational conduct or increasing Allied aerial superiority, but also concerned the attitude towards warfare that had emerged during the previous years. Throughout the war, a new approach to warfare, extending beyond the internalisation of Nazi rhetoric, had manifested itself and 'radicalised pre-existing notions of the German military ethos'.[61] National Socialism had shaped the perceptual horizon of the majority of officers to a greater extent than they realised or were willing to admit and this altered the ways in which they dealt with the demands of battle. The longer the war continued, the more grand strategy was relegated to the background.[62] Instead, the dominant approach towards military decision-making was that 'you can only see in hindsight that an enemy would have fallen, had you only pushed on a little more'.[63] This mindset influenced every strategic calculation; decisions were not based solely on an appraisal of the opposing force's strength, but were also filtered through an ideological prism.[64] On an operational level this meant, detrimentally, that even when a chosen objective proved 'seemingly' unattainable, it was nevertheless pursued, even if at the outset the costs seemed to outweigh the benefits. It was the confidence and 'willpower' of the commander in question which determined whether, say, four Red Army divisions consisting of *Untermenschen* could capture a position defended by a single German division comprising of *Herrenvolk* (master race).[65] It was the ordinary Landser who was the victim of this approach, but by and large he failed to recognise the cynicism that lay behind the commands he received. The Nazi regime was incredibly successful in repurposing the

---

[59] Waitman Beorn, *Marching into Darkness: the Wehrmacht and the Holocaust in Belarus* (Cambridge, MA., Harvard University Press, 2014), p. 209.

[60] Overmans, *Deutsche militärische Verluste im Zweiten Weltkrieg*, p. 318.

[61] David Stahel, 'The Wehrmacht and National Socialist Military Thinking', *War in History* (24) 2017, p. 336.

[62] Förster, 'From "Blitzkrieg" to "Total War"', p. 92.

[63] Williamson Murray, 'Betrachtungen zur deutschen Strategie im Zweiten Weltkrieg', in Müller and Volkmann (eds.), *Die Wehrmacht*, p. 326.

[64] Stahel, 'The Wehrmacht and National Socialist Military Thinking', pp. 336–61.

[65] Murray, 'Betrachtungen zur deutschen Strategie', pp. 318–26. See also: Müller, *Deutsche Soldaten und ihre Feinde*, p. 162.

Frontkämpferbewusstsein of the First World War, the men's almost deified awareness of being combat soldiers, with all its responsibilities and obligations. This time around, the Landser was not only tough, upright, and obedient, but his mentality was that of the 'Germanic, Aryan fighter, sacrificing himself for the Master Race in a struggle against a world of *Untermenschen*'.[66] Building Grossdeutschland demanded great sacrifices, and the German soldier was prepared to make them. Ernst Jünger's assertion that 'the truest happiness of man lies in his sacrifice, and the highest art of command is to show goals worthy of that sacrifice' resonated among the troops, and the regime willingly and knowingly exploited the troops' preparedness to fully commit themselves.[67] A lack of a clear path to victory did not change this attitude at all, and throughout 1943 and 1944 the German High Command continued to deploy its forces with little to no regard for the risk of casualties, as the death of troops was hardly worthy of sustained consideration. The resulting turnover meant that ever fewer troops knew the men that formed their chain of command, which, as we will see in Chapter 6, fostered an atmosphere of distrust and suspicion. The mounting casualties not only meant having to defend positions with fewer troops when the time came, it also meant that the surviving soldiers had to stand guard much longer and more often, leaving less time to rest and sleep.[68] Frustration grew as supply problems mounted, not only due to partisan activity but more significantly because Allied bombers started targeting railroad junctions ever further to the East, as such hampering transport to and from the front and further depressing the morale of the troops.[69]

Yet, the constant exposure to the violence of war was not viewed purely negatively. A cognitive dissonance increasingly took hold of the troops, and encouraged them, for example, to appreciate battle as 'the ultimate litmus test of a soldier's worth'.[70] Being a veteran in a tried and tested division came with numerous rewards and accolades, and new recruits would not only look up to these men but would go through great lengths to adopt their norms and habits.[71] The comradely bonds formed in combat, moreover, were incomparable to anything they had experienced in civilian life, and only became stronger in darker times. In a speech to his men, the commanding officer of Grossdeutschland veteran Guy Sajer in

[66] Bartov, *The Eastern Front, 1941–45*, p. 88.

[67] Bernd Wegner, 'Hitler, der Zweite Weltkrieg und die Choreographie des Untergangs', *Geschichte und Gesellschaft* (26) 2000, p. 493.

[68] Bartov, *The Eastern Front, 1941–45*, p. 22.

[69] See for example: BArch RH 19 VI/ 26, p. 85: Streckensperrungen 1944.

[70] Neitzel and Welzer, *Soldaten*, p. 37.

[71] Adam Lankford, *Human Killing Machines: Systematic Indoctrination in Iran, Nazi Germany, Al Qaeda, and Abu Ghraib* (Plymouth: Lexington Books, 2009), pp. 17–18.

late 1943 ensured that, even though their position was bleak, he would nevertheless 'burn and destroy entire villages if by so doing I could prevent even one of us from dying of hunger'. After that, Sajer noted, 'we loved him and felt we had a true leader, as well as a friend on whom we could count'.[72] With brutalisation flaring up whenever units were exposed to combat for longer periods of time, reconstructing the path of the divisions that would eventually defend East Prussia might help explain how the callousness their men would eventually display solidified itself among the ranks.

The Third Panzer Army, which was tasked with the defence of northern East Prussia, counted five veteran infantry divisions that had experienced the long and costly retreat from the Soviet Union: the 1st Infanterie-Division, the 56th Infanterie-Division, the 58th Infanterie-Division, the 69th Infanterie-Division, and the 95th Infanterie-Division.[73] The Army was part of Army Group Centre which, by the time it reached East Prussia's borders, mostly consisted of units that were either burned out or in desperate need of replenishing. The 56th Infanterie-Division and the 95th Infanterie-Division had been part of Army Group Centre since late 1941 while the other three divisions had recently been transferred from Army Group North. The 56th Infanterie-Division had been in action almost constantly since the start of Operation Barbarossa, and like so many others was hardly recognisable to those who had marched eastwards with it in 1941. During 1942 and into 1943 it fought bitter battles near Orel, so much so that by the summer the division had to be pulled from the front line. It was nevertheless again thrown in the fray at Cherkasy that autumn and suffered such heavy casualties that it could not be replenished. In October 1943 the division was disbanded, and its remnants were incorporated in a so-called 'Corps Detachment', Korps-Abteilung D. 'Corps Detachment' was the euphemistic designation given to an OKH-authorised amalgam of three decimated divisions that had been reduced to regiment strength, but the creation of these detachments nevertheless served an important purpose. Instead of the cadres of destroyed divisions being distributed over other weakened formations, being part of a Corps Detachment allowed them to stay together as part of a single unit, which in its very essence consisted almost exclusively of seasoned veterans. The combat experience of these men nevertheless helped little to stave off their inevitable fate. By the spring of 1944, Korps-Abteilung D took up positions in the Vitebsk area, where in July it faced the full brunt of Operation Bagration. The unit was almost

---

[72] Guy Sajer, *The Forgotten Soldier* (London: Sphere Books, 1977), p. 266.
[73] Raus and Newton, *Panzer Operations*, p. 311.

Map 2.1 The Red Army's advance from Operation Bagration to East Prussia

immediately smashed, and its pitiful remnants fell back to East Prussia. Here what had remained after two years of sustained losses formed the framework of a newly formed division which, due to the lineage of the unit, was once more raised as the 56th Infanterie-Division.[74] The story of the 95th Infanterie-Division was a similar one. In 1942 it saw action near Woronesh and in the autumn it was moved to Rshev. From there, it fought its way back via Bryansk, Gomel, Bobruisk, and Vitebsk, where

---

[74] Tessin, *Verbände und Truppen der deutschen Wehrmacht*, vol. 5, s.v. '56'; vol. 14, s.v. 'Korps-Abt. D'.

it was eventually destroyed in early 1944. As with the 56th Infanterie-Division, the remnants of the 95th Infanterie-Division were raked together with those of two other divisions to form Korps-Abteilung H. In the month following Bagration this Corps Detachment was also decimated, and as its units fell back on East Prussian soil in September 1944, they were restructured one last time to form the 95th Infanterie-Division.[75]

During this brutal two-year-long retreat from Soviet soil, the German High Command sought to ensure that the Soviet Union would be denied its resources. Whereas some units transported off as many goods as possible from areas that were about to be given up so to prevent them from falling into Soviet hands, others did not see the practical use of these evacuation measures, or struggled to carry them out.[76] These disparities prompted 'Führerbefehl 4', which the High Command issued on 14 February 1943, to ensure a 'strict execution' of 'evacuation and destruction, as well as deportation of the population during the retreat'.[77] A week later, on 21 February, the Wirtschaftsstab Ost (Economic Staff East) had worked out an elaborate dossier of so-called 'ARLZ-measures' which concerned the breaking-down, evacuation, paralysing, and destruction of military and civilian materiel threatened by the Allied advance.[78] The purpose of these measures was 'the furthest possible preservation of economic goods and manpower for the German war economy, and the weakening of the enemy's war potential through the paralysis and destruction of production facilities and their products, as well as the transporting off of manpower'.[79] The scope of the expulsion of the civilian population reveals how central the idea was that nothing had to be left once an area was abandoned. Despite the chaotic retreat and the horrendous manpower losses, Army Group Centre, of which the 56th Infanterie-Division and the 95th Infanterie-Division were part, nevertheless reported to have

---

[75] Tessin, *Verbände und Truppen der deutschen Wehrmacht*, vol. 6, s.v. '95'; vol. 14, s.v. 'Korps-Abt. H'. On the destruction of Army Group Centre during Operation Bagration, see: Rolf Hinze, *Das Ostfrontdrama 1944: Rückzugkämpfe Heeresgruppe Mitte* (Stuttgart: Motorbuch-Verlag, 1987); Frieser, 'Der Zusammenbruch der Heeresgruppe Mitte', pp. 526–603.

[76] Rutherford, *Combat and Genocide*, pp. 310–15.

[77] Norbert Müller (ed.), *Die faschistische Okkupationspolitik in den zeitweilig besetzten Gebieten der Sowjetunion (1941–1944)* (Berlin: Deutscher Verlag der Wissenschaften, 1991), p. 390.

[78] Schramm, *Kriegstagebuch des OKW Band IV*, pp. 1569–72, 'Befehl des Chefs OKW betr. Vorbereitungen für die Verteidigung des Reiches' (19 July 1944).

[79] Rolf-Dieter Müller (ed.), *Die deutsche Wirtschaftspolitik in den besetzten sowjetischen Gebieten 1941 – 1943: Der Abschlußbericht des Wirtschaftsstabes Ost und Aufzeichnungen eines Angehörigen des Wirtschaftskommandos Kiew* (Boppard am Rhein: Harald Boldt Verlag, 1991), pp. 553–80.

Figure 2.3 Soviet prisoners brought through Gumbinnen, late 1944.
Source: Author's collection

transported 535,000 Soviet civilians by late October 1943.[80] Most of them were brought to Germany in a deliberate effort to rob the Red Army of potential manpower and to increase manpower in Germany's factories.

Furthermore, to allow unrestricted movement in the area of operations and to quell partisan activity in their rear, most larger military units cleared areas up to twelve miles behind the front. Horrible scenes unfolded. Large-scale razzias ensured that larger cities were stripped of their population, while smaller villages were often simply set ablaze to force civilians out. As potential workers were of most use, mothers were separated from their children, while men who refused to leave could be shot on the spot. Often civilians were ordered to walk fifteen miles a day, with little or no food and drink, and mostly without shelter.[81]

The fighting retreat of Army Group North, Army Group Centre's left neighbour, had been more systematic and better organised by its command, although this did not mean that the treatment of the native population was fundamentally more humane. The Army Group fielded three of the divisions that would eventually defend the borders of East Prussia,

[80] Müller (ed.), *Die faschistische Okkupationspolitik*, p. 492.
[81] Pohl, *Die Herrschaft der Wehrmacht*, pp. 322–8.

the 1st Infanterie-Division, the 58th Infanterie-Division, and the 69th Infanterie-Division. The men of Army Group North had dug in in late 1941 and defended a fairly stable front line until 1943, but from that autumn onwards they would only see themselves being pushed back by superior Soviet forces. In September 1943 the Army Group had to fall back on the Panther Line, a line of defences (mostly built through forced labour of local populations) that roughly followed the old Russian imperial border.[82] In the months that followed the 58th and the 69th built the southern flank of the Army Group, and were deployed in the vital Nevel area. Although Army Group North's positions were arduous, they were still holding, while further south in Ukraine the Wehrmacht was in full retreat. Therefore, in January 1944 the 1st Infanterie-Division was transferred to Ukraine to halt the Soviet Dnieper–Carpathian Offensive. Initially it fought near Vinnitsa, but by late March saw itself surrounded near Kamianets-Podilskyi in what became known as the Hube-Pocket. In this high-stress situation, aggravated by the relentless mud season and heavy losses, the division's men nevertheless maintained morale, and after two weeks they managed to break the encirclement.[83] Meanwhile, the Red Army broke the Siege of Leningrad, forcing the 58th Infanterie-Division to be rushed north, where between February and July 1944 it participated in the battle of Narva. By September Soviet pressure along the Panther Line made holding Estonia unsustainable, and by 16 September Hitler granted permission to abandon Estonia and northern Latvia. Eleven days later, by 27 September, Army Group North had fallen back in orderly fashion to positions in the middle of Latvia.[84] By that time, the 1st Infanterie-Division had also been recalled from Ukraine and once again joined the Army Group.

The large-scale withdrawals marked an escalation of violence towards the local populations.[85] A part of the population, *Hiwis* or locals forced into collaboration (such as village elders and their families) followed voluntarily, but most villagers were quick to realise that evacuation orders spelled expulsion and exploitation, and to prevent being taken away, would regularly flee into the woods. There they would often encounter partisans, or, whenever they were caught by German troops, would be accused of being in contact with them. That accusation was enough to warrant execution or hanging or could prompt collective punishment in the form of burning

---

[82] Rutherford, *Combat and Genocide*, p. 357
[83] Karl-Heinz Frieser, 'Die Rückzugsoperationen der Heeresgruppe Süd in der Ukraine', in Frieser (ed.), *Das Deutsche Reich und der Zweiten Weltkrieg 8*, pp. 437–47.
[84] Karl-Heinz Frieser, 'Die Rückzugskämpfe der Heeresgruppe Nord bis Kurland', in Frieser (ed.), *Das Deutsche Reich und der Zweiten Weltkrieg 8*, pp. 635–42.
[85] Enstad, *Soviet Russians under Nazi Occupation*, pp. 208–11.

a village in question. This rigid approach, which the Wehrmacht readily adopted, only helped to drive these people further into the hands of the partisans.[86]

By presenting the destruction of property and the expulsion of populations during times of retreat as a way to ensure an effective German war economy, the measures were posed as pragmatic acts. Their devastating long-term effects were of little importance. At the same time, the evacuations caused a strain on the already overburdened army and were a clear indication to the ordinary Landser that the tide of war had turned. Moreover, organising these evacuations diverted the Wehrmacht from its core tasks. Having to take care of these people and decide their fate took both a mental and physical toll, as it was near-impossible for German troops not to be confronted with the moral decline of their army.[87] During his leave in early 1944, Willy Peter Reese, a veteran of the 95th Infanterie-Division, wrote a 140-page 'confession' in which he also touched on his feelings during his unit's long retreat:

We always saw the same picture: harvested fields in the storm, clouds of smoke on the horizon. Russia became a depopulated, smoking, burning, debris-covered desert, and the war behind the front depressed me still more because it affected the defenceless. I, too, was guilty of this devastation and the suffering it brought to people, responsible like all those nameless and sacrificed, like all soldiers.[88]

Nevertheless, by 1944, most soldiers had taught themselves to view morality through the lens of 'military necessity'. Therefore, rather than reflecting on their calloused behaviour they felt fairly comfortable in their numbness, especially after the 'novelty' of fighting a war of world views had worn off and was replaced with the idea that they were fighting a more traditional war.[89]

This numbness allowed violence against civilians to escalate time and again, and the ease with which the army could 'switch gears' was hardly ever considered remarkable. With partisan activity becoming more organised after the tide of the war had definitely turned, many German units had to fight a 'two-front war' – one in their rear and one on the front lines. Helped by the notion that Soviet troops were only to encounter complete destruction in the areas they reconquered, reprisals against entire communities unsurprisingly became more common again. As every retreat was accompanied by the use of scorched-earth policies, some soldiers felt

---

[86] Kilian, 'Wehrmacht, Partisanenkrieg und Rückzugsverbrechen', pp. 179–84.
[87] Pohl, *Die Herrschaft der Wehrmacht*, pp. 327–8; Nicholas Stargardt, 'The Troubled Patriot: German Innerlichkeit in World War II', *German History* (28) 2010, pp. 326–42.
[88] Willy Peter Reese, *Mir selber seltsam fremd: die Unmenschlichkeit des Krieges, Russland 1941–44* (Berlin: List Taschenbuch, 2004), 191–7 (p. 196).
[89] Rutherford, *Combat and Genocide*, pp. 374–6.

sorry for the population, although due to the misery of their retreat, most felt much more sorry for themselves. Moreover, it was not uncommon for these men to feel somewhat of a self-professed perverse pleasure in the destruction of property, if only because it gave them a glimmer of agency during a period of omnipresent hopelessness. Scorched-earth policies had long been part of military conduct, and the term 'scorched earth', an East Prussian soldier remembered about the burning down of villages, 'eased our consciences that revolted against this brutality'.[90] As a result, thousands of Soviet villages had gone up in flames by the time German troops abandoned Soviet territory.[91] Thus, no matter how much German soldiers might have felt that their adherence to notions of military professionalism served as proof of the failure of National Socialism to alter the army's long-standing structures, the behaviour during their retreat from the Eastern Front reveals that the radicalism that the regime expected in the war of annihilation, from which only one *Volk* could emerge victoriously, had become ingrained in the minds of these men.

The everyday experience of Eastern Front soldiers was, by every standard, anomalous. It was self-evidently extremely different to their previous lives as civilians, but critically also to their expectations of *Soldatentum*. In the Soviet Union, they were ordered to adhere to behavioural patterns that inevitably contributed to a radicalisation of their mindset. Soldiers' share in starvation and exploitation measures, anti-partisan actions, executions of commissars, scorched-earth policies, and evacuation drives, as well as their constant proximity to death and injury, their ideological indoctrination, and the demodernisation of their warfare, resulted in a calloused attitude unique to members of the Wehrmacht. The personal hardships of war were significantly aggravated by the institutional demands of Nazi Germany's army, which were pursued with a particular ferocity in 'the East'. The friction between the great majority of men who considered themselves to be ordinary soldiers belonging to a long and proud German military tradition, and the demands of the war of annihilation in which the High Command expected them to partake, was tangible from the earliest planning stages of Operation Barbarossa. Yet, regardless of the extent of disagreement with the many genocidal measures, the prolonged exposure to them nevertheless inevitably led to a change of attitude among the men. Troops had neither the opportunity nor the moral courage to systematically disobey the regime's criminal orders or abandon their comrades, and by and large carried out what was expected of them. Since only a small part of the men considered themselves dedicated Nazis, racist explanations

[90] Ibid., pp. 360–73. Here: pp. 371–2.
[91] Kilian, 'Wehrmacht, Partisanenkrieg und Rückzugsverbrechen', pp. 173–99.

were largely insufficient to justify the ruthlessness with which their units behaved. To rationalise their hardening conduct, soldiers internalised the notion that their actions were born out of military necessity, a notion in which they felt strengthened due to the fact that their units indeed often diverted from the regime's official course. By styling themselves as 'pragmatists', German soldiers convinced themselves that they were not merely following orders, but rather that they critically examined them. As a result, policies rooted in a calculated, and often cynical, disregard of human life based on National Socialist ideological notions were decreasingly recognised as such by those ordered to carry them out. This way of thinking, moreover, served as a defence mechanism, as it allowed soldiers to consider themselves both militarily and morally correct in a brutalising environment. By 1944, the average German soldier had become mentally adjusted to the war of annihilation he was fighting, but he often did not recognise it as such. Many of the norms and values he had once lived by had been jettisoned, and his sense of 'normality' had shifted beyond recognition as a result of his efforts to square his day-to-day behaviour with his sense of morality. This reorientation of his outlook on everyday life as a whole, the 'lowered resting heart rate of the Wehrmacht soldier', could not simply be left behind once he retreated back onto German soil.

The Changing Perception of Civilians

The warfare on the Eastern Front had introduced the Wehrmacht to a set of military standards that had prompted an overall brutalisation among its ranks. Put into place in 1941, by 1944 these had become firmly ingrained in the soldiers' collective mindset, and one of the main shifts that occurred was in the troops' perception of civilians. During the fighting in 1940 the German army had fought the French, British, Belgian, or Norwegian *armies*, while in the East the line between combatant and civilian had deliberately been blurred. By mid-1944, many a German soldier had been confronted with situations that forced him to rethink the role which civilians were to play during wartime. The wide variety of experiences on the Eastern Front, however, ensured that there was no consensus in this matter among the ranks. Yet the troops' 'lowered resting heart rate' ensured that they no longer considered civilians as mere bystanders to the Total War they were waging, but instead probed *which* role the civilian population could assume. This mindset eventually led soldiers to consider the position of their own Volksgenossen on the home front as well, and as the war continued to take a turn for the worse, more and more soldiers envisioned a role for German civilians in the defence of home soil. Obviously, the civilian population on the home front – the very people at the centre of these debates – also had their own various ideas about what their role should be. Both the resulting friction and the proposed courses of action are discussed in this section.

By the time the Red Army pushed the Wehrmacht out of the Soviet Union in the summer of 1944, it had been almost thirty years since fighting had taken place in Germany. Wehrmacht soldiers – with the exception of some generals – had only fought abroad, and little prepared them for the fighting on home soil. Neither their units' year-long routing nor their retreat into Germany had liberated them from the mental constraints that their stay on the Eastern Front had imposed on them, since the Kameradschaft that had allowed troops to maintain their staying power also made it significantly harder to divert from the norms that had defined their immediate circle. More so, during times of defeat soldiers tend to adhere more strictly to standard military practice than during times of victory, since the lessons learned during training and in the field are seen as increasing the chance of survival. Behaviour therefore becomes more ritualised and mechanic, ensuring that more and more soldiers felt 'at home' in war – even in defeat.[92] Thus, somewhat para-doxically, the more a soldier incorporated the ethos the Wehrmacht subscribed to, the more he distanced himself from the very community it was to protect.[93] Racist principles of superiority, for example, tended to spill over into overt sexism. Not only did 'Aryan' qualities such as bravery, obedience, willpower, resolve, discipline, and the willingness to sacrifice oneself distinguish them from their Slavic enemies, the duty of protector of the Heimat also placed them above their female compatriots, who, most soldiers felt, lacked these characteristics. To those men who sought to explain how their positions along a brittle front could be held, the ever decreasing support of armour and heavy weapons left little other choice but to perpetuate these clichés of masculinity.[94] One of the most common strands of this thinking presented Germany's increasingly dire plight as an opportunity and as a formative experience. In September 1944, the military newspaper *Front und Heimat* quoted from a speech Hitler had given on the occasion of the twentieth anniversary of the Beer-Hall putsch:

There are no great heroes of world history who would not have stood firm against the hardest of burdens. Everyone can tolerate sunshine, but only when it thunders and storms the tough characters reveal themselves, and only then will you

---

[92] Römer, *Kameraden*, p. 206; Fritz, *Frontsoldaten*, pp. 164–8; van Crefeld, *The Culture of War*, pp. 87–105.

[93] This holds true for virtually every army. See: van Crefeld, *The Culture of War*, ch. 3, 'Educating Warriors'.

[94] Müller, *Deutsche Soldaten und ihre Feinde*, pp. 156–66.

recognize the weakling. Only when things get difficult, you will see who a real man is, and who keep their nerves in these hours, remaining stubborn and steadfast – never thinking of capitulating.[95]

The permeation of the National Socialist military mindset, the fighting of a Total War, the close link between Heimat and Front, and the propaganda's constant tendency of presenting a one-size-fits-all, generalised ideal of the characteristics of the German Volk meant that more and more soldiers transferred their interpretations of stubbornness and steadfastness onto the civilian population, which – unsurprisingly – fell short. As a result, an increasing group of men started to have doubts about whether the German civilian shared their determination and sense of urgency.

That sense was actively fuelled by the behaviour these men observed among Soviet civilians while fighting in the East. These men and women had fought a Total War since the first days of the German invasion in the spring of 1941. In cities like Leningrad, 'volunteer' civilian militias had greatly facilitated the defence, while at Kursk the Red Army called on a 300,000-strong civilian labour force to create a massive defensive network.[96] In those Soviet areas occupied by Germans, hundreds of thousands of civilians joined the partisans. As the war progressed, the Landser's fear of partisans grew into outright terror, as thousands of bridges and trains were blown up behind the front in anticipation of a Soviet attack while straying German soldiers were killed despite the (threat of) reprisals.[97] Distrust towards Soviet citizens did not limit itself to men of fighting age: officers were instructed to pay sustained attention to 'the elderly, women, and adolescents' since it was quickly 'established' that partisans misused the fact that German troops tended to view these groups with less suspicion.[98] German soldiers had also been imprinted with the idea that the Soviets themselves cared particularly little about the value of human life, something they saw confirmed by the high casualties the Red Army was able to sustain.[99] The Soviets, many a German soldier felt, had ruthlessly deployed their civilians and had come out on top, while in Germany Front and Heimat were still 'comfortably' separated. It was

---

[95] Front und Heimat, Soldatenzeitung d. Gaues Schwaben, 3. September 1944, Nr. 91. This speech was held on 9 November 1943 at the München Löwenbräukeller.

[96] Anders Frankson and Niklas Zetterling, *Kursk 1943: a Statistical Analysis* (Abingdon: Frank Cass, 2004), p. 22; Hill, *The Red Army and the Second World War*, pp. 228–9.

[97] Shepherd, *Hitler's Soldiers*, pp. 168–70; Bartov, *Hitler's Army*, p. 104; Kenneth Slepyan, 'The People's Avengers: the Partisan Movement', in Stone (ed.), *The Soviet Union at War*, pp. 154–81.

[98] Christopher Browning, 'The Holocaust: Basis and Objective of the Volksgemeinschaft?', in Steber and Gotto (eds.), *Visions of Community in Nazi Germany*, p. 224.

[99] Amnon Sella, *The Value of Human Life in Soviet Warfare* (New York: Routledge, 1992), pp. 190–3.

a complaint that had been voiced since the first days of Operation Barbarossa. On 25 June 1941, the Gefreiter Hans Roth wrote in his diary that 'Our beloved Heimat will never fully comprehend what we have accomplished during this campaign. They do not have the slightest idea of the difficult terrain we have experienced, nor the types of battle'. Roth saw his pessimistic outlook fully confirmed some two weeks later, when

A letter received by one of our comrades is passed through the trench. In it, someone is complaining about working overtime, the shortage of beer and cigarettes, and other similar matters. How little does that idiot understand about the things that go on out here? Is that the voice of the homeland? ... Well, we are indebted to you for our great weapons and ammunition without duds, but the Russians have good weapons – sometimes even better than ours! The key factor is the spirit and bravery of the person carrying those weapons. None of you guys have any idea of these two things. Shame on you if you thought you fought these battles and have accomplished such great victories with your overtime![100]

In defeat, troops became even more unsympathetic towards the home front which they felt the regime continuously sought to shield from the heaviest burdens of war. That decision was now costing Germany dear, and came disproportionately at the expense of the fighting man and his comrades.

The SD picked up on this resentment and in early 1944 started monitoring the interaction between German soldiers and civilians. When an officer on leave was asked to leave a table at a bar as it was reserved for regular (civilian) customers, he 'wished that these people could, if only for one day, come to the forward lines at Pleskau. In Russia this would be impossible. Why? Because there are no bars there!' Another officer complained that 'Only we out there know what "Total War" means. If we were to lose the war, it is because the Heimat took this term too lightly.'[101] Yet another was frustrated by the peacetime bureaucratic attitudes:

My leave had just started, and I had hardly had the first full night's sleep, when an official gave me a piece of paper which read that the local tax office had checked the payroll tax for 1939, and found that at the time 3,12 Reichsmark too little had been deducted. I wasn't annoyed about the 3,12 Reichsmark, but about the fact that during the fifth year of the war, [which is] characterised by Total War, there is apparently still time to have an office double-check the payroll tax for 1939 for trivial amounts.[102]

---

[100] Christine Alexander and Mason Kunze (eds.), *Eastern Inferno: the Journals of a German Panzerjäger on the Eastern Front*, 1941–1943 (Philadelphia, PA: Casemate, 2010), pp. 30, 49.
[101] BArch NS 1/544, p. 28: Erörterungen der Bevölkerung über die Kriegsführung Sowjetrusslands als Beispiel für den 'totalen Krieg'. 1. Juni 1944.
[102] Ibid., 29.

That civilians did not share their sense of urgency was reaffirmed by the fact that war weariness set in among the German population well before it did among the troops. War-weary remarks were heard from 1941 onwards and were widespread by 1943.[103] Jokes such as 'whenever a soldier returned from home leave, the whole regiment came to meet him half-way' did little to convince soldiers that the population stood behind them as one.[104] Many of the men who overheard these remarks, especially the front line veterans, were 'puzzled and shocked by the bad manners of the civilian population' which even prompted Goebbels to launch a 'public politeness' campaign.[105] As a result of the scarcity of food, it was noted that some civilians 'scolded wounded soldiers because they did not eat in their hospitals, but contested the food in the restaurants'.[106] Work discipline in the factories, especially among women and adolescents, deteriorated significantly throughout the war.[107] Suicide on the home front became more common as the war continued.[108] These were implicit and explicit reminders that in the very Heimat soldiers were protecting their compatriots were losing trust that the Wehrmacht would be able to procure a favourable outcome of the war.

As the conflict continued, the climbing numbers of levels of infidelity and divorce – or even the mere fear thereof – also increasingly impacted on troops' morale.[109] An April 1944 SD report on the 'immoral behaviour of German women' explained that women who learned that not all men took their marital oath too seriously when serving abroad often felt that they 'had the same rights and were also allowed to entertain themselves'.[110] Once a soldier found out that his girlfriend had cheated on him or that his wife wanted to divorce him, the results could be devastating. The Gefreiter Günter Emanuel Baltuttis, whose unit in early December 1944 defended the East Prussian border near Gumbinnen, remembered how

two soldiers deliberately choose death, because they suffer from family conflicts. Both leave letters, from which it becomes evident that their wives divorced them. The first, who is tasked to guard the trench, climbs out one afternoon, stands up straight, and gets shot, the other leaves the shelter and walks around without

---

[103] Bankier, *The Germans and the Final Solution*, pp. 141–5; Fritz, *Frontsoldaten*, p. 182.

[104] Grunberger, *A Social History of the Third Reich*, p. 39; Steinert, *Hitler's War and the Germans*, pp. 196–8.

[105] Ibid., p. 37.   [106] Werner, *'Bleib übrig!'*, p. 331.   [107] Ibid., pp. 319, 321.

[108] Christian Goeschel, *Suicide in Nazi Germany* (Oxford: Oxford University Press, 2015), pp. 119–20.

[109] Fritz, *Frontsoldaten*, pp. 79–80.

[110] BArch NS 1/544, p. 23: Unmoralisches Verhalten deutscher Frauen, Berlin, den 13. April 1944.

taking cover in front of hill 112. He is the father of four small children. The soldiers say: 'Those women ought to be hanged!'[111]

German soldiers fought a 'total' *Weltanschauungskrieg* (war of world views) and since their sense of racial superiority had taught them to dismiss external factors as an explanation, it became more common to look for faults in their own behaviour or that of their compatriots for any shortcomings. The idea that conspiratorial and destructive forces were part of German society had been crudely force-fed to the troops fighting on the Eastern Front, and as such had much potential spillover into distrust in their own population. Veterans often directly linked poor behaviour on the home front to the military situation at the front: when a Gefreiter read a newspaper article that featured his home town but which mentioned that some of its farmers had not participated in the *Kriegswinterhilfswerk* (war winter relief for the German people), he considered these men to 'have abandoned us soldiers' and to have betrayed Führer and Volk.[112] It was at this point that the 'wavering home-front' entered – or better, re-entered – the soldiers' vocabulary. During the interwar period, the majority of German officers had managed to convince themselves that in 1918 the *Kaiserheer* (Imperial German Army) had not been defeated due to the military strength of their enemies but as a result of a betrayal of the home front: a 'stab in the back'. The military sought the reason for this betrayal in the home front's limited militarisation and realised that Total War also required the total commitment of the population.[113] The defeat of France in 1940 had erased some of the 'shame' of 1918, and the jubilant mood the German soldier encountered upon his return from the early campaigns gave him confidence that he was at the forefront of the 'fighting Volksgemeinschaft'.[114] Yet as victories failed to materialise after 1942, it became clear that the buoyancy of the Volksgemeinschaft's disposition was closely connected to military success. The sense that during times of defeat increasing parts of German society were no longer committed to the war effort prompted a fear of a repetition of twenty-five years earlier. This time, moreover, there was more at stake: the onslaught of Bolshevism posed a direct threat to the

---

[111] Günter Emanuel Baltuttis, *Auf verlorenem Posten* (Würzburg: Verlagshaus Würzburg, 2006), pp. 62–3.
[112] Kühne, *Kameradschaft*, p. 124.
[113] Geoffrey Megargee, 'The German Army after the Great War: a Case Study in Selective Self-Deception', in Dennis and Grey (eds.), *Victory or Defeat*, pp. 108, 113; Geyer, 'German Strategy in the Age of Machine Warfare', pp. 550–4. Fritzsche, *Life and Death in the Third Reich*, pp. 267–8; Schivelbusch, *The Culture of Defeat*, pp. 203–8; Bartov, 'Trauma and Absence', p. 354.
[114] Sven Oliver Müller, 'Nationalismus in der deutschen Kriegsgesellschaft 1939 bis 1945', in Echternkamp (ed.), *Das Deutsche Reich und der Zweite Weltkrieg 9/2*, pp. 38–9.

German way of life.[115] Not all soldiers felt it at the same time or with the same underlying motivations but as defeats mounted, the thought gained traction. Already in 1943, the fear of a repetition of '1918' was felt so strongly that the Ministry of Propaganda started a campaign to highlight the differences with twenty-five years earlier.[116]

Juxtaposed with the Soviet civilian, who Wehrmacht soldiers largely regarded as bearing all the trials of war without murmuring, the German counterpart fell short. To their own frustration, Eastern Front soldiers came to the realisation that 'we fight an elegant war, the Soviets a total war', and many German civilians tended to agree with this.[117] 'On one hand people hate and fear Bolshevism, but on the other admire its capacity to make the war "truly total"', an SD report noted.[118] Yet German civilians also had their qualms with the army. The SD registered complaints about the army's conservative nature, its overly complicated structure, its unnecessarily complicated weapons, and the presumed lavish lifestyle of officers. 'The population was particularly concerned about how in the Wehrmacht the "Total War" is being carried out' another SD report summarised in March 1944: 'broad parts have come to the conclusion that [in the army] necessary measures are being implemented to a far lesser extent than in the civilian sector'.[119] Some in the army agreed with this sentiment as it was widely felt that there were too many soldiers in the supply chains, the *Etappenbullen*.[120] Others were annoyed and outraged by this 'rebuttal' and suspected ungratefulness on behalf of civilians. Both ends of this spectrum, however, reached a similar conclusion: when the war moved to German soil, the role of civilians in its defence should be actively considered.

It is therefore somewhat surprising – given the regime's stress on waging a 'Total War' – that during the years immediately prior to 1944 no one at the German High Command had given sustained thought to the deployment of German civilians in the defence of the Reich. However, back in the early 1920s a group of influential military thinkers at the

---

[115] Aristotle Kallis, 'Die Niedergang der Deutungsmacht. Nationalsozialistische Propaganda im Kriegsverlauf', in Echternkamp (ed.), *Das Deutsche Reich und der Zweite Weltkrieg 9/2*, p. 246.

[116] See for example: Brochure: '1918 ≠ 1943' (Munich: Reichspropagandaleitung der NSDAP, 1943).

[117] BArch NS 1/544, p. 3: Zusammenfassung von kritische Äusserungen aus der Bevölkerung über angebliche Mißstände in der Wehrmacht. Berlin, den 23. März 1944.

[118] BArch NS 1/544, p. 26: Erörterungen der Bevölkerung über die Kriegführung Sowjetrusslands als Beispiel für den 'totalen Krieg'. Berlin, den 1. Juni 1944.

[119] Ibid., pp. 29–30; BArch NS 1/544, Zusammenfassung von kritische Ausserungen, 2–3.

[120] Bernhard Kroener, '"Frontochsen" und "Etappenbullen". Zur Ideologisierung militärischen Organisationsstrukturen im Zweiten Weltkrieg', in Müller and Volkmann (eds.), *Die Wehrmacht: Mythos und Realität*, pp. 371–84.

Truppenamt, the precursor of the OKH, had already mooted some ideas regarding the role of civilians in the defence of Germany.[121] These men had certainly not all been devoted National Socialists – some of them even passionately opposed Hitler – but their ideas had not been forgotten by the time Allied troops approached the German borders. Arguing that the First World War had blurred the line between combatant and non-combatant, they had proposed a *Volkskrieg* – a people's war – in the event of battle on German soil:

When one cannot prevent the invasion of a great power, but one makes it more difficult and more or less costly, the national defence does not just demand great resistance, but thousands of small pockets of resistance.[122]

Bringing the fight to home soil, moreover, would force the population to consider its urgency and would inevitably propel them to rise to the cause. The sentiment that even 'the frailest woman will become a heroine when the life of her own child is at stake', as Hitler wrote in *Mein Kampf*, required little explanation – and certainly not among men whose daily life revolved around battle.[123] The Volkskrieg alone however would never suffice to bring about victory and would devastate the country, but would at the very least leave an invading army highly vulnerable to German counter-offensives.[124] The Volkskrieg idea connected to the idea of a 'fighting Volksgemeinschaft', and as such satisfied fundamental requirements of National Socialism.[125] Indeed, in 1935, at the Wehrmachtsakademie, Oberstleutnant Gerhard Matzky argued in favour of a mass army, not merely out of military considerations but, since the army was an embodiment of the people in the first place, 'it was a point of national honour and dignity that the entire people should contribute to the defence in times of crisis'.[126]

What Matzky alluded to was an idea that had gained considerable traction in the interwar years: a broadly carried struggle as a road to the

---

[121] Under the auspices of Oberstleutnant (later General) Joachim von Stülpnagel, this group of thinkers included some of the most influential commanders of the future Wehrmacht, among them Werner von Blomberg, later the Supreme Commander of the Armed Forces, and Werner Freiherr von Fritsch, later the Supreme Commander of the Army. See: Matthias Strohn, *The German Army and the Defence of the Reich: Military Doctrine and the Conduct of the Defensive Battle 1918–1939* (Cambridge: Cambridge University Press, 2011), pp. 141–2.

[122] Ibid., p. 150.   [123] Stoltzfus, *Hitler's Compromises*, p. 22.

[124] Strohn, *The German Army and the Defence of the Reich*, p. 151.

[125] Megargee, 'The German Army after the Great War', pp. 105–8, 113.

[126] Strohn, *The German Army and the Defence of the Reich*, pp. 105–6. As General der Infanterie, Matzky would in 1944–5 defend East Prussia, initially as commander of the XXVI. Armeekorps, which defended the Gumbinnen area, and finally, in April 1945 as fortress commander of Festung Pillau.

redemption of Germany's stained honour. In late 1918, concurrent to the armistice negotiations, a debate had raged among Reichstag officials, Kaiser Wilhelm II, and the Supreme Command about whether to continue the war on German territory through a mass levy of civilians. If the *Entente* was shown that Germans would be prepared to continue fighting until the point of annihilation, the rationale ran, this would ensure that during peace negotiations it would refrain from making 'insufferable demands'. Although some expressed the hope 'that a *furor teutonicus* will break out in the entire land, like August 1914 had seen', eventually the government of Prince Max von Baden decided against it. A continuation of the war would wreck the country, and since there was hardly any popular support for this route it was unlikely a prolonged fight would change anything. The country nevertheless still plummeted into chaos soon after, leaving the nagging feeling that *had* the Germans continued fighting they would at least have saved their national dignity.[127]

Meanwhile, the Soviet people, through their total commitment to the war effort, increasingly gained the begrudging respect of the German troops, while Germany's traditional Western enemy, France, had in the past also successfully mobilised its population to achieve its national goals. In 1793 the French National Convention ordered a *levée en masse* (mass levy), giving birth to the 'citizen-soldier' who was to reinvigorate the revolutionary spirit of the French army after it had been dealt some devastating blows: 'Until the enemy has been chased from the territory of the Republic, all the French will be requisitioned for service of the armies', the famous proclamation ran.[128] In both cases, the civilians' rally to the flag had changed the tide of the war. Germany could boast no such example. Hitler had long expressed his admiration for France's radical decision, and already in 1923 proclaimed that 'with the collapse of France at Sedan ... the people rose in revolution to save the fallen tricolour! The war was continued with new energy!'[129] It was no coincidence that propagandists presented the construction of the Ostwall as a *levée en masse*: the people of East Prussia were to reinforce the spirit of the Wehrmacht just as the French had done 150 years earlier.[130] Although not every commander agreed with this course of action, the soldiers' 'lowered resting heart rate' caused by the barbarisation of the fighting in the Soviet Union, the perpetuation of stereotypes of masculinity, the spectres of 1918 – both the 'stab in the back' of November 1918

[127] Michael Geyer, 'Insurrectionary Warfare: the German Debate about a *Levée en Masse* in October 1918', *The Journal of Modern History* (73) 2001, pp. 459–527 (p. 474). See also: Wette, *Die Wehrmacht*, pp. 185–7.

[128] Mosse, *Fallen Soldiers*, pp. 16, 76.   [129] Schivelbusch, *The Culture of Defeat*, p. 9.

[130] Noble, *Nazi Rule and the Soviet Offensive*, pp. 103–7.

and the resulting chaos of the years that followed – and the inculcation of the National Socialist propaganda, ensured that there was certainly fertile ground for these ideas. Also in East Prussia there were segments of the army who followed these lines of thinking, as there were many men who felt that its defence necessitated the use of radical means. The mindset that underpinned the prevailing attitudes at the time nevertheless differed from region to region.

The Soldiers' Perception of East Prussia

Whether the British or American troops in the West, or the Soviet troops in the East, crossing the border of Germany was a significant event. The British Prime Minister Winston Churchill, with a 'childish grin of intense satisfaction', urinated on the Westwall position, while the US General George S. Patton urinated in the Rhine, noting that he 'didn't even piss this morning when I got up, so I would have a full load'.[131] On the other side of Germany, the later Soviet dissident Lev Kopelev ordered his men to relieve themselves as soon as they entered East Prussia.[132] The three men abhorred what Germany had become, a sentiment they shared with millions of other soldiers and politicians, even though these men also knew that in order to overcome the challenges that lay ahead it was counterproductive to tar all Germans with the same brush. Nevertheless, crossing into Germany was an important milestone, one that was celebrated by all those tasked with Germany's defeat.[133]

The event was considerably less momentous for the ordinary Landser. Crossing into East Prussia was part of a chaotic retreat and thus held a different importance. To some it was their Heimat; to others it signalled that the war was entering a final stage; to many it was a return to civilisation after years of fighting in the Soviet Union. A handful of determined individuals even considered it a final opportunity to prove themselves. Whether a veteran of the 5th Panzer-Division, a Volkssturm man, a recruit from the Oldenburg-mustered 58th Infanterie-Division, or a staff officer of the East Prussian 1st Infanterie-Division, all had vastly different views as to what East Prussia meant. At the same time, to all troops it was the location of their respective units, the area of operations,

---

[131] Alan Brooke, Alex Danchev, and Daniel Todman (eds.), *War Diaries 1939–1945: Field Marshal Lord Alanbrooke* (London: Weidenfeld & Nicolson, 2001), pp. 667–8; Terry Brighton, *Masters of Battle: Monty, Patton and Rommel at War* (London: Penguin, 2009), p. 370.

[132] Lev Kopelev, *No Jail for Thought* (London: Secker & Warburg, 1977), p. 37.

[133] On the border of East Prussia signs were erected that read: 'You are now entering the lair of the Fascist beast!'.

and the place where they were ordered to fight the Red Army. East Prussia was fought over from mid-August 1944 until late April 1945 – more than eight months – a longer time than in any other German province by a considerable margin. Building on the findings so far, we will now examine the factors that shaped the Landser's decision to defend East Prussian territory obstinately during a period in which the prospect of a favourable outcome of the war shrank day by day.

When Army Group Centre retreated into East Prussia in the summer of 1944, it had suffered extremely heavy losses during Operation Bagration, but it was certainly not defeated. By the beginning of 1945, the total strength of its three armies, Generaloberst Walter Weiss's Second Army, Generaloberst Erhard Raus's Third Panzer Army, and General Friedrich Hossbach's Fourth Army, stood at 580,000 men (of which 80,000 Volkssturm), about a fifth of the total strength of the Eastern Front.[134] What would motivate these men to keep fighting despite the perilousness of their situation was a question that occupied many at Hitler's High Command, and the preparations for the fighting in the province show that there were enough voices willing to admit that loyalty to the traditional Heimat, as opposed to the idea of a Grossdeutschland, was still important. Twelve divisions were subordinated to the Third Panzer Army (which was tasked with the defence of northern East Prussia), of which three were East Prussian: the seasoned 1st Infanterie-Division, as well as the 349th Volksgrenadier-Division and the 561st Volksgrenadier-Division. Third Panzer Army's right neighbour, Fourth Army, fielded two more battle-hardened East Prussian divisions: the 61st Infanterie-Division and the 21st Infanterie-Division. Of these five East Prussian divisions, only the 21st Infanterie-Division had reached the province without the direct interference of the High Command. In August 1944 Gauleiter Koch had personally pushed for the transfer of 5,000 East Prussian veteran soldiers and officers of the 349th Infanterie-Division from Ukraine to assist in the defence of East Prussia. The proposal found agreement at Hitler's headquarters (at that time still based in the Wolfsschanze), and one month later these men formed the skeleton of the newly raised 349th Volksgrenadier-Division.[135]

[134] Richard Lakowski, 'Der Zusammenbruch der deutschen Verteidigung zwischen Ostsee und Karpaten', in Müller (ed.), *Das Deutsche Reich und der Zweite Weltkrieg 10/1*, pp. 495, 531. In reality, the strength of the front was lower since casualty numbers for late 1944 had not yet been accounted for. See: Overmans, *Deutsche militärische Verluste im Zweiten Weltkrieg*, pp. 276–84.

[135] Deutsch-Russisches Projekt zur Digitalisierung deutscher Dokumente in Archiven der Russischen Föderation, 'Meldungen des Gauleiters Ostpreußens Erich Koch an die Führerhauptquartier', http://wwii.germandocsinrussia.org/de/nodes/2338#page/5/mode/inspect/zoom/4

In August the 1st Infanterie-Division was also transferred from Ukraine, while the 61st Infanterie-Division came over from the Kurland pocket (in western Latvia) in October. The 561st Volksgrenadier-Division was mustered in July 1944, and had such a distinctive East Prussian character that rechristening the division *Ostpreußen* was even considered, although this idea was eventually dropped.[136] As with every war, German soldiers professed to defend their loved ones rather than territory to which they had no personal attachment, and in early October 1944 a call to all branches of the Wehrmacht to defend East Prussia resulted in an additional 10,000 volunteers for the province, even though most realised that the fighting that lay ahead would be grim.[137] 'The East Prussians are glad to go to their Heimat, although the fact that the 61st [Infanterie]-Division has to fight on the Heimat gives reason for concern', the division's war chronicle noted shortly after the war.[138] Regardless, in their letters home the men of the 1st Infanterie-Division professed an uncompromising determination to defend their Heimat.[139] Then again, the fact that after the war East Prussia might be lost was something a growing number of troops evidently thought about as well. Some East Prussians, an Allied interrogation officer noted, 'didn't really care what happens to post-war Germany, as long as they are free to work and make a living'.[140] Among the tight-knit East Prussian units this view could of course never be publicly admitted.

By and large however, East Prussian troops were committed to fight for their Heimat, although this did not translate into a more steadfast defence, or higher casualty numbers, than among troops from other parts of Germany.[141] The difference in battlefield performance between the recently mustered Volksgrenadier divisions and the veteran units, moreover, was equally marginal in the province. The 349th Volksgrenadier-Division was annihilated during the fighting south of

---

[136] BArch RH 26-561/1: 561. Infanterie Grenadier-Division.

[137] Echternkamp, *Soldaten im Nachkrieg*, pp. 69–70, 79; Kunz, *Wehrmacht und Niederlage*, p. 172.

[138] Walther Hubatsch, *Die 61. Infanterie-Division 1939–1945* (Eggolsheim: Dörfler, 2004), p. 57.

[139] Martin Humburg, '"Ich glaube, daß meine Zeit bald gezählt sein dürfte": Feldpostbriefe am Ende des Krieges: Zwei Beispiele', in Hillmann and Zimmermann (eds.), *Kriegsende 1945 in Deutschland*, pp. 254–59.

[140] Karina von Lindeiner-Stráský, 'Indoctrinated, but Not Incurable? Klaus Mann's Interrogation of German Prisoners of War in 1944', *German Life and Letters* (64) 2011, p. 226.

[141] Throughout the war, soldiers from Eastern provinces did, however, die in considerably higher numbers than those from the West. This was most likely because more men from these areas were conscripted. See: Overmans, *Deutsche militärische Verluste im Zweiten Weltkrieg*, p. 231–2.

Königsberg, yet so was the 56th Infanterie-Division. The 21st Infanterie-Division was dealt some serious blows during the province's defence but was still relatively intact by early May, while the 286th Sicherungs-Division was annihilated on the Samland as late as mid-April 1945, as was the 5th Panzer-Division. The 69th Infanterie-Division was almost entirely wiped out during the fighting for Königsberg.[142] By the time of the last roll call on 7 May 1945, just prior to its surrender, Armee Ostpreußen (a purpose-built Army-command which on 7 April had absorbed all remnants of units that were still defending East Prussia) counted only 100,000 men divided between twenty-three tattered 'divisions'.[143] Regionalism, although invoked within the divisions, thus had little impact on the conduct of troops fighting in East Prussia. Whether East Prussian, Saxon, or from Weser-Ems, these men fought to the death with equal determination, which suggests that in East Prussia troops continued to adhere to similar notions as in previous areas of operations.

The attitude (*Haltung*) of most German soldiers was resolute and gritty, but we should be careful to trace this back to an elevated mood (*Stimmung*) caused by their arrival in Germany.[144] The difference between Haltung and Stimmung was epitomised by Leutnant Fritz Blankenhorn, the commander of an artillery battery of the 367th Infanterie-Division. The division fought tenaciously in East Prussia and its remnants, including Blankenhorn's unit, were among the last to surrender in Festung Königsberg in April 1945. He nevertheless wrote in the autumn of 1944 that 'every day – particularly these last weeks of retreat in East Prussia – brings new challenges, which demand the limits of my strength. What do the names of villages and localities which we march through ... even mean to me, given that our eyes almost close out of tiredness'.[145] Heinz Simat, an East Prussian soldier of the 349th Volksgrenadier-Division, also displayed a sense of detachment: 'The world is still in order, although the enemy already stands on our Heimat soil. Trench warfare also demands its casualties, as becomes clear from

[142] Tessin, *Verbände und Truppen der deutschen Wehrmacht*, vol. 1, s.v. '5'; vol. 4, s.v. '21'; vol. 5, s.v. '56'; vol. 9, s.v. '286';. vol. 9, s.v. '349'.

[143] Deutsch-Russisches Projekt zur Digitalisierung deutscher Dokumente in Archiven der Russischen Föderation, 'Verbände des AOK Ostpreußen, Stand 7.5.45', http://wwii .germandocsinrussia.org/de/nodes/2377-akte-241-angaben-des-oberkommandos-der-weh rmacht-ber-bestand-und-st-rke-der-deutsche-truppen#page/1/mode/grid/zoom/1

[144] On the difference between Stimmung and Haltung see: Steinert, *Hitler's War and the Germans*, p. 5.

[145] Fritz Blankenhorn, ... *und fah'r wir ohne Wiederkehr: Von Ostpreußen nach Siberien 1944–1949* (Reinbek: Rowolt Taschenbuch Verlag, 2006), p. 123.

the daily casualty reports.'[146] Others, such as Oberstabsvetenär Dr Johannes Hung, felt that their attitude had not changed significantly after their arrival in East Prussia but admitted that the awareness that they were now defending German soil undermined – rather than strengthened – their mood. Hung knew that he 'sat on a powder keg, about 40 kilometres away from the front':

The officer corps 'celebrated' Christmas in a casino, where an oil painting of Field Marshal von Hindenburg covered the wall, gigantic, reaching from the floor to the ceiling. Oberst Becker held an address with the motto '*Per aspera ad astra*' (Through hardships to the stars), no brash *Durchhalte*-speech, he was a much too sober soldier for that. In anticipation of the coming events, a depressed, no way Christmassy mood, prevailed.[147]

These were not isolated sentiments. The Wehrmacht that returned to Germany was not the staunch force propaganda newsreels claimed it to be. As early as 12 July, a mere three weeks after the start of Operation Bagration, Gauleiter Koch lodged complaints to Hitler about the poor morale of the troops returning from the front to his province. Appreciating the seriousness of this development, Hitler ordered East Prussia's Wehrkreis commander, General Albert Wodrig, to take 'immediate and resolute action against all phenomena that threaten discipinle within all formations'.[148] A month later Wodrig was still struggling with this task as more and more units poured into the province:

The Führer has ordered:
It must be ensured, by all means, that all units of the Ostwehrmacht that have been moved to Reich territory, or will be moved there, immediately readopt the demands of military order that the German people expect from their army.
The most pressing situation that must be dealt with is that parts of these units lie idly and without orders in German settlements, while men and boys work on defensive positions, and women and girls in the fields.
For this purpose, all units of the German Ostwehrmacht that have been billeted on Reich territory, but which are not demonstrably [and] in their entirety occupied by orders from their superior offices, are to be immediately moved to military training grounds in the eastern border area where they are to be reorganized.[149]

---

[146] Heinz Simat, *Blutiger Abschied, Tatsachenbericht über die verzweifelten Abwehrkämpfe der 349. Volksgrenadier-Division in Ostpreußen von Januar bis April 1945* (Stade: Self-published, 1986), p. 9.

[147] Johannes Hung, 'Die letzten Kriegsmonate in Ostpreußen', *Das Ostpreußenblatt*, 17 January, 1987, p. 12.

[148] Werner Rahm and Gerhard Schreiber (eds.), *Kriegstagebuch der Seekriegsleitung 1939–1945 Teil A, Band 59/I: 1. bis 15. Juli 1944* (Berlin: E. S. Mittler & Sohn, 1995), p. 268.

[149] Werner Rahm and Gerhard Schreiber (eds.), *Kriegstagebuch der Seekriegsleitung 1939–1945 Teil A, Band 60/I: 1. bis 15. August 1944* (Berlin: E. S. Mittler & Sohn, 1995), p. 257.

That morale did not spontaneously improve as the troops entered German territory was because 'fighting in East Prussia' was merely one of the many factors that shaped the soldiers' mood. Where it ranked among other factors (such as 'receiving good equipment', 'having sufficient ammunition' or 'getting properly trained recruits') depended on the individual Landser. Often the main thing still on a soldier's mind was the pursuit of ever scarcer earthly pleasures, such as food, alcohol, and women.[150] Symptomatic of an army in defeat is that previously peripheral issues assume greater importance. The German army was no different in this regard and came under intense internal pressure. Different groups within the Wehrmacht found reason to detach themselves mentally from the larger military community. Ethnic German soldiers, the Volksdeutsche, such as Austrians, Lorrainians, and Alsatians, often renounced their ties with Germany and deserted more frequently than Reichsdeutsche.[151] Men from the south of Germany started musing about a type of Bavarian–Austrian state. Troops from non-Prussian states pointed to Prussian militarism to explain Germany's dire situation.[152] Recruits from the Hitler Youth felt belittled by their superiors.[153] The rank-and-file accused the officers of cowardice; the officers accused their men of insubordination. There were plenty of soldiers for whom the location of the fighting was of little importance, especially since it was merely one of the many factors that determined their attitude.

Some of these stresses and strains within the army were illustrated by the regime-loyal Panzer-Grenadier Herbert Nerger. Nerger had volunteered for the front but was appalled by what he heard during a stopover in Königsberg during the last days of October 1944. 'The words skedaddle and vamoose ("stiften und türmen gehen") are commonplace', he wrote to a comrade of his former *SA-Standarte*. When he tried to greet his bunkmates with 'Heil Hitler', it resulted in astonishment and hostility. 'The leading sentiment is to call it quits just as soon as possible. . . . My hope is that it is different with the troops at the front, and that a healthier spirit prevails there.'[154] These tensions were further reflected in the behaviour of two company commanders of a Volkssturm battalion in late October. While one of them was brought up before a court martial on a charge of 'cowardice in face of the enemy', the other remained confident in, yet

---

[150] BArch Ost-Dok.8/579, p. 14: Wendtlandt.
[151] von Lindeiner-Stráský, 'Indoctrinated, but Not Incurable', p. 220. Volksdeutsche were people who were considered part of the 'German race', but who lived outside of the border of the Greater German Reich. They were drafted into the German army soon after their areas of residence came under German control.
[152] Ibid., p. 228.   [153] Kater, *Hitler Youth*, p. 193.
[154] BArch NS 19/813, pp. 2–4: Abschrift, Königsberg, den 28.10.1944. Lieber Walter!

critical of, the strength of the defence.[155] Higher up the chain of command, the staffs of the different armies in East Prussia were left to grapple with the magnitude of the losses that Operation Bagration had inflicted. It was work that hardly inspired confidence.

To those German soldiers who by mid-1944 still considered themselves on a path to victory, East Prussia was of vital significance. Most of Germany's U-boat crews were being trained in the province (some 25,000 crew and staff) as the Kriegsmarine had long considered the Baltic its own inland sea.[156] Grossadmiral Karl Dönitz, who had succeeded Raeder in January 1943 as the head of the Kriegsmarine, attached great importance to the province. In a meeting with Hitler at the Wolfsschanze in January 1944, as the German army was being pushed back from the Soviet Union, he successfully argued that, in order for Germany to retain control of the Baltic it had to stay put at the Kurland and East Prussia.[157] A few months later, in July, Hitler underlined that he would explicitly forbid any withdrawal from these Eastern Baltic bridgeheads due to the sea's critical role in the receipt of Finnish and Swedish ore and Estonian shale oil, both of which were of key importance to the Navy. An evacuation from the Kurland, moreover, might encourage Finland to 'jump off' the Axis alliance.[158] To Hitler, the significance of the Baltic Sea – and with that the need to maintain control of the bridgeheads – was 'completely clear'.[159] Dönitz, however, faced some backlash, both from his subordinates and the army. Not all felt that the Kurland was as important as the Grossadmiral claimed, so, to bolster his case he had report after report drawn up in which the cost and the duration of the evacuation from the area were greatly inflated. All, however, were adamant that for the Baltic to remain in German hands East Prussia had to be held at all costs.[160] Whether Hitler's and Dönitz's estimates were valid – after all, Finland did eventually switch sides – what should be clear is that the decision to stay put was grounded in thought-through 'strategic' considerations, and was not merely the result of Hitler's presumed unwillingness to yield ground at any cost.[161]

[155] Just, Rothe and Rehagen, *Hitler's Last Levy in East Prussia*, pp. 31–9.
[156] Michael Salewski, *Die deutsche Seekriegsleitung 1935–1945, Band II: 1942–1945* (Munich: Bernard & Graefe Verlag für Wehrwesen, 1975), p. 462.
[157] Gerhard Wagner (ed.), *Lagevorträge des Oberbefehlshabers der Kriegsmarine vor Hitler 1939–1945* (Munich: J. F. Lehmanns, 1972), p. 565.
[158] Salewski, *Die deutsche Seekriegsleitung*, pp. 463–4.
[159] Wagner (ed.), *Lagevorträge*, p. 565.
[160] Grier, *Hitler, Dönitz and the Baltic sea*, pp. 97–106, 141–5; Wagner (ed.), *Lagevorträge*, pp. 595–6; Salewski, *Die deutsche Seekriegsleitung*, pp. 463–4; Guderian, *Panzer Leader*, pp. 411–13.
[161] Weinberg, *Germany, Hitler, and World War II*, pp. 284–5.

Even to those troops serving under commanders who no longer believed in victory, the approaching end of the war did not necessarily mean that they would be allowed to surrender. Rather, most were encouraged to keep fighting until 'five minutes past twelve'.[162] Certain set phrases, such as holding a position 'until the last breath' or 'until the last bullet' had permeated military orders, and despite their propagandist origins could have very real consequences.[163] Some understood them figuratively, others took them more literally, but what stands out is that there were only a few commanders who opposed what one Chief of Staff of an Army on the Western Front described as 'people-devouring' (*menschenfressender*) attacks.[164] When in January 1945, during the first days of the defence of East Prussia, the company of Gefreiter Günter Baltuttis found itself in a tight spot, its commander wanted to stress that he would 'follow orders' to the end:

[Our company commander] ordered the radio operator to transmit the following message: 'Will hold the position to the last man. Long live the Führer and Greater Germany.' At the time, radio messages sent in hopeless situations read like this or in similar words. I think I know what happened in the last hours and start preparing myself. I put my *Soldbuch* in the outside pocket of my battledress, in the hope that they will find it in a counter-attack, so that my mother, whose birthday it is today, will be notified. Ten minutes later, the angry response from battalion arrives, which considers our radio message 'exaggerated'.[165]

This anecdote shows how different such orders were given and received. Baltuttis understood the order as an indicator of hopelessness and imminent death, his company commander used it to show his commitment to the National Socialist cause, while 'battalion' disagreed with its premise altogether. Yet, despite the fact that the promise to 'fight to the last man' was understood differently depending on the individual, it is clear that by the last year of the war it had become part of the soldiers' vocabulary, and had not only shaped speech patterns but also left its mark on behavioural patterns. The inculcation of this language, both during training and in the field, ensured that this kind of phraseology was readily invoked when the time came.

Especially to those senior German commanders who had fought in the First World War, preventing a repetition of the humiliating capitulation of the German Armed Forces in 1918 was, if not a guiding principle, at

---

[162] Max Domarus, *Hitler: Reden und Proklamationen, 1932–1945. II. Band: Untergang (1939–1945)* (Neustadt a.d. Aisch: Verlagsdruckerei Schmidt, 1963), p. 2056.

[163] John Zimmermann, *Pflicht zum Untergang: Die deutsche Kriegsführung im Westen des Reiches 1944/45* (Paderborn: Schöningh, 2009), pp. 282–7; Holub, 'Reception Theory'.

[164] Zimmermann, *Pflicht zum Untergang*, p. 285.

[165] Günter Emanuel Baltuttis, *Auf verlorenem Posten* (Würzburg: Verlagshaus Würzburg, 2006), pp. 105–6.

Figure 2.4 *Wochenspruch der NSDAP*, 'Anyone who prefers to die rather than lay
down their arms cannot be overcome', first week of November 1944.
Source: Author's collection

least in the back of their minds.[166] With the war no longer winnable, some
commanders felt that the only thing that was left to salvage was
Germany's honour. Displaying pure devotion to the Fatherland to the
very end was one of the few virtues still available to an army on the brink of
destruction. Propagandists had made it abundantly clear during the
previous years what constituted the purest devotion: death on the battlefield. Almost as soon as Germany laid down its weapons in 1918, com-
mentators adopted the ambiguous leitmotiv of 'purification' as a way to
explain why the casualties of the First World War had not been in vain: in

---

[166] See: Geyer, 'Endkampf 1918 and 1945'.

their sacrifice, fallen German soldiers had proven to be true patriots, absolutely pure in their devotion to the Fatherland. Nazi propagandists latched on
to this idea and pushed it with fervour. In the first week of November 1944,
for example, the mass-produced weekly quotation of the Party, the
Wochenspruch der NSDAP, read that 'Anyone who prefers to die rather
than lay down their arms cannot be overcome.'[167] During the earlier fighting
abroad, these slogans – a mixture of baseless bravado and deliberate misunderstanding of the demands of battle – would have rung hollow, but, once on
home soil, commanders were bound to come across these kind of Party
slogans with increasing frequency which, especially to those who sought to
make some sense of the mounting defeats, gave them a glimmer of purpose.
Just as pain is part of a healing process, some believed, so a soldier's death
would bring forth new life.[168] Cementing this notion was the martial idea
that the German people had a long and 'proud' tradition of suffering through
wars that had proven to be building blocks for the future 'Germany': the
Thirty Years' War that was waged in the seventeenth century was the first
major conflict that reached the homes of German civilians, followed in the
next centuries by the Seven Years' War, the Napoleonic Wars, the Wars of
Unification and finally, the First World War.[169] The preparedness to suffer
was portrayed as a German virtue, a manifestation of the stoicism that
distinguished Germans from their neighbours.

Also those commanders looking for guidance in the words of their Lord
found that death was framed as honourable and dutiful. The army-
sanctioned *Evangelisches Feldgesangbuch* had paragraphs on both 'readiness
for death' and 'loyalty until death', and had a section that read: 'My place is
at the front, no matter how difficult it is. If I fall there, what does that mean?
Tomorrow the bells ring for Resurrection Day – what a Hope! We all have
to die once, and there is no death more honourable than that on the
battlefield in faithful fulfilment of duty.'[170] Its Catholic counterpart, the
Katholisches Militär-Gebet-und Gesangbuch also stressed that a good soldier
of Christ ought to remember that 'Without loyalty until death, true soldier's honour ... cannot exist'.[171] Whether those forming the chain of
command bought into their own propaganda, or adhered to Christian

---

[167] Wochenspruch der NSDAP, Herausgeber Reichspropagandaleitung / H.A.Pro.PII /
Folge 5, 30. 1.–6.11.1944
[168] Jay Baird, *To Die for Germany: Heroes in the Nazi Pantheon* (Bloomington: Indiana
University Press, 1990), p. 208.
[169] Randall Hansen, 'War, Suffering and Modern German History', *German History* (29)
2011, p. 368.
[170] *Evangelisches Feldgesangbuch* (Berlin: Mittler & Sohn, 1939), p. 13.
[171] Franz Justus Rarkowski (ed.), *Katholisches Militär-Gebet-und Gesangbuch* (Berlin:
Wehrverlag Joseph Becker, 1939), p. 12.

themes of death and resurrection, a narrative was always in place that encouraged them to expect ever higher casualties among their men.[172]

In 1945, for Germany's honour to remain intact every member of the *Volk* had to be prepared to sacrifice himself on the altar of Germany, and contrary to the First World War, the fight on home soil meant that, this time around, that opportunity would be open to all. A March 1945 front-page editorial of the *Berliner Morgenpost*, titled 'Our spirit tested to its limit', stressed that 'the German people will be ready and must be ready to follow in this struggle for life and death', actively encouraging the idea that the last reserves of men were not the fighting troops, but rather untrained recruits, men from supply units or rearguards, and, eventually, civilians.[173] Some soldiers even seemed to have agreed tentatively with this sentiment. On the eve of the East Prussian offensive, the Gefreiter Gerhard Becker wrote home that 'If we were to lose the war, which I hope we will not, then I wish that we were all dead. But victory might be closer than we believe.'[174] If the German people were to lose, then at least it would be on their own soil, and only after having drawn on all available resources. Germany would be the stage on which the final act – the *Götterdämmerung* – would take place. Although Nazi Germany would be lost, its defiance to the very end would keep German glory intact for future generations.

Eventually, on Heroes Remembrance Day, 11 March 1945, Hitler would proclaim that 'it must be our general irreversible will, not to give prosperity a bad example like those who came before us did'.[175] This maxim was also adhered to in East Prussia. On 8 May, in the final order to the troops of Armee Ostpreußen, General Dietrich von Saucken, its last commander, already cautiously dared to 'look ahead': 'There will come a time that out of your struggle the life of our people will blossom anew.'[176] The vast majority of military orders were not this brazen, both because orders were meant to be clear rather than eloquent, and because writing cost time – a scarce commodity during battle. Finally, and most obviously, commanders knew that tying 'death' to the mission that lay ahead hardly inspired confidence among those who were to carry it out. Thus, although mostly absent in written orders, death was increasingly present in the minds of commanders; although it was never a goal in itself, preventing casualties among their men no longer drove their motivations.

---

[172] Stahel, 'The Wehrmacht and National Socialist Military Thinking', pp. 359–61.

[173] 'Geist höchster Bewährung', *Berliner Morgenpost*, 2 March 1945.

[174] Gerhard Becker, *Ich wünschte, auf einen Schlag wären alle Räder viereckig: Briefe und Postkarten 1939/1940 und 1944–1945* (Aachen: Helios, 2008), p. 211.

[175] Bessel, *Germany 1945*, p. 17.

[176] Verschiedene Materialien (Funksprüche, Fernschreiben, Befehle, Anordnungen) über die Kapitulation der Armee 'Ostpreußen' für die Zeit vom 7. bis 11. Mai 1945. http://wwii.germandocsinrussia.org/de/nodes/2390#page/1/mode/grid/zoom/1

For those soldiers searching for a rationale to keep fighting, the answer was obvious, especially to those who had been part of the army prior to the summer of 1944. What had not changed as German forces moved into East Prussia was the enemy they were facing. The sustained propaganda that painted the Red Amy soldier as a bestial Untermensch assumed a greater sense of urgency on German soil.[177] Between 1941 and 1944 the dehumanisation was so sustained that by 1945 'the Russian' was merely part of a 'flood', a 'mob', or a 'horde'. The shame of having to retreat from this 'vermin' grew with every successful Soviet push westward.[178] During the initial advance, the focus on the primitive nature of what Hitler called 'swamp humans' tempered the fear among the troops, and thus worked to their advantage. But since after three years the 'red beast' was still not slain, and indeed merely awakened and aggravated, the Red Army soldier assumed a terrifying – almost zombie-like – form.[179] The lack of a sustained dehumanising of the western Allies helps to explain why to the very last moment German troops fought so fundamentally differently on the Eastern Front than on the Western Front. In early April 1945 Stalin lamented that:

They continue to fight savagely with the Russians for some unknown junction . . . in Czechoslovakia which they need as much as a dead man needs poultices but surrender without any resistance such important towns in Central Germany as Osnabrück, Mannheim [and] Kassel.[180]

This is not to say that every soldier who fought his way back into Germany was radicalised, but the troops' steadfastness continued to rest on the premise that they were defending German interests. If anything, the defence of their Heimat confirmed the necessity of earlier genocidal practices and allowed a soldier to view himself as 'decent', even after having participated in mass murder.[181]

Many of the practices connected to the war of annihilation, moreover, continued in East Prussia. For example, although Hitler had ordered that on German territory units' reliance on Soviet *Hiwis* was to decrease, their presence in the army remained unmistakable until the very end. Filling the gaps caused by the massive losses inflicted by the Red Army, by late 1944 the Wehrmacht consisted of over 600,000 of these auxiliaries. By early 1945 even the elite 5th Panzer-Division counted 826 Hiwis among

---

[177] See Chapter 4.   [178] Bartov, *Hitler's Army*, p. 60; Shepherd, *Hitler's Soldiers*, p. 378.
[179] Kater, *Hitler Youth*, p. 174. Eric Kurlander, *Hitler's Monsters: a Supernatural History of the Third Reich* (New Haven, CT: Yale University Press, 2017), pp. xvii–iii, 52.
[180] Office of the Historian, The Chairman of the Council of People's Commissar of the Soviet Union (Stalin) to President Roosevelt, accessed 5 February 2018, https://history.state.gov/historicaldocuments/frus1945v03/d538
[181] Wette, *Die Wehrmacht*, p. 179.

its ranks, which equalled over 5 per cent of its total personnel.[182] Their presence kept the divide between *Übermensch* and *Untermensch* highly visible and served as a reminder of the continuity between the fighting in the Soviet Union and on home soil. Practices connected to genocide continued in East Prussia as well. A report to the Fourth Army's General Hossbach dated 28 December 1944 went into detail about a razzia of Poles that took place in the sector of the 541st Volksgrenadier-Division which was stationed in the south-east of the province:

All males between the ages of 16 and 60, and all females aged 16 to 30, are apprehended. The action started promptly at 6 a.m. The combing (*Durchkämmung*) is conducted by the Wehrmacht. All Poles – also those with valid work papers – are to be brought to detention camp Grajewo or to the collection camp Bogusse near Grajewo.[183]

Moreover, as soon as the Wehrmacht moved onto East Prussia, units started requesting Jews from Stutthof concentration camp. In East Prussia, the rear of Army Group Centre, Jews were forced to help in the construction of four airfields under harsh autumn and winter conditions. Army Group Centre's neighbour, Army Group North, requested and received a few hundred Jews in Libau, while along the Weichsel river Jewish inmates from Stutthof were forced to dig defensive positions.[184] German troops, some clearly inured by the previous years on the Eastern Front, oversaw their deployment, which meant that for the first time East Prussian civilians were able to see the interaction between these two groups.[185] Meanwhile, the racially motivated Vernichtungskrieg persisted in East Prussia and it is therefore hardly surprising that until the very end troops continued to execute forced Polish labourers in high numbers, while a similar fate awaited captured Red Army soldiers.[186] Troops knew (and were taught to think) that the war of annihilation was

---

[182] Nigel Thomas, *Hitler's Russian & Cossack Allies 1941–45* (Oxford: Osprey, 2015), p. 5; Rahm and Gerhard Schreiber (eds.), *Kriegstagebuch der Seekriegsleitung, Band 60/I*, p. 257; BArch RH 10/144, p. 57: Gliederung, Zustand (materielle und personelle Lage) und dgl. der Panzerdivisionen. – 5. Pz. Div. Stand 1.1.1945.

[183] Barch R 58/976, p. 95: Sicherheitspolizei und SD Sonderkommando 7b, O.U., den 28. Dezember 1944. An dem Oberbefehlshaber der 4. Armee, Herrn General der Infanterie Hossbach.

[184] Archiwum Museum Stutthof (hereafter AMS) Sygn. I-IB-3, pp. 161–2: Sonderbefehl über die Aufstellung des Baukommandos 'Weichsel'. Stutthof, den 24. August 1944; AMS Sygn. I-IB-3, pp. 199–201: Sonderbefehl über die Einrichtung der Außenlager Gerdauen, Schippenbeil, Jesau, Heiligenbeil und Seerappen, Stutthof, den 21. September 1944; Danuta Drywa, *The Extermination of Jews in Stutthof Concentration Camp* (Gdańsk: Stutthof Museum in Sztutowo, 2004), pp. 173–5, 211–12.

[185] Yad Vashem Archives O.33/8569: Memoirs of Sheva (Levi) Kopolovitz.

[186] BArch NS 19/2068, p. 37: An Reichsführer-SS Feldkommandostelle betrifft: Meldungen aus dem Ostraum, Königsberg 28.2.45.

reciprocal, a motivation to keep the scale of repression and exploitation of their mortal enemies at a constant high.[187]

It escaped few soldiers that they were now back on German territory but this knowledge hardly prompted troops to re-evaluate their daily routines. Since the immediate social environment of the Landser did not significantly change, there were few reasons – and even fewer opportunities – to alter their frame of reference.[188] Only at the highest echelons did the arrival in East Prussia prompt a change in daily practices, as Corps-, Army, and Army Group staffs were now ordered to discuss matters with other local actors.[189] Although there were some units in which morale increased after their arrival in East Prussia, the vast majority of troops simply kept fighting because ingrained military behaviours, rituals, and Kameradschaft were considered to increase their chance of survival. By and large, they fought as before and died as before, but now – thanks to the German High Command's fatalistically determined attitude – at an unprecedented rate. The heavy fighting in the province meant that troops had little opportunity to reflect on how the previous years had reshaped their outlook on life. For most soldiers, East Prussia was – above all – the last in a series of battlefields.

Conclusion

When, in the summer of 1944, after three years of fighting on the Eastern Front, the Wehrmacht moved back onto German soil, its men no longer represented the values of the army that had been victorious over France, the Low Countries, Denmark, and Norway. During their stay in the Soviet Union, they had been forced to adapt to the demands of a war that was fought in a completely new fashion, the Weltanschauungskrieg. Both the demands of their immediate superiors and the demands of their High Command were fundamentally different than before. German soldiers grew accustomed to behavioural choices unimagined and unforeseen at the outset of the war, as they systematically committed unspeakable crimes and witnessed innumerably more. Many carried out their orders willingly, but often these ordinary men struggled to navigate the morality of their actions. The vast majority nevertheless adapted remarkably quickly. 'One has to be ruthless and unmerciful', the tank gunner Karl Fuchs wrote to his wife days after the invasion of the Soviet Union: 'Don't you have the impression that it's not me but a different person who is speaking to you?'[190] The ease with which Landser detached

---

[187] Echternkamp, *Soldaten im Nachkrieg*, pp. 57, 71.
[188] van Crefeld, *The Culture of War*, p. 109. Neitzel and Welzer, *Soldaten*, pp. 208–9, 317–19.
[189] See Chapter 4.   [190] Heer, 'How Amorality Became Normality', p. 332.

themselves from the consequences of their actions was greatly facilitated by National Socialist propaganda, which permeated both their orders and the flow of information that came their way. They were consistently presented with the idea that no matter how brutal their behaviour appeared to be, it was based on a military rationale. Since the average Landser had no opportunity whatsoever to ascertain the larger picture – the magnitude of the criminality of the organisation of which he was part – this explanation was sufficient for most.

The German conduct of war nevertheless had a profound impact on the men, reshaping how the average Landser viewed his immediate environment and the roles which different actors played within it. The partisan threat blurred the line between combatant and non-combatant. In the Soviet Union it was near impossible to determine who exactly opposed German forces, and collective reprisals in the wake of partisan attacks disproportionately affected innocent villagers. Already by the end of 1941, many of the soldiers of Army Group North who were laying siege to Leningrad had convinced themselves of the military importance of shelling defenceless civilians. During retreat the mindset of the average Landser continued to harden. Both the hunger plan and the scorched-earth tactics during retreat caused the deaths of millions, and eventually even the large-scale evacuation drives, during which parents were often deliberately separated from their children, were deemed as militarily necessary. And even when soldiers reflected on the effects of their behaviour there was little opportunity to break with the system of which they were part. This inability and lack of willingness ensured that, on an individual level, a Landser's core values continued to harden. They increasingly lost the faculty to consider everyday events through a non-military prism, and commanders soon came to realise that this diminishing appreciation for humanity, the 'lowered resting heart rate of the Wehrmacht soldier', would be hard to correct.

The ever stronger dismissal of 'home' notions was epitomised in the tragedy of the defeat on the Eastern Front and became a pressing issue as the Wehrmacht retreated into Germany. The war had not only increased the physical distance between Wehrmacht soldiers and German civilians, but also the mental distance. The contrast between Soviets' large-scale use of civilians on the one hand, and the German civilians' perceived lack of support on the other hand, added to the men's doubts about the home front's appreciation for their sacrifices. With the perversion of soldiers' sense of proportionality, it is hardly surprising that an increasing number of men actively started to consider the use of civilians in the defence of their country. By and large, soldiers had been taught to consider radical measures as proportionate, and it was with this mindset that troops fell back on German soil. Both the sense that during times of crises the entire nation should stand shoulder to shoulder, as well as the need to prevent another 'stab in the back', pushed German civilians into the orbit of the military.

Although the German soldier felt differently about his compatriots than about Soviet 'subhumans', this did not mean that the retreat onto East Prussian territory markedly reshaped soldiers' collective character. Military structures did not fundamentally change, and did not have to. Both the nature of the enemy and the rationale to continue fighting remained unchanged, and troops therefore had little reason to alter their behavioural patterns. Moreover, the morale of the troops in East Prussia did not improve upon their arrival on home soil; they rather remained as dejected as before. Therefore, it seems unlikely that the army acted as a moderate counterweight to the Party, a *Radikalisierungshinderniss*, or 'obstacle to radicalisation', during the final months of the war. Although the idea that they were protecting their Heimat did influence the behaviour of some soldiers, of far greater immediate importance to the relationship between the troops and their immediate environment was a series of situational factors, such as their deployment, the quality of troops and weapons, and the preparedness of their commander to fight to the end. These factors, as we will see in the coming chapters, varied depending on time and location, and these disparities would shape the final months of the war.

3   The City As a Fortress Community

Introduction

For the German people, the Second World War became only 'total' in earnest during their country's final defence. Although Wehrmacht soldiers and German civilians had fundamentally different ideas about the fighting on German soil, both would play an active role in it. By 1945, the war's 'total battlegrounds' had moved from the fields and villages of Ukraine and Belorussia to the streets of Germany. The fighting on German soil assumed a completely different character than before, but not, as we saw in the last chapters, merely because the war's racial component fell away or because the defence of the Fatherland provoked fervent nationalism. Contrary to the earlier fighting abroad, the battles fought on home territory were primarily fought in urban environments. The decision to organise the defence on home soil in populous areas – thereby accepting a high death toll among their own civilians – reveals the desensitisation of both the German military and the Nazi regime by the final stage of the war.

Images of destroyed cities are so common that we hardly consider this decision noteworthy. In a Total War, civilian populations increasingly became acceptable targets and with that, the ordinary civilian became a significant chronicler of the wartime experience, be it with pen or camera.[1] By the beginning of the war about half of the European population lived in urbanised areas, and since they would therefore understand events within this context, the seemingly straightforward outcome – war is close to me, therefore war takes place in cities – came to predominate, leaving a distorted view of how the war was fought. Faced with immense personal hardships, it is not at all surprising that these civilians were unconcerned with the larger picture and would hardly consider the

---

[1] Dagmar Barnouw, *Germany 1945: Views of War and Violence* (Bloomington: Indiana University Press, 1996), pp. ix–xviii.

military context in which their plight should be understood. That an attack or bombardment was 'just' or 'unjust' revealed little of the underlying strategy the enemy used to subdue them.[2] As such, Total War not only changed strategy but also the way the impact of strategy is passed down through the generations.

This chapter establishes how cities came to play such an important role in the defence of Germany, and what the wider implications were of the decision to defend them. In his recollection of Königsberg's siege, Karl-Friedrich Boree asked the reader rhetorically, 'What is a city?' A city, he felt, is 'an array of fine habits and stylish traditions'. The city's demise would not only permanently change its buildings but also its figurative structures, the habits of its community. 'Everything eventually ends, but those who experience that end first hand, they lose a part of themselves.'[3] If Königsberg is to serve as a case study, it is important to establish which habits and traditions were unique to the city and which of the notions predominating during its siege can be more broadly considered. Separating local customs from behavioural patterns prompted by Total War will help us position Königsberg's community more accurately within the late-war context.

Cities at Total War

In the previous chapters, we have discussed some of the conditions that need to be met to distinguish 'limited' war from 'Total' War, but civilians often simply interpreted Total War as a war that directly impacted their immediate environment. No comprehensive effort has been made to factor 'environment' into the debate, and although the battles in Germany were fought in an urbanised environment, in densely populated cities, the 'metropolitan dimension of Total War' has largely been disregarded.[4] Within the framework of Total War, the city is above all seen as a source of industrial labour, but this is only one of its elements.[5] Cities housed Party headquarters, presses, recruitment offices, factories, governmental offices, and, eventually the fighting itself also took place in cities. This section establishes the state of thinking about cities among the

---

[2] Richard Overy, *Why the Allies Won* (London: Pimlico, 2006), pp. 125–6, 157–63; A. C. Grayling, *Among the Dead Cities: Was the Allied Bombing of Civilians in WWII a Necessity or a Crime?* (London: Bloomsbury, 2006), pp. 209–16.

[3] Karl-Friedrich Boree, *Ein Abschied* (Wiesbaden: Verlag der Greif, 1951), p. 132.

[4] Stefan Goebel and Derek Keene, 'Towards a Metropolitan History of Total War: An Introduction', in Goebel and Keene (eds.), *Cities into Battlefields*, p. 1.

[5] See for example: Rüdiger Hartmann, 'The War of the Cities: Industrial Labouring Forces', in Geyer and Tooze (eds.), *The Cambridge History of the Second World War, Volume III*, pp. 298–328.

different German actors by the time they organised their defence, which will help to explain the decisions that were made in Königsberg and the friction that existed between the Party and the Wehrmacht. As the vast majority of the troops who fought in Königsberg had fought on the Eastern Front (as had most German troops), and many of the Party members had been stationed in the occupation of Ukraine, this section will start on the Eastern Front before it discusses the cities in Germany.

When German troops entered the Soviet Union in 1941, it was clear to all that they would not only have to fight the Red Army but also the country's challenging environment. It shaped the Wehrmacht's 'mind-scape', the 'mental landscape conjured up by looking out over an area'.[6] Until the winter of 1941, vast open plains equalled victory: it was on the plains of the Soviet Union, and earlier in France, that the Wehrmacht had conducted its most successful operations. In this mindscape, the city played a subordinate role and hardly weighed in the notions of man-oeuvre. Moreover, both within *völkisch* and traditional Prussian military thinking, cities were viewed with considerable scepticism: they were considered to inspire proletarian restlessness while the proximity of different population groups made the city a *Rassengrab* – a place where racial purity would come to die. The military had long complained that city youth made a poorer stock of soldiers than their rural counterparts.[7] In Germany, cities had been hotbeds for communism until the Nazis 'stepped in', which meant that many officers tended to see the ferocious defence of cities such as Kiev, Smolensk, Mogilev, and Dnipropetrovsk as a confirmation of communism's perverted willingness to sacrifice its own habitat and civilians, rather than as the result of correct tactical consider-ations on the enemy's behalf.[8] The capture of large cities cost high casualty numbers, slowed down the speed of a German offensive or even brought it to a halt, and – especially after Stalingrad – cities became synonymous with military defeat.[9] None of Germany's great victories were achieved in cities and the fear of city fighting was heightened by Soviet operational choices. General Friedrich von Mellenthin, one of the first German commanders who sought to provide an insight in to the fighting on the Eastern Front, recalled that 'as every Russian attack was aimed at large towns (possibly with a view of attracting Stalin's notice in

---

[6] Liulevicius, *War Land on the Eastern Front*, p. 151.
[7] George Mosse, *The Crisis of German Ideology: Intellectual Origins of the Third Reich* (New York: Grosset & Dunlap, 1964), pp. 19–23, 145.
[8] Adrian Wettstein, 'Urban Warfare Doctrine on the Eastern Front', in Kay, Rutherford, and Stahel (eds.), *Nazi Policy on the Eastern Front*, pp. 52–9.
[9] Adrian Wettstein, *Die Wehrmacht im Stadtkampf 1939–1942* (Paderborn: Ferdinand Schöningh, 2014), pp. 415–21.

a Special Order of the Day) these places were avoided like the plague'.[10] These sentiments help explain why during the Second World War – as during the other conflicts of the twentieth century – there are 'remarkably few examples of the deliberate choice of an urban battlefield'.[11]

Once in German hands, the role that the Wehrmacht gave to the Soviet Union's cities was a traditional one, that of a centre for the control of the surrounding areas and their resources. Such areas, those closest to the front line, remained permanently under army jurisdiction, 'partly because of the shifting of the front line, partly because of the continued unrest in the area, and partly because ... the military resisted all efforts to transfer additional areas to civil government'.[12] The military maintained that the main purpose was strictly utilitarian, above all 'the maintenance and protection of the logistics and communication networks that served the front lines'.[13] Since the war in the East never settled, massive swaths of the Soviet Union remained under the jurisdiction of the German army rather than being passed over to German civil administration. As we saw in Chapter 2, this meant that it was the Wehrmacht more than any other official German body that was responsible for the destruction of the populations in cities in its area of operations, be it as a result of starvation policies, forced resettlement, the execution of presumed 'partisans', or retaliation measures.[14]

The cities further to the rear were governed by German civil authorities rather than by the Wehrmacht; in these cities, the Nazi occupation policy manifested itself even more clearly. Warsaw, for example, 'was stripped of her role of capital', and 'was to have no political, social, or economic significance for the Poles'.[15] Famously, once captured, Leningrad and Moscow were to be completely erased from the map.[16] Yet the large administrative framework that was in place in such cities to enable the occupation makes it easier to trace back the Wehrmacht's sociopolitical impact on them. German-occupied cities in the Soviet Union had a distinct military character, consisting of a large permanent contingent of Wehrmacht troops working in armaments, in signals, in repair and

---

[10] Friedrich von Mellenthin, *Panzer Battles 1939–1945, A Study of the Employment of Armour in the Second World War* (London: Cassell, 1955), p. 269.

[11] Gregory Ashworth, *War and the City* (London: Routledge, 1991), p. 115.

[12] Alexander Dallin, *German Rule in Russia 1941–1945: a Study of Occupation Policies* (London: Macmillan, 1981), p. 95.

[13] Mulligan, *The Politics of Illusion and Empire*, pp. 123–4.

[14] Rutherford, *Combat and Genocide on the Eastern Front*, p. 374.

[15] Joanna Hanson, *The Civilian Population and the Warsaw Uprising of 1944* (Cambridge: Cambridge University Press, 1982), p. 14.

[16] Franz Halder, *War Journal of Franz Halder* (Fort Leavensworth, KS: Archives Section, 1950), p. 212.

construction units, in military hospitals, at training courses, for the air force, or for the military police.[17] Members of the armed forces used these cities as rallying points, as part of the stopovers to the front. This assured that there was always a large military presence which in turn meant that the army believed it also had a say in their daily governance, and thus sought to exact influence on local (German occupation) authorities. Whether in Warsaw or Minsk, Wehrmacht commanders, because of their large role in assuring order and safety in these cities, did not see local German authorities as equal partners, while also the troops themselves, especially given their large numbers, 'often felt themselves the real masters of the city'. It meant that, on a day-to-day basis, 'despite numerous officially proclaimed appeals from both sides, a smooth, virtually seamless cooperation did not exist at all'.[18]

The notion that potential riots and uprisings slumbered under the surface and that the army would have to be called in to suppress them, diverting units from their core tasks, further increased the Wehrmacht's (perceived) standing. For Army Group Centre and Army Group A, which would eventually defend Eastern Germany in 1945, this was confirmed during the Warsaw uprising in the summer of 1944. As the uprising took place in their rear, thus also threatening their supply lines, and local German authorities could not quell it, they had to bring up their own troops during a period when the Soviet summer offensive, Operation Bagration, was at its height.[19] These factors further contributed to the perception of cities as a particular menace to the army.

But even though cities were perceived negatively, once the Wehrmacht returned to Germany it had to re-evaluate their military value. Germany was considerably more urbanised than the Soviet Union, which would inevitably shape the organisation of the defence. Orders regarding the Ostwall defences in East Prussia show that cities such as Königsberg and Lötzen were considered of vital importance within the overall defence scheme, but at the same time these orders reveal no deliberate effort to abandon the defence of field positions in favour of the defence of cities.[20] Although, as we will see below, propagandists placed German cities at the centre of Germany's defensive efforts, they were not considered as a self-contained system.

---

[17] Lehnstaedt, *Okkupation im Osten*, p. 36.   [18] Ibid., p. 39.
[19] John Erickson, *The Road to Berlin: Stalin's War with Germany, Volume Two* (London: Cassell, 2008), pp. 272–8.
[20] See particularly: BArch RH 2/332, pp. 57–9: Generalstab des Heeres Abt. Landesbefestigung Nr. 2145/45 geh. 6. Februar 45. Gedanken zum Stellungsbau auf Grund der Winterschlacht.

Defensive lines continued to be made across fields and built-up areas were incorporated into that defence as 'knots' in those lines.

Yet, especially in this latter phase of the war, defending cities rather than plains had some added value: Germany possessed a massive stockpile of captured guns, which were of less use in field operations, but which could be utilised from fixed positions. A rigid defence, moreover, meant less reliance on mobile warfare, which in a time of critical fuel shortage was a particularly welcome added bonus.[21] Also the Allies would not be able to fully exploit their preponderance in tanks in cities, as streets hampered their mobility. Moreover, if German commanders had learned anything from the attacks on cities like Stalingrad, it was that their destruction through aerial bombardment was certainly not guaranteed to favour the attackers and could just as well solidify a position's defence. This learning curve was seen during the German defence of the Abbey and village of Monte Cassino, which had been completely flattened by Allied bombers. German troops held out against far superior Allied forces and their tenacious defence soon became one of the favourite themes in German propaganda.[22] That 'Hitler built walls around his Fortress Europe, but he forgot to put a roof on it', as the American President Franklin D. Roosevelt told a reporter in the summer of 1943, did not have to be spelled out to Wehrmacht commanders, since by early 1944, when the fortress strategy was implemented, this had long been a given.[23] In the West, Aachen, which was to be turned into a 'German Stalingrad', and in particular 'Festung Metz', became the embodiments of this mindset. In Eastern Germany, the Lower Silesian capital Breslau was used in a similar fashion before it fell.[24]

That the defence was increasingly centred on urban areas was picked up by Germany's adversaries as well. A December 1944 article in the Red Army newspaper *Krasnaya Zvezda* instructed the troops who entered East Prussia that 'generally there are five or six hamlets per square mile. The big "townships" are no more than five or six miles apart. The enemy can

---

[21] Wettstein, *Wehrmacht im Stadtkampf*, p. 401.   [22] Ibid., pp. 392–7.

[23] Joseph Persico, *Roosevelt's Centurions: FDR and the Commanders He Led to Victory in World War II* (New York: Random House, 2013), p. 304.

[24] Peter Lieb, *Konventioneller Krieg oder NS- Weltanschauungskrieg? Kriegsführung und Partisanenbekämpfung in Frankreich 1943/44* (Munich: R.Oldenbourg Verlag, 2007), pp. 499–500. On Aachen, see: Edgar Christoffel, *Krieg am Westwall 1944/45, Das Grenzland im Westen zwischen Aachen und Saarbrücken in den letzten Kriegsmonaten* (Trier: Verlag der Akademischen Buchhandlung Interbook, 1989), pp. 122–53. On Metz, see: Ibid., pp. 222–31. The commander of the Metz garrison was captured by American forces and his conversations concerning the city's defence were tapped. See: Römer, *Kameraden*, pp. 284–99.

therefore arrange mutual fire support'.[25] Also the official American 'Handbook on German Military Forces' highlighted that 'the Germans regard towns and villages as excellent strongpoints, particularly if the buildings are of masonry. Towns are also regarded as excellent antitank positions because of the considerable infantry–artillery effort necessary to neutralize them'. But it noted that 'this passive type of defence is only an expedient due to German shortages of mobile equipment and manpower'.[26] This was an accurate observation, which fully appreciated the increased use of the city within the Total War Germany was waging.

The decision to defend its cities might have been foisted on Germany, but it nevertheless represented a final step towards 'Total War'. That the choice was made for a large part due to a lack of military alternatives was obscured by bullish language which sought to present the cities' defence as a deliberate choice. 'Nothing can be defended so outstandingly as a major city or a field of rubble. Here we must defend ... the country', Himmler told a gathering of Party members, Wehrmacht officers, and industrialists in early November 1944.[27] Given that virtually every German city by that time had been transformed into a field of rubble, such rhetoric was the only way to reformalise Germany's options. But this language is insufficient to explain the radical actions of the troops, and therefore the next section will distinguish between the city as a propagandist symbol and the city within German late-war military strategy.

Cities As 'Fortresses': Conjecture and Strategy

The above assessment offers a starting point for analysing the Wehrmacht's appreciation of cities during the final fighting in Germany itself, showing the army's ambivalent stance towards cities. This section will discuss the changes in this perception as troops moved back into Germany and examines what lay at the base of these changes. Central to this is the implementation of the fortress strategy which would come to shape the way German cities were defended.[28] As such, it continues our examination of the 'metropolitan dimension of Total War'.

[25] A. Vasilyev, 'Nemeckaja oborona v Vostochnoj Prussii', *Krasnaya Zvezda*, December 9, 1944, p. 2. This translation is taken from: A. Vasilyev, 'Siege Parties v. Blockhouses: Drawing Teeth of E. Prussian Defences', *Soviet War News*, 14 December 1944, p. 2.
[26] United States Army Center for Military History, *Handbook on German Military Forces* (Washington, DC: US War Department, 1945).
[27] Stargardt, *The German War*, p. 459.
[28] The German fortress strategy was first implemented abroad, in France and the Soviet Union. See: Sönke Neitzel, 'Der Kampf um die deutsche Atlantik- und Kanalfestungen und sein Einfluß auf den alliierten Nachschub während der Befreiung Frankreichs 1944/

Within German military history, the city had played a limited role. Even as a defensive concept, the city was largely absent from military thought.[29] The closest framework that existed for the defence of a city was the Clausewitzian notion of defending a Festung, or 'fortress', which dated from the 1830s:

Imagine a country where not only the large and prosperous towns, but every sizeable one is fortified and defended by its citizens and the farmers of the surrounding areas. The speed of military operations would be so reduced, and so much weight thrown into the scale by defending inhabitants, that the skill and determination of the enemy would dwindle almost to insignificance.[30]

In Clausewitz's theorisation of a fortress, a city's civilian population was treated as an integral part of its defence, as a resource, and as such it fitted particularly well within the notion of Total War a hundred years later.[31]

As the front line pushed towards the German borders in 1944, Clausewitz's ideas about fortresses were elevated to a fully-fledged strategy, which was introduced on 8 March 1944. The lack of innovation was not at all denied, but rather played up, as the first paragraph of Hitler's War Directive 53, which established the strategy, shows:

The fortified area will fulfil the same function of fortresses in former historical times. They will ensure that the enemy does not occupy these areas of decisive operational importance. They will allow themselves to be surrounded, thereby holding down the largest possible number of enemy forces and establishing conditions favourable for successful counter-attacks.[32]

As an avid amateur historian, Hitler would have been able to name several sieges in comparatively recent history, which due to a persistent defence, managed to turn the tide of a war, such as the siege of Sevastopol during the Crimean War, the siege of Port Arthur during the Russo-Japanese War, and the defence of Adrianople. The dogged resistance at Metz and

---

45', *Militärgeschichtliche Mitteilungen* (55) 1996, pp. 381–430; Willems, 'Defiant Breakwaters or Desperate Blunders?', pp. 353–6; Frieser 'Irrtümer und Illusionen', pp. 518–25; Gert Fricke, *'Fester Platz' Tarnopol 1944* (Freiburg: Verlag Rombach, 1986).

[29] Wettstein, *Die Wehrmacht im Stadtkampf,* pp. 54–5, 63.

[30] Carl von Clausewitz, *On War* (Princeton, NJ: Princeton University Press, 1976), p. 395.

[31] Already during the Reichswehr era, some limited attention was paid to the role of cities (and their populations) within Germany's defence. See: Strohn, *The German Army and the Defence of the Reich*, pp. 142–7.

[32] Hugh Trevor-Roper, *Hitler's War Directives 1939–1945* (London: Sidgwick and Jackson, 1964), pp. 159–63; Walter Hubatsch, *Hitlers Weisungen für die Kriegsführung 1939–1945: Dokumente des Oberkommandos der Wehrmacht* (Utting: Dörfler im Nebel-Verlag, 2000), pp. 243–50.

Paris had significantly prolonged the Franco–Prussian war and was acutely remembered by the German General Staff.[33]

The implementation of the fortress strategy poses a number of historiographical problems, especially regarding the meaning and appreciation of the word 'fortress'. The word 'fortress' today conjures up images of a medieval walled city but this is neither what Clausewitz had in mind nor what the German High Command thought it should be. Although in 1944 a fortress still had a city as its core, the general idea of it was based on the 'Prussian system' of the late nineteenth century, that of a string of forts three to six miles outside of a city that could cover each other by artillery. In Königsberg, a series of twelve forts had been completed in 1882 which had been incorporated into the province's defensive system in late 1944.[34] Relying on 'fortresses' as part of a strategy once in Germany also simply came down to a lack of alternatives: between 1830 and 1940 Germany had become highly urbanised and conducting operations while ignoring the cities was simply impossible. And so, in September 1944 Hitler propagandistically declared all German cities to be fortresses: 'Every bunker, every block of houses in a German city, and every German village has to become a fortress where the enemy either bleeds to death, or which buries those who occupy it in man-to-man battle.'[35] Yet, without a set of orders attached to the proclamation, this remained mere rhetoric.[36] The declaration, moreover, clearly echoed the 1941 infantry training regulations which stipulated that 'every man must hold a position to the last drop of blood', a conviction that the regulations repeated multiple times.[37] As such, Hitler's 'demand' for the defence of German cities, so often considered a signpost of the hardening of the final phase of the war, hardly diverged from pre-existing military practices.

Moreover, within the *Lingua Tertii Imperii* – the language of the Third Reich – the word Festung encompassed much more than merely its literal meaning. A fortress was closely connected to the safeguarding of a set of

---

[33] Hew Strachan, 'From Cabinet War to Total War: the Perspective of Military Doctrine, 1861–1918', in Chickering and Förster (eds), *Great War, Total War*, p. 19.

[34] Ashworth, *War and the City*, pp. 46–7; Lasch, *So fiel Königsberg*, pp. 13–15.

[35] BArch NS 6/ 348, p. 25: Anlage zum Rundschreiben 255/44 vom 21.9.1944.

[36] Numerous commanders nevertheless declared cities to be fortresses as the front neared, using this proclamation as a guiding principle. Often this decision did not prompt any change in warfare in the city it concerned, in which case it had nothing to do with adhering to a strategy. Rather, these men felt that their Führer expected this of them. A 'fortress' in this sense was therefore merely a propagandistic tool, and from a historiographical standpoint helped blur the line between 'strategy' and *Durchhalte*-fanaticism.

[37] Der OBH d.H./ Gen.S.d.H./ Gen.d.Inf. v. Brauchitsch, *H.Dv. 130/2a Ausbildungsvorschrift für die Infanterie (A.V.I.) Heft 2a: Die Schützenkompanie* (Berlin: Verlag Offene Worte, 1941), pp. 127, 131, 184.

values and beliefs. These in turn would bolster the defence of that fortress, especially in times of setbacks. As early as January 1932, in a major policy speech held at the Industrieklub in Düsseldorf, Hitler elaborated on this interplay:

In purely materiel terms a crisis would be felt a thousand times stronger when a people are not presented with any ideals. ... Take a fortress and bring down severe deprivation on it: as long as those in it see deliverance, believe in it, hope it will happen, they can endure the diminished rations. Take the last hope of a possible deliverance, of a better future, out of their hearts and you will see how these people suddenly view the diminished rations as the most important of their lives.[38]

A fortress was thus often used as a spiritual entity, or as a powerful metaphor, rather than as a physical location. Metaphysically, a fortress grew to be a set of values and beliefs *in itself*. Thus, even a single soldier could be a considered a 'fortress': the phrase 'every man a fortress' was said to have been coined by German troops encircled in Stalingrad, and found its way into National Socialist newspapers.[39] In his memoirs, Grossdeutschland veteran Guy Sajer likened his attitude to a fortress but attached negative connotations to it, writing about the battles of 1944 that 'although we were already beaten ten times over, our terror became a fortress of despair, which the Russians found difficult to breach'.[40]

The link between a fortress and National Socialist ideas was further strengthened by the presence of hundreds of castles that were dotted around Germany. These were readily used to romanticise warfare, connecting contemporary Germans to their ancient forefathers by underscoring the *Volk*'s martial traditions.[41] 'When people are silent, the stones speak. By means of stone, great epochs speak to the present,' Heinrich Himmler wrote in *Die Schwarze Korps* about the German castles in the East:

To all generations of the old Ordenland East Prussia – this germ cell of the German-Prussian state – throughout seven centuries, the castles of Allenstein, Heilsberg, Marienwerder and Neidenburg served as much as witnesses to hard fought-over conquest and dogged defence, as they were symbols of high German culture.[42]

---

[38] Max Domarus, *Hitler: Reden und Proklamationen, 1932–1945. I. Band: Triumph (1932–1938)* (Neustadt a.d. Aisch: Verlagsdruckerei Schmidt, 1962), p. 89.

[39] Michael Balfour, *Propaganda in War 1939–1945* (London: Routledge & Kegan Paul, 1979), p. 307.

[40] Sajer, *The Forgotten Soldier*, p. 382.

[41] Fabian Link, *Burgen und Burgenforschung im Nationalsozialismus: Wissenschaft und Weltanschauung 1933–1945* (Cologne: Böhlau Verlag, 2014), pp. 50–60.

[42] Heinrich Himmler, 'Deutsche Burgen im Osten', *Das Schwarze Korps*, 23 January 1941, p. 4.

Figure 3.1 Soldiers posing at Königsberger Schloss, early in the war.
Source: Author's collection

Meanwhile, late 1941 had seen the establishment of the concept of *Festung Europa*, which rested on two pillars. Not only was it the geographic location of Germany's New Order, but the notion that Festung Europa was embattled, 'threatened on all fronts . . . to be enslaved and dulled', was immediately connected to it.[43] By late-1944 'Festung Europa' no longer existed. The western Allies had landed in Normandy and the Soviets were pushing through Ukraine, Belorussia, the Baltics, and the Balkan. Yet the propagandist concept of Festung was still very much alive. On 1 September 1944, State Secretary Dr Werner Naumann spoke in Danzig to commemorate the fifth anniversary of the city's 'return' to the Greater German Reich. If Germany's enemies 'believe [themselves] to be at the eve of victory', Naumann vowed, 'they are mistaken. . . . Festung Germany will be defended like no fortress before has been defended – this is when our hour will come!'[44]

---

[43] Victor Klemperer, *The Language of the Third Reich: LTI – Lingua Tertii Imperii, A Philologist's Notebook* (London: Continuum, 2000), pp. 152, 212; Balfour, *Propaganda in War*, pp. 239–40. On the propagandistic limitations to the term, see: Wolfram Pyta, *Hitler: Der Künstler als Politiker und Feldherr, Eine Herrschafsanalyse* (Munich: Siedler, 2015), p. 520.

[44] 'Staatsekretär Dr. Naumann in Danzig: Unsere Gegner täuschen sich!', *Völkischer Beobachter, Berliner Ausgabe*, 2 September 1944.

The implementation of the fortress strategy in March 1944 fitted seamlessly into this rhetoric, but merely portraying the strategy as a product of Nazi propaganda would not do it justice. During its early months, however, the strategy did little more than reformalise Hitler's unsophisticated 'fall where you stand' rhetoric, as few of the directive's stipulations could be given substance to. A string of twenty-nine cities in the Soviet Union, stretching from Leningrad to the Black Sea, were designated as fortresses, but the resources allocated to them were insufficient. Although supplies started arriving in these cities after their designation as fortresses, allowing stocks to be built up, few – if any – had enough to hold out for a prolonged siege. The real problem, however, was the troops that were to defend these fortresses. Their garrisons were formed by reallocating the already diminished forces of the Army Groups under whose command they fell. This cannibalisation was much to the dismay of field commanders, who questioned the strategy's feasibility from the moment it was implemented. The materiel and personnel needed to build a fortress, they argued, would better be used to strengthen the front line. Moreover, there was a lack of trained staff officers to properly man a Fortress Staff, while the tight ammunition situation would leave fortresses poorly supplied. Most importantly, they stressed that binding troops to a city without reserves was militarily senseless.[45] 'The Army command considers that the orders designating the larger towns in the combat zone as "fortified places" are particularly dangerous', an entry in the war diary of the Ninth Army, dated 22 June 1944, read. 'The knowledge that one is chained to combat methods … whose correctness in the present circumstances one cannot in all conscience be convinced … makes one contemplate coming events with a sense of foreboding.'[46] They were soon proven correct: none of the fortresses in the Soviet Union held more than a few days after they were attacked during Operation Bagration.[47] Although as 'breakwaters' fortresses were expected to disrupt the path of the expected Soviet attack, most were simply bypassed during the first stage of the operation and the resulting pockets were subsequently eliminated by second tier units. At Army Group Centre, tens of thousands of men were trapped in the encirclements of Vitebsk, Mogilev, and Babruysk. Despite desperate urging from his generals, Hitler remained unwilling to give up these fortified places. Such precedent would abandon the strategy's core principles during

[45] Frieser, 'Irrtümer und Illusionen', pp. 518–21.
[46] Karl-Heinz Frieser, 'Errors and Illusions: the German Command's Miscalculations in the Early Summer of 1944', in Frieser (ed.), *Germany and the Second World War, Volume VIII*, p. 517.
[47] Earl Ziemke, *Stalingrad to Berlin: the German Defeat in the East* (New York: Dorset Press, 1986), pp. 316–28.

its first real test, and as such, the dictator argued, damage Germany's standing abroad – which could undermine its future negotiating position – and diminish its prestige domestically as well. Many a commander suspected ulterior motives: by refusing the abandonment of fortified places Hitler doubled down on his prerogative as commander-in-chief. The self-delusion their Führer displayed was nevertheless seconded by some commanders and executed despite their reservations, and therefore the strategy immediately became a highly divisive issue within German warfare.[48]

Yet, despite the fortress strategy's initial failure, it stayed firmly in place as Germany's main defensive strategy. Hitler's constant efforts to curb, mock, confront, suppress, and reject criticism meant that by 1944 no one at the Wolfsschanze questioned how strategic goals that had been set out at the beginning of the war could be achieved. The only 'given' was that the first step towards victory would be to turn the negative tide of the war, which for the time being simply came down to the fact that victories had to be won, one way or another. At the front line thousands of men died or were injured every day as a result of this lack of strategic vision.

Unsurprisingly, field commanders' complaints mounted with every Durchhalte-order that could not be rationally explained. The task of conveying their protestations to Hitler, by all means an unthankful task, rested on the chief of staff of the OKH, the main military advisor at Hitler's High Command on matters on the Eastern Front. As defeats continued to mount the function often became a platform for dissonant voices and opposing views, much to the Führer's chagrin.[49] Rather than taking commanders' complaints seriously, Hitler decided that they merely reflected a lack of will and determination on their part. Therefore, in the wake of the bomb plot, the dictator appointed Generaloberst Heinz Guderian, a man whom he trusted to combat the weakness of character that he felt festered among the ranks of the OKH.[50] That it was Guderian, schneller Heinz, one of Germany's most ardent advocates of mobile offensive warfare, instead of a commander with working knowledge of defensive operations – surely a prerequisite for the function in this stage of the war – reveals that the appointment was a political one rather than one based on merit.

Indeed, Guderian owed his coveted appointment above all to a set of 'soft skills' most other commanders lacked. He was one of the few German generals who grasped that Hitler was paying the piper and had long decided on the tune, and consequently had done his due diligence. Guderian was an uncompromising careerist and had taken the time to probe Hitler's attitude

[48] Frieser, 'Der Zusammenbruch der Heeresgruppe Mitte', pp. 539–57.
[49] Megargee, Inside Hitler's High Command, pp. 212–13.
[50] Kershaw, The End, pp. 45–6.

Figure 3.2 Generaloberst Heinz Guderian in discussion with Hitler near his East Prussian headquarters, the Wolfsschanze, January 1944. *Source:* bpk, Heinrich Hoffmann. Image-No. 50059195

towards warfare.[51] In 1940, his Panzer divisions had spearheaded the campaign against France and had been pivotal in its defeat, and Guderian knew the ideological and practical value of the memories Hitler held of the campaign. During his later tenure as Generalinspekteur der Panzertruppen, he had learned not to merely argue his point but to mimic Hitler's rhetoric as well: 'This war can never be decided in our favour by defence alone', he stated on 27 March 1944, days after the implementation of the fortress strategy, 'We have to attack again.'[52]

Sentiments like this met with Hitler's approval, and since in his function as Generalinspekteur Guderian was accountable to Hitler alone, he knew he had his Führer's ear. Not afraid to clash head-on with other generals and 'call out' his colleagues when it suited him, by mid-1944 he had positioned himself as one of the few generals with whom Hitler felt comfortable discussing the state of the war. Guderian, who as late as May 1944 had publicly

[51] Frieser, 'Die Rückzugsoperationen der Heeresgruppe Süd in der Ukraine', pp. 360, 449, Guderian, *Panzer Leader*, pp. 430–44; Megargee, *Inside Hitler's High Command*, pp. 196–7, 222.
[52] Bernd Wegner, 'Abkehr von Osten? Die "Festung Europa" und das Dilemma des vernetzten Krieges', in Frieser (ed.), *Das Deutsche Reich und der Zweite Weltkrieg 8*, p. 270; Frieser, 'Der Zusammenbruch der Heeresgruppe Mitte', p. 568.

accused the OKH of being 'remote from the front' and 'reluctant to take decisions' – again echoing Hitler's own convictions – was now put in charge of that very organisation, and it was in this light that the Führer entrusted him to restore the 'staying power' of the Eastern Front.[53] In his first directive to the different Army Groups in the East, distributed on 24 July, Guderian outlined the future conduct of battle as he envisioned it, immediately showing how he intended to restore the momentum the Wehrmacht had lost:

It applies to the entire Eastern Front that offence is the best defence, and every opportunity to attack should be exploited. . . . All troops are to be made clear that this battle determines the preservation of the German Heimat, and therefore they have to muster all their strength for an attack, so to solve this task. They can be sure that they are assisted by all forces available on the Heimat.[54]

Men like Guderian, who were fighting the war as if it could still be won, 'knew' that Germany would have to choose its battles carefully, and the implementation of the strategy would at least allow Germany to decide its battle grounds. With all other options exhausted, the realisation that the fortress strategy, however flawed many considered it to be, was in all likelihood Germany's best chance to force a reversal of the war's fortunes, ensuring that the strategy began to assume some genuine political and military significance. In Eastern Germany, another twenty-odd fortresses were designated from autumn 1944 onwards, and although from the beginning it was recognised that a pitched battle that centred on these Ostfestungen would catch their inhabitants in the crossfire, the OKH remained (outwardly) confident that this time the 'fortress belt' *would* tie down large numbers of Soviet forces. The main reason for this overly optimistic attitude was that in Germany conditions were considered to be fundamentally different to the Soviet Union.[55]

To harness best the opportunities the battle on German soil offered the strategy, Guderian pushed for the creation of a department within the OKH that would oversee the preparations of the fortresses' defence. Shortly after his appointment as chief of staff he revived the Abteilung Landesbefestigung – the fortification department of the OKH – which allowed the strategy to be implemented with considerably more foresight.[56] Prior to the war the department held great importance as it

[53] Bernd Wegner, 'Die Kriegsführung des "als ob": Deutschlands strategische Lage seit Frühjahr 1944', in Frieser (ed.), *Das Deutsche Reich und der Zweite Weltkrieg 8*, pp. 1172–3, 1183.

[54] Werner Rahm and Gerhard Schreiber (eds.) *Kriegstagebuch der Seekriegsleitung 1939–1945 Teil A, Band 59/II: 16. bis 31. Juli 1944* (Berlin: Verlag E.S. Mittler & Sohn, 1995), pp. 510–11, 530.

[55] Willems, 'Defiant Breakwaters or Desperate Blunders?', pp. 356–7.

[56] Guderian, *Panzer Leader*, pp. 359–60.

oversaw prominent defensive projects such as the construction of the Westwall along the French border and the Heilsberger Dreieck in East Prussia. But as the threat of invasion by foreign powers declined as the German armies pushed far beyond the national borders in the early years of the war, the department had been relegated to a small 'group'.[57] Put in charge of this newly built department was Oberstleutnant Karl-Wilhelm Thilo, a seasoned and ruthless veteran staff officer who immediately sought to align the demands of the strategy with the resources still available to Germany.

Although Guderian and Thilo were uncompromising in their attempts to strengthen the defence of Eastern Germany with 'fortresses', they were more realistic than before when considering the practicalities of their defence. Unlike in the Soviet Union, the strategy's core principle – its encirclement – was actively considered well in advance, which meant that whenever possible German fortresses were stocked in anticipation. If the destruction of the Sixth Army at Stalingrad had taught the German High Command anything, it was that supplying a besieged garrison was virtually impossible. Therefore, German cities were allocated a time to hold – smaller cities such as Kolberg and Stettin thirty days, while larger cities, such as Danzig, Breslau, and Königsberg were to hold out for ninety days – and provisions were distributed accordingly.[58] Also the supply of weapons was organised months in advance and the armament of these fortresses was meticulously kept.[59] The shorter supply lines also meant that this could be done with relative ease while the pre-existing domestic administrative structure further helped streamline this process. In the run-up to the expected Soviet offensive, Guderian held numerous meetings with different RVKs, Wehrkreis commanders, and supply officers to ensure that goods would arrive to the fortresses prior to their encirclement, and that in case of a siege everyone knew what was expected of them.[60] None of

[57] Megargee, *Inside Hitler's High Command*, pp. 57, 60, 72, 215; Dieckert and Großmann, *Der Kampf um Ostpreussen*, pp. 17–20; Rolf-Dieter Müller, *Reinhard Gehlen: Geheimdienstchef im Hintergrund der Bonner Republik, Die Biografie. Teil 1: 1902–1950* (Berlin: Ch. Links Verlag, 2017), pp. 123–5.

[58] BArch RW 4/710: Betr. Verpflegungsbevorratung der Festungen und Verteidigungsbereiche, F.H.Q. 25.2.1945; BArch RH 2/331b, p. 159: Op Abt/ Abt Lds Bef 252/45 geh. 5.1.1945. Vortragsnotiz Betr. Begriffsbestimmung der 'Festung Königsberg' sowie Arbeitseinsatz zum Ausbau der Festung; Volkssturmeinsatz in Ostpreussen.

[59] BArch RH 12–20/46: Ausbau und Armierung der Oststellungen; RH 12–20/50: Geschütze und Munition für Festungsbereich Ost, Dez. 1944–Apr. 1945.

[60] BArch RH 2/317, p. 69: Fernschreiben, gez. Guderian 7.12.44; BArch NS 19/3814, pp. 1–3: Der Chef des Generalstabes des Heeres Gen Qu./ Abt. Kriegsverw. Nr. II/2200/44 g.Kdos, H Qu OKH, den 17.12.1944 Betr. Bevorratung und ARLZ-Maßnahmen auf zivilen Sektor im Bereich der Ostfestungen. BArch RH 2/316, pp. 112–13: Der Chef des Generalstabes des Heeres Op Abt (Fest) Nr. 11 886/44 g.K. H.Qu., 11.11.44 Anweisung für den Ausbau und die Verteidigung ständiger Festungen.

this necessarily meant that by the time the front line reached these fortresses they were fully ready to withstand a prolonged siege, since the bottleneck was not the organisation but rather the availability of resources. This, however, was something that those involved did not wish to reflect upon for too long.

Obviously, the fact that these were *German* cities added tremendous value to the defence. Having to hold firm on home soil close to its own population gave a defence an immediate purpose that it had lacked in the Soviet Union.[61] More important, however, was that there would always be local expertise that could be fully relied on. War Directive 53 stipulated that a fortress commander – 'a specially selected, hardened soldier, preferably of general's rank' – was to ensure the 'ruthless utilisation' of all means available in the fortress, and was expected to procure the 'extensive use of the civilian population'.[62] That mentality was also expected on German soil. Rather than factoring in the concerns of their *Volksgenossen*, in German Ostfestungen, commanders' prerogatives were even further expanded, as they gained the authority to judge whether civilians were allowed to leave the city or whether they were needed in its defence.[63] Also the security garrisons, which had previously been formed out of the reserves of the respective Army Groups (as such sapping the strength of the front), could in Germany be formed out of lower-quality troops that had previously been written off – men with hearing loss or stomach issues were of little use on the front, as were most Volkssturm units, but they could fulfil a wide range of functions as part of a garrison.[64]

The fortress strategy thus tied civilians closer to the defence of their country, and consequently even alleviated some of the doubts that troops had about their compatriots' readiness to fight a Total War. Domestically, the strategy allowed for hardships to be shared with the population, and the sense that the people were to fall in line with the army was encapsulated in many of the strategy's principles. In the 'Guidelines for the preparation and conduct of defence of cities', passed down in November 1944 to every fortress commander, the need for 'neighbourly assistance' (*Nachbarschaftshilfe*) between military and civilians was stressed. In a besieged city, the section on the fundamental principles

---

[61] See Chapter 4.

[62] Trevor-Roper, *Hitler's War Directives*, p. 160; Hubatsch, *Hitlers Weisungen für die Kriegsführung*, p. 245.

[63] BArch NS 19/3814, p. 2: Der Chef des Generalstabes des Heeres Gen Qu./ Abt. Kriegsverw. Nr. II/2200/44 g.Kdos, H Qu OKH, den 17.12.1944 Betr. Bevorratung und ARLZ-Maßnahmen auf zivilen Sektor im Bereich der Ostfestungen (see Chapter 6).

[64] BArch RH 2/331b, p. 94; BArch RH 2/317, p. 103; BArch, RH 2/335, pp. 204–7. Dieckert and Großmann, *Der Kampf um Ostpreussen*, p. 77. These men were considered as *Festungsfähig* ('fortress-suited'). See: BArch Ost-Dok. 8/602, p. 6: Makowka.

read, 'the *Nachbarshaftshilfe* extends for Wehrmacht to Wehrmacht, from Wehrmacht to *Zivil*, and from *Zivil* to *Zivil*'.[65] The fact that once a fortress was conquered it was the civilian population which was likely to suffer more than the military (which had been the case throughout history), was completely ignored.[66] As such, the fortress strategy represented the pinnacle of National Socialist military thought during times of Total War. This was all but denied but seen as positive. A 'military-scientific' essay, printed in multiple newspapers in February 1945, eventually explained that:

The attacker will rarely succeed in ploughing through jumbled housing blocks in one go. Preparations for attack will have to be planned separately for each and every district. He then runs the risk that the impact of his shock is absorbed by the maze of streets, and that it is halted by hundreds of tricks and ambushes, halted from basements and soldiers on roofs, and worn down by time so that his infantry will come to rely on the support of the armoured cars and assault guns, which are almost defenceless in the sea of houses, exposed to Panzerfaust shots. The fight for the resistance-centre 'city' places the highest demands on the leadership, garrison, and population. When every heap of rubble is fought over man-to-man the nerves are strained to the strongest, the individual's will to sacrifice is put to the hardest test.[67]

The implementation of the strategy in Germany was further helped by the fact that many German cities that were designated 'fortresses' had played that role before. These cities often possessed a ring of Prussian forts that had been constructed throughout the previous century and had been modernised up until the First World War.[68] Although by 1944 the forts were outdated, Guderian stressed, 'even today they still offer a certain security against shelling and against tanks, and they can be brought into a state of defence in a short time'.[69] Their age, moreover, actually proved to be of added value: the vegetation that had grown on top of them over the years served as a 'pillow', which meant – much to the dismay of Red Army artillerists – that the shelling of these positions only caused minor

---

[65] For these '*Richtlinien für die Vorbereitung und Durchführung der Verteidigung von Städten*', see: Deutsch-Russisches Projekt zur Digitalisierung deutscher Dokumente in Archiven der Russischen Föderation, 'Verteidigungstaktik des Gegners: Übersetzungen von deutschen, ungarischen, rumänischen und italienischen Beutedokumenten zu taktischen Fragen', http://wwii.germandocsinrussia.org/de/nodes/1833#page/1/mode/grid/zoom/1

[66] Strachan, 'From Cabinet War to Total War', p. 22.

[67] Erich Kuby, *Das Ende des Schreckens: Januar bis Mai 1945* (Munich: Deutscher Taschenbuch Verlag, 1986), p. 54.

[68] Albert Moll, *Der Deutsche Festungsbau von Memel bis zum Atlantik 1900-1945* (Utting: Dörfler, 1988), pp. 10, 12–22.

[69] BArch RH 2/316, p. 113: Der Chef des Generalstabes des Heeres Op Abt (Fest) Nr. 11 886/44 g.K. H.Qu., 11.11.44 Anweisung für den Ausbau und die Verteidigung ständiger Festungen.

structural damage.[70] Fortresses received dozens of extra heavy artillery pieces out of the stockpiles of captured foreign guns, and these were mainly placed on these forts to complicate potential attempts simply to bypass them.[71] Also the city centres were fortified, and divided in sections, each with their own commander.[72] Throughout the last months of 1944, hundreds of thousands of mines were laid, bridges were mined, and tank obstacles were constructed. By the time the Soviet winter offensives finally commenced, most cities that had been prepared to serve as fortresses had been thoroughly transformed.[73]

What stands out, above all, in the new approach towards the German Ostfestungen, is that they lay much further behind the front line than the fortresses in the Soviet Union. The line Guderian proposed roughly corresponded with the interwar situation and followed the old Polish–German border.[74] This break with the initial conception of the strategy was one of the clearest results of his tenure as chief of staff. Establishing fortresses further to the rear meant that, in case of a Soviet attack, German territory would inevitably fall in enemy hands. Guderian's insistence on the correctness of this decision meant that he had to butt heads with his Führer, who feared that establishing fortresses further away from the front would encourage German soldiers to retreat to them. Guderian eventually got Hitler's approval, which allowed the strategy to move away from the rigid 'fall where you stand' rhetoric – to which it had previously been connected – to a strategy that dared to abandon German territory in favour of adhering to the long-term strategic 'vision' – again showing that Hitler still had every intention of winning the war.[75]

The implementation of the fortress strategy reveals the extent of the radicalisation of the Wehrmacht and the Party by 1944 and shows how interwoven their agendas had become. It was not merely a manifestation of the last convulsions of a dying regime, hell-bound to drag its citizens into a Total War. The desperate and disillusioned Wehrmacht, which, due to the regime's massive rearmament efforts, only a few years earlier had 'believed itself to live in an epoch of German military history which

---

[70] Nikolai Khlebnikov, *Pod grohot soten batarej* [Under the thunder of a hundred batteries] (Moscow: Voenizdat, 1974), pp. 355–60.

[71] BArch RH 2/316, pp. 82–3: Ob.Abt (Fest) 22.11.44. Vortragsnotiz 1.) Festungs-Artillerie.

[72] BArch RH 2/331b, p. 93: Fernschreiben, 12.1.45. gez. Guderian OKH/GenStdH/ Op Abt/ Abt. Lds Bef Nr. 445/45; BArch RH 2/331b, p. 163: Generalstab des Heeres, Op Abt/Abt Lds Bef Nr. 299/45 geh., 5.1.45; BArch, Ost-Dok. 10/890, 60: Fest. Regt. Stab Mantel. Königsberg Pr. 26.1.45.

[73] BArch Ost-Dok. 10/890, p. 25: Dieckert.

[74] Moll, *Der Deutsche Festungsbau*, pp. 28–9, 44–51.

[75] Weinberg, *Germany, Hitler, and World War II*, pp. 284–5.

had not existed "since the Great Elector"' now adhered to a strategy for the defence of Germany that deliberately exposed the civilians – who it had vowed to protect – to deadly combat in the name of that same regime.[76] The vast propaganda that accompanied the strategy had two purposes: on one hand it was the regime's seal of approval but at the same time it was meant to counter the reservations that many commanders expressed behind closed doors. As we will see in the next section, the Party elite used the Wehrmacht's critique of the strategy both as a way to point to defeatism as well as proof that the Wehrmacht questioned the regime's authority.

The Struggle for Final Authority in Germany's Defence

The army's increased presence in Germany kindled a number of fears within the ranks of the Party. Most importantly, it was feared that the armed forces would infringe upon their power. With the establishment of the Reichsverteidigungskommissar the Party had already devised a framework that curtailed Wehrmacht influence in domestic affairs, but since the army had so far mainly operated outside German borders, it had hardly been put to the test. Yet as troops moved into Germany *en masse* in the autumn of 1944, the Party became more anxious about the Wehrmacht's intentions. Since it was the Party that had most managed to increase its power inside Germany during wartime, it was the Party that had the most to lose with any change of the status quo as it had existed prior to mid-1944.[77] Friction between the Wehrmacht and the Party was bound to occur, and efforts would have to be made to reduce it.

There was little reason for the Party to see the Wehrmacht's arrival in Germany as anything but a potential challenge to its hold on domestic politics. Throughout German history, the military had been particularly successful in asserting its influence in matters of policy and had never shied away from assuming political office. One of the most recent examples of military interference in German politics, acutely remembered by the Nazi leadership, was certainly among the most brazen ones. By the summer of 1916 the First World War had taken a turn for the worse for Germany, with its forces on the defensive on every front. Up to that point, the German army had been led by General Erich von Falkenhayn, the chief of the German General Staff, a man who, entirely occupied with military

---

[76] Förster, *Die Wehrmacht im NS-Staat*, pp. 26–7. Meant is Friedrich Wilhelm, Elector of Brandenburg (1620–88) whose political and military achievements were closely entwined.

[77] On a general examination of the impact of 'infighting' during the last years of the war, see: Mommsen, 'The Dissolution of the Third Reich', p. 106.

operations, maintained his distance from politics. He nevertheless could have assumed a more political role, since already at the beginning of the war the Kaiser had declared Germany to be in a state of war (*Kriegszustand*), a measure which placed the country under martial law and as such subordinated the civilian administration to military oversight. In August, when in the absence of decisive victories his position became untenable, Falkenhayn was replaced by Field Marshal von Hindenburg, the hero of the defence of East Prussia, who brought along his subordinate, General Erich von Ludendorff. Contrary to their predecessor, the two men were fully intent on exploiting the emergency powers which martial law provided them. Trusted by the man in the street and backed by interest groups with significant political clout, these men successfully managed to pin the failings of the war on the German government. In the second half of 1916 they started targeting officials who in their opinion were not pulling their weight in the war effort. Since Hindenburg and Ludendorff maintained that the war could still be won, they consistently presented deviations from the war path as undermining morale. Eventually, in July 1917, they even managed to oust Chancellor Theobald von Bethmann-Hollweg, a man who had long been their ally but also someone who sought to explore more than one option to end the war. After Bethmann's attempts to open peace negotiations had failed, Hindenburg and Ludendorff seized their chance and strong-armed the Kaiser and parliament into asking for his resignation after having accused the Chancellor of disloyalty and harbouring a lack of faith in the military. From then on, the two men stood virtually unchallenged at the head of German state, having succeeded in creating a 'silent dictatorship' in which the government's agenda was completely shaped by the demands of the military.[78]

Military interference in domestic politics did not end after the First World War had been lost. In the turbulent immediate post-war era, different right-wing Freikorps (Free Corps) paramilitary groups sprung up all over the country, which demobilised German soldiers joined in disproportionately high numbers. These Freikorps played a vital role in the suppression of different communist uprisings in the newly established Weimar Republic, most famously the January 1919 Spartakist uprisings. In March 1920, in turn, the Freikorps-backed Kapp Putsch tried to overthrow Reichspräsident Friedrich Ebert's democratically elected government.[79] Although these veterans evidently did not return from

---

[78] Gordon Craig, *The Politics of the Prussian Army, 1640–1945* (Oxford: Oxford University Press, 1964), pp. 299–341.

[79] Hans-Ulrich Wehler, *Deutsche Gesellschaftsgeschichte: Bd. 4: Vom Beginn des Ersten Weltkrieges bis zur Gründung der beiden deutschen Staaten 1914–1949* (Munich: C. H. Beck, 2003), pp. 243–4, 406–7; Jones, *Founding Weimar*, pp. 18–19, ch. 6,

the war with a common agenda, the willingness to influence domestic policy – even after having fought abroad for years and having been largely detached from civilian life – was a purpose they shared. Also, the regular armed forces – the 100,000-man Reichswehr – had to be called in repeatedly to restore order during the fragile Weimar Republic; all the while high-ranking officers continued to occupy important positions in the different Weimar governments. During the early years of the Nazi dictatorship the army continued to maintain significant influence over internal politics, until Hitler managed to diminish its power and subordinate it to the state.[80]

The Second World War again saw the Wehrmacht in a political role, although not within Germany itself. During the occupation of the Soviet Union, it was allowed to implement the regime's vision of the occupied territories as it saw fit. Not much imagination is needed to consider the Wehrmacht on the Eastern Front a 'state', possessing far-reaching powers over a large number of subjects, controlling a vast territory hundreds of miles from Berlin, and, of course, holding a 'monopoly of legitimate and physical force'.[81] Already in October 1937 Goebbels explicitly referred to the Wehrmacht as a 'state within a state', fearing that, since 'politically the generality had learned nothing', it would present a dissonant voice within his propaganda.[82] Certainly the implications of the Wehrmacht as an independent pillar within the National Socialist society – a notion initially championed by Hitler himself – remained a constant worry throughout the war.[83] Even as the tide of war turned against Germany, and the Wehrmacht was pushed out of the Soviet Union, it maintained many of its 'state-like' qualities. It possessed a vast police apparatus, its own justice system (to which we will return in Chapter 6), and its own press corps and presses (Chapter 4). Moreover, the army possessed one of the most sophisticated communication networks which not only served to pass down orders from unit to unit, but could also be used to communicate the military's demands directly to the war economy.[84] Furthermore, the Wehrmacht had an organisational structure in place specifically designed

'Atrocities and Mobilisation', ch. 7, 'Weimar's Order to Execute'; Dirk Schumann, *Political Violence in the Weimar Republic 1918–1933: Fight for the Streets and Fear of Civil War* (Oxford: Berghahn Books, 2012), pp. 3–11.

[80] Craig, *The Politics of the Prussian Army*, pp. 415–96.

[81] Merriam-Webster s.v. 'state'; Max Weber, *The Essential Weber: a Reader*, Sam Whimster (ed.) (London: Routledge, 2004), pp. 131–2.

[82] Förster, *Die Wehrmacht im NS-Staat*, p. 25; Elke Fröhlich (ed.), *Die Tagebücher von Joseph Goebbels, Teil I Aufzeichnungen 1923–1941, Band 4: März – November 1937* (Munich: K. G. Saur, 2000), p. 379 (28 October 1937 entry).

[83] Förster, *Die Wehrmacht im NS-Staat*, pp. 22, 25–6.

[84] Andreas Kunz, 'Die Wehrmacht in der Agonie der nationalsozialistischen Herrschaft 1944/45. Eine Gedankenskizze', in Hillmann and Zimmermann (eds.), *Kriegsende 1945*

to perform well under duress, and would therefore be well suited to the challenges posed in 1945. Underpinning all this, from divisional level downwards, army units consisted of men with all the civilian skills to operate independently from the state, such as butchers, cobblers, vets, doctors, and so on. Trying to fit this massive organisation into Party and state structures was therefore unfeasible, especially given that – despite the high casualty numbers – military structures remained more or less intact, while German civilian society itself was steadily crumbling. Moreover, as we will see in Chapter 4, the Party was well aware of its waning popularity, and in order to drum up popular support had itself championed a Total War society that closely linked the Heimat to the front, a *Kampfgemeinschaft*. As a result, the army still enjoyed a certain popularity among the German population that the Party had long not enjoyed.

The main tool at the disposal of the Party to prevent the Wehrmacht from gaining undue influence in the political sphere was to accuse it of a lack of loyalty towards the Volksgemeinschaft. The Wehrmacht was portrayed as a milieu that the regime had failed to penetrate, a hotbed of *Resistenz* that allowed for an 'inner emigration' from the regime.[85] The Party elite presented the failures on the Eastern Front as a form of betrayal and a failure of National Socialist spirit among the Wehrmacht's ranks.[86] Hitler, throughout his career, remained sceptical of the army's willingness to fight for the regime, especially at times when commanders had been unwilling to follow his orders.[87] Likewise, although after the assassination attempt of 20 July the plotters were presented as 'a very small clique of . . . criminally stupid officers', behind closed doors the matter was treated as an almost characteristic – to some extent anticipated – manifestation of a larger problem among the ranks of the military.[88] Although the Wehrmacht's lack of loyalty to the community was mainly used as a pretext to prevent it from assuming too much power, it was nevertheless a powerful accusation that brought about a reaction that was very real. An internal 'clean-up', nothing short of a minor purge, was requested by the army itself and followed shortly after the assassination attempt in an effort

---

in Deutschland, pp. 108–9. A diary entry of the OKW chief of operations, Alfred Jodl, mentions '120,000 long distance calls and 33,000 telegrams' on 26 January 1945 alone.

[85] Martin Broszat, '*Resistenz* and Resistance', in Gregor (ed.), *Nazism*, pp. 241–4.

[86] Heinz Boberach (ed.), *Meldungen aus dem Reich: Die geheimen Lageberichte des Sicherheitsdienstes der SS 1938–1945, Band 17* (Herrsching: Pawlak Verlag, 1984), p. 6653 (22 July), pp. 6686–7 (28 July), p. 6700 (10 August); Stargardt, *The German War*, p. 453; Steinert, *Hitler's War and the Germans*, pp. 270–3.

[87] Wilhelm Keitel and Walter Gorlitz (eds.), *The Memoirs of Field Marshal Keitel* (London: William Kimber, 1965), 166–7; Kershaw, *The End*, pp. 197–203.

[88] Stargardt, *The German War*, pp. 452–4.

to restore its tainted honour.[89] This autumn purge not only affected the General Staff and interior military positions, it placed field commanders under scrutiny as well. An elaborate British intelligence report of autumn 1944 read that in East Prussia 'the political morale of all the personnel is being very carefully checked'. It further noted: 'In addition to this, a drastic purge among all officers from the rank of major up is taking place in both [the Sixteenth and Eighteenth] Armies as a result of the belief at Hitler's HQ that the officers were mainly to blame for the German collapse in the Baltic States. Courts of enquiry are conducting a detailed investigation into the activities of all officers, from battalion commander inclusive, upwards.'[90] Moreover, the sight of the chaotic army pouring into East Prussia did little to strengthen its role in the province's hierarchy, and served as further 'proof' of the Wehrmacht's unreliability.[91]

Yet Hitler's unwillingness to trust the Wehrmacht's political reliability was largely unfounded. Despite the personal reservations that some of the commanders felt towards the regime, virtually none of them considered renouncing their oath to the Führer.[92] In November 1944 a British intelligence report concluded that 'there are no indications in East Prussia of any desire, either on the part of the personnel of the armed forces or of the civilian population, to overthrow the Nazi regime, although Hitler personally, and the Nazi Party as a whole, are universally unpopular'.[93] Although these conclusions might have been somewhat overstated, the middle-ranking and lower-ranking Party officials – Bonzen – were indeed largely despised among the troops.[94] In particular there was resentment over the role these men – many of whom were considered to be bragging dilettantes – occupied in the country's defence. After the war, Eberhard Knieper, a former staff officer in Königsberg's fortress staff, reflected that one of the main frustrations among the top ranks of the army was that they felt that the Party undeservedly sought to lay sole claim to the right to rally the population for the city's defence.[95] One of the main fears of the Wehrmacht was to appear 'soft', and understandably it saw these kind of calls as 'warning shots', since they implied that the Party was trying to assume even more powers at the army's expense.[96] For the discredited army, addressing the potential weaknesses

---

[89] Max Domarus, *Hitler Reden und Proklamationen 1932–1945, II. Band Untergang (1939–1945)* (Neusstadt a.d. Aisch: Verlagsdruckerei Schmidt, 1963), p. 2137.

[90] TNA HW 1/3341, Germany: Morale of Armies in East Prussia, 22-11-44. On the 'troubled conscience' of German troops during the latter half of the war, see: Stargardt, 'The Troubled Patriot'.

[91] Meindl, *Ostpreußens Gauleiter, Erich Koch*, p. 440.   [92] Römer, *Kameraden*, pp. 306–9.

[93] TNA HW 1/3341, Germany: Morale of Armies in East Prussia, 22-11-44.

[94] Römer, *Kameraden*, pp. 79–90.   [95] AKO 22304-4: Oberleutnant Eberhard Knieper.

[96] Bessel, *Germany 1945*, p. 36.

of too large a role for the Party thus not only served to organise the defence of Germany, it was also a way to show its teeth and hold its own against its major rival.

Two issues stand out in the way the Wehrmacht sought to prevent further inroads from the Party while on German territory. Firstly, as we have seen, the Wehrmacht had always been in charge of the so-called 'area of operations' close behind the frontline, whereas the Party possessed no expertise whatsoever in this respect.[97] It was entirely plausible that this lack of experience would hasten a quick collapse of an area's defences when under attack, since inexperienced Party officials were likely to lose their heads. In this respect, the Wehrmacht possessed a mighty tool: especially up until mid-February 1945, it possessed virtually sole authority over summary courts martial. This meant that they could round up everyone in the areas of operation – including Party officials – who they felt had failed to do their duty during critical moments. The presence of two independent justice systems operating alongside each other was considered a dangerous precedent, and in early February 1945, Gauleiter Joachim Eggeling of Halle-Merseburg advised Reichsleiter Bormann to address the matter. The sight of Wehrmacht officers sitting in judgement over wavering Party officials threatened to undermine the Party's standing, and Eggeling believed that this practice should be avoided.[98]

Secondly, generals were quick to stress that there was no war weariness among troops, and there had been no 'revolutionary manifestations' among the troops in 1945 as there had been in 1918.[99] Military morale among troops was said to be consistently higher than that of German workers.[100] Although this was not the same as possessing a National Socialist spirit, 'assuring victory' was the Wehrmacht's core task within Germany's Weltanschauungskrieg (war of world views), and one that from late 1944 gained in importance given that the other aims of the war (annihilation, exploitation, and domination of the East) could not be achieved during the defence of Germany.[101] Moreover, the generals,

---

[97] See Chapter 5.

[98] IfZArch Akten der Partei-Kanzlei der NSDAP: 13202379. Beleg Nr. 5, p. 10. Febr. 1945 An die Partei-Kanzlei z. Hd. Herrn Reichsleiter M. Bormann. gez. Eggeling Gauleiter.

[99] Neitzel, *Abgehört*, p. 189.

[100] Timothy Mason, *Social Policy in the Third Reich: the Working Class and the 'National Community'* (Oxford: Berg, 1993), p. 334.

[101] Förster, *Die Wehrmacht im NS-Staat*, pp. 59–60. Förster asserts that 'to achieve the gigantic "purpose of war" of the German people – victory, annihilation, exploitation and domination – four instruments, so-called pillars, were envisaged: Wehrmacht, SS, Four-Year Plan, and administration. In order to effectively master this important task, the areas of Hitler's "4 commissioners" were not clearly separated, but closely interlinked'.

most of whom had experienced the First World War and its aftermath, still felt a sense of guardianship over Germany, and the idea that during the previous war the army had not been defeated on the battlefield but as a result of a stab in the back by a war weary and traitorous home front, was – as we saw – deeply embedded in the Wehrmacht.[102] Meanwhile, war-weariness was increasingly observed on the home front and the Party was seen giving in to the demands of the population, for example by postponing cuts in rations. Party elites were unwilling to subordinate everything to the demands of the military, so the Wehrmacht could reasonably argue that it was once again being held back.[103] These conflicts were not unwelcome to the Wehrmacht. Indeed, Hitler 'was generally unwilling to resolve disputes by coming down on one side or the other, much preferring parties in a dispute to sort it out themselves', after which he could support the side that had managed to come out on top.[104] The Wehrmacht had most to gain by stirring up the current state of affairs, and thus had a vested interest in creating a conflict in order to enhance its position within the state.

Yet these conflicts were not decisive in the way these men behaved towards each other: their frame of reference was shaped above all by the circumstances, opportunities, and limitations that presented themselves. How these men were to behave towards each other was specified in various orders. It was at a local level that the interaction between most Party officials and Wehrmacht officers actually took place, and with more and more cities designated as fortresses, the regulations concerning fortress cities offers a representative view of how at this level the divide between Party and Army was to be bridged. In late 1944, a fair number of Eastern Germany's larger cities were declared fortresses, among them Danzig, Königsberg, Lötzen, Gotenhafen, Thorn, Graudenz, Oppeln, Breslau, Glogau, Schneidemühl, Posen, and Pressburg. More would be later added to the list, such as Olmütz, Frankfurt am Oder, and Berlin. The measures taken for the fortress cities offer us the clearest indication of the interaction between Wehrmacht and Party in Germany's cities. In particular, the problem of ultimate authority needed to be solved. The most comprehensive attempts to tackle this came from the OKH, led by

---

[102] On the activities of prominent Wehrmacht generals during the period immediately following the First World War and during the Weimar Republic, see: Hürter, *Hitlers Heerführer*, pp. 86–111; Geyer, 'Endkampf 1918 and 1945', pp. 35–68; Bessel, *Nazism and War*, pp. 164–6, 179–81.

[103] Mason, *Social Policy in the Third Reich*, pp. 362–6.

[104] Ian Kershaw, *The Nazi Dictatorship: Problems and Perspectives of Interpretation* (London: Edward Arnold, 1991), p. 75.

Generaloberst Heinz Guderian. In mid-December 1944 Guderian proposed the establishment of a Gemeinsamer Arbeitsstab in every
fortress.[105] Under this system, for every fortress Gauleiter would desig-
nate a *Festungsbeauftragte der NSDAP* (Fortress-commissioner of the
NSDAP) who would be responsible for its political matters, as well as
the care of civilians:

> In case of an encirclement this commissioner stays in the fortress and is subordin-
> ate to the fortress commander. From then on, he will be particularly tasked to do
> everything to strengthen the indomitable will of the troops to resist (in cooper-
> ation with the NSFO) and to deploy the Volkssturm units present in the
> fortress.[106]

The RVK, at the same time, would appoint a Referent (consultant) for 'all
civilian Reich defence measures, particularly supply and ARLZ-
measures'.[107] The Leiter der Gemeindeverwaltung (head of local government, normally the Oberbürgemeister – mayor) was also to find a place on
the combined staff, but all the civilian officials were to be subordinated to
the fortress commander.[108] The proposal fitted into Guderian's belief
that a fortress commander should be 'master over life and death of all
persons present in the fortress'.[109] However, the Party disagreed with this
scheme, arguing that in Germany fortress commanders should merely
have 'the right to give instructions, but no subordination structure which
grants the rights to judge about life and death of all persons in the fortress.
That was true for fortresses abroad, but not for Germany'.[110] What the
army demanded was thus a much greater degree of autonomy than the
Party was willing to allow. The Party's foot-dragging was closely connected to the authority it claimed the Wehrmacht lacked in regard to

---

[105] BArch NS 19/3814, pp. 1–5: Der Chef des Generalstabes des Heeres Gen Qu./ Abt.
Kriegsverw. Nr. II/2200/44 g.Kdos, H Qu OKH, den 17.12.1944 Betr. Bevorratung
und ARLZ-Maßnahmen auf zivilen Sektor im Bereich der Ostfestungen.
[106] Ibid., pp. 2–4.
[107] Ibid., p. 2. *ARLZ*-Arbeitsstäben (*Auflockerung, Räumung, Lähmung und Zerstörung* or
Task Forces for Breaking-down, Evacuation, Paralysing and Destruction).
[108] Ibid., pp. 2, 5.
[109] BArch RH 2/316, pp. 112–13: Der Chef des Generalstabes des Heeres Op Abt (Fest)
Nr. 11 886/44 g.K. H.Qu., 11.11.44 Anweisung für den Ausbau und die Verteidigung
ständiger Festungen.
[110] BArch RW 4/704, p. 5: WFSt/Qu 2 (Ost) Nr. 0150/45 geh. F.H.Q., den 6.1.1945 Betr.:
Rücksprache mit dem Sachbearbeiter der Parteikanzlei für Evakuierungsfrage. The
issue was eventually resolved on 17 February 1945 when Bormann distributed the
final memorandum concerning the 'Command structure for cut off troops and rules
on fortresses, defensive areas etc.', drawn up by Field Marshal Keitel. Party members
were partially placed outside of the authority of the fortress commander. See: BArch NS
6/ 354, pp. 71–80: Der Leiter der Partei-Kanzlei Führerhauptquartier, den 17.2.1945,
Rundschreiben 88/45g Betrifft: Befehlsführung bei abgeschnittenen Truppenteilen und
Bestimmungen über Festungen, Verteidigungsbereiche usw.

governing a city's population. But at the end of the day much would come to depend on local 'moral authority'. This meant that moral authority could only be asserted during the defence of the city in question.

Towards a New Community

With the conscious decision to defend Germany's cities, war reached the pinnacle of totality for much of the German population. Never had so many Germans been so close to warring belligerents and the dynamics in these cities helped shape the nature of late-war violence.[111] Cities were environments where people of different social strata and beliefs could easily gather together, and friction was never far away. Nowhere is this better conveyed than in an alarming report, written by a certain Leutnant Haussleiter, a National-Socialist Leadership Officer of the Fifteenth Army, which fought in Western Germany. His report reached Guderian (who as 'Chef der OKH' was mainly concerned with the Eastern Front) via the Oberbefehlshaber West, Field Marshal Gerd von Rundstedt. Guderian had immediately sent the report to Bormann, who in turn passed it on to Himmler.[112] The findings can rightly be considered as broadly accepted among those men within the Party and the Wehrmacht that were willing to fight to the end.

The decent soldier remains at the front. Nobodies and shirkers, however, leave their lines. They already form a dangerous mass in the large cities, and upon the dissolution of order immediately turn into agents of sinister movements. These masses at the same time spread rumours and negative attitudes. They obviously represent the scum of the nation.

These men, who 'loaf around for weeks' on stations throughout the country, were defeatists whose message, Haussleiter observed, found large audiences in 'every jam-packed waggon or hairdresser'. They could easily disappear into these crowds when they were called out, something Haussleiter found when he tried to catch one of these men. Some of the workers that listened to the stories, in turn, told troops that their factories had ceased to work while women openly discussed hiding them.[113] In his report, Haussleiter repeatedly expressed the need to set examples to counter the behaviour, clearly adhering to the notion of

---

[111] By 1936, according to the *Statistisches Jahrbuch für das Deutsche Reich*, 30.2 per cent of the German population lived in cities of over 100,000 people.

[112] The function of the NSFO, the Nationalsozialistischer Führungsoffizier, will be discussed in Chapter 4.

[113] IfZArch Akten der Partei-Kanzlei der NSDAP: 10700993. Führerhauptquartier, den 1. März 1945 Bo/Lch. Herrn Reichsführer-SS Himmler Betrifft: Beobachtungen im Heimatkriegsgebiet; IfZArch Akten der Partei-Kanzlei der NSDAP: 10700994-

'violence as a means of communication'.[114] Although Haussleiter's report is almost grotesque in its analysis and proposals, it demonstrates why cities and their immediate environment serve as the best possible framework to examine the wave of violence that swept over Germany. The urban presence of dissenters with a wildly different outlook to the official discourse made German cities into pressure cookers in which the use of violence became a readily accepted valve.

In Königsberg there were enough men and women who fit Haussleiter's description and the dynamics he described certainly also manifested themselves in the city. Traditionally the hard line pursued on the ground to deal with these 'defeatists' is traced back to Nazi hardliners, but what immediately stands out in the assessment of Königsberg's siege is that the Wehrmacht vastly outnumbered Party officials. The military's arrival shaped behaviour patterns in the city and its members knew how to use their authority vis-à-vis the Party to impact life in the city. Establishing the working relationship between the main actors will eventually allow us to determine the grounds on which they based the decisions they took during the two-month siege. We will briefly address the main actors that arrived in the city in late January 1945 as well as those who were already there but subsequently assumed a different role.

On 27 January 1945 General der Infanterie Otto Lasch (1893–1971), the former Wehrkreis commander of East Prussia, was appointed as fortress commander of Königsberg.[115] The minutes of the military conference at Hitler's headquarters on 27 January 1945 show that Generaloberst Guderian, who knew General Lasch from earlier military conferences, personally recommended him to Hitler, referring to Lasch as 'the most notable personality we have up there'.[116] Lasch was the

---

10701000 Geheime Kommandosache, Abschrift von SSD-Fernschreiben Chef des Genstb. Ob. West/ NSFO Nr. 75/45 g.Kdos. von 28.II.45 an Chef OKW

[114] Keller, *Volksgemeinschaft am Ende*, p. 422.

[115] BArch PERS 6/251, p. 34: Heeres-Personalamt. Personalakten für Lasch, Otto. The message of his appointment reached Lasch on the morning of 28 January. See: Lasch, *So fiel Königsberg*, p. 37–8. During peacetime, Wehrkreis I (the East Prussian military district) mustered a Korps, the I. Armeekorps, headed by Generalkommando I., which had its in seat Königsberg. When the Korps was mobilised (prepared for deployment) the command remained in place but without troops attached to it. As such, during wartime it became a Stellvertretender Generalkommando, which oversaw the Wehrkreis's remaining military administration. It was headed by a Stellvertretender Kommandierender General. General Lasch was the last to hold this position, until 22 January 1945.

[116] Helmut Heiber and David Glantz, *Hitler and His Generals, Military Conferences 1942-1945: the First Complete Stenographic Record of the Military Situation Conferences, from Stalingrad to Berlin* (London: Greenhill, 2002), pp. 632–3; BArch RH 2/317, p. 69: Fernschreiben gez. Guderian Generaloberst und Chef des Generalstabes des Heeres 7.12.44.

archetypical Wehrmacht general, and, although after the war Lasch distanced himself from the Nazi regime, he owed a lot to it, and was certainly a perfect fit for the appointment. Otto Lasch had been born on 25 June 1893 in the Upper Silesian town of Pless (now Pszczyna), a town with a predominantly Polish population that was actively being discriminated against by German authorities.[117] He enrolled in the army as a cadet at age nineteen, and on 7 August 1914, the week of Germany's general mobilisation, was promoted to Leutnant. Lasch considered the First World War an 'adventurous time' during which he held numerous different positions, while his daring even won him the *Ehrenbecher für den Sieger im Luftkampf* (a goblet of honour for the victor in aerial combat). It nevertheless garnered little attention from his superiors as he only reached the rank of Oberleutnant in March 1918.[118] Immediately after the war he went to the East Prussian town of Lyck where his brother was the Erster Bürgermeister (mayor), to join 'Freikorps Himburg'.[119] This decision to join a Freikorps helps to understand Lasch's outlook on German society, as well as the place he felt violence occupied in it.[120]

For the Freikorps in contested Eastern German territories, violence was 'both a symptom and a constitutive element', and it is therefore highly unlikely that Lasch was opposed to it.[121] Around the same time as his arrival in Lyck, a wave of Polish nationalism threatened the German character of his birthplace of Pless, and the only way to curb these Polish nationalist tendencies was to increase German (para-)military presence. It nevertheless proved insufficient, as two pro-Polish uprisings – in August 1919 and August 1920 – would eventually help secure a Polish majority in the March 1921 plebiscite, after which Lasch's Heimat fell under foreign rule.[122] For men like Lasch, the sense of feeling embattled was therefore acute, which meant that the threshold to resort to open violence and brutality was lowered.[123] As experienced veterans of the First World War, Freikorps men considered themselves authorities in the

---

[117] Christian Koller, 'Racisms *Made in Germany*: Without "Sonderweg" to a "Rupture in Civilisation"', in Hund, Koller, and Zimmermann (eds.), *Racisms Made in Germany*, pp. 20–1.

[118] Lasch, *So fiel Königsberg*, pp. 7-11; BArch PERS 6/251: Heeres-Personalamt. Personalakten für Lasch, Otto.

[119] Reinhold Weber, 'Zuerst lagen dort Schwarze Husaren', *Das Ostpreußenblatt*, 20 August, 1988, p. 10.

[120] Other prominent members of Freikorps Himburg were the later General Hans Jordan and Generalleutnant Otto Hellmuth Böhlke.

[121] Annemarie Sammartino, *The Impossible Border: Germany and the East, 1914–1922* (Ithaca, NY: Cornell University Press, 2011), p. 46; Jones, *Founding Weimar*, pp. 18–19.

[122] T. Hunt Tooley, 'German Political Violence and the Border Plebiscite in Upper Silesia, 1919-1921', *Central European History* (21) 1988, pp. 92–4.

[123] Jones, *Founding Weimar*, pp. 18–19.

proper use of violence, a 'given' that allowed them to disregard civilian concerns and objections. Rather than to give credence to these sentiments, the 'misunderstanding and rejection that Freikorps fighters believed greeted them in Germany' only convinced these men of the naivety of those civilians they 'protected', a notion which was seemingly confirmed given that local authorities never sanctioned their actions.[124]

Indeed, Lasch was also rewarded for his loyalty to the Reich. After the plebiscite of July 1920, during which Lyck's inhabitants voted with an overwhelming majority to stay part of Germany, Lasch became a Polizei-Oberleutnant in the city. In 1921 he became Polizei-Hauptmann, leaving Lyck three years later, in 1924. In the decade that followed, Lasch was posted to Magdeburg, Sensburg, and Breslau, where on 1 May 1933 he joined the NSDAP. The early membership, in the wake of the *Machtergreifung* (the Nazi seizure of power), was most likely a career move, since neither friend nor enemy described him as a particularly fanatical Party supporter.[125] Men like Lasch were recognised by *Alte Kämpfer* as opportunistic *Märzveilchen*, or 'March Violets', but it nevertheless benefited his career, and in November 1933 Lasch became a Polizei-Major.[126] Two years later, in October 1935, shortly after Hitler had openly broken with the military restrictions imposed by the Versailles Treaty, Lasch was transferred back into the army.[127]

As with his Party membership, the arrival of Lasch's cohort in the army was viewed with scepticism, this time by the senior officers of the old Reichswehr. These men rightly feared that the army's social cohesion would be diluted by the vast inflow of 'reactivated ex-officers, reserve officers, transferred police officers, and SA leaders', whose lack of military qualities were evident but had to be overlooked to accommodate the growth of the armed forces.[128] Regardless whether Lasch was personally bothered by the division between 'old' and 'new' officers – in his memoirs he goes to some lengths to stress his 'Prussianism', implying that, despite

---

[124] Sammartino, *The Impossible Border*, p. 56.
[125] BArch PERS 6/300107: Lasch, Bernhard Otto; Michael Wieck, *Königsberg Zeugnis vom Untergang einer Stadt* (Augsburg: Bechtermünz Verlag, 1998), p. 218. Wieck is highly critical of General Lasch's decision to fight to the last man but explains this as militarily motivated and not as rooted in National Socialist conviction. For the Soviet attitude towards Lasch, see: Ivan Bagramyan, 'The Storming of Königsberg', in Erickson (ed.), *Main Front*, pp. 242–3.
[126] BDC M0087 Lasch, Otto. Mitglieds Nr. 2056645. Geboren 25.6.93, Ort: Pless, Beruf: Pol. Hptm.; Verheiratet; Eingetreten: 1.5.33; Lasch, *So fiel Königsberg*, pp. 7–11.
[127] Lasch was one of the 1,200 police officers to be absorbed into the Wehrmacht in 1935–6. See: Förster, *Die Wehrmacht im NS-Staat*, p. 87; Wilhelm Deist, 'Die Aufrüstung der Wehrmacht', in Deist (ed.), *Das Deutsche Reich und der Zweite Weltkrieg, Band 1*, p. 421.
[128] Grunberger, *A Social History of the Third Reich*, pp. 138–9; Malinowski, *Vom König zum Führer*, pp. 500–3.

his rather standard call to the colours, he was part of the former group – opportunism was no longer a dirty word. In fact, without the 'mental flexibility' of men like Lasch, the breakneck expansion of the Wehrmacht would not have been possible, something of which its top echelons were acutely aware.[129]

After his transfer to the army Lasch rose steadily through the ranks, and by the beginning of Operation Barbarossa in June 1941 he had reached the rank of *Oberst*. His daring and willingness to take risks were, contrary to during the First World War, recognised and appreciated.[130] He received the Knight's Cross for the capture of Riga in 1941 while serving as regimental commander in the (East-Prussian-raised) 1st Infanterie-Division. It brought him to the forefront of the army elite and he featured on the army calendar as 'conqueror of Riga' exactly three years after the feat, and had a street named after him in Riga as well.[131] There should be no doubt that during the fighting for the city Lasch became aware of the war's genocidal ramifications. A pogrom, incited by men of Einsatzgruppe A, erupted in Riga as his regiment – temporarily bolstered with a detachment of SS and SD-men – fought its way through the city. The perpetrators of this pogrom were mainly men of nationalist Latvian 'self-defence units', who dragged Jews from their houses in public spectacles, which Lasch and his men must have noted. When he returned to the city on the first anniversary of its 'liberation', his brother-in-arms during Riga's capture, Generalleutnant Walter Braemer, had written a feature in the monthly *Ostland* celebrating the events of those days, even euphemistically describing how, as soon as the battle was over, 'the civilian population takes to the streets, some of them armed. These are Latvians, who want to track down and destroy the still-hidden Bolshevists'.[132] Within a year, the pogrom had become part of the story of the liberation of Riga, rather than a secret of the SS that was carefully kept from the regular troops. As guests of honour, Lasch and Braemer would have reminisced about their feats in those days and the progress the German presence had brought about, while their host, the scrupleless Reichskommissar für das Ostland Hinrich Lohse, might have contributed to the conversation by praising the Wehrmacht for its part in the

---

[129] Shepherd, *Hitler's Soldiers*, pp. 6–11.

[130] The above-mentioned military feats were not found in Lasch's memoirs, but in Lasch's Wehrmacht personnel files. See: BArch PERS 6/251: Heeres-Personalamt. Personalakten für Lasch, Otto.

[131] Yad Vashem Photo Archives 1603/2: Riga, Latvia, A festive parade of German soldiers on the anniversary of the city's occupation; 'Lasch-Bunker' Kaliningrad, interview with Süsskind-Schwendi. Today, the 'Oberst Lasch Straße' is called the Jura Alunãna iela.

[132] Walter Braemer, 'Zum Tage der Befreiung Rigas', *Ostland: Monatschrift des Reichskommissars Ostland*, 1 July 1942.

Figure 3.3 Far away from home: Lasch's regiment is deployed south of Leningrad, 1,000 kilometres from Königsberg, early 1942. *Source:* Author's collection

destruction of the city's Jewish population.[133] Lasch's memoirs betray consent, if not downright agreement, with the events of those days. Lasch specifically notes that during the battle of Riga also 'Bolshevik scum ['gesindel'] in civilian clothing took part in it', which leaves little doubt that many of these combatants, in line with the Barbarossa-Decree, would have been shot as partisans afterwards.[134]

In August 1942 Lasch was promoted to Generalmajor and a month later he was given command of the 217th Infanterie-Division, yet another unit consisting mainly of East Prussians. The unit was part of the Eighteenth

[133] Angrick and Klein, *The 'Final Solution' in Riga*, pp. 61–7, 76–8.
[134] See: Römer, 'Im alten Deutschland wäre solcher Befehl nicht möglich gewesen'.

Army, which besieged Leningrad – a siege that would result in the deaths of over one million civilians. Lasch's men were not directly facing the city but deployed some 50 miles to the south-west, emboldening Lasch in the post-war years to strongly dismiss the notion that he had been part of this war crime, which the siege had been classified as at the 1946 Nuremberg International Military Tribunal.[135] Given his career, it is extremely unlikely that this dismissal was routed in empathy or respect for his opponents. In November 1943 his 217th Infanterie-Division was disbanded after it was almost completely annihilated in the fighting in the Leningrad sector. Most of its staff were brought to St Omer in northern France, where later that month the 349th Infanterie-Division was built around them. Still commanded by Lasch, the newly formed division was sent to the Eastern Front in April 1944 and put into action in northern Ukraine, where the unit, once again consisting of a core of East Prussians, was destroyed within four months.[136]

After a week of leave in late August he was ordered to head to Dijon, France, where he was to head the LXIV. Korps. On his way, Lasch's column had to fight off 800 defected men from an *Ostbattalion*, which once again reinforced Lasch's profound mistrust in 'Russians'. His tenure as Korps commander was cut short, probably as a result of jaundice which took him away from the front, and in early November Lasch was ordered take up the position of Wehrkreis commander of East Prussia.[137] The new function, an administrative role, was initially not to Lasch's liking as he felt that it was not the best use of his skills. With the High Command's 'promise' that fighting would reach East Prussia soon enough, Lasch left for the province. Having fought a losing battle to defend the encroachment of the Slavs in his late twenties, he now found himself on the same crossroads, having to defend his adopted home of East Prussia, the place of birth of his wife and two daughters.[138]

Lasch's appointment as fortress commander took place during an unfolding crisis, which arose on 23 January 1945 when Soviet troops of the Third Belorussian Front crossed the river Deime, the last natural

[135] International Military Tribunal Nuremberg, *Trial of the Major War Criminals before the International Military Tribunal: Nuremberg 14 November 1945–1 October 1946, Volume VIII Official Text in the English Language, Proceedings 20 February 1946–7 March 1946* (Nuremberg: International Military Tribunal, 1947), pp. 112–31; Otto Lasch, *Zuckerbrot und Peitsche: Ein Bericht aus russischer Kriegsgefangenschaft: 20 Jahre danach* (Ilm: Ilmgau Verlag, 1965), pp. 67, 70–3.

[136] Tessin, *Verbände und Truppen der deutschen Wehrmacht, vol. 8*, s.v. '217'; Tessin, *Verbände und Truppen der deutschen Wehrmacht, vol. 9*, s.v. '349'; Lasch, *So fiel Königsberg*, p. 21.

[137] Dermot Bradley, Markus Rövekamp, and Ernes Henriot, *Deutschlands Generale und Admirale: Teil IV/ Band 7: Die Generale des Heeres 1921–1945. Knabe – Luz* (Osnabrück: Biblio-Verlag, 2004), pp. 395–6.

[138] BArch PERS 6/300107: Lasch, Bernhard Otto; Lasch, *So fiel Königsberg*, pp. 7, 17–23.

barrier before Königsberg. They had started their offensive into East Prussia seventy-five miles further to the east only ten days earlier.[139] Although the appointment was an army matter, Gauleiter Koch immediately sought to enhance his role. In the late hours of 27 January, he summoned Lasch and told him about a phone call he just had with Hitler. Stressing that Hitler had asked the Gauleiter about Lasch's 'qualification and reliability', Koch implied that his approval was needed in the process.[140] But in his memoirs, Lasch claims that when he was summoned by Koch, he told him that 'there would, in my opinion, be only one use [for me], which is as fortress commander'.[141] This implies both that Lasch was prepared to stand up to the Party and that he had already given sustained thought as to what was expected of him as a soldier.[142]

On the first evening of his appointment Lasch called several Party members and army commanders to his headquarters for a meeting. The general, according to Dr Eugen Sauvant, one of the officials present, spoke in a serious tone of the Führerbefehl to hold the city 'until the last bullet', thus stressing the gravity of the situation and in turn implying the existence of a direct link between Hitler and himself.[143] By doing so, he further diminished Gauleiter Koch's role in the fortress, but it was chiefly Koch's own behaviour that undercut his authority. By the time that Lasch held the meeting, Koch had already made a number of decisions that were not only frowned upon by the army, but by Party members as well. Since the Party was responsible for the population's evacuation, its actions were closely observed. When on 21 January Koch ordered the families of Gauleitung employees to be evacuated by a special train, panic struck among the population.[144] It was a decision that alarmed some of the more committed Party members. It seemed to confirm the pessimist prediction of propaganda ministry officials, who 'judged some 80 per cent of the 7 to 8 million Party members to be "driftwood", awaiting defeat'.[145] To add to this, on 27 January Koch suddenly announced the general evacuation of Königsberg, preparing neither the population nor the Party for it. Not

---

[139] BArch Ost-Dok. 8/510, p. 15: Dieckert; Erickson, *The Road to Berlin*, pp. 455, 465–9.

[140] Lasch, *So fiel Königsberg*, pp. 37–8, 128; Archiv Kulturzentrum Ostpreußen (hereafter AKO) 22034–4, Hauptmann d. Res. Sommer: *Vermerk*.

[141] Lasch, *So fiel Königsberg*, p. 37.

[142] On the establishment of an independently thinking German officer corps and its importance in the Second World War, see for example: Hürter, *Hitlers Heerführer*, p. 63; Römer, *Kameraden*, p. 297; See also: David H. Kitterman, 'Those Who Said 'No!': Germans Who Refused to Execute Civilians during World War II', *German Studies Review* (11) 1988, pp. 241–54.

[143] AKO 22034-4: Sauvant: *Die letzten Tage von Königsberg*, 2.

[144] AKO 22034-4: Aufzeichnungen des Hauptschriftleiters der *KAZ* Wegener; Max Hastings, *Armageddon: the Battle for Germany, 1944–45* (London: Macmillan, 2004), p. 322.

[145] Hancock, *The National Socialist Leadership and Total War*, p. 142.

only were Soviet troops already within striking distance by then, the temperature at the time was well below minus twenty degrees.[146] Meanwhile, Koch was absent from Lasch's meeting since he had 'relocated' to Pillau.[147] This behaviour damaged his reputation among three of his closest remaining subordinates, Waldemar Magunia, Kreisleiter Ernst Wagner, and Deputy Gauleiter Ferdinand Grossherr.[148] As the front neared Germany in late 1944, Gauleiter were drilled on the fact that they were expected to set the example of steadfastness for the rest of the population, assuring that the German population would 'feel personally responsible for contributing to the Volk's defence in its hour of mortal peril'.[149] They would repeatedly be reminded of this duty in the months that followed, and throughout 1945 Bormann would occasionally send telegrams and memorandums stressing that they were expected to 'fight or fall within their areas of responsibility'.[150] Koch's thinly veiled flight corroded his authority as well as that of those Party officials who 'relocated' with him.

A comparison with Gauleiter Karl Hanke of Lower Silesia immediately shows the close link between authority and the decision to stay put. Hanke did not leave his besieged capital of Breslau, earning him numerous accolades. His ability to hold sway over, and even to dismiss, the fortress commander of Breslau was in sharp contrast with Gauleiter Koch's attempts to do the same.[151] It had long been commonly held within Party circles that the Party's 'spirit' rested on the willingness of its committed members to take things into their own hands which had proven of vital importance in the early days of its existence, the *Kampfzeit*. That theme was dusted off as the tide of the war turned, and from 1943 onwards 'Party propaganda spoke relentlessly of the crucial experience of the Kampfzeit, through which obstacles should be overcome'.[152] Thus, although Koch had boasted that Königsberg was to be held to the last man, he now appeared insincere, cowardly, and

---

[146] BArch Ost-Dok. 8/580, pp. 2–3: Zerahn; BArch Ost-Dok. 8/588, p. 9: Dr. Will; Lasch, *So fiel Königsberg*, 36.

[147] Edgar Lass, *Die Flucht, Ostpreussen 1944/45* (Bad Neuheim: Podzun-Verlag, 1964), p. 196.

[148] Werner Terpitz, *Wege aus dem Osten. Flucht und Vertreibung einer ostpreußischen Pfarrersfamilie* (Munich: Oldenbourg Wissenschaftsverlag, 1997), p. 46; Meindl, *Ostpreußens Gauleiter Erich Koch*, pp. 92–3, 445; AKO 22034-4: Magunia: *Abschrift*, 3; AKO 22034: Dorfmüller: *Zusammenstoß*. Wagner was sent to the fortress on the night of 27–8 January 1945: Lasch, *So fiel Königsberg*, p. 65.

[149] Yelton, *Hitler's Volkssturm*, p. 26.

[150] Earl Beck, *Under the Bombs: the German Home Front 1942–1945* (Kentucky, University Press of Kentucky, 1986), pp. 187–8.

[151] Noble, *Nazi Rule and the Soviet Offensive*, pp. 202–4, 221–5. Most noteworthy is Hanke's appointment as Reichsführer-SS in late April 1945 after Heinrich Himmler lost his credibility to Hitler.

[152] Mommsen, 'The Indian Summer and the Collapse of the Third Reich', pp. 116–19.

irresponsible.[153] The remaining Party members realised that it was the army, headed by Lasch, which actually followed up on the promises.[154] Privately Lasch had his doubts about holding the city, but he did not share these with Party members. According to Dr Sauvant, the general told him that 'we know what awaits us. We can probably hold the city for some time, but Germany is lost. We can no longer hope for the city to be relieved in the current war situation. What happens next, the gods know.'[155] This uncertainty was omnipresent in all branches of the Wehrmacht during these days in Königsberg.

Gauleiter Koch's move to Pillau effectively cut East Prussia's Party elite in two, as it created a clear dividing line between those who left and those who stayed behind. The remaining Party members now had more in common with the army commanders in Königsberg, and this notion shaped their perception of the unfolding events. Yet these Party members saw that, besides the Party, army units also abandoned Königsberg, and had already noticed similar behaviour before, notably in Ukraine and on the borders of East Prussia the previous summers.[156] Luftwaffe men were seen retreating through Volkssturm lines and blew up their cannons before having fired a single shot.[157] The *Kriegsmarine* had a number of warships sail to the western Baltic, near Denmark, while orders were passed down to destroy docks and other harbour installations.[158] Most of the army staffs left Königsberg as well.[159]

Although the remaining Party members condemned the departure of their colleagues, they were much more forgiving in their assessment of the armed forces. They seemed relatively unconcerned by the Wehrmacht's behaviour and focused on those who remained in Königsberg instead. To explain this behaviour, a few general observations might be made. By and large, in Party circles personal loyalty trumped any reliance on

[153] BArch Ost-Dok. 8/588, p. 9: Dr. Will; Meindl, *Ostpreußens Gauleiter Erich Koch*, p. 436.
[154] Lasch, *So fiel Königsberg*, pp. 41–64; Rendulic, *Gekämpft, gesiegt, geschlagen*, pp. 337-40; Werner Haupt, *Als die Rote Armee nach Deutschland kam* (Friedberg: Podzun-Pallas-Verlag, 1981), p. 19.
[155] AKO 22034-4: Sauvant: *Die letzten Tage von Königsberg*, p. 2.
[156] Noble, *Nazi Rule and the Soviet Offensive*, p. 100.
[157] BArch Ost-Dok. 8/510, p. 26: Dieckert; TNA HW 1/3495: BONIFACE report, 30 January 1945; AKO 22034-4: Aufzeichnungen des Hauptschriftleiters der *KAZ* Wegener, p. 2.
[158] TNA HW 1/3479: Intelligence Report 25 January 1945; TNA HW 1/3495: BONIFACE report, 30 January 1945.
[159] On the evacuation of the Third Panzer Army, see: BArch Ost-Dok. 8/557, p. 10: Müller-Hillebrand. On Luftwaffe evacuation see: Dieckert and Großmann, *Der Kampf um Ostpreussen*, p. 216. On the evacuation of the Wehrkreis staff, see: Lasch, *So fiel Königsberg*, pp. 10, 35. On the general chaos among staff in late January 1945, see: BArch Ost-Dok. 8/510, p. 26: Dieckert.

institutional patterns.[160] Gauleiter Koch's move west was undoubtedly considered disloyal by those – and to those – who stayed behind. Furthermore, it was evident to even the staunchest National Socialist that once a Soviet offensive was set in motion, the German army could not easily halt it. The army was above all responsible for the protection of Reich territory, and the Wehrmacht's departure from the city might thus be a bitter necessity, while the *Parteiflucht* inherently meant self-preservation at the expense of the civilian population they left behind.[161] On 18 January 1945, an editorial in the *Königsberger Allgemeine Zeitung* stressed that 'the strength of a people never solely lies in its weapons. Wars are always and only decided by the inner strength and the will of a people.'[162] Whereas the army showed a willingness to defend the city, most Party members did not express this at all. Moreover, from the first moment Lasch actively involved Königsberg's Party members in the city's defence it not only ensured that they believed they were taken seriously, it also placed them against the Party members who had fled.[163]

Friction continued to exist throughout the siege between the Party and the Wehrmacht but at the same time the two sides tried to reach something of a 'civil truce' in order to mobilise the local population.[164] Despite their hopeless situation, the Party–state–Wehrmacht collaboration in besieged Königsberg continued to be characterised by a willingness to continue to function as before, even though the insistence on the continuation of the city's governmental machinery could not really be rationalised, nor its use easily explained.[165] Shortly after his appointment as fortress commander, Lasch moved to the Oberpostdirektion, the regional post administration, at the Hansaring in the north-west of the city. Although Gauleiter Koch still disagreed with the Party's subordinate role in Königsberg, he nevertheless appointed Kreisleiter Ernst Wagner as *Festungsbeauftragte der NSDAP* among the lines of Guderian's scheme.

Wagner almost immediately reached out to Lasch: although the Kreisleiter could have chosen to move into the Gauhaus on the Grosse Schlossteichstrasse, he instead set up his 'post' in the Rundfunkhaus, across the street from Lasch.[166] Wagner was a committed and proud National

---

[160] Mommsen, *The Indian Summer and the Collapse of the Third Reich*, p. 112; Martin Broszat, *The Hitler State: the Foundation and Development of the Internal Structure of the Third Reich* (London: Longman, 1981), p. 44.

[161] AKO 22034-4: Schäfer: *Der Fall Königsbergs*, p. 2.

[162] 'Die Stärke', *Königsberger Allgemeine Zeitung*, 18 January 1945.

[163] AKO 22034-4: Magunia: *Abschrift*, pp. 3–4.   [164] Broszat, *The Hitler State*, p. 22.

[165] Werner, *'Bleib übrig!'*, pp. 350–2.

[166] AKO 22034-4: Wegener: *Der Untergang von Königsberg*; Telefonbuch Königsberg 1941: s.v. 'Nationalsozialistische Deutsche Arbeiterpartei Dienststellen in Königsberg'; BArch Ost-Dok. 8/580, p. 4: Zerahn.

Figure 3.4 Kreisleiter Ernst Wagner (in his function as Volkssturm-Führer Nord) at an office of a Volkssturm unit near the East Prussian border, November 1944. *Source:* akg-images / Sammlung Berliner Verlag / Archiv

Socialist, a true 'guarantor of the National Socialist revolution'.[167] He had interrupted his political career to serve in the 1st Infanterie-Division and returned from active service in January 1944 to assume his role once again as Kreisleiter of Königsberg. As such, he possessed the perfect mix of ideology and military spirit needed for his new appointment a year later.[168] Wagner became Lasch's point man for civilian matters and, even twelve years after the fact, the general noted that Wagner 'did his duty in every respect'.[169]

---

[167] Barbara Fait: 'Die Kreisleiter der NSDAP – nach 1945', in Broszat, Henke, and Woller (eds.), *Von Stalingrad zur Währungsreform*, p. 224.

[168] Tilitzki, *Alltag in Ostpreußen*, p. 267. The interruption of his political career might not have been completely voluntary, but within the assessment of his loyalties by 1945, this is irrelevant.

[169] Lasch, *So fiel Königsberg*, p. 65.

Königsberg's Oberbürgermeister (mayor), Dr Hellmuth Will, also stayed behind in the city.[170] Will was a career civil servant who had been Königsberg's mayor since 3 May 1933. He was one of the few big city mayors who did not owe this position to his loyalty to the NSDAP and joined the Party only two days prior to his appointment. As this fact surely exposed him to accusations of opportunism, he 'would be very dependent on the Gauleiter', and the appointment might very well have been a shrewd calculation on Koch's behalf.[171] Whether Will truly internalised National Socialist teachings in the years that followed can therefore be questioned, but he nevertheless symbolises the preparedness of the state to fight when called upon: Will offered city hall to be made available as a Volkssturm collection point, and later as department for the 'Health service in combat sector Festung Königsberg'.[172] Dr Will himself led a Volkssturm battalion, remained in close contact with General Lasch, and eventually went into Soviet captivity, where he stayed until 1955. He received widespread praise, but his presence was largely symbolic: Will was subordinated to Kreisleiter Wagner, while the city's day-to-day administration was largely left to Rechtsanwald Dr Kurt Eske.[173]

The Wehrmacht, for its part, reached out as well. After hearing that the cooperation between the Wehrmacht and the Party was poor, 'especially in East Prussia' (a clear reference to Gauleiter Koch), the Party chancellery asked for the appointment of 'a liaison officer between the Army Group and the *Gauleiter und RV-Kommissaren*'. It would be his task to keep the Gauleiter informed on the military situation, and generally to liaise with the Party.[174] On his first day as fortress commander Lasch appointed Major der Reserve Gunther Ipsen to this position. The National Socialist credentials of Ipsen, who during peace time had been a sociology professor at the Albertina University in Königsberg and in Vienna were beyond dispute. He had joined the NSDAP in 1937, the same year in which he claimed to consider laws protecting minorities as an invention of the Jews, and as a metaphorical 'order of battle against the German people's will to live'.[175] Moreover, during the war Ipsen had

[170] BArch Ost-Dok. 8/588: Dr. Will.
[171] Jeremy Noakes, 'Oberbürgermeister and Gauleiter. City Government Between Party and State', in Hirschfeld and Kettenacker (eds.), The 'Führer State', pp. 198–9.
[172] Die NSDAP Ostpreußen, 'Hier spricht die Partei', Festung Königsberg, 2 February 1945.
[173] Will, for example, was used as a figurehead in the call to use gas and electricity in moderation. AKO 23304-2: Kemsies: Stimmungsbilder aus Königsberg.
[174] BArch RW 4/704, p. 3: WFSt/Qu 2 (Ost) Nr. 0150/45 geh. F.H.Q., den 6.1.1945 Betr.: Rücksprache mit dem Sachbearbeiter der Parteikanzlei für Evakuierungsfrage.
[175] BArch Ost-Dok. 8/586, p. 3: Werbke; Christian Tillitzki, 'Wie ein versunkenes Vineta, Albertina 1944–1945', Ostpreußenblatt, 25 September 1999, p. 12; Ingo Haar, Historiker im Nationalsozialismus: deutsche Geschichtswissenschaft und der 'Volkstumskampf' im Osten (Göttingen: Vanderhoeck & Ruprecht, 2002), p. 309.

proved to be an outstanding soldier as well, receiving the German Cross in Gold and the *Nahkampfspange* (close-combat clasp) while serving with the 1st Infanterie-Division, which meant that he had even participated in days-long hand-to-hand combat.[176]

Ipsen was one of the three officers Lasch brought with him from the Wehrkreis command to become part of Königsberg's fortress staff. The two other men were Oberst Hugo Freiherr von Süsskind-Schwendi and Oberstleutnant Dr Eugen Sauvant.[177] Von Süsskind-Schwendi – an aristocratic Berliner who had been part of the 100,000-man Reichswehr – became the fortress's chief of staff, having earlier served under Lasch in northern Russia as chief of staff of the hard-pressed 217th Infanterie-Division. The two men greatly respected each other. After the war, von Süsskind-Schwendi remembered with some pride the 'tug of war' leading up to his appointment: no one less than Field Marshal Wilhelm Keitel saw him fit to become the chief of staff of an Army, but he eventually took up the position of Lasch's chief of staff after the latter's 'expressly pronounced wish' to work with his former subordinate.[178] Lastly, Dr Eugen Sauvant came over from the Wehrkreis command as a seasoned quartermaster. The responsibilities of quartermasters were generally broadly defined, but above all concerned matters of logistics. During the first days of Königsberg's fortress era, however, Lasch entrusted Sauvant with a specific task that was peripheral to this function: the restoration of order through means of summary courts (see Chapter 6).[179] These six men – General Lasch, Kreisleiter Wagner, Oberbürgermeister Will, Major Ipsen, Oberst von Süsskind-Schwendi, and Oberstleutnant Sauvant – formed the nucleus of the fortress staff. The careers of these men had been shaped by National Socialism and they had internalised (in some cases propagated) its values. The more unique denominator these men shared and prided themselves on, service in an East Prussian military unit, meant that a martial, 'Prussian' mindset would most likely predominate.

---

[176] BArch Ost-Dok. 8/591, p. 42: Heysing.

[177] BArch Ost-Dok. 10/888, p. 30: Dieckert; Lasch, *So fiel Königsberg*, pp. 128–9.

[178] Hugo Frhr. von Süßkind-Schwendi: 'Aus meinem Soldatenleben – Teil V', *Deutsches Soldatenjahrbuch* (41) 1993, p. 350. Although his conviction is undeniably sincere, this reading should be treated with some care. Von Süsskind-Schwendi steers away from saying that he was asked by Lasch to serve as the fortress's chief of staff, although he actively implies it. In reality, Lasch first asked him to become his chief of staff at the *Stellv. Gen. Kdo. I.* in early January 1945, and it appears that von Süßkind-Schwendi simply followed Lasch to his new appointment. See: BArch Pers 6/282148: Personalakten Frhr. von Süßkind-Schwendi, Hugo.

[179] Lasch, *So fiel Königsberg*, pp. 57–9.

During the first days of Königsberg's siege, Party and Wehrmacht established a local balance of power. More than anything else, a fairly pragmatic assessment of the situation 'on the ground' shaped the behavioural patterns at the fortress command. In this rapidly changing environment Berlin was far away, which meant that ideological commitment – although it manifested itself in the fortress staff's behaviour – was of limited immediate concern. In this sense, their behaviour was reminiscent of the *Kampfzeit*, during which National Socialism might have served as an ideological fundament, but one's initiative was of key importance to overcome challenges. The process was not sophisticated: Gauleiter Koch and General Lasch played a local power game. But this nevertheless had important stakes: the moral authority over the city. The flight of the Party provided Lasch with enough leverage to assume authority. After the war he would define Königsberg's community as 'one big family that worked together for better and for worse' (within the German martial tradition, rooted in patriarchy, this made him the 'father' of this community).[180] Kreisleiter Wagner saw it as a 'clean and tough community of hardship'.[181] Both descriptions – especially Lasch's – are self-serving, but nevertheless show that the Total War experience of the civilians in Festung Königsberg was defined by those present in the city itself, rather than by distant Party officials and Wehrmacht commanders, or by broadly defined regulations. Indeed, the cooperation between the two actors shows that the dynamics in Festung Königsberg should not be framed as 'fanatical Party versus an unwilling Wehrmacht'. Although the two actors might have had different motivations to keep fighting as the city was being encircled by late January 1945, that willingness *in itself* was strongly present among the Königsberg's Party elite as well as the Wehrmacht commanders charged with the city's defence.

Conclusion

A fortress is a structure that is built to withstand attacks from outside. When, during a siege, those inside the fortress think and act in unison, they have the best chance to withstand it. In a country dotted with castles this conception was considered self-evident, and it did not take long before Nazi propagandists realised that 'Festung' could also serve as a powerful metonymy for the defensibility of the Volksgemeinschaft itself. The term won in popularity as the war progressed and in its figurative

---

[180] Lasch, *So fiel Königberg*, p. 64.
[181] Ernst *Wagner*, '*Aufruf an der Königsberger Volkssturm*', 5 February 1945, quoted in Lasch, *So fiel Königberg*, pp. 139–40.

sense became part of the Third Reich's vocabulary. From 8 March 1944 onwards 'Festung' also assumed a literal meaning as the German High Command implemented the fortress strategy. Initially in the Soviet Union, but from autumn 1944 onwards also in Germany itself, urban areas were incorporated into larger defensive systems, a process that served as a clear harbinger that Total War was about to impact on the population's immediate environment. The defence of cities themselves was unparalleled in modern German history, but as the country was highly urbanised there were no other valid options. Moreover, since both the German High Command and the members of Hitler's intimate circle ruled in favour of an active involvement of civilians in the defence of their Heimat, they pushed forward with the strategy.

The decision to defend German cities was not well received. Troops had long dreaded fighting in cities and equated them with military setbacks, with Stalingrad as the most obvious example, a notion that was only confirmed during Operation Bagration. In the summer of 1944 fortresses had been overrun or encircled with the death or capture of their German garrisons as a result. Local Party elites, in turn, saw their authority being challenged by the increasing powers the military was granted to organise the defence of cities on home soil. To prevent further inroads into their power, Party members repeatedly questioned the Wehrmacht's loyalty to the Volksgemeinschaft. This constant hammering of reliability linked actual authority over cities to the issue of 'moral authority'. Yet when in January 1945 the fighting for 'fortress Königsberg' was about to commence, numerous Wehrmacht staffs and significant elements of the Party elite, including Gauleiter Koch himself, left the city. Those who remained only concerned themselves with immediate problems and sought to find common ground in the mutual determination to keep the city out of Soviet hands. That utilitarianism required a fortress-specific vocabulary which diverted from the regime's official line. The next chapter will examine the language that was used in the fortress and determine the extent to which Königsberg's garrison broke with the visions of the Volksgemeinschaft, and what motivations lay behind that process.

4   Redefining Königsberg: Historical Continuity in Practice

Introduction

By late January 1945 the Soviet offensive into East Prussia had success-fully managed to cut off Königsberg and its wider environs from the rest of Germany. The exodus of Party and military authorities caused a brief power vacuum but with the establishment of the fortress staff, governance returned. After these turbulent days, the local administration resumed and would remain firmly in place until the final storming commenced on 6 April.[1] This chapter seeks to answer how and why those in charge during this period sought to define their community. Whereas military and Party authorities in some areas surrendered without a single shot, others, like in Königsberg, decided to fight to the last bullet. This cannot be solely explained by an assessment of the opposing forces involved and concerns about the post-war era; self-image, as we will see, was of decisive importance. Significant energy was expended to propagate the 'new' values of Festung Königsberg that better presented the fighting. On 31 January 1945, within a few days of Königsberg's encirclement, *Die Festung Königsberg*, the 'battle-paper for labourers, soldiers, and men of the Volkssturm', was published for the first time.[2] That tagline hinted at a search for identity. Indeed, a week later this message had been altered, while the official Party newspaper of East Prussia's NSDAP branch, the *Preußische Zeitung*, presented itself as a 'paper for the entire Volksgemeinschaft', which was explained as 'Wehrmacht, Volkssturm and population'.[3] Königsberg would be defined by a set of values on which those in the city could agree rather than by values imposed on them by Berlin.

The need to define a communal 'fortress-identity' had emerged in late 1944, when military and Party authorities discerned a drop in morale and

---

[1] Dieckert and Großmann, *Der Kampf um Ostpreussen*, p. 151; AKO 22034–4: Aufzeichnungen des Hauptschriftleiters der *KAZ* Wegener, 3; AKO 22034–4: Magunia, *Abschrift*, 10: Lasch, *So fiel Königsberg*, p. 35.
[2] BArch Ost-Dok. 10/890, pp. 176–7: Dieckert.   [3] *Preußische Zeitung*, 8 February 1945.

a lack of discipline among both population and troops. This negative mood surfaced mainly because few of those remaining in East Prussia still bought into the idea of a clear path to victory, which prompted propagandists to search for an alternative message. Among the general populace, the authorities estimated, a deep-rooted attitude persisted that the defensive war fought on home soil lacked favourable prospects or a deeper purpose. To counter these sentiments, and to cement its rule, Königsberg's fortress command tapped into a traditional discourse of 'banal nationalism', thereby allowing the army to once again perceive itself as the guarantor of the country's historical continuity.[4] Yet, in order to eventually link the new state of affairs in Königsberg to the violence it engendered, this chapter goes beyond an analysis of the new propagandist course. For the people trapped in Königsberg, the siege saw the transformation of their society from a Volksgemeinschaft to a Kampfgemeinschaft, with Kampf in turn changing from a conceptual 'struggle' to an actual 'battle' (i.e. from a 'community of struggle' to a 'battle-community'). Whether they agreed with the new course or could identify with this newly imposed identity is less known. This chapter will examine whether the parameters of the new Kampfgemeinschaft indeed represented Königsberg's community.

Towards a Closer Collaboration

On 12 and 13 January 1945, the Second and Third Belorussian Fronts started the East Prussian offensive. The artillerist Kurt Orgel, who after being wounded awaited transport from the port of Pillau, initially misjudged it as a 'small, local counter-attack', showing the success of the propagandist efforts at downplaying the threat.[5] On 16 January, the Königsberger Allgemeine Zeitung described the 'German soldiers as a wall around East Prussia', promising that the attackers would 'bleed to death' on the positions that had earlier been dug.[6] Two days later, as the offensive still showed no signs of slowing down, the newspaper adopted a more cautious tone, and steeped its lead article in military jargon. It was claimed that, due to the sheer mass of forces, the offensive was bound to gain some initial ground, but 'the defence needs to set aside a certain amount of time to deploy its operational and tactical reserves'.[7] The

---

[4] Malešević, Identity As Ideology, pp. 146–50, 204–6.
[5] Stargardt, The German War, pp. 492–3.
[6] 'Deutsche Soldaten wie eine Mauer um Ostpreußen', Königsberger Allgemeine Zeitung, 16 January 1945.
[7] 'Verbissener Widerstand gegen Massenansturm', Königsberger Allgemeine Zeitung, 18 January 1945.

Map 4.1 The Red Army's advance through East Prussia in January 1945

Soviets, however, kept pushing even after the reserves had been deployed: the Third Belorussian Front captured Tilsit on 20 January and Gumbinnen on 21 January, while on 23 January troops of the Second Belorussian Front reached the Frische Haff lagoon east of Elbing, cutting off the troops north-east of it from the brunt of the German forces.[8] On 29 January Soviet troops completed the encirclement of Königsberg. This had a big impact on morale.[9] 'The awareness of being trapped severely

---

[8] Grier, *Hitler, Dönitz, and the Baltic Sea*, pp. 109–12.
[9] BArch Ost-Dok. 8/588, p. 2: Dr. Will.

affected the mood', a company commander later noted about the atmosphere in his unit.[10] The remaining civilians were even more affected by the new circumstances. Suicide was openly discussed, making it abundantly clear how little trust the population had in the defenders.[11] Indeed, in the first two weeks of the encirclement about 120 people committed suicide, largely out of fear for their imminent future at the hands of the Soviets.[12]

In turn, the presence of large numbers of soldiers who were often openly hostile to Party members emboldened many civilians to express their aversion, something that until a few weeks earlier had only been possible in private.[13] Growing numbers lost trust in the sincerity of official propaganda, eroding the fundaments of the National Socialist system. Furthermore, not only were local Party members seen to be dodging military service throughout the war, but it was evident that Gauleiter Koch and his Kreisleiter had been shamelessly enriching themselves during times in which the average standard of living continuously dropped.[14] All this added to stresses within the fortress.

There was also a growing external threat. With the front pressed against Königsberg, the Soviets made sustained attempts to influence its garrison and population.[15] The lead role in this effort was reserved to the NKFD, the Nationalkomitee Freies Deutschland, an anti-fascist movement consisting of former German prisoners of war and left-wing German émigrés. The main task of the NKFD in East Prussia was to convince its population to turn their backs on the Nazi regime, a course it had pursued since early 1944.[16] Throughout 1944 their means had been too limited to make any impact, while Goebbels' atrocity propaganda had undermined their credibility: they were no longer merely seen as consorting with Germany's enemies, but rather as facilitators of their bestial behaviour. 'Russian

[10] BArch Ost-Dok. 10/889, p. 60: Dieckert.
[11] Schieder, *Dokumentation der Vertreibung der Deutschen aus Ost-Mitteleuropa I, Band 1*, p. 83; Von Lehndorff, *Ostpreußisches Tagebuch*, p. 24.
[12] BArch Ost-Dok. 10/888, p. 32: Dieckert; Goeschel, *Suicide in Nazi Germany*, pp. 156–66.
[13] Hensel, *Medizin in und aus Ostpreußen*, pp. 72–3.
[14] Kater, *The Nazi Party*, pp. 213–15; Meindl, *Ostpreußens Gauleiter Erich Koch*, pp. 191–4; Dieckert and Großmann, *Der Kampf um Ostpreussen*, p. 43.
[15] 'The refutation of enemy propaganda' was of increasing importance during this stage of the war. See: IfZArch MA 757: Persönlicher Stab Reichsführer-SS, Schriftverwaltung Akt.Nr. Geh./ 353. H.Qu., den 23. Februar 1945. Oberkommando der Heeresgruppe Weichsel, Via/ NSF: Richtlinien für die Arbeit des NSFO.
[16] Perry Biddiscombe, '"Freies Deutschland" Guerrilla Warfare in East Prussia, 1944–1945: a Contribution to the History of the German Resistance', *German Studies Association* (27) 2004, pp. 45–62; See also: Gerd Ueberschär (ed.), *Das Nationalkomitee "Freies Deutschland" und der Bund Deutscher Offiziere* (Frankfurt a.M.: Fischer Verlag, 1996).

propaganda in East Prussia', a British intelligence report noted in November 1944, 'is now a complete failure. Nobody pays the slightest attention to it'.[17] But during the two-month siege of Königsberg the NKFD became more accepted as an alternative news source. Loudspeaker cars were used on a large scale to stress the hopelessness of Königsberg's garrison, interspersed with tempting promises to those who were willing to give up the fight. On other occasions reports of the Sovinformburo (Soviet Information Bureau – the Soviet state news agency) were read out, describing the Soviet advance or the conclusions reached at the Yalta Conference.[18] The artillery spotter Wolfgang Eisenblätter was repeatedly exposed to this propaganda, and after the war acknowledged that 'the arguments were indeed plausible to us', although, at the same time he stressed that 'they did not have the intended motivational effect'.[19]

Finally, creating mood-raising propaganda to bolster the soldiers' resolve was considered a military necessity. Commanders realised that troops' dejected mood, stemming from the massive casualties suffered during the previous weeks, severely threatened combat performance. Elevating this mood meant stressing that at all times a soldier was part of the Wehrmacht – 'the strong protector and shield for the life of the people and the existence of the Reich' – and conduct himself accordingly.[20] With the military ethos distorted by the years of brutal warfare, during which commanders unceasingly demanded disproportionate sacrifices of their soldiers, even the clear absence of a path to victory did not change the preparedness of higher commands to expose the troops to enormous risks.[21] What mattered above all was that soldiers would always know how to muster the courage and willpower to serve as a 'strong protector and shield'. The idea that numerical or technological superiority was of only subordinate importance to fulfil his duty had been drilled into a man's mind since his first days as a recruit: rather than focusing on the development of specialist skills, German military training was structured in such a way that men would learn to endure the strain of

---

[17] TNA HW 1/3341, Germany: Morale of Armies in East Prussia, 22 November 1944.
[18] Louis Clappier, *Festung Königsberg* (Cologne: Kiepenheuer & Witsch, 1952), p. 132; Balfour, *Propaganda in War*, p. 360; Guido Knopp, *Der Sturm: Kriegsende im Osten* (Berlin: Econ, 2004), pp. 90–1; AKO 22034–4: Banneitz: *Erlebnisbericht*, p. 2; Alexander Marinov, *Komsomol v soldatskoj shineli* [Komsomol in a soldier's overcoat] (Moscow: Voenizdat, 1988), p. 98.
[19] Ostpreußisches Landesmuseum (hereafter OL): XI E 2 Eisenblätter Eis, Wolfgang Eisenblätter *Von Königsberg nach sonstwohin, Aus dem Leben einer Ponarther Familie*, p. 23.
[20] Hermann Foertsch, *Der Offizier der deutschen Wehrmacht: Eine Pflichtenlehre* (Berlin: Verlag E. Eisenschmidt, 1942), p. 12.
[21] Stahel, 'The Wehrmacht and National Socialist Military Thinking', p. 339.

war. By putting young men under stress, so the reasoning went, they would discover their inner reserves, as such permanently boosting their confidence, elevating their morale, and teaching them to cope with the war's psychological dimensions.[22] With the opportunity to properly train recruits dropping to an absolute minimum by 1945, raising morale by means of propaganda gained even more importance. With the Party possessing the necessary means to do so (which, moreover, left more troops to focus on the army's core task of fighting), there was certainly scope from the army's point of view for a closer collaboration.

The fortress command was forced to craft its own message because of the largely failed appeal of national propaganda, the military necessity of providing troops with tangible reasons to keep fighting, and, to a lesser extent in view of their traitorous reputation, the need to counter the propaganda of the NKFD. In the face of seemingly imminent defeat, their efforts might appear senseless, but as shown by the often illogical ways in which the public reacted to adverse wartime experiences, human nature leaves ample scope to exploit the widespread uncertainty amongst the broader population.[23] These illogical consequences of the uncertainty were fully acknowledged by both soldiers and propagandists independently of one another. On both the British and the German home front, whenever communities experienced adverse events, their inhabitants, rather than being dejected, almost immediately showed clear signs of resilience and adaptability. It escaped few propagandists that residents of bombed-out neighbourhoods consistently showed a level of determination unrivalled by their compatriots. Goebbels often visited these areas, and drew a strong parallel between experiences on the home front and those of the fighting troops; he notably explained to a group of 'Sebastopol heroes' in August 1942 that morale was highest in German districts which had suffered the most, much like the military, where morale similarly was always higher at the front than at the rear.[24] This line of reasoning likened the 'front' to the 'home front', and, since military thinking principally determined the state of affairs in Königsberg, it did not take long for this reasoning to be adopted and taken to the extreme.

The second pillar of propaganda in Königsberg was built around its local identity. This course could not be pursued in every part of Germany since it inevitably placed the city or town in question on a more equal footing to the regime, which could have unanticipated corollaries. Highlighting the importance of a city's history, culture, and architecture

[22] Hew Strachan, 'Training, Morale and Modern War', *Journal of Contemporary History* (41) 2006, pp. 211–7.
[23] See: Tversky and Kahneman, 'Judgment under Uncertainty'.
[24] Balfour, *Propaganda in War*, p. 286.

might encourage individuals to devote all their energy to ensuring its preservation, rather than fighting for Germany or National Socialism. It would, moreover, draw attention to an alternative which more and more people were starting to contemplate: rather than their city becoming a battleground for the preservation of National Socialism, would it not be better to consider Allied rule if it meant sparing their city? In the parts of Western Germany that were still in German hands, some newspapers even cautiously started to refer to a post-war world, deliberately overlooking whether this was a world under Allied or Nazi rule.[25] In Königsberg, where the alternative was Soviet rule, the number of people who pursued this line of thought was negligible.

The new direction propagandists in the city took did not necessarily represent a deliberate break with the earlier Nazi propaganda, but merely placed different emphases on topics than the earlier propaganda, while other topics were downplayed or disregarded. The course they chose can best be described as the adoption of 'banal nationalism', a locally oriented Kampfgemeinschaft which harked back to Königsberg's past. Banality, it should be stressed, should not be confused with harmlessness: 'banal nationalism' serves to reproduce 'institutions which possess vast armaments' that 'can be mobilised without lengthy campaigns of political preparation'.[26] During the siege of Königsberg this nationalism was used to search for 'continuity' in German history by increasing the impact historical feats had on its garrison and the population while also downplaying the influence of National Socialism.

The previous chapter showed that by late January 1945 the balance of power in the fortress had tipped in favour of the Wehrmacht. That two army propaganda companies (Heereskriegsberichterzug Mitte and Propagandakompanie 689) arrived with the retreating troops further increased the army's influence.[27] Yet it was the Party that presided over Königsberg's press and radio. According to the war correspondent Günther Heysing, the Reichssender Königsberg (where Kreisleiter Wagner had set up his command post) remained the 'voice of the fortress' throughout Königsberg's siege.[28] As a timely evacuation of the staff and the printing presses of the Preußische Zeitung to Fischhausen (a village that fell under Gauleiter Koch's authority) had failed, they also remained

---

[25] Fritz, *Endkampf*, p. 35.

[26] Michael Billig, *Banal Nationalism* (London: Sage, 1995), pp. 6–7.

[27] Jörg Wurdack, 'Propagandatruppen des Heeres', www.lexikon-der-wehrmacht.de/Glie derungen/Propaganda/Propaganda-R.htm

[28] BArch Ost-Dok. 8/591, p. 49: Heysing; Grunberger, *A Social History of the Third Reich*, pp. 401–2.

available to the fortress.[29] Thus the army had to work with the Party in this task. The new collaboration could best be observed at the Ostpreußische Druckerei. Not only did it print the official Party newspapers and provide the administrational documents (such as ration cards), it also started printing divisional newspapers and military pamphlets. When the power supply in the fortress became unreliable, the army in turn supplied the press with one of its own generators to keep it going.[30] As a result, from the beginning of the siege sustained efforts were made to convey a message on which both the Wehrmacht and the Party could agree. The next sections will examine what this message entailed.

Abandoning the Greater Good

For many of those trapped in Festung Königsberg, the East Prussian offensive confirmed the negative image of the regime that had matured during 1944. It lay bare the regime's limitations, above all showing that its role as the 'guardian of the Volksgemeinschaft' was, by 1945, grossly misplaced. Elements of four battle-hardened divisions reached the city before the Red Army surrounded it in late January: parts of the 1st Infanterie-Division, the 5th Panzer-Division, remnants of the 69th Infanterie-Division, and the 367th Infanterie-Division. Other divisions would arrive in the city throughout the siege. Most of these men, as we saw in Chapter 2, defended the province without adhering to greater ideals. The other significant group of actors that found itself trapped in the city, initially numbering around 200,000, was the civilian population, which consisted of local inhabitants and refugees. Within these groups a wide range of (predominantly negative) attitudes could be discerned, although the one common denominator was that all considered the situation to be bleak. Königsberg's defence, in short, lacked purpose, yet the anticipated siege would demand a strong moral backbone of civilians and soldiers alike. A siege, after all, is meant to force the hand of the defenders: often it is not the anticipated destruction of the troops inside the besieged city but rather the spectre of a starving and suffering population that would sway a commander to surrender. At the fortress command, headed by General Lasch (who had served as a high-ranking commander with Army Group North as it besieged Leningrad) these dynamics were well understood. Moreover, it was clear that many in the city were tired of war and cared little about the role Königsberg played

---

[29] AKO 22034–4: Aufzeichnungen des Hauptschriftleiters der *KAZ* Wegener, p. 4.

[30] Otto Dikreiter, 'Das letzte Kapitel, 10000 Milchkarten für Säuglinge', *Das Ostpreußenblatt*, 22 July 1967.

Figure 4.1 A view along the destroyed Kneiphöfsche Langgasse with Königsberg's castle in the back, ca. September 1944. *Source:* Archiv Stadt Königsberg

within the strategic vision of 'Berlin'.[31] Overcoming the widespread resignation and instilling the importance of the city's defence would become the main purpose of the fortress's propaganda. To do so, local propagandists opted to embrace the idea of a locally oriented Kampfgemeinschaft. As the war progressed, German propagandists had presented Germany as an embattled Kampfgemeinschaft, and within this, *Kampf* was interpreted as a metaphysical struggle to secure the country's world views.[32] As we will see, propagandists in Königsberg definitively broke with this broad interpretation, redefining both the meaning of Kampf and the scope of the community.

Within this new identity, geopolitics were less important. The most striking political event that took place during Königsberg's fortress era, the Yalta Conference, was largely ignored by Königsberg's press. On 18 February, the *Nachrichten des Oberkommandos der Wehrmacht*, a newsletter for high-ranking commanders, reported on the conference's outcome, but its details were 'not meant for publication, but only meant

[31] Walzer, *Just and Unjust Wars*, pp. 161–3.
[32] See: Browning, 'The Holocaust: Basis and Objective of the Volksgemeinschaft?'

to inform the higher [military] departments'.[33] Elsewhere, Yalta was trivialised and mainly used to 'uncover' the growing tensions between the Allies rather than as ammunition to keep on fighting.[34] According to the *Preußische Zeitung*, the conference merely proved 'that England had completely got stuck between the two millstones of the plutocratic imperialism of the USA and the Bolshevik imperialism of Moscow'. In turn, attention was drawn to the 'adventure politics' of the United States, which was 'indifferent to the fate of Europe'.[35] It was reported that millions of German slave labourers were to be sent to the Soviet Union to repay the war-debt while Germany would be occupied until the year 2000.[36] Yet these stories were merely consigned to the paper's back page.

The new line instead focused on a simple message: fight for the survival of the city. This was in itself not an easy 'sell'. Königsberg had suffered heavily from two Allied bombardments in late August 1944, which destroyed 53 per cent of the built-up areas, especially the city centre.[37] Soviet artillery further reduced much of the city to ruins during the two-month siege. 'There was a dull atmosphere of the downfall of the world', the writer Rudolf Naujok recalled over a decade later. 'The feeling of walking through a mortuary was impossible to get rid of.'[38] Nevertheless, the approach local propagandists took from the very beginning was to emphasise that everyone in the city was in the same boat. The fact that the city was surrounded and constantly shelled from late January onwards was presented as a test. Posters distributed throughout the city, co-signed by General Lasch and Kreisleiter Wagner, read: 'In the thunder of guns, the stout hearts prove themselves. There is no going back here.' The encirclement would give birth to an 'unconditional battle community' consisting of 'soldiers, men, and women', which would be invincible. These posters also linked the anticipated steadfast behaviour in Königsberg directly to the preservation of the rest of Germany: 'That's how we will do it. All of us together will hold Königsberg until the time that the Reich achieves victory over our mortal enemies.'[39] A similar message could be found on specially designed Volkssturm posters. In Königsberg, these posters featured two men holding weapons while the silhouette of Königsberg's castle

---

[33] BArch RW 4/352, pp. 3–4: Oberkommando der Wehrmacht. Nachrichten des Oberkommandos der Wehrmacht. Berlin, den 18.2.1945.

[34] '"Ich sagte Jalta, nicht Malta!"', *Preußische Zeitung*, 21 February 1945.

[35] 'Die Lehren von Jalta', *Preußische Zeitung*, 19 February 1945.

[36] 'Bis zum Jahre 2000!', *Preußische Zeitung*, 19 February 1945.

[37] Charles Webster and Noble Frankland, *The Strategic Air Offensive Against Germany 1939–1945, Volume IV Annexes and Appendices* (London: HMSO, 1961), pp. 484–86.

[38] Rudolf Naujok, 'Das Mädchen von Königsberg', *Ostpreussen-Warte*, June 1958, p. 11.

[39] AKO 22032–3: Pamphlet: *Haß unsere Pflicht, Rache unsere Tugend*.

could be seen in the background.[40] These messages were consolidated by defiant speeches. On 5 February Kreisleiter Wagner highlighted that for 'better or for worse we are connected to the fate of fortress Königsberg'. On 1 March he focused on 'the fate of our city and the freedom of our East Prussian Heimat'.[41] By rallying people to the defence of their Heimat, an almost tangible, emotionally laden concept, they were contributing to the more indefinable 'Reich' as well.

Alongside this, there was to be an illusion of normality. Large swaths of the *Preußische Zeitung* were reserved for seemingly mundane everyday matters. Thus, Wagner himself would often provide short articles about how to run a household ('Residues of dry bread can be used to make tasty bread soups').[42] Meanwhile, it was reported that at least three cinemas remained open during the siege, showing films on a daily basis, of which one of these was a special *Soldatinenkino*.[43] At Reichssender Königsberg, which kept broadcasting until 7 April, significant effort was put into the rearrangement of the record collection. To supplement these musical offerings, a seventy-strong symphony orchestra was formed, consisting partly of foreign labourers and prisoners of war.[44] But despite these initiatives, the Party continued to be looked upon with suspicion within the Königsberg fortress. Party speakers were treated with hostility and in the areas that housed large numbers of refugees they were hardly given the chance to speak. In the working-class neighbourhood Liep, a former stronghold of the Kommunistische Partei Deutschland (KPD) they were booed and laughed at, while dogs were encouraged to bark whilst they talked.[45] Clearly, more space needed to be put between the old message of the regime and the new local realities.

---

[40] Newsreel 'Aus der Festung Königsberg', *Die Deutsche Wochenschau*, 22 March 1945.

[41] Ernst Wagner, '*Aufruf an der Königsberger Volkssturm*', 5 February 1945, quoted in Lasch, *So fiel Königsberg*, pp. 139–40; Günther Heysing, 'Der Geist von Königsberg: Festung der Waffen und Herzen', *Berliner Morgenpost*, 3 March 1945.

[42] Ernst Wagner, 'Der Bevollmächtigte Kommissar des Gauleiters gibt bekannt', *Preußische Zeitung*, 19 February 1945, p. 2.

[43] 'Die Kinospielzeiten', *Preußische Zeitung*, 20 February 1945; David Welch, *Propaganda and the German Cinema 1933–1945* (Oxford: Clarendon Press, 1983), p. 217–22; Hensel, *Medizin in und aus Ostpreußen*, p. 71. In his memoirs, which concern Dresden, Victor Klemperer puts forward the idea that cinemas in Germany were shut in February 1945 to prevent people from gathering. The opposite was true for Königsberg. See: Victor Klemperer, *To the Bitter End: the Diaries of Victor Klemperer 1942–45* (London: Phoenix, 1999), p. 489.

[44] BArch Ost-Dok. 8/591, p. 49: Heysing; AKO 22034–4: Wegener, *Der Untergang von Königsberg*, p. 3; Ruth Geede, 'Die Vergangenheit ist noch längst nicht vergangen', *Das Ostpreußenblatt*, 29 Janaury 2000.

[45] Hensel, *Medizin in und aus Ostpreußen*, pp. 72–3.

The Search for Continuity

On 15 February 1945, the former Berlin correspondent, Alfred Brattel, wrote an inflammatory article about Königsberg in the Aberdeen-based *Press and Journal*. 'Königsberg, not Berlin, is the real and spiritual capital of Prussia and all that it stands for', Brattel believed, continuing that 'to Prussians, it is what Mecca is for the Arabs and what Reims means to the French'. The article went on to list every negative cliché about the city, which explained the article's subheading: 'Königsberg, Mecca of Prussians, Deserves What She'll get'.[46] By choosing this wording, Brattel attributed guilt to Königsberg *itself*, raising the premise that the city had 'provoked' certain treatment throughout its history, and still did so. What Brattel omitted – and every Allied journalist or Nazi propagandist those days with him – was that Königsberg was also known as Immanuel Kant's 'city of pure reason', and as a bridge between Europe and the East.[47] That the city's martial heritage was emphasised within the fortress in 1945 was perhaps predictable, but it is interesting to reflect on the impact of this on the garrison's behaviour. Since 'war altered the physical city, often at a stroke, and, at the same time, opened up new spaces of thinking about the metropolis', connecting the material 'Festung Königsberg' to the perception and interpretation of it helps us to further the examination of the 'metropolitan dimension of Total War'.[48] Therefore, what follows is an assessment of the manner in which Königsberg's history was framed and conveyed, since, 'when built from a traditional knowledge base', propaganda was at its most successful.[49]

That traditional knowledge base of Königsberg was that it was the *alte Krönungsstadt*, the coronation city of Prussian monarchs, and the city of Immanuel Kant, to which we will return shortly. Days after the encirclement, Herbert Schnellhammer, a fanatical Obergefreiter, wrote the article 'Our Duty!' for the *Festung Königsberg* newspaper, in which he spurred on his comrades by tapping into the city's history. 'Königsberg! City of Prussian military tradition, centre of Prussian duty and Kantian philosophy – Königsberg! The city that during unfortunate times brought Prussia together against the Napoleonic enemy: the proud history of

---

[46] Alfred Brattel, 'Red Army's Road to Berlin', *Press and Journal*, 15 February 1945, p. 2.

[47] Hans-Werner Rautenberg, 'Der Zusammenbruch der deutschen Stellung im Osten und das Ende Königsbergs. Flucht und Vertreibung als europäisches Problem', in Bernhart Jähnig und Silke Spieler (eds.), *Das Königsberger Gebiet im Schnittpunkt deutscher Geschichte und in seinen europäischen Bezügen* (Bonn: Kulturstiftung der deutschen Vertriebenen 1993), pp. 115–16.

[48] Goebel and Keene, 'Towards a Metropolitan History of Total War', p. 2.

[49] Müller, *Deutsche Soldaten und ihre Feinde*, p. 91.

Prussia will these days be tested through deep inner commitment.'[50] The Prussian military heritage was omnipresent in Königsberg. The fourteen forts of Königsberg's fortress belt read as a who's who of the Wars of Liberation and the defiance against the French in the early 1800s, with names such as 'Gneisenau', 'Friedrich Wilhelm III', 'Stein', and so on, while the inner city was protected by 'Der Wrangel' and 'Der Dohna'.[51] The 1st (Ostpreussische) Infanterie-Division was even mustered in East Prussia, Königsberg having been the garrison city of one the division's regiments since 1716. The vast majority of the divisional general staff officers that entered Königsberg in January came from noble Prussian backgrounds.[52]

Some even saw the uniquely Prussian character of the city as a challenge to the Nazi regime. 'Prussian' Königsberg lent itself to serve as a counterweight to 'National Socialist' Berlin, and Hitler himself was thoroughly aware of that. In late January 1945, as Generaloberst Lothar Rendulic, whose Army Group North fought in East Prussia, recalled in his memoirs, 'Hitler conveyed his concern to me, that in case of a loss of Königsberg the so-called Seydlitz group would establish a rival government in the old Prussian coronation city under Russian patronage.'[53] In Berlin the rumour also circulated that a rival government would be established in Königsberg, although in reality by 1945 Stalin had long given up on the idea.[54] The Soviets also sought to appeal to the garrison's sense of Prussian history. According to the Soviet Colonel-General Nikolai Khlebnikov, leaflets were shot into the city, urging 'the enemy soldiers and officers to lay down their arms and surrender in order to avoid vain bloodshed, as the same already happened with Königsberg on January 22, 1758 when Russian troops entered the city'.[55] Indeed, during most of the Seven Years' War (1756–63), Königsberg had been occupied in an orderly fashion by Russian troops after the city submitted to

---

[50] Herbert Schellhammer, 'Unsere Verpflichtung!', *Festung Königsberg*, 2 February 1945.

[51] Hannsjoachim Koch, *A History of Prussia* (London: Longman, 1978), pp. 160, 188–92; Lasch, *So fiel Königsberg*, p. 15.

[52] Walther Grosse, 'Königsberg (Pr.) als Garnisons- und Festungsstadt', *Deutsches Soldatenjahrbuch* (15) 1967, p. 229. Besides the chief of staff of Königsberg Oberst von Süsskind-Schwendi, Ia of 5th Panzer div.: Major von Knyphausen, Ia of 69th Inf. Div.: Major von Witzleben, Ia of 561st VGD.: Major von Wangenheim.

[53] Rendulic, *Gekämpft, gesiegt, geschlagen*, p. 338.

[54] Wolfram Wette, Ricarda Bremer, and Detlev Vögel, *Das letzte halbe Jahr, Stimmungsberichte der Wehrmachtpropaganda 1944/45* (Essen: Klartext Verlag, 2001), p. 253: 'Once Königsberg falls, a provisional German government will be proclaimed in which Paulus and Seydlitz should get senior posts'. Pyta, *Hitler: Der Künstler als Politiker und Feldherr*, p. 606.

[55] Nikolai Khlebnikov, *Pod grohot soten batarej* [Under the thunder of hundred batteries] (Moscow: Voenizdat, 1974), p. 360.

Empress Elisabeth I of Russia.[56] However, such capitulation was strongly opposed by the army and while Deputy Gauleiter Grossherr might have entertained the idea, General Lasch distanced himself from any such surrender (see Chapter 5).[57]

The Prussian military heritage – stripped from any Nazi connotation – became one of the pillars of the fortress's propaganda.[58] Königsberg, many officers felt, had not been tainted by Nazism in the same way as in Potsdam and Berlin, and the departure of many Party activists only strengthened this notion: Königsberg became even more pure in its Prussianism.[59] Therefore, when Königsberg's propagandists used the concept of *Kampfzeit* they did not invoke political parallels of 'struggle'. Instead, Kampfzeit referred to the fighting for the city itself as part of the Prussian virtues of obedience and determination and was not linked to the 'battle of the streets' of the 1920s and early 1930s. Although street fighting seemed inevitable in the near future, and Nazis had regularly and violently clashed with communists during the Kampfzeit, this parallel was not explored.[60] Rather, 'Prussian anecdotes' were printed in the *Preußische Zeitung*, further underlining Prussian military values.[61] Local military authorities were not at all unfamiliar with this course: the bulletin of the East Prussian military district – of which General Lasch had been commander since November 1944 – bore the (somewhat anachronistic) name *Soldat im Ordensland Preußen*, referring both to the German Order which had conquered the area in the thirteenth century and the Prussian military tradition that emerged centuries later.[62]

The change to a Prussian military-dominated propaganda had advantages for the Party as well. Nazi Party officials seemed to have been aware of the limits of their power and popularity to a greater extent than is often acknowledged. The overt Nazi propaganda angered large parts of the

---

[56] Rautenberg, 'Der Zusammenbruch der deutschen Stellung im Osten', pp. 119–20.

[57] AKO 22034-4 Dorfmüller: *Ferngespräch des Kreisleiters Wagner*. See Chapter 5.

[58] Interestingly, not the entire Prussian heritage was adopted. Otto von Bismarck, for example, remained completely unmentioned. As Chancellor, Bismarck was at odds with the Prussian officer corps and often clashed with generals, repeatedly complaining that they were withholding vital information.

[59] For the reception of Hitler's speech in the Garnisonskirche in Potsdam in 1933 and the link to Field Marshal von Hindenburg, see: Gordon Craig, *The Politics of the Prussian Army 1640–1945* (London: Oxford University Press, 1964), pp. 470–1. Moreover, according to Brattel, Königsbergers had two hundred years earlier 'coined the mock phrase "Every second Berliner comes from Breslau", meaning that there is no such thing as a pure-blooded Prussian in Berlin'.

[60] Bessel, *Political Violence and the Rise of Nazism*, pp. 87–9; Gause, *Die Geschichte der Stadt Königsberg*, pp. 114–16.

[61] 'Preußische Anekdoten', *Preußische Zeitung*, 21 February 1945.

[62] Soldat im Ordensland Preußen, Nachrichten aus Heer, Kriegsmarine und Luftwaffe im Wehrkreis I.

population and was widely scorned. Since Stalingrad, the official explanation of Nazi propaganda for the mounting losses had been that a near defeat always preceded eventual victory.[63] The infamous radio speech of Goebbels, 'Hannibal ante portas!', which drew a historical parallel with Hannibal's advance on Rome and the subsequent Roman victories which led to the eventual destruction of Carthage, was considered as shameless by some of the more critical listeners.[64] Also Veit Harlan's (historically inaccurate) epic *Kolberg*, which focused on the town's siege by French troops in 1807, was shown in Königsberg. The movie was flown into the city to bolster the garrison's fighting spirit but was received with mixed feelings. *Kolberg* showed the city's defence as organised by the steadfast mayor, Joachim Nettelbeck, and the energetic major (later field marshal) August Neidhardt von Gneisenau, who prevailed due to their willingness to make deep sacrifices for the greater good.[65] Again, the historical parallels were so obvious that a doctor who viewed it considered it as a 'weird imposition', asking himself: 'Are we supposed to look upon our Kreisleiter as a Nettelbeck?'[66] The answer to that question came on 3 March when the article 'The Spirit of Königsberg: Fortress of Weapons and Hearts' opened with the lines: 'Nobody here thinks about softening up. A Kolberg-mood prevails.'[67] This official Party propaganda was never abandoned but was pursued less rigorously. A parallel propaganda, subtler in its National Socialist wording, was adopted instead. A more martial tone was adopted, and as such the Party was once again able to validate its role in *Menschenführung* (people management).

In the meantime, the army's increasing influence over the fortress's line of propaganda at the expense of the Party worried Gauleiter Koch. His view of Königsberg as a kind of 'military dictatorship' in the midst of his province – exactly what the increasing powers of the Reichsverteidigungskommissar had sought to counter – explains his sustained efforts to undermine the new state of affairs.[68] These

---

[63] Dietrich Orlow, *The History of the Nazi Party: Volume II 1933–1945* (Newton Abbot: David & Charles, 1973), p. 414.

[64] von Lehndorff, *Ostpreußisches Tagebuch*, p. 51.

[65] Welch, *Propaganda and the German Cinema*, pp. 225–34. The willingness to persevere in a besieged fortress for the sake of the people was further stressed by the fact that the movie was flown into La Rochelle in France (a Festung cut off by the Allies since September 1944), where it symbolically premiered at the same time as in Berlin, on 30 January 1945. In a broadcasted telegram to Goebbels, the fortress commander Vice-Admiral Ernst Schirlitz, expressed 'our gratitude for the dispatch of the film on 30 January and our pledge to emulate the courageous struggle at home'.

[66] Hensel, *Medizin in und aus Ostpreußen*, p. 71.

[67] Günther Heysing, 'Der Geist von Königsberg: Festung der Waffen und Herzen', *Berliner Morgenpost*, 3 March 1945.

[68] Meindl, *Ostpreußens Gauleiter Erich Koch*, pp. 415–16.

efforts increased after the recapture of the area between Königsberg and Pillau in late February 1945. Shortly afterwards, during one of Koch's rare visits to Königsberg, he pointed out to Magunia that, had the army not abandoned the trenches he had dug, the situation would have been considerably better.[69] To further his influence, Koch dispatched twelve Kreisleiter to Königsberg. They took over some of the tasks the military had previously overseen but also spread a joke to discredit the army: 'Es steht schlecht um die Festung. Der Kommandant ist lasch und sein Stabschef ein Süsskind'. (It is looking bad for the fortress. The commandant is *lasch* and his chief of staff a *Süsskind*). Lasch here refers to General Lasch, but at the same time the word translates as 'feeble' or 'lax', whereas Süsskind refers to Hugo Freiherr von Süsskind-Schwendi, the chief of staff of the fortress, but also translates as 'sweet child', as such portraying him as helpless and inadequate.[70] In Berlin, Koch continued to discredit Lasch and passed on the joke to Goebbels, who must have taken it on board, noting in his diary on 25 March 1945 that 'he [Lasch] does justice to his name'[71] In turn, among the ranks of the army, Koch was referred to as the 'Satrap of Neutief'.[72] Not only did the saying underline his continued absence from Königsberg, it was also a jab at the vulgarity and lack of sophistication of Koch, who, many knew, started his career as a railway worker. In his earlier role as Reichskommissar of Ukraine, he had occupied a castle in Rovno, which his visitors felt merely served as a 'drab décor' from where he organised opulent hunting trips, and where his white-gloved servants silently poured tea 'in a manner modelled on cinema counterfeits of life among the *haut monde*'.[73] Even the Soviets picked up on this feud, shooting pamphlets into the city which informed the population that Gauleiter Koch was the 'first Volkssturm man' to leave Königsberg, an example they should follow.[74] It is therefore perhaps less of a surprise that, in his post-war analysis of the fortress era, Oberbürgermeister Will claimed to have felt that the resistance of the fortress was more diminished by political intrigue than by military decisions.[75]

[69] BArch Ost-Dok. 8/594, p. 6: Magunia; BArch NS 19/2606, p. 52.
[70] Thorwald, *Die Ungeklärten Fälle*, pp. 169–71.
[71] Goebbels, *Tagebücher 1945*, pp. 377–8. 'Er tragt seinen Namen zu recht'. A week later Goebbels fell out with Koch, due to his absence from Königsberg, see: Ibid., p. 510.
[72] Thorwald, *Die Ungeklärten Fälle*, p. 171.
[73] Gerald Reitlinger, *The House Built on Sand: the Conflicts of German Policy in Russia 1939–1945* (London: Weidenfeld and Nicolson, 1960), pp. 175–6; Grunberger, *A Social History of the Third Reich*, pp. 60–1.
[74] BArch NS 19/2068, p. 62; AKO 22304-4: Kemsies: *Stimmungsbilder aus Königsberg*, p. 9.
[75] BArch Ost-Dok. 8/588, p. 5: Dr. Will.

Losing Faith in the Führer

As the tide of war turned, propagandists had to reconcile Germany's mounting defeats with Hitler's infallibility. Throughout his career Hitler had time and again defied the odds (bringing freedom from Versailles, full employment, and the restoration of national honour), and it seemed that whenever Germany was at its lowest, Hitler was able to rise to the occasion. Setbacks provided the opportunity to rally behind him, and the defeats of the second half of the war were once more used to place him in the role of the country's saviour. The year 1944 saw propagandists promoting slogans like 'Adolf Hitler ist der Sieg' (Adolf Hitler is victory) in an attempt to pin Germans' hopes to their Führer one final time.[76] By 1945, however, to many Germans the setbacks simply seemed irreversible; not only had faith in the Nazi Party largely crumbled, ever larger parts of the population openly ventilated criticism of Hitler as well. Germans felt abandoned by the Nazi leadership, which in the case of East Prussians was even literally so. According to Field Marshal Wilhelm Keitel, Hitler's presence in his military headquarters in Rastenburg had always had 'a very soothing effect on the population' of East Prussia, but after Hitler's departure in November 1944 this illusion of safety also fell away.[77] Similar to Stalin's reaction to the mounting losses in the summer of 1941, Hitler had largely retreated from the public eye by mid-1944. The purpose of this decision was twofold: first, it meant that he did not have to face collective dissent which might damage his carefully constructed cult of personality. Moreover, the fact that he kept his distance from tragedy and interceded only sporadically upheld the notion that local disasters could have been resolved 'if only the Führer knew'.[78] Overall, however, the outcome was negative, meaning that, as Goebbels noted in his diary, 'neither the Führer in person, nor the National Socialist concept, nor the National Socialist movement are immune from criticism'.[79] As a result of his less frequent appearances in the press, Hitler became 'a distant, shadowy figure' to more and more Germans.[80] In East Prussia this was no different, with rumours circulating in late 1944 that Hitler was sick or possibly even dead. His New Year's speech in 1945 at least soothed some of these sentiments but did little to restore his 'charismatic leadership'.[81] Among the troops in particular, his 'strategic genius' was being questioned, even though he remained closely

---

[76] Stahel, 'The Wehrmacht and National Socialist Military Thinking', pp. 347–8.
[77] Keitel, *The Memoirs of Field Marshal Keitel*, pp. 190–1; Kershaw, *Hitler 1936–45*, pp. 737–41.
[78] Kershaw, *The 'Hitler Myth'*, pp. 94–5. Stolzfus, *Hitler's Compromises*, p. 9.
[79] Stephen Fritz, *Endkampf: Soldiers, Civilians, and the Death of the Third Reich* (Lexington: University Press of Kentucky, 2004), pp. 34–5.
[80] Kershaw, *The End*, p. 389; Kershaw, *The 'Hitler Myth'*, pp. 219–25.
[81] Noble, *Nazi Rule and the Soviet Offensive*, p. 182.

Figure 4.2 Better memories of Hitler: the Führer arrives at Königsberg's Devau
airfield, 9 May 1933, together with Reichswehrminister Werner von Blomberg.
Gauleiter Koch can be seen immediately to von Blomberg's right.
Source: Photo by ullstein bild / ullstein bild via Getty Images

involved in the developments concerning Königsberg. As several reports of
staff meetings show, Hitler repeatedly highlighted the city's importance and
ensured that weapons and ammunition would arrive in the city, but none of
this was used to encourage a renewed respect for their Führer.[82]
During Königsberg's siege, Hitler featured prominently in the newspapers
on only three occasions. The first time was on 31 January, when large parts of
his speech commemorating the seizure of power in 1933 were published.
The second time was on 25 February, a day after the twenty-fifth anniversary
of the proclamation of the Party programme, when his speech (which was
read out by Secretary of Propaganda Hermann Esser, rather than by Hitler
himself) and a telegram to Gauleiter Koch, were printed in the *Preußische
Zeitung*. Hitler's final appearance in the newspapers came on 20 March when
he was reported to have received Hitler Youth boys at the Reich
chancellery.[83] The demise of the 'Hitler-myth' has been studied in depth,

---

[82] BArch RH2/335, p. 137; BArch RH2/335, p. 221; BArch RH2/335, p. 223.
[83] BArch Ost-Dok. 10/890, pp. 176–7; 'Ich prophezeie den Sieg des deutschen Reiches!',
Preußische Zeitung, 25 February 1945; '20 tapfere Hitlerjungen vor dem Führer',
Preußische Zeitung, 20 March 1945.

yet how the hole caused by the departure of Hitler's personality cult was filled has received less attention. The need to redefine role models (perhaps precisely because the Hitler-myth had been so all-embracing) was clearly visible in Königsberg. The short history of unified Germany had left the country with few worthwhile heroes (with Immanuel Kant himself already in the late eighteenth century stating that the Germans did not possess national pride).[84] Therefore, the role models that the fortress propagandists chose were local ones.

In the first and only divisional newspaper of the 561st Volksgrenadier-Division, *Die Sturmglocke*, an entire article was devoted to General Ludwig Yorck von Wartenburg, the Prussian hero of the Wars of Liberation of 1813, including his picture and some quotations that were as appropriate in 1945 as they were in 1813. The impact of his (distilled) legacy is not to be underestimated, as in Königsberg military decisions were sometimes even judged through the eyes of Yorck, even when the resulting actions were contradictory to Hitler's view. To East Prussians, Yorck's claim to fame was his decision in 1812 to declare himself neutral at the Battle of Tauroggen north of their province when he was supposed to fight alongside the French. By doing so, he went against the wishes of his king, Frederick William III, effectively changing sides. Königsberg played an important role in these events: five days after his deed, Yorck entered Königsberg and urged the members of the Ostpreussische Landtag, which had gathered without the King's permission, to arm the people, triggering the Wars of Liberation that ended the loathed French rule. When Kreisleiter Wagner was sounded out about his willingness to overthrow Gauleiter Koch, he was asked to consider a 'Yorckish deed' by imprisoning Koch and declaring Königsberg an open city.[85]

Another local role model, by far the most famous son of the city, was the philosopher Immanuel Kant, whose legacy was reinterpreted to fit the propagandist aims of 1945. In 1941, S. D. Stirk, a German graduate from both Oxford and Breslau universities who had migrated to Britain before the war, wrote a 'war book', seeking to explain some of the uses of Prussianism in National Socialist thought. He summed up how Kant's notion of 'duty', which in his eyes was meant as an 'integral part of a noble conception of man as an independent and autonomous being', had been hollowed out: 'It has

---

[84] Fritz, *Endkampf*, p. 63.

[85] Koch, *A History of Prussia*, pp. 194–7; AKO 22032-2: '*Die Sturmglocke*', Divisional newspaper of the 561st VGD, March 1945; AKO 22032-2: Strahl: *Erlebnisse*; Grosse, 'Königsberg (Pr.) als Garnisons- und Festungsstadt', p. 231; Ruth Wagner and Hans-Ulrich Stamm, *Die Letzten Stunden daheim: Ostpreussens Schicksal in schwerer Zeit* (Cologne: Staats- und Wirtschaftspolitische Gesellschaft, 1972), p. 97. The actions of men like Yorck were part of the 'collective memory of the officer corps' and forced an officer to act according to 'God and his conscience'. See: Hürter, *Hitlers Heerführer*, p. 63.

really been emptied of its ethical content and has come to mean blind obedience to the letter of the laws and to the command issued by the state and those in authority'.[86] The propagandists of the Third Reich did not venture beyond Stirk's observation, with the *Königsberger Allgemeine Zeitung* already stating before the siege that 'Kant's notion of duty is embedded in each and every German soldier and German worker, even if he has never read a single line of Kant'.[87] Along similar lines, Professor Eduard Baumgarten, dean of the philosophic faculty of the Königsberg's Albertus University, broadcast a message from the fortress 'in the memory of Kant', condemning Churchill's post-war ideas and rallying people to fight.[88]

More contemporary local role models were used as well. The recipients of the Knight's Cross, Germany's highest award for valour, were announced in the *Preußische Zeitung*, with East Prussian recipients receiving special attention.[89] Best known in Königsberg was Ernst Tiburzy, one of only four Volkssturm members ever to receive the Knight's Cross. During a Soviet attack on the city on 2 February, Tiburzy knocked out five tanks with a Panzerfaust, although the Soviet advance towards the city continued. Staying put, despite being wounded, he knocked out four more tanks after which the attack was called off. This limping man with one eye remaining, but still in action, was the epitome of a fight until the end: this was exactly the kind of tangible heroism propagandists were looking for.[90] Indeed, on 5 February Kreisleiter Wagner devoted a large part of a speech to him, while in that same speech Hitler was mentioned only once in passing.[91] A few days later the *Preußische Zeitung* opened with the celebration of Tiburzy's feat and reported his divisional commander's speech, which tied the soldier's bravery into the 'greater-German' context:

As first Gau of Greater Germany East Prussia has, as a result of true popular support [and] due to the leadership of its Gauleiter, not only preceded all other *Gaue* in the construction of positions and the raising of the Volkssturm, it now also has an East Prussian Volkssturm leader that is the first to be awarded this distinction of bravery.

Wagner's rather brief supplement, 'Gauleiter Koch is proud of you, and sends his regards!', reveals that the Party was taking its lead from the army.[92]

---

[86] S. D. Stirk, *The Prussian Spirit: a Survey of German Literature and Politics 1914–1940* (London: Faber and Faber, 1941), pp. 82–3.

[87] Kossert, *Damals in Ostpreussen*, p. 136.

[88] AKO 22034–3: Aus der Rundfunksprache von Professor Baumgarten.

[89] See, for example, the *Königsberger Allgemeine Zeitung* of 18 January 1945 and the *Preußische Zeitung* of 21 and 24 February 1945, and of 20 March 1945.

[90] Kissel, *Der Deutsche Volkssturm*, p. 63; Newsreel 'Ernst Tiburzy', *Die Deutsche Wochenschau*, 22 March 1945.

[91] Lasch, *So fiel Königsberg*, p. 140.

[92] Wilke, 'Ein Ostpreuße erster Ritterkreuzträger des Volkssturms', *Preußische Zeitung*, 16 February 1945, p. 1. The reference to a divisional commander, moreover, shows

Figure 4.3 The first Volkssturm member to receive the Knight's Cross, Battalion Commander Ernst Tiburzy. *Source:* Unknown photographer

The 'Volkssturm man' in himself was another propaganda tool. All necessary virtues could be allocated to him, including steadfastness, discipline, and courage. The values of the East Prussian Volkssturm were presented as a continuation of Prussianism, rather than as National Socialist traits, with Waldemar Magunia claiming that 'the East Prussian Volkssturm man had the discipline of this ancient Prussian *Soldatenland* in his bones'.[93] Addressing the different local Volkssturm units, Wagner – himself a native East Prussian – avoided speaking about Germany, but focused exclusively on the people of

that in Königsberg the Volkssturm was fully incorporated in the Wehrmacht command structure, and did not operate as separate battalions anymore. See Chapter 6.

[93] AKO 22034–4: Magunia: *Der Volkssturm in Ostpreußen 1944/45.* See also: Wagner and Stamm, *Die Letzten Stunden daheim,* p. 75: 'The watchword "every man for himself" does not belong in the East Prussian dictionary'.

Königsberg. When he spoke to the units he often spoke of 'us' or 'we' to indicate the local collective identity.[94]

Interestingly, General Lasch kept a low profile locally in the propaganda effort. Although he was featured prominently in *Die Deutsche Wochenschau* in the last week of March 1945, side by side with Gauleiter Koch, no 'forced-upbeat' interview with Lasch appeared in local newspapers and no propaganda pamphlets bearing his name were distributed. With limited personal links to the city, he seems to have restricted himself to one appeal to the troops, which mainly seemed to have served to convey his appointment as fortress commander.[95] Local personalities were thus placed at the forefront of Königsberg's propaganda. This manifested itself in both Party outlets, such as the *Preußische Zeitung*, and in military newspapers. To establish to what extent Königsberg was unique in pursuing this approach, the next section will continue to examine this theme by addressing more directly the role of the spoken word within late-war propaganda.

The NSFO and the *Mundpropaganda*

In order to bolster the army's fighting spirit during times of defeat, 1943 had seen the introduction of the NSFO, the Nationalsozialistischer Führungsoffizier, or National Socialist Leadership Officer, whose task it was to transfer the National Socialist world view to the troops.[96] During the fighting in Germany, Hitler stated that 'the National Socialist world view and political attitude must be used as the strongest weaponry'.[97] Eventually, groups of NSFOs were even dispatched to hard-pressed areas of the front to discourage troops from retreating.[98] Although these men were presented as a vital link between the regime and the army, and as support for the notion that the army was willing to embrace National Socialist principles, it is hard to define an archetypical NSFO. Some officers in Königsberg took their appointment as NSFOs very seriously, while others, such as Leutnant Bodo Kleine, only took up the function

---

[94] AKO 22034–4: Pamphlet 9 February 1945: *Aufruf! Packt alle an!*; Lasch, *So fiel Königsberg*, p. 140.

[95] Lasch, *So fiel Königsberg*, p. 139. Interestingly, the Soviets immediately used Lasch as a tool. He was forced to sign a pamphlet that was shot in large numbers into the Pillau pocket, prior to the offensive of that grouping, from 13 April 1945 onwards.

[96] Waldemar Besson, 'Zur Geschichte des nationalsozialistischen Führungsoffizier', *VfZ* (9) 1961, pp. 76–116; Gerhard Weinberg, 'Adolf Hitler und der NS-Führungsoffizier (NSFO)', *VfZ* (12) 1964, pp 443–56; Förster, 'Motivation and Indoctrination in the Wehrmacht', pp. 264, 271.

[97] Besson, 'Zur Geschichte des nationalsozialistischen Führungsoffizier', p. 114.

[98] Ibid., p. 83.

after being ordered to do so. Kleine subsequently questioned whether his talks had any effect on the troops at all.[99]

These men were at the forefront of one of the most important dilemmas of those days: was the defence of Germany of overriding importance or were National Socialist teachings to be upheld during Germany's gravest hour, no matter the cost?[100] Many commanders in Königsberg decided – or were forced to decide due to circumstances – on the former. For example, even though the Volkssturm was initially a Party-led organisation, its East Prussian units had received little political education. The overriding need to halt the Soviet offensive into East Prussia in October 1944 meant that its men received weapons training only.[101] That in hard-pressed fortresses even fewer soldiers were interested in politics seemed to have dawned on some of the more realistic members of the Wehrmacht. It is worth quoting at length an instruction, dated 15 February 1945, to NSFOs who were serving inside a fortress.

At least once a week, troops are to be given a political address, during which it should be made clear to them that fortress garrisons are not forgotten, but that in most cases the homeland is much harder hit than the fortresses. It should be impressed upon the troops that further reserves are to be expected, but that these will have no softening effect on the homeland. Commissars are to stick to the truth, and they are told that it is better to appear ignorant on certain points rather than to tell lies. There is to be no instruction of the troops on political themes. National Socialist leadership is what counts, not National Socialist education. The object is not to know, but to will. Appeal is to be made to the troops' emotional and traditional values. Soldiers are never concerned with theories, but only with immediate problems. The superiority of National Socialism to reactionary plutocracy and destructive Bolshevism is to be stressed. The final objective of such talks must be to produce confidence that the Germans can still win and that the will to see it through is thoroughly inculcated.[102]

Different NSFOs, however, gave different emphases to their roles. The NSFO who contributed to the newspaper of the XXVIII. Korps, *Die Samlandfront*, did not seek to pursue a political line with his readers. He merely painted a picture of the recent recapture of the Samland peninsula, Operation Westwind (which we will discuss in Chapter 5), and stuck

---

[99] Bodo Kleine, *Bevor die Erinnerung verblaßt, Infanterist an der Ostfront: zwischen Woronesch und Königsberg – Kriegsgefangenschaft in Rußland 1942/1948* (Aachen: Helios, 2004), p. 85.

[100] IfZArch MA 757: Persönlicher Stab Reichsführer-SS, Schriftverwaltung Akt.Nr. Geh./ 353. H.Qu., den 23. Februar 1945. Oberkommando der Heeresgruppe Weichsel, Via/ NSF: Richtlinien für die Arbeit des NSFO

[101] Seidler, *'Deutscher Volkssturm'*, p. 155.

[102] TNA HW 1/3523: Boniface report, 15 February 1945: Memorandum from the German Naval Command in the West, on Political Leadership, with particular reference to the tasks of National-Socialist Political Commissars with Fortress Commandants.

to military events and statistics. On the back of the same pamphlet, the Korps' commander, General Hans Gollnick, praised his troops by focusing on their diverse German origins and their combined mission of evicting the Soviet troops, who were – somewhat surprisingly – not portrayed as Germany's subhuman mortal enemies, but rather as 'dogged' (*verbissen*) and strikingly human opponents.[103]

The course that the NSFOs in Königsberg took can also be distinguished by their implementation of *Mundpropaganda*, 'mouth-' or 'whisper-propaganda', in the city. With the decreasing availability of news through ordinary channels, the German population increasingly dared to – but at the same time had to – rely on rumours and hearsay.[104] This had not gone unnoticed by propagandists, and in late 1944 they adopted the rumour as an official propaganda tool. Special Wehrmacht-propaganda officers were appointed at Wehrkreis-level, whose task it was 'to strengthen public confidence in the leadership, and to substantiate the public's belief that this war must be won at all costs, and can only be ended with our victory'.[105] In Königsberg the Wehrmacht introduced a set of rumours in late February–early March 1945 as part of the Mundpropaganda efforts. Some civilians and some soldiers saw through them but many of these rumours were taken seriously.[106] The rumours focused exclusively on local matters that preoccupied the people in Königsberg. A post-war evaluation of the mood in the city, written by Walter Kemsies, an intelligence officer who was present at the time, speaks about the introduction of a rumour indicating that the Russian troops had become demoralised, having underestimated the strength of the garrison of Königsberg. Instead, the Russian troops in East Prussia had gathered for an attack on the German troops surrounded in Kurland, further to the north, and therefore would have no troops left to attack Königsberg. Apparently, the fact that other parts of the German army were now threatened was of little consideration for the propagandists, as long as the situation in the city was eased. A similar pattern can be detected in other rumours spread: encircled German troops in Insterburg and Tilsit were said to have linked up and were marching towards Königsberg while some 500,000 men of the Wlassow Army had broken out from an area near Warsaw and were also heading to the city.

[103] BArch RH 24–28/106: Tagesbefehl des Gen. d. Inf. Gollnick, 1. März 1945.
[104] Müller, *Deutsche Soldaten und ihre Feinde*, p. 89.
[105] Wette, Bremer and Vögel, *Das letzte halbe Jahr*, pp. 17–20.
[106] IfZArch ZS/A-2/ 04–140: Gerhardt Kretschmer, Nuernberg-Zabo, d. 11.4.49. On the natural tendency to try to extract meaning from a confusing environment, and the role rumour plays in this tendency, see: Ralph Rosnow, 'Psychology of Rumor Reconsidered', *Psychological Bulletin* (89)1980, pp. 582–5.

Himmler was also claimed to be gathering his army and would approach the city via Danzig. According to an SS intelligence report, this rumour resonated particularly well among the troops. On top of that, it was rumoured that 500 Tiger tanks had been offloaded in the port of Pillau and were shortly to be made available to bolster the city's defence.[107] The Mundpropaganda and the activity of the NSFOs thus reflected the tendency to focus on local threats, and as such reveal that enough institutional flexibility existed to allow for this. The next section will examine the most infamous sub-genre within Nazi propaganda – atrocity propaganda – to determine whether these findings can be extended into this field as well.

Atrocity Propaganda

For better or for worse, Nazi propagandists had committed themselves to bringing Soviet atrocities to the attention of the German public. By early 1945, however, there were ever louder voices, also coming from the Party elite, that urged that they be presented in a more nuanced light.[108] The representation of atrocities formed a key element in German propaganda during the last year of the war. East Prussians held a special place in this propaganda, being the first to experience the rage of 'Moscow's hangmen'.[109] Yet the backlash caused by the 'Nemmersdorf' campaign showed that the German Volksgemeinschaft did not wholeheartedly embrace this course. Moreover, at times the propaganda contributed to a further corrosion of German society, with people in Western Germany being unmoved by the death of 'a couple of people in East Prussia'.[110]

Initially, in late January–early February 1945, the fortress command too seemed to have failed to grasp that the basic emotional response to atrocity propaganda by those remaining in Königsberg was fear rather than steadfastness. A general feeling of defencelessness prevailed among the civilians in the city: two-thirds of them were refugees, of which the vast majority were women, children, and elderly.[111] The first pamphlet that General Lasch and Kreisleiter Wagner drafted, however, did not address their fears and insecurities but simply attacked the 'Bolshevik hordes' instead. Addressed to 'soldiers, men, and women of Festung Königsberg', it told that 'courage and steadfastness are our honour,

---

[107] AKO 22034–4: Kemsies: *Stimmungsbilder aus Königsberg*, p. 9. AKO 22034–4: Aufzeichnungen des Hauptschriftleiters der *KAZ* Wegener, 3; BArch NS 19/2068, p. 60.

[108] IfZArch Akten der Partei-Kanzlei der NSDAP: 13202379. Beleg Nr. 5, 10. Febr. 1945 An die Partei-Kanzlei z. Hd. Herrn Reichsleiter M. Bormann. gez. Eggeling Gauleiter.

[109] Longerich, *Goebbels*, p. 907.

[110] Steinert, *Hitler's War and the Germans*, pp. 304–5.

[111] AKO 22034–4: Kemsies: *Stimmungsbilder aus Königsberg*, p. 4.

hate and revenge the watchwords!'[112] This wording had long been commonplace among the barbarised German Eastern front soldiers and for most of them the tone of the pamphlet was justified: some of the soldiers who retreated into Königsberg had also seen action around Nemmersdorf. General Lasch himself had been appointed East Prussia's Wehrkreis commander in the very week that the events surrounding the village were presented to the wider public, making 'Nemmersdorf' one of his first experiences in the province.[113] Civilians on the other hand were thoroughly upset by the pamphlet. 'Herr General, what do you hope to obtain by the appeal we have found posted up everywhere, with your signature appended?', Hans Graf von Lehndorff protested in a letter about the pamphlet: 'You are not going to bamboozle anybody with "Heil Hitler" anymore.'[114] Although von Lehndorff cherished little hope that his letter would have any impact, newspapers show that in the weeks that followed, the topic of atrocities was pushed more into the background.

This approach towards atrocities changed in late February in the wake of Operation Westwind, during which German troops recaptured large areas between Königsberg and Pillau. The first village that was recaptured was Metgethen, just west of Königsberg, where large numbers of corpses were discovered that showed signs of mutilation and rape.[115] This did not mean, however, that propagandists immediately sought to exploit the 'opportunity' with which they were presented. During the first days after the recapture of the Samland area the topic was ignored, for which there was an obvious reason. A sense of euphoria dominated among the civilians in Königsberg, the soldier Heinz Stendtke remembered about those days.[116] This was confirmed by two SS reports describing the mood of the population as 'confident' on 21 February and still, a week later, on 26 February noting that 'due to the successes on the Samland the mood of the people is good'.[117]

---

[112] AKO 22032–3: *Haß unsere Pflicht, Rache unsere Tugend.*

[113] Lasch, *So fiel Königsberg*, p. 24; Müller, *Deutsche Soldaten und ihre Feinde*, pp. 91–114; Bartov, *The Eastern Front, 1941–45*, pp. 76–92.

[114] Translation taken from: Hans von Lehndorff, *East Prussian Diary: a Journal of Faith 1945–1947* (London: Oswald Wolff, 1963), p. 23. The pamphlet actually did not read 'Heil Hitler', but 'Es lebe der Führer!'.

[115] Large parts of post-war testimonies can be found in: Kulturstiftung der Deutschen Vertriebenen, *Vertreibung und Vertreibungsverbrechen, 1945–1948: Bericht des Bundesarchivs vom 28. Mai 1974, Archivalien und ausgewählte Erlebnisberichte* (Bonn: Kulturstiftung der Deutschen Vertriebenen, 1989) and: Alfred-Maurice de Zayas, *Anmerkungen zur Vertreibung der Deutschen aus dem Osten* (Stuttgart: Kohlhammer, 1986), pp. 67–71: AKO 22034–4: Magunia: *Abschrift*; AKO 22034–4: Banneitz, *Erlebnisbericht.*

[116] Knopp, *Der Sturm*, p. 83.

[117] BArch NS 19/2068, pp. 18–19, 34. An Reichsführer-SS Feldkommandostelle Betrifft: Meldungen aus dem Ostraum, Königsberg 21.2.45; Königsberg 27.2.45: BE: SS-Stubaf. Friedrichs.

However, General Lasch ordered an investigation into Metgethen, probably with the purpose of handing over the findings to the Wehrmacht War Crimes Bureau, as had happened in Nemmersdorf.[118] The local Sicherheitsdienst prepared a 'photo report of the murdered and desecrated Germans by the Bolsheviks in Metgethen'.[119] One source indicates that 'Gaupropagandaleiter W. followed the advancing German troops, made pictures on the spot and interrogated liberated civilians. Two days later he wrote the memorandum "Revenge for Metgethen".'[120] The first article on the subject, 'Metgethen … ! Metgethen … !', was written by the war correspondent Günther Heysing and appeared on 25 February on the second page of the Preußische Zeitung, a week after the area had been recaptured.[121]

Over the following days, a two-stage process can clearly be distinguished: soldiers knew much earlier than civilians about the events at Metgethen. Walter Kemsies noted: 'What the advancing soldiers saw surpassed by far the propaganda up till now.'[122] Anton Detlef von Plato, a former general staff officer of the 5th Panzer-Division, wrote in the post-war divisional history that as their tanks passed through the village, soldiers immediately wrote 'Revenge for Metgethen' on their vehicles. Testimonies about the number and state of the people the soldiers found vary widely. Numbers were inflated as high as 3,000 victims, although no wartime source has survived with a figure that comes even close to this. The SS report mentions that ninety-one bodies were found by the SD.[123] But even if the real number was lower, the shock that was caused as a result of it bolstered the fighting spirit in the entire region, with the same report mentioning a 'boundless rage' among the troops, assuring that 'virtually no' Soviet prisoners were made.[124]

The next step was to present the atrocity to the local population, but the information they would receive about Metgethen was extremely limited.

---

[118] Alfred-Maurice de Zayas, 'The Wehrmacht Bureau on War Crimes', *The Historical Journal* (35) 1992, p. 385.

[119] Library of Congress, 'Bildbericht über von den Bolschewisten ermordete und geschändete Deutsche in Metgethen', www.loc.gov/pictures/item/2005675708/

[120] Kemsies, *Stimmungsbilder aus Königsberg*, 8. This pamphlet did appear, but the role of Gaupropagandaleiter Maertins is unknown. As Kemsies refers to him as 'Gaupropagandaleiter W.' it could also have been a completely different person. On the role of Gau propaganda leaders, see: Daniel Mühlenfeld, 'Between State and Party. Position and Function of the Gau Propaganda Leader in National Socialist Leadership', *German History* (28) 2010, pp. 167–92.

[121] Günther Heysing, 'Metgethen … ! Metgethen … !', *Preußische Zeitung*, 25 February 1945.

[122] AKO 22034–4: Kemsies: *Stimmungsbilder aus Königsberg*, pp. 7–8.

[123] Kulturstiftung der Deutschen Vertriebenen, *Vertreibung und Vertreibungsverbrechen, 1945–1948*, p. 146; BArch NS 19/2068, p. 37.

[124] Christian von Oppel and Hartmut Mathieu (eds.), *Im Rücken des Feindes: Erinnerungen von Edgar Burger 1925–1945* (Schwalbach: Books on Demand, 2004), pp. 85–7; BArch NS 19/2068, p. 37.

Figure 4.4 *Metgethen Rache*, Revenge Metgethen propaganda poster,
February 1945. *Source:* Unknown designer

The *Preußische Zeitung* provided no detailed account of the massacre itself, and looking at the available sources, it appears that civilians were kept away from the village in the days that followed its recapture. 'Metgethen' was kept in the realm between myth and reality. Banners that read 'revenge for Metgethen' were hung throughout the city, while posters appeared with 'METGETHEN RACHE' (Metgethen revenge), which depicted a Soviet skeleton, clinching a knife between his teeth, holding a barely dressed and emaciated woman, which he obviously had killed. Like before, the sight of these posters caused a backlash, and many of them were removed by the population, fearing that upon entering the city the Soviets would in their turn be enraged by them.[125]

For the civilian population of Konigsberg, Metgethen became the embodiment of doom and immediately replaced Nemmersdorf as such.[126] It was a final pillar of Königsberg's embattled Kampfgemeinschaft. The brutality of the Soviets that was observed by German troops meant that the nationwide notion of Kampfgemeinschaft was stripped of any deeper meaning: it was insufficient to represent 'Kampf' as 'struggle': the events at Metgethen showed that Kampf could only mean 'battle'. Whereas the proverbial 'struggle' lacked urgency (as we saw, the 'struggle with the East' had been going on for centuries and had most of the time not been a struggle at all), the immediate need to 'battle' against an enemy that stood within ten miles of Königsberg's city centre was now clear to all.

Conclusion

During the two months of Königsberg's siege, army commanders and Party officials decided on a communal message that was centred on the willingness to fight for Königsberg, rather than for Germany as a whole. They realised that few civilians in the city believed that the promise of the Volksgemeinschaft could be achieved in the foreseeable future and were well aware that people's concerns did not venture beyond their immediate environment. The result of these realisations was that they embraced the idea of a locally oriented Kampfgemeinschaft.

The course that was decided on was a product of trial and error, but eventually broke with some of the accepted themes of Nazi propaganda. Overall, propaganda in Königsberg became more locally focused, and

---

[125] Hensel, *Medizin in und aus Ostpreußen*, p. 72; Thorwald, *Die Ungeklärten Fälle*, pp. 156, 166; Wieck, *Königsberg, Zeugnis vom Untergang einer Stadt*, p. 176; Ursula Cheeseman, *Unter der Zeitbrücke: Aufzeichnungen einer Ostpreußin* (Germany: Books on Demand, 2000), p. 91.

[126] An examination of the editions of the *Völkischer Beobachter* in the period following the discovery of the crimes shows that Metgethen was not even mentioned once on national level.

appealed to the population's sense of 'banal nationalism'. A distinct effort was made to closely connect the Festung Königsberg to the traditional martial perception of the city. The concept of final victory, *Endsieg*, was pushed to the background, and perseverance, *Durchhalten*, was linked to the city itself, rather than to Germany as a whole. With the Führer-myth undermined, the remaining civilians were asked to look to their 'own' history, from where Kant and Yorck were encouraging them to assist in the defence of Königsberg. Meanwhile, in regard to the issue of atrocities, the message of hate and revenge was not haphazardly repeated, as propagandists gave much thought to how and to whom to present it. Only when proof of atrocities was found in nearby Metgethen did they evoke the hate and revenge rhetoric, but still only after a week-long embargo on the news.

The fortress's propagandists created an easy-to-follow idea: everyone in Königsberg was expected to persevere in order to prevent the city from falling into enemy hands. The way this new line was supposed to be interpreted was unsophisticated but effective: soldiers understood this as defending the population of the city while the population of the city understood this as aiding soldiers. Rather than defending some greater German ideals until final victory, the simple fact that one could look others directly in the eye created an acute sense of personal responsibility. Certainly, not all German cities could be turned into such a community. Königsberg's strong regional pedigree and its designation as a fortress enabled this, while the 'willingness' to become part of this new society also arose due to lack of other options. The relative ease with which the National Socialist world view was reshaped to fit a mould of traditional nationalism thus means that the maltreatment of the civilian population – the central issue of the following two chapters – did not necessarily have to be rooted in Nazi fanaticism.

5   The Evacuation of East Prussia

Introduction

In his memoirs, the Grossdeutschland veteran Guy Sajer painted a depressing picture of the refugees whom he encountered in the port of Pillau. While waiting to be transported in March 1945, Sajer, who had taken part in some of the most intense fighting on the Eastern Front, was upset by the 'heart-wringing' plight of the children he saw there. 'Many were lost. When they tired of calling their mothers, they collapsed into floods of tears which nothing and no one could console. These were the smallest ones, too young to grasp any explanations. Their faces dabbed with tears, which instantly froze, remain one of the most pathetic images of that time.'[1] Tragic stories like these are abundant; tens of thousands of refugees were waiting to be evacuated from Pillau between January and April 1945. Both at the time, and particularly in the early post-war era, Wehrmacht commanders, civilians, and scholars alike blamed the misery of Eastern Germany's population on the poor organisation of the Party, a view which has persisted.[2]

These contemporaries failed to grasp the impact of the Wehrmacht itself on the decisions that were taken in the province. The Eastern Front had been a 'school for violence', whose lessons defined the way both rank-and-file troops and the officer corps regarded the evacuation of their own population.[3] The German army even provided material which precisely elucidated what could be learned from the enemy, as with a pamphlet entitled 'The Soviet Measures for the Successful Defence of Leningrad'. Stripped of any racial preconceptions, its authors stated that, prior to and

---

[1] Sajer, *The Forgotten Soldier*, pp. 528–9.
[2] Lasch, *So fiel Königsberg*, pp. 76–8; Dieckert and Großmann, *Der Kampf um Ostpreussen*, pp. 119–22; Karl Dönitz, *Zehn Jahre und Zwanzig Tage* (Bonn: Athenäum-Verlag, 1958), ch. 22. 'Regierungschef'; Noble, *Nazi Rule and the Soviet Offensive*, pp. 99–100; Kershaw, *The End*, pp. 108–12, 176–7.
[3] Römer, *Kameraden*, p. 410.

during the siege of Leningrad, 'the evacuation was ruthlessly carried out. Only those qualified for the defence were allowed to remain in the city'.[4] The pamphlet also indicated that many parents did not know where their children were evacuated to which added to the general confusion, but this was considered inevitable. This not only reveals the intention of the army to take an active part in the evacuation but it also makes clear that the well-being of the civilian population was of secondary importance.[5] This chapter, therefore, seeks to restore agency to the Wehrmacht in the organisation of the evacuation. By reconstructing the motivations of the different actors, as well as the environment in which they operated, it will show that from the moment the German troops entered East Prussia in mid-1944, the evacuation of civilians was fully subordinated to the demands of the Wehrmacht.

Considering the Evacuation of East Prussia

Up to the summer of 1944, when German troops reached the borders of their country, the Wehrmacht had overseen a series of mass evacuation efforts. As we saw in Chapter 2, during the retreat from the Soviet Union it had forcibly expelled millions of Soviet citizens; although these evacuation drives were portrayed as militarily necessary, they were still considered as hard, unfamiliar, and often unpleasant measures. In this light it is perhaps more understandable that after the war army commanders stressed that the evacuation of German civilians in late 1944 was organised by the Party and that they themselves only played an advisory role once back in Germany.[6]

On paper, the evacuation measures in Germany were clearly delineated: RVKs bore the final responsibility for the evacuation of civilians while the army was tasked with the evacuation of goods.[7] Yet this division

---

[4] BArch NS 19/2721, p. 3. Die sowjetischen Maßnahmen zur erfolgreichen Verteidigung Leningrads. The document is undated, but other documents of the same series, 'Befehle der Heeresgruppe Weichsel, insbes. zur Stärkung des Kampfgeistes' [Orders of Army Group Vistula, in particular for the strengthening of the fighting spirit], are all dated between 10 and 20 February 1945.

[5] On this topic, see particularly the research of Heinrich Schwendemann. Heinrich Schwendemann, 'Strategie der Selbstvernichtung. Die Wehrmachtsführung im "Endkampf" um das "Dritte Reich"', in Müller and Volkmann (eds.), Die Wehrmacht, pp. 224–44; ' 'Deutsche Menschen vor der Vernichtung durch den Bolschewismus zu retten': Das Programm der Regierung Dönitz und der Beginn einer Legendenbildung', Hillmann and Zimmermann (eds.), Kriegsende 1945 in Deutschland, pp. 9–34; 'Tod zwischen den Fronten', Spiegel Special (June 2002), pp. 42–7; 'Inferno und Befreiung: "Schickt Schiffe!"', Die Zeit, 13 January 2005.

[6] Dieckert and Großmann, Der Kampf um Ostpreussen, pp. 72–81. Noble, Nazi Rule and the Soviet Offensive, pp. 128–45.

[7] Schramm, Kriegstagebuch des OKW Band IV, p. 1567.

of responsibilities was not as strict as it appears: according to East Prussia's Regierungspräsident, Dr Paul Hoffmann, an evacuation plan had been drawn up in late 1943 and evacuation routes had been 'coordinated with the armed forces in order to avoid congestion of roads'.[8] In addition, for Königsberg and other fortresses, well before any Soviet offensive Wehrkreis commanders were to inform local Gauleiter 'how many and what civilian population is required in the fortresses to achieve the objectives of the fortress commander, which population is allowed to stay, or is yet to be taken in'.[9] Although in East Prussia the military thus had a say in the organisation of the evacuation of German civilians, attitudes towards safeguarding their own population were nevertheless detached. This stance had its roots much earlier in the war. When in September 1938 tensions rose in anticipation to the German invasion of Czechoslovakia, hundreds of thousands of German civilians living along the French frontier, fearing a French attack in answer to the German campaign, took it upon themselves to leave the area and evacuate their homes. These people subsequently clogged the roads, wandered into military zones, and generally disrupted military planning, much to the frustration of commanders. A year later, prior to the invasion of Poland, these movements were even greater, with people trying to get away from both the Polish and the French border regions. In both cases the army pushed for regulations that would demand civilians' orderly evacuation, but Hitler was unwilling to do so. Official evacuation orders, he feared, would link the regime too closely to the increasing demands of the war, while the coercive measures that would have to be taken in order to carry out the evacuation would moreover undermine the regime's popularity. The 'option' to evacuate was to be presented as a gesture of a benevolent regime looking after its people's welfare, rather than as a forced measure. As a result, both the departure from, and the return to, these areas remained an individual choice. Eventually, military authorities ordered the evacuation from these areas themselves, but since there were no repercussions for disobeying these orders few civilians acknowledged them.[10] These events taught the military two important lessons about domestic evacuation efforts: firstly, they would not be able to count on

---

[8] BArch Ost-Dok. 8/536, p. 3: Hoffmann. On the role of the Wehrkreis command in the evacuation measures in Königsberg, see BArch Ost-Dok. 8/560, p. 2: Marquardt.

[9] BArch NS 19/3814, pp. 2–4: Der Chef des Generalstabes des Heeres H.Qu OKH, den 17.12.1944 Gen Qu / Abt. Kriegsverw. Nr. II/2200/44 g.Kdos Betr. Bevorratung und ARLZ-Maßnahmen auf zivilem Sektor im Bereich der Ostfestungen.

[10] Stoltzfus, *Hitler's Compromises*, pp. 209–14; Torrie, *'For Their Own Good'*, pp. 6–8.

their compatriots' resolve and cooperation, and secondly, forcing Hitler's hand on the matter would be nearly impossible.[11]

In late 1944, Soviet forces started to gather along the East Prussian borders in ever greater numbers and there was little doubt that in the case of a main attack German forces had to yield ground. Commanders anticipated that East Prussia might be cut off, and that they eventually would have to fall back on the defences that shielded the Samland, which, due to its large hinterland, lent itself perfectly for a prolonged defence. This was conveyed to Gauleiter Koch, and as inter-Gau evacuation was deemed unfeasible in the case of a main attack and while the threat of the Soviet offensive also had to be downplayed, the Party pushed for an evacuation within the province itself.[12] During these months, the possibility of a successful Soviet advance through the province that would necessitate full-scale seaborne evacuation was never seriously considered.[13] Already on 12 July 1944, three weeks after the start of Operation Bagration, the Wehrmacht and the Kriegsmarine discussed matters of evacuation and supply in case the fighting would reach the Baltic Sea region. The navy was given six tasks:

1. Fortification of the Baltic Sea coast
2. Replenishing Army Group North and the Twentieth Mountain Army in Northern Finland
3. Adaptation and adjustment of bases for naval forces to meet the new circumstances
4. Preparations, and if necessary, implementation of evacuation measures in the area of the Twentieth Mountain Army and Army Group North
5. Breaking down, and if necessary, evacuation of bases in the East as well as relocation of training grounds. These measures could apply to Libau, Memel, but possibly also to Pillau and, in the most unfavourable case, to Danzig and Gotenhafen.
6. Evacuation of civilian population and assets.[14]

The military ranked the evacuation of civilians as the absolute lowest of priorities, but this did not mean that local commanders were not informed about the state of the evacuation. Documents of the IX. Korps show that the Party's evacuation measures were clearly

---

[11] Ibid., pp. 208–41.
[12] Tilitzki, *Alltag in Ostpreußen*, pp. 283–4, 292–3. OL: IV M 4 DIE, 4: Erich Diester, Zur Tagung der Kulturwarte am 6. u. 7. März 1965 in München: Verjagt – beraubt – geschändet – erschlagen! 'Kreis Schlossberg is cleared between 17 and 23 October. The reception district is Wehlau. Continuing the Treck is fundamentally prevented'.
[13] Schwendemann, 'Der deutsche Zusammenbruch im Osten 1944/45', p. 129.
[14] Rahm and Schreiber (eds.), *Kriegstagebuch der Seekriegsleitung, Band 59/I*, p. 267.

communicated to the army on a regular basis. Some information between the Gauleiter and the Kreisleiter was even forwarded to the different divisions of the Korps in order to keep them up to speed on the movement of the East Prussian population in and near evacuated areas.[15] Much of this communication dealt with the matter of reluctant evacuees since many East Prussians were long-established ('sehr bodenständig') in the province and hesitant to leave their homes.[16] Over 1,700 families stayed behind in and around the city of Memel alone, a decision that was influenced by the fact that many of these people – especially the rural population – possessed a horse-drawn cart which they felt allowed them to evacuate themselves at short notice.[17] Many inhabitants either ignored the evacuation orders or returned as quickly as possible. Oberst Schaefer, who oversaw many of the evacuation measures, noted shortly after the war:

> As the front continued to hold more and more people trickled back into the evacuated border areas to complete the autumn harvest. Whereas these were initially only men with horses and farm implements, eventually entire families returned, who remained on their farms even after completion of their work in the fields, so the evacuation of the border districts had to be ordered again once the Russian winter offensive commenced.[18]

Men like Schaefer, however, must have been aware of the army's role in the drafting of the evacuation orders that led to this. Guidelines on evacuation were passed down by the IX. Korps as far as regimental and even battalion level, and were linked to the fighting that lay ahead. For example, many of the male farmers were ordered to return to collect the harvest in threatened areas, and despite a strict ban their wives generally accompanied them, a practice that the army was ordered to curb: 'The evacuation of the civilian population from the threatened areas is a hard but necessary measure. Your operational conduct is only guaranteed if it is carried out strictly according to the instructions given by the Party.'[19] Soldiers were forbidden to bring civilians into the restricted areas, 'no matter how compelling the reasons are in some cases'.[20] Inevitably, the army had to deal with these matters near the front. On 5 November 1944, the staff of the IX. Korps received instructions concerning Koch's evacuation orders. The divisions stationed in the area were tasked with the

---

[15] BArch RH 24–9/ 137, p. 194: Generalkommando IX. Armeekorps Ia K.Gef.Stand, den 18.11.1944 Betr. Rückkehr von Zivilisten in das Räumungsgebiet.
[16] Tilitzki, *Alltag in Ostpreußen*, p. 287.   [17] Kibelka, *Ostpreußens Schicksalsjahre*, p. 29.
[18] BArch Ost-Dok. 8/565, p. 2: Schaefer.
[19] BArch RH 24–9/212, pp. 6–9: Generalkommando IX. A.K. Abt. IIa/IIb Nr.3762/44 geh. K.Gef. Stand, den 29.10.44 Korps-Tagesbefehl Nr. 10.
[20] Ibid.

Figure 5.1 Wehrmacht troops assist with the evacuation of cattle, late 1944.
Source: Unknown photographer

evacuation of the population immediately behind the front while the evacuation of areas further to the rear was to remain the task of the civil administration, although the local Kreisleiter bore the final responsibility in both cases.[21] To ensure that civilians actually stayed away from the evacuated areas, troops were now ordered to report everyone they encountered without valid papers, after which these people were transported to the nearest Kreisleitung (district office), escorted by a non-commissioned officer.[22]

Perhaps most striking is that the orders to the army leave no doubt that the evacuation drive should first seek to get the cattle to safety before it concerned itself with the civilian population. Assuring that cattle were brought out of harm's way was considered a priority, and special attention was paid to the rural population, which was taken in – with their livestock, of course – on the Samland.[23] The minutes of a meeting on 6 January

[21] BArch RH 24–9/ 293, p. 27: Generalkommando IX. Armeekorps Qu./Iva/VII K.H.Qu., den 5.11.44. Anlage 13.
[22] Ibid. For similar orders in Western Germany, see: Schumann and Groehler (eds.), *Deutschland im Zweiten Weltkrieg 6*, p. 245.
[23] BArch 24–9/137, p. 27: Generalkommando IX. Armeekorps Qu./Iva/VII K.H.Qu., den 5.11.44. Anlage 13; BArch RH2/316, 118: Op Abt (IH) 11. November 1944,

1945 between the OKW and high-ranking officials of the Party further illustrated that ordinary civilians were considered expendable:

For both housing and supply the limits of capacity are almost reached, substantial further evacuation measures within the Reich territory are not possible anymore. On this point the Party chancellery has the same view as the OKW, [namely] that a too extensive evacuation will put the people who are to be evacuated, and eventually also the remaining Volksgenossen, in a difficult position. ... If necessary, leaving behind the civilian population in territory to be occupied by the enemy must be accepted.[24]

This hardening approach towards their own civilian population can be explained by considering the 'cumulative radicalisation' that took hold of the Party and the Wehrmacht as they were confronted with each other's jurisdictions. The concept of 'cumulative radicalisation' proposes that 'the outwardly conjured unity to strengthen the political will nurtured the rivalry of those officials seeking expansion of their competencies and extension of their power'.[25] Throughout the Nazi dictatorship, Hitler had consistently played out different offices against each other and by proposing ever more radical measures, these offices sought to ensure their Führer's ultimate approval. Hitler was notoriously reluctant to put his most extreme demands on paper, and often his true intentions could only be gauged. Pushing for the most radical line, as such outdoing their rival, was one of the clearest ways these offices could convey their loyalty and show their added value.[26] By 1945, this meant that if the Party wanted to maintain its influence over domestic defence it would have to follow the hard line that the Wehrmacht had grown accustomed to on the Eastern Front. The army, in turn, was expected to carry out these increasingly hardening measures. In other words, none of these parties was unwilling to execute radical orders, and none was ignorant of their potential consequences.

Evakuierung Ostpreussen; Schieder (ed.), *Dokumentation der Vertreibung der Deutschen aus Ost-Mitteleuropa I, Band 1*, pp. 15E, 65.

[24] BArch RW 4/704, pp. 7, 8: WFSt/ Qu 2 (Ost) Nr. 0150/45 geh. F.H.Qu., den 6.1.1945. Betr. Rücksprache mit dem Sachbearbeiter der Parteikanzlei für Evakuierungsfragen.

[25] Hans Mommsen, 'Der Nationalsozialismus. Kumulative Radikalisierung und Selbstzerstörung des Regimes', in *Meyers Enzyklopädisches Lexikon, Band 16* (Munich: Lexicon Verlag, 1976), p. 786. I dismiss Mommsen's notion of the Wehrmacht as one of the 'moderating influences of the traditional ruling groups'. Instead, Peukert's findings that Party, administration, SS, police, business, and Wehrmacht all 'had [their] vassals and a relatively secure power base, but each tended to interfere with the areas of responsibility of the others' comes much closer to this notion. See: Detlev Peukert, *Inside Nazi Germany: Conformity, Opposition, and Racism in Everyday Life* (London: B. T. Batsford Ltd., 1987), p. 30.

[26] Kershaw, 'Working towards the Führer'.

In the run up to the final Soviet offensives both the higher Party officials and the higher echelons of the Wehrmacht were acquainted with, and agreed upon, the domestic evacuation procedures and subsequently executed them. In the Soviet Union, the overriding importance for army commanders was the clearance of their area of operations, and evacuation measures had been executed with a virtual disregard for their human consequences. Yet, unlike in the Soviet Union, evacuations on home soil were not marked by racially motivated mass violence; this agenda fell away as German troops crossed back into East Prussia. This did not mean, however, that members of the Wehrmacht approached evacuation policies fundamentally differently than before. In fact, the army's hardening mindset, born out of the experiences on the Eastern Front, often prevented a measured approach towards many of the practices connected to evacuation. The effects of the years of brutalisation can clearly be distinguished among the ranks of the army during its stay in East Prussia. The next section will therefore examine how the 'lowered resting heart rate' of the Wehrmacht shaped the attitudes towards evacuation in the province.

Evacuation and the German Soldier

The flight of East Prussia's population in early 1945 is one of the darkest chapters in the province's history. During this period, the Wehrmacht was not only in charge of the defence of the province, but as we saw, it also played a central role in the evacuation. The concept of 'evacuation', like so many others, had undergone a moral devaluation as the war progressed, as the set of 'criminal orders' had been incredibly successful in creating a heightened sense of indifference among the troops. The average Wehrmacht soldier returned to Germany with a 'lowered resting heart rate', which meant that he had become indifferent to the violence he committed and also often became incapable of recognising the effects of his behaviour. The Landser's remarkable aptitude for adjusting to the hardening of German warfare ensured that he grew ever further detached from civilian life, and increasingly viewed his behaviours through a military prism. This section explores the consequences of this mindset with regard to evacuation. Contrary to what their compatriots might have expected, to the military, evacuation was a means, not an end. As before, it was part of a wider agenda which sought to ensure the continuation of the fight. The evacuation of civilians was not a stand-alone issue; it was undertaken in concert with other preparatory defensive procedures, the aforementioned 'ARLZ-measures'. Therefore, before we examine the military's treatment of civilians during the evacuation of East Prussia, we will place it in the wider context of these measures and examine how considerations regarding them shaped behavioural patterns prior to the Soviet offensive.

When in August 1944 the front reached East Prussia, the German military had just been engaged in some of the heaviest fighting of the entire war. The once formidable Army Group Centre had been mauled during the Soviet summer offensive, Operation Bagration. For over two months it had faced the brunt of four Soviet 'Fronts' in battle after battle in Belorussia and the Baltics, and was now in complete disarray.[27] As it fell back on German soil, the army – already poorly regarded due to its failure to fend off the Soviet offensive – drew much negative attention. Many of the troops who retreated into East Prussia had lost their confidence in final victory and, as East Prussia's propaganda office in mid-July complained, their subsequent mood 'severely distressed the population' as well.[28] To a certain extent, the troops were aware of their negative impact. Although optimistic in public after the war, Major Kurt Dieckert privately noted that it had been 'a gypsy-like sight when support units arrived, and one believed to be in the Thirty Years' War, rather than a modern one, fought with tanks and planes'.[29] As a result, as commanders realised, the troops' presence on home soil would in itself not be enough to change the mood and attitude of the German soldier.[30]

As more and more Wehrmacht units moved into the province, the complaints intensified. A lower-ranking Party official was so confounded that he wrote a six-page report on the troops and described what he saw as 'sabotage': 'On the vehicles, one can find mostly chickens, ducks, geese, pigs, cows, sofas, armchairs, mattresses, bed frames, and so on, but little place is reserved for equipment that is necessary to fight a war.' On these cars, he noted, only few officers could be found. However, they could be found in bars.[31] In early August, Koch wrote to Reichsleiter Bormann that 'as a result of the contact with the people from the East, the troops apparently seem to have forgotten that they are no longer in the occupied eastern areas, but in the Reich'.[32] Koch's observations, although undoubtedly meant to discredit the army, cannot simply be dismissed as such, as there are certainly grounds for them. For well over a year the

[27] John Erickson, *The Road to Berlin* (London: Cassell, 2008), pp. 200–30; 411–30.

[28] Römer, *Kameraden*, p. 16–18, 205–16; BArch R55/616, p. 107: Sondermann, 14 July 1944.

[29] BArch Ost-Dok. 8/510, p. 4: Dieckert. On the demodernisation of the German Army, see: Bartov, *Hitler's Army*, pp. 12–28.

[30] See Chapter 2.

[31] BArch NS 19/2606, Abschrift Nationalsozialistische Deutsche Arbeiterpartei Kreisleitung Scharfenwieze, Scharfenwieze, den 12.7.1944, pp. 6–11.

[32] Hahn and Hahn, *Die Vertreibung im deutschen Erinnern*, p. 263.

army had been forced to yield ground to the advancing Red Army, and it had received comprehensive orders on how to treat the immediate environment during times of retreat. As we saw in Chapter 2, throughout 1943–4, 'destruction' and 'evacuation' had become two sides of the same coin: what could not be evacuated, was to be destroyed. 'Evacuation' became an umbrella term for increasingly radical measures: millions of Soviets were expelled from their homes while German troops prevented spring sowing and destroyed crops, turning much of Belorussia into a 'desert zone'. Rather than this destructive behaviour being punished, it was actively encouraged.[33] After one-and-a-half years of retreating, the organised destruction of property near the front was thus not only considered as normal but as essential. By mid-1944, the concept of evacuation had been largely detached from its traditional meaning, the safeguarding of populations.[34]

This callous attitude towards evacuation clearly manifested itself in East Prussia as well. Wishing to avoid being caught between fleeing civilians and the advancing Red Army, commanders pushed for the evacuation of the East Prussian border districts.[35] Communities were often evacuated in their entirety in so-called *Trecks*, or wagon trains. Permission to evacuate by means of wagon train came from local authorities, which gave the orders (*Treckbefehle*) in consultation with the army. In August 1944 the areas north of the river Memel, as well as the northeastern border districts Tilsit, Ragnit, Pillkallen, Stallupönen, and Goldap were evacuated, with few exceptions. In mid-October 1944, German troops of the Third Panzer Army repelled the first major attack of the Third Belorussian Front on East Prussian territory. The front line then stabilised along the northern border of East Prussia, although Soviet troops did manage to capture a strip of land thirty miles into the East of

[33] Alexander Werth: *Russia at War* (London: Barrie and Rockliff, 1964), pp. 773, 863.

[34] Both Hague Conventions (1899 and 1907) do not pay attention to the evacuation of civilians during times of war. Already in the 1930s, 'evacuation' was closely linked to military actions. See: *Der Große Brockhaus*, 15th ed. (1933), s.v. 'Räumung', im Militärwesen das Aufgeben einer Stellung oder eines Gebiets, mit dem Zweck, sich einer drohenden Niederlage zu entziehen ... Eine entschiedene Maßnahme ist die Abschiebung der Bevölkerung aus den Kampfgebieten (Evakuation). Sie dient neben den milit. Zwecken auch der Sicherheit der Bevölkerung selbst; Meyers Lexicon, 8th ed. (1937), s.v. 'Evakuierung' (lat.), zwangsweise Entfernung von Bevölkerungsteile auf Zeit aus ihrem Wohngebiet, z.B. wenn dieser Kriegsschauplatz zu werden droht. Pohl, *Die Herrschaft der Wehrmacht*, pp. 122–23.

[35] Meindl, *Ostpreußens Gauleiter Erich Koch*, p. 434; BArch RH 24–9/137, p. 30: FS an PZ. AOK 3 Bezug: Pz. AOK 3 – Ia Nr.10261/44 geh. 20.10.44. Little evidence suggests that actual concern for the population played any role of significance in this decision. The commander of the IX. Armeekorps also derogatorily noted that he felt that the inferior-deemed *Trosse* were to be sent far away ('weit abzuschieben') from the front so as not to hamper the manoeuvrability of the fighting troops in case of an attack.

the province.[36] This led to a second evacuation drive, which took place in late October. A further strip of twenty miles in depth, which included the eastern half of the Allenstein district and most of the Gumbinnen district, was evacuated, uprooting over 600,000 people, or one-quarter of the East Prussian population.[37]

The evacuees had to leave behind the majority of their enterprises, as most of these could not be dismantled and transported away. Much private property, such as furniture, also had to remain behind, both because evacuation orders were given at short notice and because there was limited space on the wagons of the *Trecks*. Shortly after the war, a refugee from Memel reflected on the confusion during the final hours before the evacuation: 'Suddenly, around 4 August, an evacuation order came in, according to which the entire population was to be transported immediately, and with them the most important inventory and especially the livestock.'[38] Since a too early evacuation order could be interpreted as a sign of defeatism, houses often had to be abandoned in great haste, leaving their inhabitants little opportunity to clear them properly. This meant that during the months that separated these evacuation drives from the Soviet winter offensive, everything that refugees had to leave behind was left to the discretion of the Wehrmacht. Its troops, however, had neither the time nor the inclination to consider the (sentimental) value of the property they were to protect. This was mainly the result of the attitude that prevailed at the High Command. As the likelihood of a defence of home soil increased, it started to push for regulations which as before would allow the army to conduct unrestrained operations. As early as July 1944 Field Marshal Keitel ordered preparations for the 'ARLZ-measures' to be taken on German territory. Just as earlier in the Soviet Union, the measures, which were fully implemented in September 1944, ignored the devastating effects their implementation would have on the population.[39]

The first major East Prussian city to suffer from these measures was Memel, in the far north of the province. On 22 November 1944 the city was declared a fortress, an order which was accompanied by guidelines, 'according to which the Wehrmacht bears responsibility for the defence and execution of destructive measures of all objects that immediately

---

[36] Dieckert and Großmann, *Der Kampf um Ostpreussen*, pp. 60–1.

[37] Schieder (ed.), *Die Vertreibung der deutschen Bevölkerung aus den Gebieten östlich der Oder-Neiße, Band I*, p. 15E.

[38] Ibid., p. 1.

[39] Schramm, *Kriegstagebuch des OKW Band IV*, pp. 1569–72: Befehl des Chefs OKW betr. Vorbereitungen für die Verteidigung des Reiches (July 19, 1944); Moll (ed.), *Führer-Erlasse*, pp. 456–7: Doc. 363: *Zweiter Erlass des Führers über die Befehlsgewalt in einem Operationsgebiet innnerhalb des Reiches vom 20. September 1944.*

Figure 5.2 In Memel, engineers of Panzergrenadier-Division Grossdeutschland blow up buildings to allow their own artillery a better field of fire, November 1944.
Source: SZPhoto, Image ID: 00384941

serve military conduct' to be used to ensure 'the principally unrestricted demolition of [Memel's] chimneys and church towers'.[40] The results were clearly visible. Shortly after the city's capture in late January 1945, the Lithuanian architect Lapė assessed the damage in the city, which had fallen into Soviet hands virtually without a fight: 'The tower of the reformed church lay across the Litauischen Strasse but the houses around the church were undamaged', Lapė noted, which gave him and his team the impression that it had been demolished deliberately, possibly to rob enemy artillery of a point of orientation.[41]

Similar damage could be observed in Memel's port, the destruction of which had been discussed in even greater detail as a result of its strategic value. The Marine Oberkommando Ost (Navy Command East), which was responsible for the defence of the Baltic Sea, had as early as August 1944 passed down orders to prepare for the destruction of Memel's

---

[40] BArch RH 2/317, p. 81: Fernschreiben mit Anschriftenübermittlung, gez. Wenck, 22.11.44.
[41] Vygantas Vareikis, 'Klaipėda (Memel) in der Nachkriegszeit 1945–1953', *Annaberger Annalen* (3) 1995, p. 52. After the war Memel would become the Lithuanian city of Klaipėda.

harbour, as well as for those further to the west, such as Pillau, Elbing, Danzig, and Gotenhafen.[42] Eventually it was decided that Memel's port facilities were to be rendered unusable although they were not to be destroyed.[43] Demolition of important objects prior to the Wehrmacht's abandonment of a city became so common that, judging by the destruction of industrial installations, Soviet commanders already knew with some certainty when a city was about to be given up or whether the Wehrmacht intended to fight for it.[44] With impending defeat, almost all port facilities suffered a similar fate. On 26 March 1945, the Seekriegsleitung (Maritime Warfare Command), the German body that led the planning and execution of naval warfare, ordered that:

The ports of Gotenhafen, Hela, and Pillau are to be destroyed, mined, and blocked off without limitation. Focus on destruction of the breakwaters.

The ports of Danzig, Königsberg, Stettin, and Schwinemünde are to be effectively mined and blocked off. Offloading equipment and cranes are to be destroyed.[45]

Similar orders were passed down in Königsberg where, for example, the defenders deliberately flooded parts of the Nasser Garten suburb to prevent Soviet troops from advancing too rapidly.[46] In March 1945 engineers blew up the façade of the university since the statues on it posed a safety concern in case of Soviet shelling, and during the final storming the railway bridge was detonated as well.[47] This behaviour was by no means restricted to the east of Germany. For example, on 8 February, under the command of Field Marshal von Rundstedt, engineers blew up the Heimbach hydroelectric power station in Gau Köln-Aachen, near Germany's western border, with the purpose of halting the American advance.[48]

To explain why, during the final battles on German soil, the army had repeatedly been seen damaging and destroying German property, after the war military commanders were quick to point to the 'Nero Decree' of 19 March 1945. Counting on the fact that the chaos of the war's final months resulted in a muddied perception of the chronological order of the

---

[42] Rahm and Schreiber (eds.), *Kriegstagebuch der Seekriegsleitung, Band 60/I*, p. 20.

[43] TNA HW 1/3495: Boniface Report 30 January 1945.

[44] Ivan Bagramyan, *Tak shli my k pobede* [Thus we achieved victory] (Moscow: Voenizdat, 1977), p. 310.

[45] Werner Rahm and Gerhard Schreiber (eds.) *Kriegstagebuch der Seekriegsleitung 1939–1945 Teil A, Band 67: März 1945* (Berlin: Verlag E. S. Mittler & Sohn, 1997), p. 382.

[46] Lasch, *So fiel Königsberg*, p. 60.

[47] Gause, *Die Geschichte der Stadt Königsberg*, p. 167. Sumowski, *'Jetzt war ich ganz allein auf der Welt'*, pp. 67–8.

[48] Hans-Dieter Arntz, *Kriegsende 1944/1945 – Zwischen Ardennen und Rhein* (Euskirchen: Kümpel, 1986), pp. 169.

period's events, virtually all destruction measures on German soil were traced back to the decree. The decree, after all, came straight from Hitler and could thus be portrayed as the brainchild of a radicalised dictator who had lost all sense of humanity.[49] The decree called for 'all military-, transport-, communications-, supply-, and industrial facilities, as well as anything ... within Reich territory that in any way might be used by the enemy for the continuation of his fight', to be destroyed.[50] Apart from envisioning Gauleiter and RVKs as playing an active role in this process (as such immediately identifying a scapegoat in the post-war era), the decree did not represent any change in military conduct, nor did it divert from pre-existing rationales. The language of the Nero Decree was similar to that of the earlier ARLZ-measures and served little purpose beyond rubber-stamping a practice that was already commonplace throughout the country. As before, Wehrmacht commanders destroyed or kept intact German property depending on military necessity. Nevertheless, after the war army commanders presented their 'unwillingness' to fully embrace the decree as an act of defiance against Hitler. Königsberg's Oberstabsintendant Friedrich Dorfmüller, for example, claimed to have discussed it with the fortress's chief of staff, Oberst von Süsskind-Schwendi, who, as a dramatic gesture, threw the order in a stove. The places that were earmarked for destruction – the waterworks at Peyse and the city's mills – were guarded from then on to discourage overzealous Party fanatics from attempting to put them out of action.[51]

The High Command's calculated disregard for German civilian property also filtered through to the rank-and-file. Indeed, in their day-to-day treatment of German property, the troops' 'lowered resting heart rate' could clearly be observed. The different divisions of the IX. Korps, which defended the northern part of East Prussia, were ordered by its commander, General Rolf Wuthmann, to build *Erfassungskommandos* (appropriation commandos). Wuthmann instructed that 'every house and every barn is to be searched. All kinds of stocks, equipment, finished goods, raw materials, machinery, whose return is worthwhile, are to be collected at stations in nearby places'.[52] As long as it benefited the *Kampfführung* (conduct of battle) appropriation was permitted. Yet too much was

---

[49] International Military Tribunal, *The Trial of German Major War Criminals: Proceedings of the International Military Tribunal Sitting at Nuremberg, Germany, Part 17* (London: HMSO, 1948), pp. 34–39; Albert Speer, *Erinnerungen* (Berlin: Propyläen Verlag, 1969), pp. 450–5.

[50] Moll (ed.), *Führer-Erlasse*, pp. 486–7: Doc. 394: *Zerstörungsmaßnahme im Reichsgebiet (sog. 'Nerobefehl')*, 19 March 1945.

[51] AKO 22034–4: Dorfmüller, *'Verbrannte Erde'*; AKO 22034–4: Banneitz: *Erlebnisbericht*.

[52] BArch RH 24–9 /293, p. 27: Generalkommando IX. Armeekorps Qu./IVa/VII K.H.Qu., den 5.11.44. Anlage 13.

appropriated, or 'salvaged' under the rubric of Kampfführung, something that was quickly picked up on by Wuthmann.[53] Not only were troops careless and disrespectful towards German property, searching houses led to plunder: 'Those who appropriate objects that are not directly needed for the conduct of battle or the preservation of the troops' effectiveness, such as jewellery and furniture, will be punished for looting.'[54] Looting, however, simply increased after it became apparent that only a small fraction of the goods could be evacuated.[55] Although the distances between factory and front were getting shorter with the day, the army's supply situation was nevertheless deteriorating. By 1944, Allied bombers had begun targeting previously untouched areas, disrupting agriculture and rail junctions ever further to the east.[56] It meant that more goods had to be transloaded, which was a time-consuming process. The state of the Wehrmacht further prevented the steady arrival of goods to the front line. Especially among the less battle-hardened troops in the rear the faith in 'final victory' dwindled, and more and more soldiers went into hiding or roved through Reich territory.[57] By the end of the year, the supply chain, the Etappe, was collapsing, often leaving German soldiers near the front little choice but to explore the opportunities that presented themselves in their direct environment.

The notion that 'everything will fall into the hands of Ivan anyway', as a soldier told an evacuee from Tilsit, removed many of the soldiers' reservations.[58] This behaviour worried army commanders, and in a lecture one of the staff officers of the IX. Korps stressed that 'the continuation of the fight on German soil means protection of German property. Unfortunately, many soldiers are still not yet clear about this'.[59] Civilians, governmental bodies, and Party offices all expressed concern, frustration, and outrage. In the Volksgemeinschaft, plunder during times of war ranked among the most despised acts. The punishments for those caught (considered Volksschädlinge, or 'public vermin'), were notoriously high.[60] Soldiers, on the other hand, normally got away with it and often 'covered up' for each other (a practice known as Deckungskameradschaft). They

[53] BArch NS 6/135, p. 83: An den NS-Führungsstab der Wehrmacht II P – No/Kg. 14.3.45.
[54] BArch RH 24–9/ 294, p. 60: Generalkommando IX. A.K. Ia/Qu/IVa K.H.Qu., den 24. Oktober 1944. Abschrift Betr. Landesausnützung.
[55] On the limited means available for the evacuation of goods, see: BArch RH 24–9/291, p. 10: Kriegstagebuch IX. Armeekorps Nr. 11, 1944.
[56] Hancock, The National Socialist Leadership and Total War, p. 128.
[57] Kroener, '"Frontochsen" und "Etappenbullen"', pp. 378–9, p. 382; Bessel, Germany 1945, pp. 42–3.
[58] Hugo Linck, Königsberg 1945–1948 (Leer: Verlag Rautenberg & Moeckel, 1952), p. 12.
[59] BArch RH 24–9/137, p. 195. Vortrag Ic über Lage. Undated, most likely second half of November 1944.
[60] Süß, Tod aus der Luft, pp. 152–3.

allowed each other to 'organise' (steal) food and goods, not only abroad, but in East Prussia as well.[61] As before, 'organising' was hardly considered as theft but rather as an admirable and useful skill. During his swim in an East Prussian lake, Leutnant Fritz Blankenhorn had his pistol stolen by a soldier of a neighbouring unit. Surely, he was annoyed, but he was hardly surprised, as he explained:

'Organising' is one of the tools of the trade for a soldier. The better someone understands how to get hold of certain items that others don't have, and which make life easier for him, the higher he is held in esteem by those who are too stupid or too unsuited to do it. Stolen? No. Only brought. *Organised*.[62]

The young housewife Charlotte Gottschalk experienced this injustice at first hand. 'We noted one Sunday morning that our stables had been cleared out, rabbits and poultry were gone. The police could – or would – do nothing because the trail led to the nearby railway tracks, where until earlier in the morning a military train had stood. "German soldiers do not steal", was the comment! Well, that was the end of it'.[63] Visiting the evacuated town of Ostenburg in mid-October, the president of Königsberg's higher regional court, Dr Max Draeger, was appalled to see that in its courthouse German troops had plundered most of the furniture and furnishings.[64] Just over a month later, on 24 November, Draeger visited the towns of Tilsit and Ragnit, where he found that 'most houses, even the courts, have been looted terribly, allegedly by soldiers and Volkssturm men. All doors and cabinets are broken, drawers are pulled out, everything lies on the floor like a deserted mess; a horrible sight'.[65] A scathing report sent to SS-Standartenführer Dr Rudolf Brandt, who was part of the personal staff of Reichsführer-SS Heinrich Himmler, concerned the observations of another official who visited the evacuated areas as well. It described how houses were being stripped by German troops 'to build bunkers or make fire', while the nearby forest was ignored. Their behaviour was closely linked to the radicalisation on the Eastern Front: 'The troops, who for many years have been deployed in the non-German Eastern territories, seem not at all clear about the fact that they are once again on German soil and that they are to defend German values.'[66]

---

[61] Kühne, *Kameradschaft*, pp. 117–18.
[62] Blankenhorn ... *und fahr'n wir ohne Wiederkehr*, pp. 44–5.
[63] Charlotte Gottschalk, email message to author, November 2009.
[64] Tilitzki, *Alltag in Ostpreußen*, p. 282.   [65] Ibid., pp. 298–9.
[66] BArch NS 19/2606, p. 39: Der Reichsführer-SS als Sonderbeauftragter f. Pflanzenkautschuk, 9. Dezember 1944.

In the Soviet Union, plunder had become completely accepted. Predating Operation Barbarossa German officials had pushed for the implementation of the 'Hunger Plan', which was a double-edged sword. By seizing food from the Soviet countryside, millions of racially inferior Slavs were expected to perish, while this 'living off the land' also meant that the Wehrmacht's stay in the Soviet Union would have less impact on the food situation back in Germany. Plunder was presented as a natural part of the soldiers' everyday life, and the behaviour could not be shaken off easily once back in Germany.[67] It is therefore of little surprise that General Wuthmann feared that the scale of plunder of his Korps' troops in East Prussia would 'damage the reputation and standing of the German soldier'.[68] In a circular, Wuthmann called for luggage checks of soldiers on leave prior to their departure as well as for more thorough checks of the *Feldpost*, since cases had already been discovered where German soldiers had mailed German property to their relatives.[69] In fact, NSFOs were to instruct their men on the treatment of German property near the front: 'The property of each evacuated Volksgenosse is sacred, and every soldier has to treat and protect the possessions of each Volksgenosse as if it were his own.'[70] Plunder was also witnessed in Königsberg. In late January 1945, for example, soldiers were seen kicking in doors searching for alcohol and tobacco upon returning from the front.[71] The intelligence officer Walter Kemsies reported that some troops appeared to have no respect for private property in the city:

Unclean elements were still trying exploit the plight and predicament of the poorest: stole and plundered from them, lied to them and mocked them. Regrettably, most of them were German soldiers – thankfully the majority of them were the scum of the Wehrmacht, deserters and cowards – who laid hands on the refugees or on their paltry possessions, who confused the poor refugee woman who had lost her nerves, who unhitched the refugees' horses, took their vehicles, [and] stole their last jewellery.[72]

Plunder would remain an unresolved issue until the end of the war and reports about the army's behaviour remained commonplace.[73] The belief

[67] Tooze, *The Wages of Destruction*, pp. 476–80; Götz Aly, *Hitlers Volksstaat: Raub, Rassenkrieg und nationaler Sozialismus* (Bonn: Bundeszentrale für politische Bildung, 2014), pp. 114–58; Bastiaan Willems, 'Nachbeben des Totalen Kriegs: Der Rückzug der Wehrmacht durch Ostpreußen und seine Folgen', *VfZ* (66) 2018, pp. 403–33.

[68] BArch RH 24–9/137, p. 18: Generalkommando IX. Armeekorps Ia Nr. 3832/44 geh. K. Gef. Stand, den 1.11.44 Hinweise Nr. 5.

[69] Ibid.

[70] BArch RW/62–1, Der politische Soldat, Januar 1945: Deutsches Eigentum im Frontgebiet.

[71] BArch Ost-Dok. 8/602, p. 5: Makowka.

[72] AKO 22034–4: Kemsies: *Stimmungsbilder aus Königsberg*, p. 2.

[73] BArch NS 6/135, p. 83: An den NS-Führungsstab der Wehrmacht II F – No/Kg. 14.3.45; BArch NS 6/354, pp. 100–1: Rundschreiben 156/45 g. Betrifft: Plünderungen

of many troops that defeat (either of Germany or of their own unit) was imminent only seems to have encouraged them to continue plundering; of those who plundered, the notion that they were looting *German* goods hardly seemed to have mattered. In the Soviet Union, troops had been taught to appropriate property as they saw fit with little regard to the human consequences of their behaviour. Although in comparison to the Soviet Union the scale was certainly more limited in East Prussia, this behaviour clearly continued once back in Germany.

Since troops had long learned to detach evacuation from its humanitarian context, plunder was little more than a kneejerk reaction, a clear manifestation of a set of ingrained behaviours. The bar to resorting to plunder was further lowered by the fact that the supply chain, the *Etappe*, had collapsed, forcing the German soldier to 'organise' his living by scourging his direct environment. The behaviour, although frowned upon by civilians, fitted within the set of values of the Wehrmacht that had matured during its stay on the Eastern Front. Moreover, a string of orders portrayed it as necessary: the decision to implement the destructive ARLZ-measures on German soil also leaves no doubt that during the defence of the Heimat the Wehrmacht did not consider the plight of civilians of immediate importance. There were few orders from above that conveyed the need to exercise restraint in regard to damaging behaviour; if anything, the continuing execution of the ARLZ-measures argued the polar opposite. Compounding this was that the dejected mood and the long-established dynamics within the respective units left troops little opportunity to reflect on their changing environment. German soldiers received mixed signals, to say the least: while on one day commanders ordered their troops to defend German property, on another those same commanders could instruct their men to destroy it. As before, German warfare prioritised the fighting itself while the long-term effects on the civilian population were all but disregarded.

Plenty of German soldiers will have changed their behaviour out of a certain respect to their Volksgenossen but we should be careful not to give the individual Landser too much agency in this matter. For Wehrmacht troops, the main difference between the Soviet Union and Germany was that in the former they had operated in an environment that – especially when it concerned the treatment of civilians – had been effectively lawless from the very start, whereas in the latter they were expected to adhere to much stricter rules. However, there was a clear discrepancy between the

durch deutsche Soldaten in geräumten Gebieten, 24.3.1945. No less than 890 copies of this document were distributed, which was prepared by Reichsleiter Bormann, written 'by order of the Führer', and signed by Field Marshal Wilhelm Keitel.

orders and directives that were being passed down by the highest military and Party echelons and their implementation during battle in faraway villages in East Prussia. The next section will dissect this discrepancy and address the root causes of these diverging decisions.

East Prussian Refugees Within German Defensive Warfare

Military behaviour during the unfolding humanitarian crisis in East Prussia can be explained along two main strands: regime conformity and military utilitarianism. The prior mainly concerns itself with decisions taken by the High Command, the latter is rooted in choices made by field commanders who had to base their decisions on the situation 'on the ground'. Ideally, the two would mostly overlap – which would imply agreement between field commanders and the High Command. Yet after the war, those commanders who sought to champion themselves as defenders of refugees had little choice but to claim that they had turned their backs on the OKW and OKH since the orders these bodies passed down in late 1944 and early 1945 left little doubt that the refugee question was hardly more than a side issue. To commanders in the East moreover, the OKW and OKH were welcome scapegoats, if only because by the end of the war they also seemed to be losing their grip. Albert Speer, who as one of Hitler's closest confidants in February 1942 had been appointed as Minister of Armaments and War Production, noted 'that the [OKH] had definitively given up informing Hitler correctly and instead occupied itself with war games'.[74] Guderian remembered meetings at which the entire OKH staff was drunk, so much so that they were even standing on the tables.[75]

More and more commanders reacted to this development by bypassing the chain of command and adopting – in their view – a more pragmatic and utilitarian approach to warfare that better suited the demands on the ground. They did so by 'reinterpreting' the orders and directives they received, a development that was not lost on Hitler. On 19 January 1945 he ordered that every intended operational movement down to divisional level had to be put before him, and that he expected to read nothing but the 'unvarnished truth'.[76] The order shows the widespread distrust that was mutually felt between field commanders on one hand and the German High Command on the other. A similar tendency can be

---

[74] Kunz, *Wehrmacht und Niederlage*, pp. 93–4.
[75] Duffy, *Red Storm on the Reich*, p. 46.
[76] BArch RH2/ 331a, p. 149: Geheime Kommandosache Der Führer Nr.00688/45 g.Kdos. 19. Januar 1945.

observed among local Party dignitaries who saw themselves caught between the increasingly delusional demands of 'Berlin' and the plight of the population they were faced with on a daily basis. However, any instance of 'unwillingness' to adhere to Hitler's orders during this stage of the war should be treated with care. Most commanders had been imbued with the principles of *Auftragstaktik* and still adhered to them – not as a form of silent protest, but rather out of habit. Party offices meanwhile had to be managed with a complete lack of resources, making it impossible for their functionaries to carry out their tasks. Nevertheless, both Party and Wehrmacht in East Prussia – despite what was happening in front of their very eyes – continued to operate as if the war could still be won. The East Prussian refugee thus became trapped between a misguided sense of duty and a baseless determination to keep fighting.

Perhaps the main reason that field commanders conformed to the policies of the High Command is precisely because they suited their own warfare particularly well: occasions where the OKW considered the fate of civilians over that of the troops are scarce. During a main attack, for example, the OKW took over control of the railway, and ranked the refugee matter as fifth and last in importance, which, as its war diary noted, 'practically meant that all refugee trains were cancelled'.[77] Behind this lay a grim reality. At least six East Prussian military hospitals were evacuated in orderly fashion after the East Prussian offensive had commenced, and their staffs arrived by train in Königsberg without significant delays along the way.[78] Yet at the same time many civilian refugees desperately tried to head west as well, but found that for them transportation by rail was extremely limited. In Königsberg, armed soldiers blocked the access to the station for refugees, and those trains that were eventually destined for refugee transport were often shunted into sidings for days to allow for unhindered military movement.[79] People were desperate to get to Pillau, on the westernmost tip of the Samland, from where ships were said to be leaving to safety.[80] In despair, parents who were denied access to the trains pushed their children through the windows while fights on the train erupted in the search for a place. The trains were packed so tight that many people lost consciousness.[81] The conditions in the trains heading south-west – via

[77] Schramm, *Kriegstagebuch des OKW Band IV*, pp. 1150, 1322–3: 20–2 and 6–3-1945: 1. Wehrmacht-transports (operational and supplies); 2. Coal; 3. Food; 4. Notprogram of RuK-ministry; 5 Refugees.
[78] BArch RH 53–1/27, p. 1: Wehrkreisarzt I Bericht!
[79] Kershaw, *The End*, pp. 177–8; Schwendemann, 'Tod zwischen den Fronten', pp. 44–5.
[80] Today, Pillau is the Russian town of Baltiysk.
[81] BArch Ost-Dok 8/602, p. 4: Makowka; Knopp, *Der Sturm*, pp. 73, 75.

Elbing to the Reich – were even worse. Unaware that Elbing had been captured on 23 January, they kept heading in that direction. As a result, some trains halted for days in the blistering cold. Many refugees suffered from hypothermia and several even died inside the trains.[82]

Fleeing via road was even harder. During the operations in East Prussia, German army officers increasingly complained about carts of refugees hindering military traffic. Along the streets south of the river Pregel, an officer of the 5th Panzer-Division wrote of endless lines of refugees heading west and congesting the roads to Königsberg, and as the fuel had to come from that direction, only limited amounts of the badly needed supplies reached the troops.[83] The troops on the spot regularly took the law into their own hands. Heinz Simat, a veteran of the 349th Volksgrenadier-Division, recalled the behaviour of his unit at the small town of Norkitten, where congested lines of refugees tried to cross the Pregel: 'Often the military vehicles rigorously drove the refugee carts off the road, and the largest vehicles time and again

Figure 5.3 A road sign warning Trecks to stay on the right side of the road and not to hinder military traffic, November 1944. *Source:* SZPhoto, Image ID: 00067569

[82] Schieder (ed.), *Die Vertreibung der deutschen Bevölkerung aus den Gebieten östlich der Oder-Neiße, Band I*, pp. 67–8.

[83] Anton Detlef von Plato, *Die Geschichte der 5. Panzerdivision: 1938 bis 1945* (Lüchow: Gemeinschaft d. Angehörigen d. Ehem. 5. Panzerdivision, 1978), pp. 377, 379.

ignored their right of way.'[84] Thus, a few days after the offensive had commenced, civilians were forbidden to use the province's main roads, Reichsstrasse 1 and Reichsstrasse 138.[85] In addition the roads in the area between the river Deime and the road between Königsberg and Cranz were made off limits for civilians. When the fighting neared Königsberg, even its Ringchaussee was closed off for civilians.[86]

Miss G.K. hastens through the no man's land between the fronts. She reaches Konigsberg, together with her neighbour, his wife, and their ten children. German soldiers close off the entrance streets. 'Königsberg is a fortress. No civilians are allowed to enter.' Miss G.K. pleads, begs, cries. In vain. She, too, must join the refugee stream that continues westwards.[87]

On 23 January, at the height of the flight of East Prussia's inhabitants, even the road between Königsberg and Pillau – the main artery used by these refugees – was closed to civilians.[88] The refugees were therefore forced to use byways or even go through fields.[89] In effect, it meant that their Trecks did not even reach walking speed and many were unable to reach the shelter of a town or village by the end of a day. During the last two weeks of January, when the temperature almost constantly fell below minus twenty or even minus thirty degrees, many refugees froze to death.

On 23 January Soviet troops reached the Frische Haff near Elbing, which meant that all Germans east of it were cut off. From then on, the seemingly most straightforward way to escape East Prussia was by boarding a ship from the port town of Pillau, on the westernmost tip of the Samland, to the Danzig/Gotenhafen area or directly to reception areas in northern Germany and Denmark.[90] As we saw, by then the choice had long been made to give absolute priority to the transport of military materiel and personnel, and the military continued to persist in this view during the unfolding humanitarian crisis.[91] On 22 January, Grossadmiral Dönitz and Hitler discussed the evacuation question in depth, since, as the war diary of the Seekriegsleitung noted, 'the rapid

---

[84] Simat, *Blutiger Abschied*, p. 27. For a similar story, observed by the commander of Army Group Centre, see Kershaw, *The End*, p. 199.
[85] Kreisgemeinschaft Wehlau, *Heimatbuch des Kreises Wehlau Alle-Pregel-Deime-Gebiet I. Band* (Leer: Verlag Gerhard Rauterberg, 1975), p. 568–9.
[86] AKO 22034–4: Kemsies: *Stimmungsbilder aus Königsberg*, p. 2.
[87] Lass, *Die Flucht*, p. 200.
[88] Heinz Schön, *Ostsee '45: Menschen – Schiffe – Schicksale* (Stuttgart: Motorbuch Verlag, 1984), p. 94.
[89] AKO 22034–4: Kemsies: *Stimmungsbilder aus Königsberg*, pp. 1–2.
[90] Danzig and Gotenhafen are today the Polish cities of Gdańsk and Gdynia.
[91] See for example: BArch RH 2/332, p. 242: Fernschreiben OKH/ GenStdH/ Op Abt (roem. 1a) Nr. 2373/45 g.Kdos 24.2.45; BArch RH 2/335, 106–107: Fernschreiben Betr. Abtransport aus Ostpreußen OKH/ GenStdH/ Op Abt röm. 1a Nr. 4167/45 g. 4.4.45.

deterioration of the situation in East Prussia, especially the large influx of refugees in the ports, has led to "cries for help" from civilian agencies'.[92] The outcomes of the discussions would shape the way the evacuation of the province would be carried out during its defence.

The Reich Commissioner for Shipping [Gauleiter Karl Kaufmann] can, without disturbing the current transport movements, provide a total of eighteen ships in the home area for evacuation, but these depend on the coal stocks available in the eastern areas [of Germany]. Here lies the bottleneck. There is still sufficient coal to continue transport tasks (replenishment of divisions, supply of Army Group Kurland) for three weeks, for the rail transport of troops for only ten days … Since the consignment of divisions and the supply of Army Group Kurland would come to a standstill in no time without replenishment and must necessarily take precedence, nothing remains but to dispense with the evacuation of refugees.[93]

Hitler agreed with Dönitz's evaluation and prioritisation of the supply of the fighting troops and decided that 'the remaining coal stocks must be reserved for military tasks, and may not be used for the evacuation of refugees'.[94]

After the war, the Grossadmiral nevertheless placed the navy at the centre of the evacuation efforts.[95] Between late January and early May 1945 hundreds of ships did indeed shuttle between the eastern German ports of Königsberg, Pillau, Gotenhafen, and Danzig to the ports in the west of the Reich and Denmark.[96] Eventually over a million refugees were transported by the merchant navy and the Kriegsmarine, allowing former naval officers in post-war Germany to push a narrative in which they suggested that the navy's rescue of civilians was a deliberate and concerted operation, known as Operation Hannibal.[97] This version of events portrayed the Kriegsmarine as unblemished and selfless, a narrative readily adopted by refugees from the former eastern provinces who used the supposed magnitude of Operation Hannibal as a way to have their plight acknowledged.[98] Yet, regardless of the individual courage of ships' captains and crew, the war diary of the Seekriegsleitung leaves no doubt about the marginal place 'Hannibal' occupied at the naval headquarters

---

[92] Werner Rahm and Gerhard Schreiber (eds.) *Kriegstagebuch der Seekriegsleitung 1939–1945 Teil A, Band 65: Januar 1945* (Berlin: Verlag E.S. Mittler & Sohn, 1996), p. 403.

[93] Wagner (ed.), *Lagevorträge*, p. 636; Schramm, *Kriegstagebuch des OKW Band IV*, pp. 1600–1.

[94] Wagner (ed.), *Lagevorträge*, p. 636.

[95] Dönitz, *Zehn Jahre und Zwanzig Tage*, pp. 398, 430–45.

[96] Heinz Schön, *Ostsee '45: Menschen – Schiffe – Schicksale*, Motorbuch Verlag Stuttgart, 1984, pp. 677–85.

[97] Ibid., pp. 84–7.

[98] Douglas Peifer, 'Selfless Saviours or Diehard Fanatics? West and East German Memories of the Kriegsmarine and the Baltic Evacuation', *War & Society* (26) 2007, pp. 110–12.

in Kiel. On 23 January, the morning after his meeting with Hitler, Dönitz discussed with his staff the possibility of implementing 'Rotdorn Case B': the transfer (in reality the evacuation) of naval forces from the ports of East and West Prussia to the west. 'Rotdorn' was the codename for a series of evacuation plans (A, B, and C) of Kriegsmarine troops from the eastern Baltic, and the possibility of implementing 'Case B' had already been discussed some days earlier, on 14 January.[99] Hans-Georg von Friedeburg, the commanding admiral of the U-Boat arm, had anticipated this move, and according to the war diary of the Seekriegsleitung indicated during the meeting that 'using the codename "Hannibal" he had already issued advance orders for "Rotdorn" to the troops under his command'.[100] Thus, 'Hannibal' was certainly not at an all-encompassing operation that sought to safeguard the civilian population, but rather one of the many orders aimed at transferring the forces in the area westwards. Dönitz and von Friedeburg agreed that as many civilians as possible should be taken along yet there was 'full clarity' among the Seekriegsleitung that 'military transports and tasks must take precedence over all other tasks, especially at this stage'.[101] How low refugees were on the list of priorities of the Kriegsmarine is well encapsulated by a passing remark of 12 February in the war diary of the Seekriegsleitung which noted that the OKW 'announced that a Party chancellery representative for refugee transports is appointed at the Marine Oberkommando Ost'. The passive wording suggests that the navy saw this as outside interference – which it had not requested – and it is therefore hardly surprising that the matter was neither elaborated on during the meeting nor was acknowledged or followed up on even once in the weeks that followed.[102] Dönitz would stick to this principle throughout the final months of the war. On 28 January he reiterated that 'the refugee transports by sea can be carried out only as far as they do not hamper the transportation of combat troops to and from Kurland and Norway', two areas that were still occupied by German forces.[103] Not only did the evacuation of civilians receive the least priority, which meant that hardly any resources were allocated to it but also, from the moment the Soviet offensives commenced, the army repeatedly pushed for a Führer-order to forbid the 'manifold hectic evacuations' which in their eyes only 'jeopardised military operations'.[104]

---

[99] Rahm and Schreiber (eds.) *Kriegstagebuch der Seekriegsleitung, Band 65*, p. 244.

[100] Ibid., p. 418. This is the only mention of 'Hannibal' in the war diary of the *Seekriegsleitung*.

[101] Ibid., pp. 418, 442.

[102] Werner Rahm and Gerhard Schreiber (eds.), *Kriegstagebuch der Seekriegsleitung 1939–1945 Teil A, Band 66: Februar 1945* (Berlin: Verlag E.S. Mittler & Sohn, 1996), p. 116.

[103] Schramm, *Kriegstagebuch des OKW Band IV*, p. 1602.

[104] Schwendemann, 'Der deutsche Zusammenbruch im Osten 1944/45', p. 138.

Hitler, however, went in a different direction. The unfolding refugee crisis, the enormity of which could be gauged after a few minutes in his map room, prompted him on 5 February to issue a Führer order. The order, which concerned the 'transport of refugees from the East to Denmark', demanded that refugees who were stuck in East Prussia and in the Danzig area were to be moved by sea, while refugees in Pomerania, near Stettin and Swinemünde, were to be evacuated by rail. The order ended with the assurance that 'the armed forces will provide every conceivable support', but since it also stipulated that these transports were to be carried out 'without impairing the day-to-day movement of troops and supplies', the order was nullified even before the ink was dry.[105]

The prioritisation of military concerns over those of refugees meant that most East Prussians were stranded in Pillau. After the departure of the Party leadership from Konigsberg, Pillau had become the domain of the Party. The town, with a pre-war population of 10,000 could not cope with the tens of thousands of refugees who arrived there and steadily swelled to 50,000 by mid-February.[106] In this period, Gauleiter Koch organised a *Gauleiteraktion zur Erhöhung der Lebensbilanz* (Gauleiter campaign for the increase of living standards) in Pillau, although the results were limited.[107] When asked by his long-standing subordinate, Waldemar Magunia, why he had chosen to set up his post in Pillau rather than return to Königsberg, Koch explained that his presence at the port town allowed him to oversee the evacuation of East Prussia's population more effectively.[108] Although this conveniently meant that he was kept away from the front line, during the last months of Koch's rule his focus would indeed remain on the evacuation question rather than on the defence of East Prussia. In Berlin, he started lobbying – without success – for additional shipping space for refugees.[109] Karl Friedrich, a representative of Gauleiter Koch later wrote: 'The disastrous situation around Danzig and Gotenhafen meant that for weeks no ship even came to Pillau. Even the

---

[105] Hubatsch, *Hitlers Weisungen für die Kriegsführung*, p. 302. According to the deputy chief of the OKW's operations staff, General Walter Warlimont, by the end of the war these directives merely 'derived from impressions or necessities of the moment', and were therefore hardly taken seriously anymore. See: Walter Warlimont, *Im Hauptquartier der deutschen Wehrmacht 1939 bis 1945, Grundlagen – Formen – Gestalten, Band 2* (Koblenz: Weltbild Verlag, 1990), p. 433.

[106] BArch R55/616, p. 184: Komm. Leiter Pro Ref.: MR Imhoff, Berlin, den 15. Februar 1945 An den Herrn Staatssekretär Betr.: Lage in der Evakuierung.

[107] AKO 22034-4: Aufzeichnungen des Hauptschriftleiters der *KAZ* Wegener, p. 1.

[108] BArch Ost-Dok. 8/594, p. 6: Magunia. Gauleiter Koch, whose headquarters were on the Frische Nehrung at Neutief, had firstly ensured his own safety. At all times, two ice breakers were ready to sail out west. See: Klement, 'Eisbrecher "Ostpreußen" jetzt auf der Elbe', *Das Ostpreußenblatt*, 13 March 1954, p. 8.

[109] Meindl, *Ostpreussens Gauleiter Erich Koch*, p. 446–8.

few ships that brought cargo (war materiel and food) to Pillau, were not allowed to take any refugees on board and had to leave Pillau empty.'[110] In the light of the armed forces' priorities, all Koch's efforts to secure additional cargo space for refugees were thus doomed to fail from the start.

In mid-February, Reichsleiter Bormann passed a circular to the Gauleiter, showing his agreement with the measures that had so far been taken by the military in Eastern Germany. If anything, he implied that the measures to limit evacuation were not far-reaching enough. Large-scale evacuation as a result of the Allied offensive in the west, he foresaw, 'would meet in the Reich interior the stream of fugitives from the East, thus hampering military and civilian movements'. Therefore 'even women and children [are] to remain, but nobody capable of working for the Allies [is] to be left. Elements of the population remaining behind [are] no longer to be regarded as traitors'.[111] As a result, by February 1945, 80,000 East Prussian civilians were already in Soviet hands according to estimates of Königsberg's fortress command. Meanwhile, in early March, when the refugee crisis in East Prussia was at its height, Dönitz once again stressed that 'assuring the control of [sea] ways, maintaining maritime transports, and the support of land fronts by naval artillery remain our most important tasks in the Baltic Sea, the fulfilment of which must be striven for with all available means'.[112]

The effects of these decisions can clearly be seen in Pillau. The man responsible for the evacuation of the port city was Deputy RVK Dr Bruno Dzubba, who, despite his earlier role in the evacuations of Memel, Tilsit and Zichenau, was poorly regarded, but whose views seemed to correspond much closer to those of the army than to his immediate superior, Gauleiter Koch.[113] Louis Clappier, a French prisoner of war, typified Dzubba's attitude towards refugees as follows: 'Refugees are people, who don't want to fight ... Refugees are people that want to flee at all costs because they fear cannons or Russians. For this kind of people there is no urgent interest. They are to be got rid of so that the battle area does not clog because of an unnecessary accumulation of civilians.'[114] Around the same time, Reichsführer-SS Himmler, in his ultimately disastrous turn as commander of Army Group Vistula, put it even more succinctly: 'we are organising the defence, not the flight [das Davonlaufen]'.[115] Throughout

---

[110] BArch Ost-Dok. 8/508, p. 3: Friedrich.   [111] TNA HW 1/3520, 15 February 1945.
[112] BArch NS 6/354, p. 171: Anlage 3 zur Bekanntgabe 162/45 g. von 27.3.1945. Abschrift! 26. Kurzlage des Ob.d.M. vom 9.3.1945.
[113] AKO 22034-4: Aufzeichnungen des Hauptschriftleiters der KAZ Wegener, p. 1.
[114] Clappier, Festung Königsberg, pp. 50–1.
[115] Schwendemann, 'Strategie der Selbstvernichtung', p. 238.

February, March, and April, the care for the refugees in Pillau thus remained poor, even though the refugee crisis grew ever more pressing. Here we see evidence of this kind of 'cumulative radicalisation' as Party interests converged with those of the military.

East Prussian refugees became the victims of a general mindset among the top ranks of the Party and the Wehrmacht that firmly subordinated civilian life to the defence of territory. The disregard of human life was no longer part of a genocidal agenda, as it had been in the Soviet Union, but it *was* the result of a warped sense of utilitarianism and military 'professionalism' that had matured during the years prior. For all intents and purposes, by 1945 especially, the military commanders were morally numbed and 'sound' operational conduct trumped humanitarian concerns. Their behaviour was not rooted in resigned 'self-destructiveness',[116] but appears as a navigation between their allegiance to Germany and their oath to Hitler on one the hand and the need for self-preservation and their loyalty to their troops on the other hand. These considerations, as they had been during the earlier defensive battles in the Soviet Union and the Baltics, were largely unconcerned with civilians. This section also reveals that the behaviour of Party members in Germany in 1945 might partly be explained by the fact that many of them felt that they had to come into line with military necessities. The solutions that were favoured became increasingly radical in nature which ended in a deliberate choice to rank the needs of civilians ever lower. To explore these decision-making processes further, the next section will therefore examine how the evacuation in Königsberg was organised and what considerations lay at its core.

Evacuation Policy in Königsberg

Examining the way that the evacuation from Festung Königsberg was carried out can teach us a lot about what transpired in 1945. Firstly, with the Wehrmacht and the Party both assuming prominent roles in the city (with the Wehrmacht taking over control of parts of local government and the Party adopting more military tasks), we can measure the effects of 'cumulative radicalisation' in Königsberg's evacuation measures. Secondly, a study of the city's evacuation can help us to understand the military imperatives that drove General Lasch, as well as the relationship between the wider fortress authorities and the local population.

The evacuation process under examination here needs some brief clarification. During the East Prussian offensive, the different Soviet armies had lost a significant part of their manpower and materiel, and in

---

[116] Schwendemann, 'Strategie der Selbstvernichtung'.

early February their commanders convinced the Front command of the immediate importance of regrouping and replenishing their exhausted units.[117] They therefore strengthened their positions around the city and held a tight grip on it, but on the other hand did not launch any sustained attacks on German positions. Since Königsberg was virtually completely encircled during this period, evacuation could only take place by ship, using the sea lane between Königsberg and Pillau. Soviet artillery was positioned on the coast and could target these ships which meant that they could only sail at night, so the number of evacuees during this period was low.[118] It is thus more worthwhile to examine the period when the fortress command had the means at its disposal to organise a more effective evacuation.

Therefore, the starting point of this section is Operation Westwind, the German military operation that would come to define Königsberg's fortress era. The aim of the operation was to restore the lost link between Königsberg and Pillau. For the operation to be effectively overseen, the seasoned General Hans Gollnick was put in charge of the purpose-built Armee-Abteilung 'Samland', which comprised all German forces on the peninsula.[119] The operation had been planned from the moment the link was lost in late January, it was supported by the Kriegsmarine, and it commenced on 19 February, when four divisions attacked from the area around Pillau eastwards while three divisions attacked westwards from Königsberg.[120] A day later the units linked up and on 25 February the area was secure enough to restart the rail link between Königsberg and

---

[117] Bagramyan, *Tak shli my k pobede*, pp. 513–15; Kuzma Galitsky, *V boyakh za Vostochnuyu Prussiyu: Zapiski komanduyushchego 11-y gvardeyskoy armiyey* [In the battles for East Prussia: Notes of the Commander of the 11th Guards Army] (Moscow: Naika, 1970), pp. 344–5.

[118] IfZArch Akten der Partei-Kanzlei der NSDAP: 13201458 Komm.Leiter Pro Ref. MR. Imhoff. Dem Herrn Staatssekretär. Berlin, den 21. Februar 1945. Betr.: Lage der Evakuierung. Report states that between 29 January and 19 February 33,000 people were evacuated by means of sea transport.

[119] Armee-Abteilung 'Samland' absorbed all divisions that had earlier been subordinated to the Third Panzer Army, whose staff on 19 February was transferred to Army Group Weichsel (Vistula). The staff of Armee-Abteilung 'Samland' was that of General Gollnick's XXVIII. Korps, which had earlier defended Festung Memel, and in late January 1945 had retreated via the Kurische Nehrung to take up positions on the western tip of the Samland. The designation as Armee-Abteilung reveals that even at the High Command it was clear that the strength of the units remaining in East Prussia no longer represented that of an army.

[120] BArch RH 2/328, p. 235: OKH/GenStdH/ Op Abt (röm 1a) Nr. 450081/45 g.K. Chefs. 7.2.45. Weisung für Heeresgruppe Nord!; Grier, *Hitler, Dönitz and the Baltic Sea*, pp. 112–13; Christopher Duffy, *Red Storm on the Reich: the Soviet March on Germany, 1945* (New York: Da Capo Press, 1993), pp. 164–6.

Map 5.1 Operation Westwind, late February 1945

Pillau.[121] In his memoirs, General Lasch claimed that Operation Westwind sought 'to create the opportunity to transport away large parts of the clustered civilian population' and get new supplies in, although an extensive report on the goals of Army Group North, sent one week after the start of Operation Westwind, does not refer to the care for civilians.[122] We will therefore examine to what extent the operation benefited the civilian population and how, in the period that followed, the authorities used the opportunities created by the operation to ensure the civilians' evacuation from the area.

On 17 February 1945 General Gollnick ordered Lasch to assign the 1st Infanterie-Division and parts of the 5th Panzer-Division to Operation Westwind.[123] Lasch, however, decided to commit significantly more troops to the operation. He would deploy the entire 1st Infanterie-Division, the entire 5th Panzer-Division, as well as the 561st Volksgrenadier-Division, leaving only two divisions, the 367th and 69th Infanterie-Divisions, to defend the city. This decision was met with opposition from his superiors as it left the fortress dangerously exposed, but the general willingly accepted responsibility in case of failure.[124] His initiative was criticised by his army colleagues even though it would contribute significantly to the eventual success of the operation.[125] This 'conflict' shows that, even by 1945, the spirit of Auftragstaktik was still alive: Lasch, who was junior to Gollnick, significantly altered the plan of attack that was put in front of him, and although Gollnick voiced his objections, he let Lasch carry out his mission as he saw fit. However, this turn of events also means that Lasch's post-war complaints of being restricted in his operational freedom by the OKH and OKW should be approached with a certain scepticism: not only did he refuse to address Gollnick's concerns; he knew that by ignoring the order he also snubbed the commander of Army Group North, Generaloberst Rendulic, as well as Gauleiter Koch, who both had direct contact with Hitler.

What factors determined Lasch's decision to commit three divisions and disregard the wishes of his superior? Most likely, a commander's concern for the welfare of his troops would have weighed heavily on his mind.

---

[121] Dieckert and Großmann, *Der Kampf um Ostpreussen*, pp. 158–9; Lasch, *So fiel Königsberg*, pp. 68–75; Grier, *Hitler, Dönitz and the Baltic Sea*, pp. 118–19; Kurt Mehner, *Die geheimen Tagesberichte der deutschen Wehrmachtführung im Zweiten Weltkrieg 1939–1945, Band 12: 1. Januar 1945 – 9. Mai 1945* (Osnabrück: Biblio Verlag, 1984), p. 222.

[122] Lasch, *So fiel Königsberg*, p. 69; BArch RH 2/ 328, pp. 242–5: Fernschreiben an Chef des Gen St d H, gez. Rendulic Obkdo. H.Gr. Nord Ia Nr.1543/45 g.Kdos. Chefs.

[123] Lasch, *So fiel Königsberg*, p. 68; Kabath and Forstmeier, 'Die Rolle der Seebrückenköpfe beim Kampf um Ostpreussen', pp. 334–5.

[124] Lasch, *So fiel Königsberg*, pp. 68–70.

[125] von Plato, *Die Geschichte der 5. Panzerdivision*, p. 384.

Lasch, in particular, was a deeply paternalistic officer. Generaloberst Erhard Raus, under whom Lasch served half a year earlier, wrote in an assessment that Lasch was a 'very good officer who knew how to quickly transform his newly established division into a solid unit. However, [Lasch] sometimes puts the interests of his troops too much in the foreground'.[126] Moreover, Lasch, like most commanders, felt that the defence of Königsberg could only end in the garrison's capture by Soviet troops. He, on the other hand, was one of the Wehrmacht's experts with regard to the breakout from pockets. A year earlier, he had broken out of the Brody pocket in western Ukraine, bringing his troops back to a safe line.[127] What was more, something similar had been undertaken in late January 1945, three weeks before Operation Westwind, by the commander of the Fourth Army, General Friedrich Hossbach. On 23 January Soviet troops reached the Frische Haff near Elbing which meant that the German troops east of it were cut off. Hossbach knew that being encircled made supplying his army a considerably harder challenge and therefore wanted to restore a connection with the main German lines. Without consulting the OKH, the general thus started to prepare a breakout westwards, but when the news of his attempted breakout came out, the commander was sacked.[128] Lasch thus knew that he could not abandon the city, but he was keen to open a route to Pillau. But such an operation risked leaving Königsberg's entire population exposed.[129]

To understand the enormous danger Lasch put Königsberg's population in, we should address the city's topography. Königsberg was cut into a northern and a southern half by the river Pregel. The southern half was almost completely encircled by Soviet troops, so German units there had considerably less opportunity to retreat since they would have to cross the

---

[126] BArch PERS 6/300107: Lasch, Bernhard Otto: 16.8.44 Raus, O.B. 1. Pz.Armee This loyalty worked two ways, and his funeral in 1971 was attended by a number of his subordinates. See: F. G. 'Abschied von General a.D Lasch', *Das Ostpreußenblatt*, 15 May 1971, p. 13.

[127] BArch PERS 6/300107: Lasch, Bernhard Otto: 1.8.44. Balck, Kom.Gen. XXXXVIII. Pz.K.

[128] Schwendemann, 'Tod zwischen den Fronten', p. 42–3; Kershaw, *The End*, p. 199. Hoßbach's decision to abandon that part of East Prussia also meant that he abandoned the other German units that were fighting in the area, notably the Third Panzer Army which contributed to the outrage at Hitler's headquarters. See: Guderian, *Panzer Leader*, pp. 400–1. Schumann and Groehler (eds.), *Deutschland im Zweiten Weltkrieg 6*, p. 511: The chief of staff of Army Group Centre, Generalleutnant Otto Heidkämper noted on 24 January, 'Hossbach does not care about the Third Panzer Army, which he wants to abandon … 'if it means he can only save his Fourth [Army]'.

[129] In his self-serving telling of the events in Festung Königsberg, von Süßkind-Schwendi chose not to devote any attention at all to the motivations that lay behind the breakout. See: Hugo Frhr. von Süßkind-Schwendi: 'Aus meinem Soldatenleben – Teil V', *Deutsches Soldatenjahrbuch* (41) 1993, pp. 347–52.

Pregel to get to safety. Lasch left the defence of southern Königsberg to the battle-worn 69th Infanterie-Division, which he 'bolstered' with inferior Volkssturm and police units with little to no combat experience. The north connected to the Samland, and it was from there that the operation was launched westwards. It was also there that Lasch placed the 367th Infanterie-Division, the strongest remaining formation in the city. Had Königsberg been attacked by Soviet forces in response to Operation Westwind, it is likely to have fallen almost immediately, given the limited forces left to defend it.[130] As General Lasch was fully aware of the danger he put the city in, he clearly did not have the safety of the population as uppermost in his mind.[131] Operation Westwind can therefore hardly be considered a conscious attempt to secure the safety of civilians trapped in the city.

What, then, transpired between 25 February and early April, when Königsberg was eventually stormed by Soviet forces? What first needs to be stressed is that in their treatment of civilians, Königsberg's fortress command and East Prussia's Party elite should not be seen as isolated actors, since the OKW was well-aware of the situation in the province. Officials in East Prussia did not operate in a vacuum and were dependent on decisions taken higher up the chain of command, as we saw in the previous section. Around 20 February 1945, a report was discussed at the OKW which addressed East Prussia's refugee crisis. Some 2.3 million inhabitants were said to have been living in East Prussia when the Soviet invasion commenced, many of whom were displaced by the time the report was compiled. Estimates of their whereabouts showed the following numbers: 320,000 in the Danzig area; 500,000 in Pomerania; 200,000 in Saxony; 140,000 in Mecklenburg; 100,000 in Schleswig-Holstein; and 100,000 in other parts of the Reich. This totalled approximately 1,400,000 inhabitants. The report stated that 'of the residual 900,000, around 500,000 serve in the Wehrmacht, Volkssturm, and so on. The final 400,000 inhabitants still have to be evacuated from East Prussia. 135,000 of them are in Königsberg, 200,000 in the Heiligenbeil Pocket, 40,000 on the Samland peninsula'.[132] The OKW estimated that the evacuation of these 400,000 people would take fourteen days.

Days after the recapture of the southern Samland, Gauleiter Koch dispatched ten Kreisleiter to the city to once again take over the civilian administration, much to the frustration of the Wehrmacht commanders.[133]

---

[130] Lasch, *So fiel Königsberg*, pp. 96–9; Blankenhorn, *... und fahr'n wir ohne Wiederkehr*, pp. 164–70.

[131] AKO 22034–4: v. Natzmer: *Einsatz der 4. Armee*, p. 2; Lasch, *So fiel Königsberg*, pp. 68–70. The assessment of the Volkssturm follows in Chapter 6.

[132] Schramm, *Kriegstagebuch des OKW, Band IV*, pp. 1326–7.

[133] AKO 22034–4: Schäfer, *Der Fall Königsbergs*, p. 2.

The Party started pushing for evacuation, but with little means at its disposal it would require the help of the Wehrmacht. Although the army eventually took the credit, there is little evidence to suggest that the fortress command devoted sustained attention to the evacuation of Königsberg's civilian population.[134] The ability of the fortress command's officers to compartmentalise is as astounding as it is cruelly negligent; despite a refugee crisis of epic proportions unfolding in front of them, they failed to draft any order that addressed the plight of the civilian population head-on. Theoretically, Königsberg's evacuees were to be brought to the port of Pillau, from where they could be transported to the west. The first days after Operation Westwind showed that authorities had the potential to evacuate civilians, as resources – most importantly ships' cargo space – were made available to the fortress command.[135] On 26 February the evacuation of Königsberg began with the evacuation of 14,000 inhabitants and the following day another 17,000 were evacuated from the city. Yet many of them were merely brought to the adjacent Samland. In Pillau however there was insufficient space to house the refugees. To accommodate them, four transit camps were set up on the western Samland, in the villages of Peyse, Fischhausen, Neuhäuser, and Rauschen. In practice, this meant that, rather than leaving the province, evacuees were unceremoniously dumped into an administrative no-man's land between Pillau and Königsberg. The camps soon started to become overcrowded since they could not absorb the massive number of refugees, not only from Königsberg but also from the Heiligenbeil Pocket. Hunger became rampant as a result of the complete neglect to organise the provision of food, and it did not take long for epidemics to break out. A medical commission dispatched to the camps warned that if hygiene did not improve immediately the camps would see 'a mass mortality of women and children'.[136] Dysentery duly broke out and caused many deaths, and only the late arrival of doctors managed to contain the epidemic from spreading further.[137] Conditions grew so bad that several thousand refugees prepared to go on a 'hunger march' to Königsberg as a way of protest. Meanwhile, none of the

---

[134] Ibid, p. 4.
[135] BArch NS 19/2068, p. 32. An Reichsführer-SS Feldkommandostelle Betrifft: Meldungen aus dem Ostraum, Königsberg 26.2.45; BArch NS 19/2068, 34. An Reichsführer-SS Feldkommandostelle Betrifft: Meldungen aus dem Ostraum, Königsberg 27.2.45.
[136] BArch NS 19/2068, p. 59. An Reichsführer-SS Feldkommandostelle Betrifft: Meldungen aus dem Ostraum, Königsberg 9.3.45; BArch NS 19/2068, 71. An Reichsführer-SS Feldkommandostelle Betrifft: Meldungen aus dem Ostraum, Königsberg 17.3.45; Hensel, *Medizin in und aus Ostpreußen*, pp. 72–3.
[137] BArch Ost-Dok. 8/602, pp. 8–9 Makowka; Meindl, *Ostpreußens Gauleiter Erich Koch*, p. 450; Wilhelm Starlinger, *Grenzen der Sowjetmacht im Spiegel einer West-Ostbegegnung hinter Palisaden von 1945–1954* (Würzburg: Holzner-Verlag, 1955), pp. 41–2; Hensel, *Medizin in und aus Ostpreußen*, p. 72.

prominent Party members dared to visit the camps as they feared they could be attacked by an angry mob. Instead, lower-ranking Party officials were dispatched to talk to the evacuees.[138] As these men were poorly informed about the situation at hand, they were of little use in aiding the refugees.

According to Oberfeldarzt Dr Paul Schroeder, a medical liaison officer to the fortress staff, many thousands actually flooded back from the camps to Königsberg when the situation became unbearable.[139] General Lasch confirmed that 'before long, the women that were accommodated there showed up to me with their children and prams and asked me, wringing their hands, to allow them back in their houses and lodgings, since they at least had something to eat there'.[140] Lasch, reluctant to inform the returnees about the true state of the defence, but eager to point to the shortcomings of the Party, allowed most of them back in. One of the more critical officers to arrive in Königsberg, Gerhardt Kretschmer, described the atmosphere in the fortress command by late March: 'Everyone discreetly cursed the Gauleiter, who was supposedly somewhere in Pillau ... not taking care [of the population] at all; yet no one stuck his hands out themselves even the slightest'.[141] The poor evacuation of civilians stood in stark contrast to that of wounded soldiers. Throughout late February, March, and early April, commanders in East Prussia would continue to put their men first. On 7 March the navy noted that, due to the heavy fighting in Eastern Germany, the army was suffering some 7,100 wounded per day: around 3,000 from Danzig, 2,500 from Pillau, 800 from Kurland, and 800 from Army Group Vistula. These men had to be evacuated by means of sea transport yet the daily capacity of the available hospital ships reached a mere 2,000. Commanders sought to 'remedy' this situation at the expense of civilians: refugee ships were co-opted to accommodate 1,000 wounded soldiers a day, as such putting even more strain on the tightly budgeted spaces allocated to the evacuees.[142] In the morning of 6 April, just hours before the anticipated final storming of Königsberg, Lasch ordered a train with 10,000 slightly wounded troops to leave the city.[143] These troops were part of a

---

[138] Hensel, *Medizin in und aus Ostpreußen*, p. 72.

[139] Starlinger, *Grenzen der Sowjetmacht*, pp. 41–2. See also: Diechelmann, *Ich sah Königsberg sterben*, pp. 9–10.

[140] Lasch, *So fiel Königsberg*, pp. 76–7; BArch Ost-Dok. 8/531, p. 19: Klaus von der Groeben, Landrat des Kreises Samland. Das Ende in Ostpreußen. Den Ablauf der Geschehnisse in Samland. (1.10.1952).

[141] IFZArch ZS/A-2/ 04–140, Gerhardt Kretschmer, Nuernberg-Zabo, d. 11.4.49.

[142] Rahm and Schreiber (eds.) *Kriegstagebuch der Seekriegsleitung, Band 67*, p. 103.

[143] Lasch, *So fiel Königsberg*, p. 80; BArch Ost-Dok. 8/598, p. 102: Klein; Schwendemann, 'Der deutsche Zusammenbruch im Osten 1944/45', p. 142. Between 1 and 20 March 1945, over 60,000 wounded of Army Group North, meticulously documented, were evacuated from the ports of Pillau (19,299), Danzig (21,039) and Gotenhafen (21,718).

Figure 5.4 Tired-looking German troops are evacuated by ship, March–April 1945. *Source:* Author's collection

contingent of over 150,000 soldiers who, after being wounded, were evacuated out of East Prussia to the west by well-organised transports; a measure which served to maintain battle morale.[144]

After the war, men like Lasch maintained that they could do little but follow orders.[145] However, the worsening military situation did not necessarily mean that the hands of army commanders were tied. As there was an appreciation of the situation on the ground at the OKH and OKW, commanders were given the flexibility to make decisions based on their own discretion. But they constantly subordinated civilian concerns to those of the military. During a period in which apparently no shipping space for civilians could be found, Army Group North nevertheless managed to successfully transfer dozens of units from East Prussia.[146] Shortly after the conflict, Landrat Klaus von der Groeben remembered: 'We negotiated with the various departments ... for sufficient transport possibilities and the construction of a pontoon bridge over the Pillauer Tief. The commander of Pillau considered it important that

See: BArch RH 2/333, p. 116: Op Abt. I M/K 22.März 1945 Vortragsnotiz. Betr.: Verwundetenabtransport H.Gr. Nord (Nach Angabe MVO).

[144] Schwendemann, 'Der deutsche Zusammenbruch im Osten 1944/45', p. 142.
[145] Lasch, *So fiel Königsberg*, p. 23. 'Aber der Mensch denkt und das OKH lenkt'.
[146] BArch RH2/332, p. 214: Abschrift von Fernschreiben vom 21.2.45 An OKH / Gen St d H / Op Abt.

some precaution was taken but vigorously opposed the idea that Pillau could be used as a passage for refugees at all.'[147] A 500-metre pontoon bridge from Pillau to the Frische Nehrung would have provided a road from Königsberg to Danzig that refugees could pass on foot. Yet, as it hampered the supply to the Heiligenbeil Pocket, the plan never material-ised. Furthermore, although it is hard to quantify, the unwillingness of both Wehrmacht and Party to overcome petty quarrels also had a detri-mental effect on the evacuation. On the Frische Nehrung, for example, where the command structure was unclear, the deployment of police units led to arguments as to who was accountable. Gauleiter Koch stressed that since their job was to assist in the evacuation of civilians, these men should be subordinated to him. On the other hand, General Oldwig von Natzmer, the commander of Army Group North, considered the deployment area to be the main factor in determining their place in the command structure, in which case they were under the authority of the army. The deputy Höhere SS- und Polizeiführer Nordost, SS-Gruppenführer Otto Hellwig, eventu-ally sided with the army but not before voicing his discontent in two reports – one of them to Himmler himself – about the state of affairs.[148] Thus, the success of the combined effort did not merely rest on the availability of resources; their poor deployment, resulting from local feuds fought out over the heads of the civilian population, severely hampered both East Prussia's evacuation and its defence as well.

The poor attitude of commanders and Party officials in East Prussia towards evacuation determined the behaviour of Königsberg's civilian population. Some twenty daily situational reports – written by officials of the Königsberg-based SS-Oberabschnitt Nordost to Reichsführer-SS Himmler between 15 February and 23 March 1945 – have survived, and make it abundantly clear that during this period the population widely opposed evacuation. On 21 February it was noted that 'the popu-lation generally refuses to be evacuated because Konigsberg is considered as safe. Moreover, people believe that presently nothing can happen [to them], since many of those [officials] who left Königsberg during the critical days have returned'.[149] Stories about the sinking of the liners *Wilhelm Gustloff* and *Steuben*, two of the biggest naval disasters in history, made people wary of travel by sea.[150] 'Meanwhile', Karl Friedrich

[147] BArch Ost-Dok. 8/531, 4: von der Groeben.
[148] BArch NS19/2606, pp. 52–3: Der Höhere SS-u.Polizeiführer Nordost, O.U., den 12.2.1945, An Reichsführer-SS Persönlich; BArch NS 2606, p. 57: Der Höh.SS u. Pol. Führer Nordost, Pirel, den 14.2.1945.
[149] BArch NS 19/2068, p. 19. An Reichsführer-SS Feldkommandostelle Betrifft: Meldungen aus dem Ostraum, Königsberg 21.2.45.
[150] Schön, *Ostseehäfen 1945*, pp. 169–70; On the sinking of the Steuben, see: Schön, *Ostsee '45*, pp. 261–309.

remembered, 'news about the conditions in Pillau had spread in Konigsberg, so several transports left Königsberg empty or only half full.'[151] Certainly, as we will see in the next chapter, the living conditions in Königsberg were considerably better than on the Samland. On 4 March, for example, only 4,000 of the 16,000 people showed up to be evacuated.[152] Also, as the war progressed, more and more reception areas were in immediate danger of being threatened by the western Allies, while in early March the Volksgruppenführer in Denmark, Jens Möller, advised against housing refugees in Denmark, since 'for the German refugees a forced quarter with Danish families is significantly worse than the most primitive mass accommodation in collective accommodations'.[153]

People who were earmarked for evacuation sometimes hid for days so as not to be evacuated. The pleas of Party officials fell on deaf ears. Evacuation staff often faced heavy resistance and had to use force to get the people to move out of their lodgings, making the Party even more unpopular.[154] Indeed, the reports suggest that the fortress command only took evacuation seriously between 24 February and 10 March, after which it was 'postponed until further notice' due to 'technical issues'.[155] Meanwhile, the atmosphere at the Königsberg's Party headquarters became increasingly isolated.[156] The majority of the brought-in Party members, who had already cared little about evacuation in late January, resorted to an ostrich-like policy and, according to Wegener, held feasts that included loose women and high-quality food and employing their own winemaker, chef and butlers.[157] As March progressed, fewer and fewer Party officials bothered to devote any attention to Königsberg's evacuation. The insouciance of Party officials and the unwillingness of the Army to discuss the issue reveals that no one in the fortress command felt the need to evacuate any further inhabitants. There was the belief that evacuees would be going from the 'frying pan into the fire', and there seems to have been no willingness to challenge this assumption. Moreover, as virtually all local men were ordered to assume defensive roles in Königsberg, most families had to make the decision whether or not to

---

[151] BArch Ost-Dok. 8/508, p. 7: Friedrich.
[152] BArch NS 19/2068, p. 47. An Reichsführer-SS Feldkommandostelle Betrifft: Meldungen aus dem Ostraum, Königsberg 4.3.45.
[153] BArch RW 4/705: Osten Operationsgebiet Reich, allgem. Schriftverkehr Febr. April 1945 Befehlsreglung im Osten des Reichsgebietes, Jan. 1945.
[154] BArch NS 19/2068, p. 47; Hensel, *Medizin in und aus Ostpreußen*, p. 72.
[155] BArch NS 19/2068, p. 60. An Reichsführer-SS Feldkommandostelle Betrifft: Meldungen aus dem Ostraum, Königsberg 10.3.45.
[156] Hensel, *Medizin in und aus Ostpreußen*, p. 72.
[157] AKO 22034–4: Aufzeichnungen des Hauptschriftleiters der *KAZ* Wegener, pp. 3–4.

stay together.[158] For example, the family of Irene Schumacher weighed up the options of staying behind against the possibility of being captured by the Soviets: 'My father had never been in the Party. Through documents it could be proven that he had been dismissed in 1934 as a teacher because he had turned against the Hitler regime. The Russians would also recognise this.'[159] Many families of Volkssturm men and regular troops decided to stay by the side of their husbands or fathers and take their chances.[160]

This leaves the question of how many German civilians remained in Königsberg by the time of the final storming in early April. The highest number of civilians in the city was recorded at the beginning of the siege at the end of January 1945. The intelligence officer Walter Kemsies estimated that there were some 200,000 civilians in the city at this time (40,000 to 50,000 inhabitants, and about 150,000 refugees from the East of the province), while Waldemar Magunia placed this number slightly higher, at 210,000.[161] This number decreased throughout February and early March, and by 24 March Army Group North reported that a mere 70,000 people were still present in the city – the lowest number recorded during the siege.[162] In the latter half of March, for reasons discussed later in the chapter, this number increased again so that directly prior to the final assault some 100,000 civilians were left behind in the city.[163] These civilians lived primarily in the neighbourhoods of Juditten, Amalienau, Speicherdorf, Balleith, Rosenau, Ponarth, Kalthof and Lauth, which were mostly Königsberg's suburbs.[164] There was also possibly a further hidden element. Oberfeldartzt Dr Paul Schroeder noted that many returning refugees from the Samland 'did not seek to get ration cards because they did not want to become registered, be it for digging trenches, for the Volkssturm, or other tasks'.[165] He

---

[158] We will return to this in Chapter 6.
[159] Schön, *Ostseehafen*, p. 166. As a *Times* article pointed out, this line of reasoning often backfired: 'Germans are anxious to establish the belief that their previous political affiliations were above suspicion and that their acquiescence in the Hitler regime was enforced. They seem quite unaware how angry they make the Russians with their futile cries of *'Rotfront!'* or their protestations that they had once voted Communist'.; TNA FO 371/ 46859. Paper clipping, 7 March 1945: Herrenvolk no More, Russian Impressions from the Occupied Zones.
[160] Cheeseman, *Unter der Zeitbrücke*, p. 91.
[161] AKO 22034–4: Kemsies: *Stimmungsbilder aus Königsberg*, p. 4; AKO 22034–4 Magunia, *Abschrift*, p. 6.
[162] Schramm, *Kriegstagebuch des OKW, Band IV*, p. 1326; BArch, RH 2/333, Bl. 46, Operationsabteilung (Op) Abt IN/K Vortragsnotiz, 24.3.1945.
[163] Starlinger, *Grenzen der Sowjetmacht*, p. 36; BArch Ost-Dok. 8/588, p. 9: Dr. Will.
[164] AKO 22034–4: Kemsies: *Stimmungsbilder aus Königsberg*, p. 5; OL XC Königs3c Mat: Hermann Matzkowski: Bericht über die Vorkommnisse und Zustände in Königsberg/ Pr. seit der Einnahme durch die Sowjettruppen im April 1945 (Bremen, 2. Mai 1946).
[165] Starlinger, *Grenzen der Sowjetmacht*, p. 41.

thus estimated that around a third of the remaining population (which he put at approximately 130,000) went into hiding until after the storming in early April.[166] These people had to survive in conditions reminiscent to those of cave-dwellers.[167]

From a humanitarian standpoint, the evacuation of Königsberg can only be considered a failure. Many thousands of people remained in the besieged city even though many of these people could have been evacuated during February and March 1945. However, viewing the evacuation measures purely through this lens misses the point, since for the fortress command this was not the main issue at all. In 1945 the chain of command rapidly eroded in the face of military events and prevented its effective control over its areas of operation – a process known as the 'atomisation' of warfare.[168] This fractured state increasingly encouraged military commanders like Lasch to act according to their own discretion. Their loyalty seemed to have primarily remained with the troops they had commanded throughout the war. Ensuring that his men would live to see the end of a war had always been part of the unwritten understanding between a general and his troops, and with the end of the war only weeks away there was little reason to divert from this ethos in the spring of 1945. The choices that Lasch made in preparation for Operation Westwind showed the danger to which he was willing to expose civilians, but the priorities of the Wehrmacht and the Party became even clearer in the six weeks that followed. There was little concrete action taken in regard to the evacuation question and the refugee camps that were established on the Samland received only marginal attention. Shortly after the war, Kurt Jacobi, a former Ministerialdirigent (Assistant Secretary) in the Reich Ministry of the Interior, aptly summarised these considerations: 'As far as the evacuation in 1945 was concerned, the question of ordering the evacuation and the need to defend the Heimat were mutually exclusive demands. An appeal to evacuate would have made the ... defence of East Prussia impossible from the outset'.[169] The 'cumulative radicalisation' translated into a reluctance to allocate resources to the matter, which led to negligence and eventually to a resigned attitude among both parties. This mentality, fostered by the execution of the different 'criminal orders' on the Eastern Front, dominated the fortress command throughout the siege, which meant that when the final storming of Königsberg commenced there were many civilians who would find themselves caught between belligerents in a heavily fought-over city war zone.

---

[166] Ibid., p. 42.
[167] Rudolf Naujok, 'Das Mädchen von Königsberg', Ostpreußen-Warte, June 1958, p. 10.
[168] Kunz, Wehrmacht und Niederlage, p. 96.   [169] BArch Ost-Dok. 8/507, p. 3: Jacobi.

The Inability to Surrender

By the beginning of April, the fortress command was well aware that the final storming was only days away.[170] In his memoirs, Lasch stated that few officers, not even himself, cherished any hope that the assault could be fended off.[171] The 55,000 men under Lasch's command certainly stood no chance against the four Soviet armies that opposed them.[172] The OKH, however, made it clear that Königsberg was to be held 'under all circumstances'.[173] For three days, from 3 April to 5 April, the Soviet artillery conducted a preliminary bombardment and on 6 April the actual storming commenced. The Eleventh Guards Army attacked from the south, the Forty-third and Fiftieth Army attacked from the north and east. West of the city, the Thirty-ninth Army cut the connection between Königsberg and the Samland. In the early afternoon of 8 April troops of the Forty-third and Eleventh Guards Army met in the Amalienau suburb west of the city centre, completing the encirclement. On the night of 9 to 10 April, General Lasch surrendered the fortress.[174] On 10 April, the report of the OKH concluded that 'the overall impression (final radio messages from the fortress, aerial reconnaissance, enemy reports) is that the garrison of Königsberg, after brave battles in the rubble of the burning city, has been defeated by the onslaught of three Armies'.[175] Those last

---

[170] BArch RH 2/2026, p. 32: Funkspruch Abgegangen: 15.3. ObKdo.H.Gr.Nord roem 1 c/AO Nr.802/45 geh.; BArch RH 2/ 335, p. 133: Op Abt / Ia 4.4.45 Notiz nach Führervortrag Nacht 3./4.4.45; BArch RH 2/335, p. 174: Op Abt IN/K 6.4.45 Abschrift von FuFe vom 6.4, 13.00 Uhr AOK 4 Ia Nr. 4489/45 geh.

[171] Lasch, *So fiel Königsberg*, pp. 78–9.

[172] Appendix 1: Strength of Garrison Festung Königsberg immediately prior to the final storming, April 6, 1945. See further: Bastiaan Willems, 'Mezhdu souchastnikom i zhertvoy: opyt grazhdanskogo naseleniya pri osade kreposti Konigsberg v 1945 godu' [Between Accomplice and Victim: Civilians During the Siege of Königsberg in 1945], *Vestnik Baltiyskevo Federal'nevo Universiteta im. I. Kanta* (12) 2015, pp. 43–51; Gennadii Kretinin, 'Implitsitnaya pamyat', ili Vnov' o nemetskom naselenii Konigsberga vo vremya osady kreposti v fevrale – aprele 1945 goda' [Implicit Memory, or Once Again on German Civilians in Königsberg During the Fortress' Siege in February–April 1945], *Vestnik Baltiyskevo Federal'nevo Universiteta im. I. Kanta* (12) 2016, pp. 16–22; Bastiaan Willems, '"Krepost" Konigsberg v 1945 godu: garnizon i naseleniye. Otvet na zamechaniya G.V. Kretinina' [Festung Königsberg in 1945: the Garrison and Its Population. A Reply to G.V. Kretinin's Remarks], *Vestnik Baltiyskevo Federal'nevo Universiteta im. I. Kanta* (12) 2016, pp. 23–31.

[173] BArch RH2/335, p. 231: Adjutant des Chefs des Generalstabes des Heeres Nr. 1250/45 g.K. H.Qu.OKH, den 7.4.45. Notizen nach Führervortrag am 7.4.5 nachm.(*sic*) The phrase 'Until the last drop of blood', which is often used by scholars to point to radicalisation in late-war Germany, is a propagandist concept and does not feature at all in these kind of orders.

[174] Lakowski, *Ostpreußen 1944/45*, pp. 201–15.

[175] Mehner, *Die geheimen Tagesberichte der deutschen Wehrmachtführung*, p. 367. Incidentally, this report also tells something about the state of German intelligence at the time since there were actually four Soviet Armies.

radio messages, some wired by Lasch himself, certainly tell a story of a 'heroic defence', but also tell another story: 'Due to aerial bombardment and constant artillery shelling the entire city is as good as destroyed. As a result of personnel and material losses the battle strength of the troops has been strongly reduced. High casualty numbers among the civilian population.'[176] This section will focus on how these people died and why their deaths should be seen as the result of the army's preparedness to fight – quite literally – to the last bullet. It will also assess if the fortress command was criminally negligent.

Immediately prior to the storming the fortress command had a number of options to consider, although certainly not every alternative carried as much weight as the other. Although virtually every fortress was ordered to hold to the very end, most of their commanders plotted their own course. In France in 1944, for example, some commanders of encircled fortresses established contact with their Allied besiegers to organise the evacuation of French civilians, which in some cases was successful. Although little evidence suggests that this was done on humanitarian grounds, it was already more than Königsberg's fortress command was willing to consider.[177] General Lasch – like most fortress commanders in Eastern Germany – categorically refused to parley with the Soviets, as he fully expected Soviet troops to act barbarously. Moreover, as we have seen, he had actively sought to create a polarising atmosphere that ruled out any contact between the two belligerents. Also, a distrust in the population's willingness to keep fighting, which will be discussed extensively in Chapter 6, certainly was a factor. In Aachen, for example, war-weary German civilians guided Allied forces to hideouts and had betrayed the location of German positions, much to the dismay of the city's commander.[178] Closer to Königsberg, in mid-January, Soviet forces had shelled positions on the Deime river at Labiau after these had been disclosed by civilians.[179] As civilians were closely involved in the defence of Königsberg, there was no doubt that, were they to fall in to Soviet hands, Soviet intelligence would be able to extract information from them which would have impeded the city's defensibility.

Another option was surrender. Few German cities surrendered without a fight, although it did happen. On the American axis of advance, the Kampfkommandant of Feste Platz Gotha, Oberstleutnant Josef Ritter von Gadolla, surrendered the city on 4 April. A week later the front line

---

[176] BArch RH2/2027, p. 45: Funkspruch Abgegangen 7.4. um: 2325. Absendende Stelle: Fest .Kdt. Königsberg.
[177] Lieb, *Konventioneller Krieg oder NS-Weltanschauungskrieg?*, pp. 488, 497–8.
[178] Ibid., p. 500.
[179] Afanasii Belobodorov, *Vsegda v boju* [Always in the Fray] (Moscow: Voenizdat, 1978), p. 314.

had reached the city of Wernigerode but its Kampfkommandant, Oberst Gustav Petri, refused to incorporate it in the combat zone. Instead, on 12 April, he also decided to surrender the city without a fight. Both men were summarily executed the day after their surrender by order of local Army headquarters.[180] In Eastern Germany, the 30 April surrender of Greifswald stands out. Between January 1945 and April, the city's dignitaries, headed by the rector of Greifswald University, had appealed to the newly appointed Stadtkommandant, Oberst Rudolf Petershagen to surrender Greifswald peacefully. Like Lasch, Petershagen was a highly decorated Eastern Front veteran who in the aftermath of the First World War had fought in a Freikorps. On the other hand, Petershagen had not served during the First World War, but *had* been part of the Reichswehr and had married a woman of noble descent – all factors that would shape his decision in April 1945. The resolution of local authority figures to approach a hardened veteran unknown to them, their subsequent persistent attitude in the face of the accusation of defeatism, and Petershagen's eventual courage to disobey the order to defend the city to the last bullet resulted in a completely different outcome than in Königsberg, as such saving the lives of countless people.[181]

Also in Königsberg, the options of surrendering the Festung or declaring it an open city were discussed. Contrary to what is often thought, it was Königsberg's Party elite that was the first to a call for a cessation of the fighting. As soon as the fighting had begun on 6 April, Deputy Gauleiter Grossherr proposed to Gauleiter Koch that Königsberg should be declared an open city and that a new front be established to the north.[182] A day later, on 7 April, Kreisleiter Wagner also called on Koch to demand that the fighting cease in Königsberg. This conversation was overheard by Oberstabsinterdant Friedrich Dorfmüller: 'Tell your friend – he probably meant the Führer – that the troops have fought heroically; in Königsberg everything that was humanly possible was accomplished. It would be madness and a crime against the civilian population to continue to fight.'[183] Koch, however, had no intention of declaring Königsberg an open city or asking for its surrender. But in any case, this would have met with strong opposition from the army; another indication of 'cumulative radicalisation'. Indeed, whereas throughout 1943 and 1944 a number of prominent foreign

---

[180] Helga Raschke, *'Damit Gotha leben kann, muss ich sterben'. Ein Grazer Offizier: Josef Ritter von Gadolla und die letzten Kriegstage in Gotha* (Raschke: Gotha, 2007); Peter Lehmann, *Geachtet – Geleugnet – Geehrt. Oberst Gustav Petri, Retter von Wernigerode* (Berlin: Lukas-Verlag, 2013), pp. 80–134.

[181] Bessel, *Germany 1945*, p. 139; Rudolf Petershagen, *Gewissen in Aufruhr* (Berlin: Verlag der Nation, 1957).

[182] AKO 22034–4: Dorfmüller: *Ferngespräch des Kreisleiters Wagner*; AKO 22034–4: Sinzig: *Meine Erinnerungen*.

[183] AKO 22034–4: Dorfmüller: *Ferngespräch des Kreisleiters Wagner*.

cities – Rome, Florence, Athens, and Paris – had been declared open cities in late 1944, either on the initiative of their commanders or with the full knowledge of Hitler, Himmler proclaimed that 'no German city will be declared an open city. Every town and every village will be defended at all costs'.[184]

Going against this maxim required moral courage but it was not unprecedented during the defence of Germany, with Aachen perhaps best epitomising the different attitudes among the German officer corps towards declaring a German city an 'open city'. Initially tasked with its defence was the famous Windhund-Division (116th Panzer-Division), whose aristocratic commander, Generalleutnant Gerhard von Schwerin (1899–1980), had served during the First World War and had advanced through the ranks of the Reichswehr. He was a commander of the old style, and had certainly not internalised all 'new' attitudes towards warfare. Estimating that the evacuation of the 40,000-strong civilian population on the eve of battle would prove disastrous, and that the fighting would destroy Aachen's historic centre, he ignored Hitler's express orders and had his men take up positions to the north-west of the city. He wrote a note in English to the approaching American forces which a postal clerk was to deliver to the first Allied officer who would enter the city:[185]

To the commanding officer of the US Forces occupying the town of Aachen: I stopped the stupid evacuation of the civilian population and ask you to give her relief. I'm the last commanding officer here.
Gerhard Count von Schwerin
13 September 44, Lt. General

The American advance, however, proved slower than von Schwerin expected and Aachen remained in German hands. The note fell into Himmler's hands, after which von Schwerin was removed from his command and interrogated. Despite the gravity of his insubordination, von Schwerin did not face serious charges but was instead transferred to Italy where he was eventually even promoted to general.[186] Meanwhile, by mid-October, the final defence of Aachen was entrusted to Oberst Gerhard Wilck (1898–1985). Wilck – like Lasch – had fully internalised the National Socialist attitudes towards warfare, claiming to surrender only as 'remnants of the defence of the German Kaiserstadt are fighting in hand-to-hand combat at the command post'. Although from the moment Wilck was

---

[184] Alexander Gillespie, *A History of the Laws of War: Volume 2: the Customs and Laws of War with Regards to Civilians in Times of Conflict* (Oxford: Hart Publishing, 2011), p. 25.
[185] Robert Baumer, *Aachen: the U.S. Army's Battle for Charlemagne's City in World War II* (Mechanicsburg, PA: Stackpole Books, 2015), p. 21.
[186] Charles Whiting, *Bloody Aachen* (Staplehurst: Spellmount, 2000), pp. 25–9, 37–9; Baumer, *Aachen*, pp. 18–53.

appointed as Stadtkommandant it was clear that Aachen would fall, he only capitulated on 21 October 1944 after weeks of dogged urban warfare.[187]

Königsberg's fortress command also adhered to the maxim of 'defending a city at all costs' without question. A major difference with Aachen – of course – was that Königsberg was situated on the Eastern Front which certainly contributed to its garrison's incapability to capitulate. The complicity of men like Lasch in Germany's war of annihilation was unmistakable, and his familiarity with the war's genocidal aspects and the Eastern Front's 'criminal orders' is beyond dispute.[188] These factors certainly were important in Lasch's inner circle but, especially since he maintained that he believed he had done nothing wrong while in the Soviet Union, they can only provide a part of the reason why Königsberg's fortress command fought on for four days before it finally decided to surrender.[189]

For the German army, honour was at stake. What the OKW seemed to have grasped very well was that surrender in the first place was a personal decision in which personal and psychological factors trumped purely military considerations.[190] The German army had sought to connect surrender to dishonour as early as the fall of France in the spring of 1940, when – as a final humiliation – the French army was forced to accept Germany's armistice terms at the exact spot near Compiègne and in the same railway carriage where Germany had been forced to do the same in 1918.[191] By 1942 the tables had started to turn and from 1943 onwards it was the German army that found itself surrendering. For example, the capitulation of the Sixth Army at Stalingrad in early 1943 was considered a national tragedy and was followed by the establishment of the communist-led NKFD and BDO (Bund Deutscher Offiziere) under General Walther von Seydlitz and Field Marshal Friedrich Paulus, acts that were perceived as a stain on the prestige of the Wehrmacht.[192] By 1945 some commanders had decided to commit suicide rather than surrender unconditionally, with Field Marshal

---

[187] Henke, *Die amerikanische Besetzung Deutschlands*, pp. 154–5.

[188] Erhard Lucas-Busemann, *So fielen Königsberg und Breslau* (Berlin: Aufbau Taschenbuch Verlag, 1994), pp. 92–4. See also Chapter 3. Lasch does not deny that the German military had committed war crimes and explicitly mentions that the commander of the Fourth Army, General Friedrich-Wilhelm Müller, whom he thoroughly disliked, was executed by the Greeks in 1947.

[189] Lasch, *Zuckerbrot und Peitsche*, pp. 67, 70–3.

[190] Niall Ferguson, 'Towards a Political Economy of Military Defeat: Prisoner Taking and Prisoner Killing in the Age of Total War', *War In History* (11) 2004, pp. 152–3.

[191] Julian Jackson, *France: the Dark Years 1940–1944* (Oxford: Oxford University Press, 2003), p. 127.

[192] Jürgen Förster, 'Die Niederlage der Wehrmacht: Das Ende des "Dritten Reiches"', in Foerster (ed.), *Seelower Höhen 1945*, p. 8.

Walter Model choosing to shoot himself in a forest rather than having to oversee the capitulation of his Army Group.[193] In Königsberg, no commanders committed suicide, but surrendering a fortress, a 'symbol of the nation's unwavering willingness to fight', ranked among the most dishonourable acts a general could contemplate.[194] A surrender was deemed unworthy of the German military tradition. Already in February 1944, a month before the defence around fortresses was elevated to strategy, Field Marshal Wilhelm Keitel used a classic 'fall-where-you-stand'-rhetoric to convey what he expected of commanders that had been entrusted with the defence of a city or area: 'Capitulation, ceasing the resistance, evasion or retreat do not at apply to fortress- and battle commanders. The fate of the fortress- and battle commanders is connected with the area entrusted to them. The commander of a ship also goes under with it, with the flag in mast. The history of German soldiery has never known a different view.' To show the seriousness of the order, the memorandum's preamble pointed out that two commanders had already been executed after they had left their positions.[195]

Lasch could have been in no doubt about his duty to uphold the honour of the Wehrmacht. Being entrusted with the defence of a city like Königsberg (and the same goes for other fortresses) was a high point in a military career, and violating the trust of the men that had enabled this career tarnished that.[196] On 8 April 1945, hours before communication broke down with the outside world, he received a telegram from General Friedrich-Wilhelm Müller, the commander of the Fourth Army, under which authority Festung Königsberg fell, stressing that Lasch's officers' honour bound him to hold Königsberg to the last bullet.[197] This is most likely why in his memoirs, whilst he was keen to emphasise that he had decided to capitulate 'to bring an end to the terror' for the sake of the population, he also went to great lengths to show that when the surrender of Königsberg took place, the city had almost completely been overrun except for some small isolated pockets of resistance.[198] In the face of

[193] Goeschel, *Suicide in Nazi Germany*, p. 152.
[194] Kunz, *Wehrmacht und Niederlage*, p. 224.
[195] BArch NS 19/3118, p. 8: O.U. den 7.2.1944 gez Keitel Feldmarshall OKW/WFSt/ Op (H) Nr.0906/44/geh.
[196] A peculiar story features in the *Kriegstagebuch des OKW*. According to Percy Ernst Schramm, who kept the OKW war diary, '2 officers who swam through the *Haff* stated that, contrary to the reports, the Commander of Königsberg, General Lasch, was still fighting as enemy tanks appeared in front of his command post'. Schramm states that he was forced to add that these statements were 'probably wrong' but claimed to have considered Lasch an 'upright man' with a 'sense of responsibility for the soldiers entrusted to him'. See: Schramm, *Kriegstagebuch des OKW Band IV*, pp. 54, 1246.
[197] AKO 22034–4: Sinzig: *Meine Erinnerungen*.   [198] Lasch, *So fiel Königsberg*, p. 107.

defeat, Lasch, like most commanders, did not subscribe to the idea of 'dying with honour' which Hitler had sought to instil among the troops.

There was certainly a discrepancy between the string of orders envisaging a soldier dying 'with a weapon in his hand', and commanders' resolve to base their decisions on the tactical situation.[199] Königsberg was not the first fortress to surrender, and Lasch's behaviour was in line with German military behaviour elsewhere. In September 1944, for example, after Hitler's initial protestations, Army Group North was evacuated from Estonia, so Festung Reval (Tallinn) and Festung Wesenburg (Rakvere) fell without a fight.[200] Famously, in August 1944 Festung Paris was surrendered without Hitler's consent and against his explicit will.[201] In East Prussia, Festung Lötzen, one of the cornerstones of the province's defence, was left virtually undefended.[202] As a result, by 1945 Hitler's trust in army commanders had almost completely vanished in regard to the fortress strategy. On 26 March he ordered that from then on only naval officers could be appointed as fortress commanders, 'since already many fortresses [have fallen], but still no ship has been lost without a fight to the end'.[203] The order undoubtedly hurt the pride of the top ranks of the army, but it is unlikely that it led to more determined fortress staffs.

To further 'encourage' commanders to fight to the end, the practice of *Sippenhaft*, family liability punishment, was greatly expanded during the last year of the war: in cases such as surrender or desertion, a soldier's family risked imprisonment on his behalf.[204] This also weighed on Lasch's mind. Army General Ivan Bagramyan observed that during interrogation of the captured German generals, 'the fortress commander looked particularly downcast and wretched. ... We had learned from radio monitoring that the imbecile Führer had declared him a traitor for the surrender of the fortress and ordered the arrest of his family.

---

[199] Neitzel and Welzer, *Soldaten*, pp. 244–61.

[200] Frieser, 'Die Rückzugskämpfe der Heeresgruppe Nord bis Kurland', pp. 635–42.

[201] Schramm, *Kriegstagebuch des OKW*, pp. 346–8, 358, 472; Manfred Overesch, *Das III. Reich 1939–1945, Eine Tageschronik der Politik, Wirtschaft, Kultur* (Augsburg: Weltbild Verlag, 1991), pp. 525–8.

[202] Duffy, *Red Storm on the Reich*, pp. 171–2; Guderian, *Panzer Leader*, p. 400.

[203] John Zimmermann, 'Die deutsche militärische Kriegsführung im Westen 1944/45', in Müller (ed.), *Das Deutsche Reich und der Zweiten Weltkrieg 10/1*, p. 347. Apparently, Hitler had forgotten, or chose to ignore, the battle at River Plate of December 1939 during which the captain of the *Admiral Graf Spee*, decided to scuttle his ship off the coast of Montevideo rather than to attack the British force of three Royal Navy cruisers. See: Neitzel and Welzer, *Soldaten*, pp. 257–9.

[204] Loeffel, 'Soldiers and Terror', p. 516. As Germany continued to 'shrink' in 1945 the measure lost its appeal, mainly because family members were often already in areas captured by the Allied forces. See: Erich Kuby, *Das Ende des Schreckens* (Hamburg: Deutscher Taschenbuch Verlag, 1986), p. 64; Kunz, *Wehrmacht und Niederlage*, p. 271.

Obviously, General Lasch was depressed by this'.[205] The nature of an encircled fortress made it impossible for anyone outside of it to prevent its capitulation, but by systematically linking surrender to the breaking of trust and the military tradition, and to the threat of punishment of family members, the OKW nevertheless built in some 'delaying factors' in regard to the surrender of a fortress.

A further consideration was the practical difficulty of assuring a surrender. The reputation of one of the best understood signs of surrender, the white flag, had steadily diminished throughout the war.[206] Probably the most infamous example took place on 29 December 1944, when – according to the Sovinformburo news agency – in two Budapest neighbourhoods two Soviet envoys, both carrying white flags, were killed, even though their arrival at the German lines had been announced well in advance.[207] The German High Command approached the matter by stressing that the international coverage of the shooting of the parleys was nothing but a 'mendacious version of events' that only sought to accuse the German army of breaching international law. To prevent this kind of negative press in the future, parleys would 'no longer be received, but have to be sent back before reaching our lines'.[208] In effect, this order made capitulation talks significantly harder to organise.

There was similar pushback when Wehrmacht troops themselves considered the use of white flags, with some commanders even forbidding their men to prepare them.[209] By 1945, even as the potential for surrender was obvious to everyone, sustained efforts were made to discourage troops from contemplating it. To prevent capitulation talks, Field Marshal Walter Model, the commander of Army Group B, went as far in late March 1945 as to order that 'manifestations of subversion and acts

---

[205] Bagramyan, 'The Storming of Königsberg', p. 242; See also: Eberhard Beckherrn and Alexei Dubatov, *Die Königsberg Papiere, Schicksal einer deutschen Stadt, Neue Dokumente aus russischen Archiven* (Munich: Langen Mueller, 1994), pp. 16–17: 'Oberstleutnant Iwanow asked the captured General Lasch during interrogation: "Do you already know, that a Hitler-court has sentenced you to death?" The General replied "I am not really troubled by that". Only the situation of his family, which had been evacuated to Denmark, worried him'.

[206] Officially recognised during the Hague convention of 1907. See: 'Laws of War: Laws and Customs of War on Land (Hague IV); October 18, 1907', accessed 11 July 2016. http://avalon.law.yale.edu/20th_century/hague04.asp Annex to the Convention Art 32.

[207] Sovinformburo, 'Murder of Soviet Negotiators in Budapest Area', *Soviet War News*, 1 January 1945, pp. 2–3.

[208] BArch RH2/ 331a, p. 176: OKH / GenStdH / op Abt (röm 1 a) Nr. 796/45 g.Kdos. 22.1.45.

[209] Römer, *Kameraden*, p. 366.

of sabotage at the command post, regardless whether the offender is a soldier or a civilian, are to be prevented by armed force'.[210] Model's portrayal of commanders willing to consider negotiations as offenders (*Täter*) symbolises the widespread dismissal and scepticism towards the practice. It should therefore be questioned whether Himmler's infamous 'flag order' of 3 April ('when a white flag appears from a house, any male inside is to be shot'), which has generally been linked to the National Socialist *Durchhalte*-terror, had any additional impact.[211] Although in all likelihood army envoys in Königsberg were fired on by Party members, the opposition to the use of a white flag was by then already widespread in the Wehrmacht. For example, Obergefreiter Sinzig, Oberst von Süsskind-Schwendi's orderly, was ordered to put up the white flag over General Lasch's command post only 'once the first Russian machine gun fire coming from the Paradeplatz can be heard'. Furthermore, Sinzig remembered that even though Lasch's bunker lay directly under the Paradeplatz, which meant that Soviet troops were only dozens of metres away by the time the flag went up, there was still opposition to it from soldiers:

> There I see a little boy hop from funnel to funnel and suddenly the little fellow (I guess he is 16 or 17 years old) is in front of me and points to the white flag that I had now hoisted and said: "What kind of nonsense is this? Our comrades are out there, defending and bleeding to death, and you hoist the white flag here.[212]

This type of defiance meant that fighting went on long after the military situation had become hopeless. When on 8 April the city was cut off after the link-up between the Forty-third and Eleventh Guards Army, Marshal Alexander Vasilevsky immediately ordered leaflets to be thrown over the city in order to persuade Lasch to surrender, but Lasch still refused to do so and continued to fight.[213] That decision brought battle into the midst of the civilian population where there was a fight 'for houses and streets with extreme severity'.[214] It is at this point that any of Lasch's post-war assurances that he had taken into account the safety of the population fall flat. The garrison's self-propelled guns were so close to field hospitals that doctors had to ask them to move so as to respect the rules of the international Red Cross, while some of the German troops who passed

---

[210] Elisabeth Koolhaas, '"Aus einem Haus, aus dem eine weiße Fahne erscheint, sind alle männliche Personen zu erschießen": Durchhalteterror und Gewalt gegen Zivilisten am Kriegsende 1945', in Arendes, Wolfrum, and Zedler (eds.), *Terror nach innen*, pp. 65–6.
[211] Ibid., pp. 65–6.   [212] AKO 22034–4 Sinzig: *Meine Erinnerungen*.
[213] Alexander Vasilevsky, *Delo vsej zhizni* [The Matter of My Whole Life] (Moscow: Politizdat, 1978), pp. 464–5; Galitsky, *V boyakh za Vostochnuyu Prussiyu*, p. 414.
[214] Mehner, *Die geheimen Tagesberichte der deutschen Wehrmachtführung*, p. 364.

Figure 5.5 Red Army forces advance along the Pregel, April 1945.
Source: Unknown agency, Mikhail Ivanovich Savin

through them meanwhile continued to fire on enemy combatants.[215] In his memoirs, Michael Wieck, one of the few 'certified Jews' (a *Geltungsjude*) that had remained in Königsberg by 1945, called Lasch out on this 'discrepancy': 'Had you, General Lasch, really cared about the civilian population and the preservation of human life, like you claimed afterwards, you should have capitulated much earlier. Not only when the Russians were already at the Paradeplatz in front of your bunker, or near to it.'[216]

General Lasch eventually decided to surrender on the morning of 9 April. By that time the garrison was almost out of ammunition and only parts of the inner city were still in German hands.[217] All contact with the outside world had been lost.[218] Moreover, Lasch knew that the 5th Panzer-Division, which had stayed behind on the Samland after Operation Westwind, would not attempt to relieve the fortress's garrison,

---

[215] Deichelmann, *Ich sah Königsberg sterben*, p. 17; von Lehndorff, *Ostpreußisches Tagebuch*, p. 62; Günter Braunschweig, 'Untergangstage in Königsberg', *Jahrbuch der Albertus-Universität zu Königsberg, Pr.* (3) 1953, p. 200.
[216] Wieck, *Königsberg: Zeugnis vom Untergang einer Stadt*, p. 218.
[217] Lasch, *So fiel Königsberg*, p. 104.
[218] Mehner, *Die geheimen Tagesberichte der deutschen Wehrmachtführung*, p. 364.

while a final westward breakout attempt by troops north of the river Pregel had also failed. That attempt, conducted around midnight on 8–9 April, was supposed to remain secret from the population but word nevertheless got out, and as more and more civilians gathered near the area from which the attack was to be launched the element of surprise was lost. Soviet artillery started shelling the gathered masses, inflicting a large number of casualties.[219] It was another indictment of the negligence of the army and Party.

The general, thus, fought on as long as it made any military sense, although – and this is where he broke with the National Socialist rhetoric – he had no intention to sacrifice his life or those of his staff in the process. Nevertheless, even in this dire situation, the call for surrender caused a backlash among some of the troops. In his memoirs, Lasch plays up the role of the SS, which wanted to continue the fight, but among other troops who wanted to continue were the staff of the 69th Infanterie-Division which had retreated into the city in late January.[220] Such defiance was not unique in East Prussia. A week later, in mid-April, a group of officers of the 5th Panzer-Division, faced with depleted ammunition stocks and limited operational space, believed that 'the division's best bet would be to destroy its tanks and infiltrate southwards through Soviet lines in order to launch a partisan campaign, or perhaps to form small battle groups and independently march back to German lines'. The division's commander decided against it, and many of the troops subsequently mutinied.[221] Thus, the decision to (dis)continue a defence of Königsberg rested significantly on local actors and circumstances. For Königsberg's fortress command, the decision to surrender came at the last possible moment. Yet, still thirty years after the war, the fortress's chief of staff, Süsskind-Schwendi, felt the need to stress that what the fortress command effectively intended was 'not a capitulation of the fortress. Konigsberg had already fallen. It was a surrender of the remaining troops'.[222]

To arrange the surrender, envoys were dispatched from the different strongholds in order to make contact with Soviet troops.[223] After a few hours, during which time the fighting continued, envoys sent by the

---

[219] Lasch, *So fiel Königsberg*, pp. 95–103; Blankenhorn, *... und fah'r wir ohne Wiederkehr*, pp. 164–73.

[220] Perry Biddiscombe, *Werwolf!: the History of the National Socialist Guerrilla Movement, 1944–1946* (Toronto: University of Toronto Press, 1998), p. 215. Lasch, *So fiel Königsberg*, p. 42.

[221] Biddiscombe, *Werwolf!*, p. 110.

[222] Hugo Freiherr von Süßkind-Schwendi, 'Kurze Ruckschau auf die militärischen Ereignisse in Königsberg (Pr.)', in Kalusche (ed.), *Unter dem Sowjetstern*, p. 226.

[223] Lasch, *So fiel Königsberg*, pp. 104–6.

commander of the Trommelplatz barracks, Oberstleutnant Bruno Kerwin, finally managed to reach Soviet lines. After initial contact had been established, Kerwin was summoned to a Soviet regimental headquarters where he had to convince the commander of the sincerity of the message. Again many hours passed. Eventually he guided Soviet representatives through German lines, and in the late evening he arrived at Lasch's command post with the words 'General, as ordered I have executed a soldier's saddest task. Here is the Russian envoy'.[224] Kerwin's sentiments underline just how deep-seated the aversion to surrendering was within the army hierarchy.

Finally, around 2 a.m. on 10 April the capitulation was signed.[225] The terms of surrender offer a final glimpse into General Lasch's motivations and concerns and leave no doubt that military considerations were of significantly more importance than the care for the population. None of the ten points listed in the document concerned Königsberg's remaining civilians.[226] Instead the document opened with three points guaranteeing officer privileges: assuring that they could keep their blade weapons, an orderly, and their kit.[227] Moreover, the document did not put an end to the fighting. Lasch stressed that 'eliminating remaining strongholds is the task of the Russian army', and, as a result, isolated pockets, large enough to be seen by the Army Group reconnaissance air planes, kept fighting until days after the fortress's capitulation.[228] Eventually the fighting moved to the basements, which during the siege had been interconnected. As the capacity of the air-raid shelters built in the war was limited, many people had taken shelter in these basements. To clear them, Soviet soldiers used flamethrowers and grenades, further contributing to the civilian death toll.[229]

Due to three days of preliminary bombardment, four days of heavy street fighting combined with continuous artillery bombardment and aerial bombardment by 2,400 aircrafts, and the mopping up of isolated units in the days that followed the capitulation, the high civilian casualties

---

[224] Bruno Kerwin, 'Dokument der Geschichte: Königsberg im April 1945', *Das Ostpreußenblatt*, 14 July 1979, p. 10.

[225] IfZArch ZS/A-2/ 04–34: Bruno Kerwin, Herford/ Westfalen, Bruchstrasse 6, den 9. April 1949. Different times of surrender are also mentioned because German sources adhere to local time and Soviet sources adhere to Moscow time.

[226] Appendix 2: The Capitulation of Königsberg.

[227] Eventually his kit was stolen, and Lasch would complain about it until deep in the 1950s to Marshal Vasilevsky in person. Especially as he left behind a burning city, 'his complaints about personally suffered hardships in captivity, which after all are part of the occupational hazard of an officer, appear embarrassing'. See: Hannsferdinand Döbler, 'Das Gepäck des Generals', *Die Zeit*, 20 August 1965.

[228] Mehner, *Die geheimen Tagesberichte der deutschen Wehrmachtführung*, p. 369.

[229] Biddiscombe, *Werwolf!*, pp. 215–16.

in Königsberg are understandable.[230] The more important question of why, despite the presence of a corridor to Pillau, so many civilians were still in the city by April, has nevertheless remained largely unaddressed. Even after it became clear that the final assault was only days away, the fortress command devoted little attention to the evacuation of the civilian population. Meanwhile, opportunities to come to some arrangement with the Soviets to spare civilian lives were spurned. The fortress command categorically refused to take civilian considerations into account, did not declare Königsberg an open city, and rejected multiple possibilities to discuss the surrender of the garrison. The final capitulation still reveals no sign of empathy towards the remaining population. Therefore we can only conclude that the Wehrmacht took a conscious decision to expose civilians to the violence of urban warfare. It was the German military itself that was largely responsible for the deaths of thousands of their own civilians.

Conclusion

As the Red Army approached the borders of East Prussia, Party and Wehrmacht were forced to take a position on the evacuation of civilians. Even though it was clear that in case of a main attack – of which the question was 'when', rather than 'if' – Soviet troops would reach populated areas within days, neither Party nor Wehrmacht pushed for large-scale evacuation measures that would ensure the safety of civilians. Out of fear of the accusation of 'defeatism' both were reluctant to prepare for the population's organised departure from threatened areas. For the different Wehrmacht commanders, moreover, another major factor shaped their view on evacuation. During their stay on the Eastern Front, the concept of evacuation had been steadily hollowed out. With German warfare largely unconcerned with racially inferior Untermenschen, the 'evacuation of goods' became a euphemism for theft, while an order to evacuate civilians from a threatened area normally resulted in their forced expulsion. In East Prussia this racist component fell away, although it nevertheless became clear that commanders had 'untaught' themselves to care for civilians. As a result, as the different Army-, Korps-, and divisional staffs prepared the province's defence, they only considered the evacuation of goods in detail. This, however, did not mean that the Wehrmacht left the evacuation of civilians solely to the Party. The evacuation of civilians was

---

[230] Author collective, *Sovetskiye Voyenno-vozdushnyye sily v Velikoy Otechestvennoy voyne 1941–1945 gg* [The Soviet Air Force in the Great Patriotic War of 1941–1945] (Moscow: Voenizdat, 1968), pp. 360–1.

discussed at all levels: both between the High Command and the RVKs, as well as between individual divisions and the Kreisleiter of the areas in which they were situated. As long as the Wehrmacht was ensured man-oeuvrability in the area of operations, it willingly followed the orders and requests of the Party. The chaos of the first weeks of the East Prussian offensive – so often blamed on the Party and the Soviets – was therefore anticipated by the Wehrmacht.

Limited evacuation drives were eventually conducted in the autumn of 1944, ensuring that a quarter of the population was moved out of imme-diately threatened areas. In these areas it soon became clear that a great many soldiers had problems adjusting to the fact that they were once again on German soil. Indiscriminate destruction and plunder of German property was extremely common, and it did not take long for command-ers and officials to realise that the soldiers, brutalised by years of serving in the Soviet Union, had problems shaking off the ingrained behavioural patterns of the Eastern Front. The 'lowered resting heart rate of the Wehrmacht soldiers', caused by the nature of the brutalising orders and the extraordinariness of the situations they were asked to deal with during the previous years, ensured that many men were altogether incapable of properly recognising the effects of their behaviour. This moral disorien-tation was compounded by the fact that the retreat into East Prussia did not mark a fundamentally different approach to the practices connected to retreat and defeat. The ARLZ-measures remained firmly in place since they served a purpose that was as urgent in the Soviet Union as it was on home soil. As a result, church spires were blown up, neighbourhoods were flooded, agrarian enterprises were dismantled, and cattle moved out. With orders like these reaching troops on a recurrent basis, it is little surprise that they often neglected to consider the ethical ramifications of their actions.

Once the East Prussian offensive commenced in January 1945, Koch lost most of his power, and local army commanders became finally responsible for the province but continued to disregard the plight of the population. The deployment of able-bodied civilians at the Ostwall, which we discussed in Chapter 1, has already illustrated that the care for the civilian population was of subordinate importance, and this only became worse during the retreat. As the behaviour of General Lasch shows, the misery of civilians was not merely the collateral damage of operational conduct. The main roads in East Prussia were closed to civilians, a measure that was ruthlessly enforced. Commanders also left the evacuation of civilians to the Party after the front had stabilised in late January, even though it was clear that the Party could not handle the developing refugee crisis. The Wehrmacht expressed no intention of coming to the aid of the struggling Party authorities. At national level, the OKW and OKH ranked the evacuation as least important, and instead pushed for the transport of military materiel. To a certain extent, the choices for Königsberg's fortress command were thus limited, but the sheer absence of attention to the local refugee question – especially the situation in the refugee camps on the Samland – is nevertheless striking. This should not necessarily simply be traced to the unwillingness of men like Lasch and Wagner; more likely, this mindset resulted from the indifference the matter caused as a result of the incapability to align the refugee question with the defence of the city. Therefore, in the period between Operation Westwind and the final storming of Königsberg in April 1945, neither Party nor Wehrmacht was willing to devote adequate resources to it.

Königsberg's final days under German control, however, showed that military commanders, when it was demanded of them, were not merely utilitarian in their approach to civilians, but – as before – criminally negligent. Moreover, it shows the profound impact a limited number of local actors could have on the way fighting was brought to an end. The decisions that were taken immediately prior to and during the final storming in April reveal a deep unwillingness to surrender, even when it was clear that this 'determination' would come at the expense of civilians. Different alternatives to 'fighting to the last bullet' were discussed but these were readily dismissed. Both at the fortress command and to Gauleiter Koch, Deputy Gauleiter Grossherr put forward the idea to declare Königsberg an 'open city', but this proposal gained little traction. Even after the Red Army's announcement that the storming was imminent, the fortress command still did not go over to a full-scale evacuation: the ensuing chaos would disrupt military preparations and there was also the fear that civilians would give away military secrets. The fortress command did, however, find the time and resources to evacuate some 10,000 wounded soldiers on the day prior to the storming. Two days into the final storming on 8 April, the city was cut off, but this knowledge still did not encourage General Lasch to capitulate. Lasch, like so many other German commanders, lacked the moral courage to do so. Eventually he surrendered when Soviet troops reached his command post, and the terms of surrender make clear that the safety of the civilian population was at best of secondary importance. Von Süsskind-Schwendi's post-war emphasis on the fact that Lasch had not capitulated the fortress but merely surrendered the troops under his command serves as a sombre testament to the fact that a warped sense of military necessity and military pride continued to trump the concerns for the civilian population.

Whereas in the summer of 1944 Party and Wehrmacht at least sought to form a coherent, albeit limited, evacuation policy, by the spring of 1945 neither concerned itself with the plight of the civilian population. This chapter has sought to explain this change through the lens of 'cumulative radicalisation'. There had long been disputes between the Wehrmacht and the Party concerning the different overlapping authorities and responsibilities, both domestically and abroad. But rather than being a mitigating factor, upon their return from the Soviet Union the Wehrmacht brought with it an institutionalised disregard for civilians and their property as it returned from the Soviet Union, instead devoting all possible resources to fighting defensive battles. Party officials, in turn, believed that they had no option but to follow suit. By 1945, both Party and Wehrmacht had thus manoeuvred themselves into a position where the only way to demonstrate their value was by focusing on Germany's defence rather than assuring the safety of its population.

6   Königsberg as a Community of Violence

Introduction

So far this work has mainly examined the indirect repercussions of the Wehrmacht's presence in Germany. This final chapter will venture beyond these findings and examine the role of the Wehrmacht in the direct violence during the final months of the National Socialist regime. It analyses how the defence of Königsberg was organised and will focus particularly on the role of violence against civilians as a means of coercion. It was in this stage of the war that the violence and terror of the Eastern Front returned to Germany. Especially given the fractured state of Germany at this point, 'violence not only affected its direct victims, but communicated unambiguous messages to others, displaying the sway and dominance of the new *and* social order that was to be'.[1] The brutality of 1945 – during the months in which the regime had lost its monopoly on violence – was committed by a variety of actors with the members of the Wehrmacht playing a major part. The concerns of German troops and Party officials on the one hand, and the civilians they were ordered to protect on the other, differed fundamentally. Examining the agendas of the different actors allows us to reconstruct their place within Königsberg's society during the final months of the war. The year 1945 engendered a wave of German intra-ethnic violence that has largely been pinned on Nazi officials, and to a lesser extent on stubborn, indoctrinated troops. Challenging this means prying into an open wound, since the question of why Germans continued to fight in 1945 tends to assign blame.[2] Yet given the diminishing reach of the state during the last year of the war, a top-down explanation seems inadequate to understand the scope of the violence. This chapter explores this hypothesis.

---

[1] Keller, 'Volksgemeinschaft and Violence', p. 227.   [2] Bessel, *Germany 1945*, p. 3.

Military Law in the War Years

Königsberg had been a fortress since late 1944 but one of its defining characteristics, the complete transfer of judicial power to the fortress commander, was only introduced as Soviet troops approached the city. Instead of countrywide martial law, in the beginning of the war Hitler had opted for a system of Reich Defence Commissioners (see Chapter 1), thereby curbing the domestic influence of the armed forces. Only areas that were immediately threatened – the areas of operations – would be subject to martial law. With the front line moving deeper and deeper into Germany, German areas under complete martial law became more numerous. In these areas local commanders used, in addition to regular military courts, drumhead courts-martial whose verdicts were immediately enforceable.[3] In Königsberg, General Lasch bore the final responsibility for the judicial process as Gerichtsherr (Master of Court), a function which was part of every fortress commander's responsibilities.[4] Yet the authority to pass judgement was typically exercised by staff officers and military judges and certainly did not only lie with Lasch. By the time the city was encircled, the juridical process had become decentralised and many courts had sprung up that adhered to parallel standards of justice. As the war went into its final stage, military justice had become less about the letter of the law and more about its 'spirit', and the outcome of a trial therefore became highly dependent on those conducting it.

Already by the beginning of the Second World War, the German military court system had been aligned with National Socialist thought, and throughout the war sentencing became harsher. Death sentences were mainly reserved for cases of desertion and the 'decomposition' of military strength (*Wehrkraftzersetzung*) and as such they differed little from earlier military courts. What was different was the way that a verdict was reached. From August 1939 onwards, judges were ordered not necessarily to base their judgements on the facts put in front of them alone, but rather to give a verdict that would serve the 'people's and military community' (*Volks- und Wehrgemeinschaft*).[5] After November of that year, judges were even allowed to pronounce death sentences for all

---

[3] Peter Lutz Kalmbach, '"Das neue Recht ermöglicht energisches Vorgehen"', *Deutsche Richterzeitung* (93) 2016, p. 29.

[4] BArch RH 2/332, 14: OKH/GenStdH/Op Abt/AbtLds Bef Nr. 1877/45 geh. 2.2.45 J.A. gez. Wenck 'Commander of Festung Königsberg, Gen. d. Inf. Lasch, has the right of ratification and repeal [in proceedings before the military tribunal] (Bestätigungs-und Aufhebungsrecht im Verfahren vor dem Feldkriegsgericht) as described by gem. § 79, Abs. 3, Ziff. 2 KstVo. (Kriegsstrafverfahrensordnung) Compare service instructions for fortress commandants'.

[5] Ulrich Baumann and Magnus Koch, *'Was damals Recht war . . . ' Soldaten und Zivilisten vor Gerichten der Wehrmacht* (Berlin, Be.Bra verlag, 2008), pp. 27, 30.

'criminal acts that threaten discipline or the commandment of soldierly courage', regardless of their seriousness, as long as the judgement would help 'maintain discipline, or [when] the security of the troops requires it'.[6]

As some judges prior to the court proceedings already knew that they would pass the death sentence, they were known to resort to political tirades rather than explaining their verdict along judicial lines.[7] Military courts allowed themselves significant leeway by basing death sentences on the rather broad concepts of abetting the enemy or causing a disadvantage to their own military, and by the end of 1944 army courts had presided over the execution of 26,000 to 27,000 people, 18,500 of whom were soldiers.[8] The traumatic defeat of the First World War, during which only forty-eight German soldiers had been sentenced to death for desertion, severely impacted the conduct of the National Socialist military justice system. This supposedly lenient approach was seen as an important factor for Germany's defeat and was sharply attacked even before the Nazis assumed power.[9] During the Second World War it was thoroughly rooted out, while the Wehrmacht itself also enforced much stricter self-discipline even without pressure from National Socialist bodies.[10] The severe punishments were not only considered necessary because they ensured 'absolute obedience and discipline' but also because desertion revealed the soldier's inability to grasp the importance of the Volksgemeinschaft. A deserting soldier was labelled a *Wehrmachtsschädling*, a military parasite, which often sealed his fate even before the trial itself, as fewer and fewer judges set out to discover the individual motives of the deserters in front of them.[11]

The hard German military justice was not only practised in courts but increasingly in the field as well. When the prosecution of these cases

---

[6] Reichsgesetzblatt Teil I, Nr. 218, 4 November 1939. 'Erste Verordnung zur Ergänzung der Kriegssonderstrafrechtsverordnung', p. 2131.

[7] Wolfram Wette and Detlef Vogel, *Das letzte Tabu: NS-Militärjustiz und 'Kriegsverrat'*, (Bonn: Bundeszentrale für politische Bildung, 2007), p. 32.

[8] Manfred Messerschmidt and Fritz Wüllner, *Die Wehrmachtjustiz im Dienste des Nationalsozialismus. Zerstörung einer Legende* (Baden-Baden: Nomos Verlagsgesellschaft, 1987), 78–9. Wette and Vogel, *Das letzte Tabu*, p. 23.

[9] Manfred Messserschmidt, *Die Wehrmachtjustiz 1933–1945* (Paderborn: Ferdinand Schöningh, 2005), p. 21; Stephen Welch, '"Harsh but Just?" German Military Justice in the Second World War: a Comparative Study of the Court-Martialling of German and US Deserters', *German History* (17) 1999, p. 376; Kershaw, *The End*, p. 220; Bessel, *Germany 1945*, p. 63.

[10] Robert Loeffel, 'Soldiers and Terror: Re-evaluating the Complicity of the Wehrmacht in Nazi Germany', *German History* (27) 2009, pp. 514–30. Using *Sippenhaft*, or family liability punishment, Loeffel proposed that rather than reflecting the desire of the Gestapo, 'it was the *Wehrmacht* itself that drove the attempt to apply terror' against its own troops.

[11] Welch, 'Harsh but Just?', pp. 381–3.

would not allow for a delay, commanders of regiments and upwards were given the authority of *Gerichtsherr* in *Standgerichte*, or 'drumhead courts-martial'. These courts-martial (whose name derived from the early use of a drumhead as a table top during court proceedings) tried offences that had occurred in action and which demanded summary justice, such as cowardness, insubordination, and attacks on superiors, as well as cases of plunder and riot.[12] Although these courts were meant as exceptions to the rule, the sheer size of the Wehrmacht and its constant deployment made them a staple of military life.[13]

Once the tide of war turned, the German High Command changed its attitude towards Standgerichte, fully recognising their capacity to pass swift justice. Attributing the mounting defeats to a wavering attitude among the German troops, in November 1943 the German High Command established the so-called OKW-*Feldjäger*.[14] The OKW-Feldjäger consisted of three Feldjägerkommandos (one on the Western Front, two on the Eastern Front), of which one, Feldjägerkommando I, was formed in Königsberg. Every such Kommando oversaw one Feldjäger-regiment which consisted of five Feldjäger-Abteilungen. These, in turn, comprised fifty patrols – known as *Streifen* – that were made up of four men, one officer, and three experienced non-commissioned officers.[15] Feldjäger were given almost complete authority at the immediate rear of Army Groups. The purpose of these men, who were directly subordinated to the OKW, was to maintain military discipline among the troops that were retreating or falling back and to return them to their units. To ensure this, Feldjäger had the power to immediately enforce the death sentence. Beyond powers of enforcement, these commandos, drafted from decorated and long-serving combat veterans, had investigative and judicial powers, as such uniting the entire process of justice. Feldjäger differed from the regular military police in one major aspect: whereas the task of the regular military police was to bring people in front of a court, Feldjäger units had judges attached to them which passed their judgement by order of the commanding officer.[16] Many of

---

[12] Merrion Webster s.v. 'drumhead court-martial'.

[13] Messerschmidt, *Die Wehrmachtjustiz*, pp. 410–11.

[14] BArch RH 48/52: General der Flieger Wilhelm Speidel, Kurze Denkschrift über meine Aufgabe und Tätigkeit als Befehlshaber Feldjägerkommando III von Mitte März 1945 bis Juni 1945.

[15] Gordon Williamson, *German Military Police Units 1939–45* (London: Osprey, 1989), p. 12.

[16] Peter Lutz Kalmbach, 'Polizeiliche Ermittlungsorgane der Wehrmachtjustiz', *Kriminalistik*, February 2013, p. 120; Peter Lutz Kalmbach, 'Feldjäger, Sicherheitsdienst, Sonderkommandos Polizeiorgane und Standgerichtsbarkeit in der Endphase des Zweiten Weltkriegs', *Kriminalistik*, July 2014, pp. 454–5.

the roughly 1,000 men of Feldjägerkommando I operated in East Prussia, allowing every major road and many of the byways in the province to be permanently controlled. As a result, more and more judgements in the field moved away from judges (who could already hardly be considered impartial) and came to rest with hardened veterans.

On 23 September 1944, the OKW, in an effort to steel the front along the borders of the Reich, passed down 'measures against disintegration in the troops', which heralded the era of indiscriminate public violence that was to come in the months that followed. From then on, Feldjäger-Kommandos were given the explicit order 'to crack down on the spot against signs of disintegration . . . with extreme severity'. At all costs, they were to prevent soldiers from detaching themselves from the front line and just loaf around in the rear to await defeat, as had happened in 1918.[17] The collective trauma of the final days of the First World War still had its grip on the conduct of these men. The Standgerichte, as it were, 'avenged' 1918; by striking down on everyone who considered ending the fight, they would prevent a surrender that would once again set Germany on path of chaos and humiliation.[18] As such, the Standgerichte performed a significant but often ignored function: they helped create a 'false consciousness' of a supposed 'internal enemy' by shifting the blame for Germany's defeat from the High Command to the rank-and-file.[19] This mindset, bolstered by the language found in the different orders, encouraged these men to act both autonomously and extremely ruthlessly.

From mid-1944 onwards, with the front line running through parts of Germany, the fear of desertion grew, since it was correctly assumed that soldiers could more easily go into hiding with the help of local people who spoke the language.[20] Moreover, during the relative calm that predated the East Prussian offensive many soldiers had taken part in anti-partisan actions. Those caught were mostly dressed in civilian clothing, or worse still, in German military attire, cementing the eerie feeling that a foe could look the exact same as a friend.[21] The fear of men wearing the same uniform can best be explained by considering the casualties of that year: the massive number of casualties had to be made up by equal numbers of new recruits, and the man in the next foxhole was increasingly a

---

[17] Schumann and Groehler (eds.) *Deutschland im Zweiten Weltkrieg* 6, p. 96: 'Befehl des OKW gegen Auflösungserscheinungen in den Truppenverbände (Auszug)'. Two months later, the tone again hardened. See: BArch, NS 6/354, Maßnahmen zur Ausrottung von Etappenerscheinungen.- Befehl des Chefs des OKW vom 28. Nov. 1944.- B 19/45g.

[18] Keller, *Volksgemeinschaft am Ende*, p. 421; Geyer, 'Endkampf 1918 and 1945', pp. 42–3.

[19] On 'false consciousness' during wartime, see: Walzer, *Just and Unjust Wars*, p. 36.

[20] Bessel, *Germany 1945*, pp. 42–3.   [21] BArch Ost-Dok. 8/519, pp. 2–3: von Bredow.

stranger.[22] Especially worrying was the turnover of officers: tens of thousands of men were hurriedly trained to fill the depleted ranks, although a majority of these men, according to a report of an officer course, 'lack the inner calling of a military and political leader, many even [lack] the willingness to become an officer'.[23] The turnover, in turn, meant that ever fewer troops knew the men that formed their chain of command. On 11 November 1944 the OKH passed down an order concerning 'defensive measures against infiltration of hostile or treacherous elements', which explained how troops should verify orders from unknown officers. The order had already been distributed before, in early August that year, but 'given the imminent new main attack on the Eastern Front', troops were again to be taught on the matter.[24]

The OKH was certainly not wrong to do this: one of the Soviet Union's most famous dissidents, Lev Kopelev, whose unit – a political department of a Soviet Front, responsible in East Prussia for 'propaganda and psychological warfare against the enemy' – recalled how special members of the NKFD, dubbed 'commissars of panic', were dropped behind German lines in order to 'spread rumours about the Soviet advance, to yell, "the Russians have broken through!", "Tanks behind us!", and the like at opportune moments and generally to spread confusion in the German ranks'.[25] Still unwilling to pin the mounting defeats on the quality of the Soviet operational conduct, the Wehrmacht and Party kept searching for hostile elements among its own ranks to explain the situation.[26] A circular distributed on 1 February 1945 instructed that 'suspicious persons, whether they wear the uniform of the German Wehrmacht, Organisation Todt, or a Party uniform, are to be carefully checked by the police or the appropriate Wehrmacht patrols. All vehicles that are moving out westwards are therefore to be checked with particular care'.[27] Yet, all civilians headed west, fleeing ahead of the Soviet troops, and every

---

[22] Overmans, *Deutsche militärische Verluste im Zweiten Weltkrieg*, pp. 238, 318. Over 560,000 soldiers fell in July and August 1944, at the height of Bagration. In January 1945, as the final Soviet offensives commenced, the number of casualties peaked at 450,000. In February, March and April, between 280,000 and 300,000 German soldiers died each month.

[23] Kunz, *Wehrmacht und Niederlage*, pp. 177–81.

[24] BArch RH 2/316, pp. 125–6: OKH/GenStdH/ Op Abt (roem. 1a) Nr.7009/44 g.Kdos. roem.2. Ang. 10.11.1944.

[25] Kopelev, *No Jail for Thought*, pp. 15, 35.

[26] By 1945, however, the Red Army had long taught itself to reflect on its past mistakes and learn from them and was no longer recognisable as the 'disorganised' force it had been in 1941. See, for example: M. V. Frunze Military Academy, *Durchbruch der Schützenverbände durch eine vorbereitete Verteidigung* (Berlin: Ministerium für Nationale Verteidigung, 1959).

[27] BArch NS 6/354, p. 54: Der Leiter der Partei-Kanzlei, Führerhauptquartier, den 1.2.1945. Rundschreiben 47/45 g. Betrifft: Feindpropaganda. The 'Organisation Todt'

time a unit fell back it was westwards. As such, any move to safety could be deemed as suspicious.

What compounded matters was that the German rank-and-file was given increasing leeway in judging whether actions they observed were a threat to fighting strength. In November 1944, the OKH passed down orders concerning deserters stating that soldiers intending to desert were to be fired upon by their own comrades.[28] This was once again stressed in the 'Provisions on the Conduct of Officers and Men in Times of Crisis', better known as the *Katastrophebefehl* (catastrophe-order), distributed on 28 January 1945. Not only was the use of deadly force encouraged if this was considered the only way to maintain discipline, the provisions also opened the door for further indiscriminate violence: 'He who, in the case of major breaches of duty, acts courageously and responsibly . . . shall not be held accountable, even if he exceeds his powers'.[29] This measure potentially allowed every soldier to become judge, jury, and executioner, and effectively gave soldiers carte blanche – echoing earlier attitudes towards the civilian populations in the occupied East. Pushing much further than any domestic law thus far, the order ensured that wherever soldiers were, military values became the measuring rod in judging whether someone performed his or her duty in Germany's struggle.

Despite the apprehensive atmosphere that was present in the army, and despite the fact that these men – often stressed and burned out after long periods of fighting – could hardly be considered as objective, they were still actively conditioned to look at their surroundings for signs of defeatism and sabotage.[30] Thus, fanatics within the army were not only enabled to kill suspicious alien elements, they were also encouraged to be active participants in maintaining discipline among their own ranks and act upon it personally when breached. For example, the Volkssturm hero Ernst Tiburzy was not only hailed by Kreisleiter Wagner for knocking out Soviet tanks, he was also praised for having shot a platoon commander who had ordered his man to fall back.[31] Similarly, in a post-war questionnaire, Oberstleutnant Hans-Heinrich Wendtlandt, a regimental

(OT) was a civil and military engineering group that worked in close cooperation with Nazi authorities.

[28] BArch RW 4/725, p. 14: Maßnahmen gegen Überläufer, Landesverrat in der Kriegsgefangenschaft

[29] Der Chef des Oberkommandos der Wehrmacht: 'Bestimmungen über das Verhalten von Offizier und Mann in Krisenzeiten', 28 January, 1945. Printed in: Rudolf Absolon, *Das Wehrmachtstrafrecht im 2. Weltkrieg – Sammlung der grundlegenden Gesetze, Verordnungen und Erlasse* (Kornelimünster: Bundesarchiv, Abt. Zentralnachweisstelle, 1958), pp. 93–4.

[30] Omer Bartov, 'The Conduct of War: Soldiers and the Barbarization of Warfare', *The Journal of Modern History* (64) 1992, pp. 35–8.

[31] Lasch, *So fiel Königsberg*, p. 140.

commander, told how in late January 1945 he put a Luftwaffe major in front of a courts-martial after he had lost his nerves, although, Wendtlandt claimed, 'the verdict [had] not become known' to him.[32]

These two cases show signs of what is referred to as 'forward panic', when, after a period of relative passivity (as had been the case in the months leading up to the anticipated Soviet offensive), the built-up tension could finally be released, often in an emotional rush.[33] Not only did this 'embolden' the defenders; on occasions when this violence could not be directed at the enemy who had caused the panic, it was directed at the "next-best" threat: cowards or shirkers. An SS situation report from Königsberg dated 17 February 1945 seemed to illustrate the widespread willingness of troops to have their say in matters of life and death: 'Among the troops there is huge outrage about the flight of doctors and the hospital personnel. It is being demanded that those who fled, as well as the officers of the [abandoned and ignited] ammunition depots, who have also fled, are to be executed.'[34] Some soldiers nevertheless contemplated abandoning their comrades. In a surrounded fortress with a stable front, moreover, defecting – as such becoming part of the *Verrätergesindel* (traitor scum) – was even more likely to occur since troops had more time to weigh their options.[35] Every man who eventually decided to defect played into his comrades' confirmation bias.

The function and position that fortresses occupied in Germany's defence, moreover, made it more likely that soldiers with mental health problems were garrisoned there, which in turn increased the chance of violence. As the war progressed, doctors saw a sharp increase in chronic stomach disorder, which was often a symptom of deeper psychological problems. From mid-1943, special 'stomach battalions' were established which were to occupy positions away from the front. Some of the garrisons of Königsberg's forts consisted of these kinds of units.[36] Moreover, being encircled in fortresses – unflatteringly referred to as 'Kessel' (boilers) – weighed heavy on troops, and in a number of cases even led to a phenomenon referred to as *Kesselpsychose* (boiler psychosis).[37]

---

[32] BArch Ost-Dok. 8/579, p. 9: Wendtlandt.
[33] Randall Collins, *Violence: a Micro-Sociological Theory* (Princeton, NJ: Princeton University Press, 2008), p. 85.
[34] BArch NS 19/2068, p. 7. An Reichsführer-SS Feldkommandostelle, Betrifft: Meldungen aus dem Ostraum Königsberg, 15.2.45.
[35] BArch NS 19/2068, p. 62. An Reichsführer-SS Feldkommandostelle, Betrifft: Meldungen aus dem Ostraum Königsberg, 13.3.45; 'Verachtung dem Verrätergesindel', *Preußische Zeitung*, 11 February 1945.
[36] Cocks, *Psychotherapy in the Third Reich*, p. 316; Lasch, *So fiel Königsberg*, p. 111.
[37] Frieser, 'Irrtümer und Illusionen', pp. 521–4.

Alongside this, as we have examined in depth in Chapter 2, the concept of 'civilian' had been hollowed out during the years of combat and occupation on the Eastern Front. The way civilians were dealt with fell well outside the traditional rules of war. Collective punishment had been instituted as German troops invaded the Soviet Union in the summer of 1941 and mass executions, mostly under the rubric of quelling incipient guerrilla activity, became standard practice.[38] The many pictures of hanged Soviet partisans – either real or supposed – taken by German soldiers suggest that there was a kind of gratification in their open display, if not to say some pride. By the time the Wehrmacht moved onto East Prussian territory, many German soldiers had developed a tendency to consider civilians as a legitimate threat. Although this should certainly not be seen as an excuse for the excessive amounts of violence in the Soviet Union, or the violence that lay ahead, it might help to explain the behaviour of German troops in 1945.

For most of the war the home front and front line were separated by hundreds of miles, but in late 1944 the two came into contact with each other. This meant that the domestic justice system and the military justice system 'met', as did their perceptions of 'civilians'. It is worth pointing out that up to this point, Wehrmacht courts had been responsible for the deaths of most of the Volksgenossen. Surely, domestic courts had convicted thousands of people, but most of these were 'social outsiders', racially inferior, *Rassenschänder*: people, in other words, who the court system did not consider German, or those who by their actions had 'forfeited' their rights as Germans.[39] The terror that German troops had felt on the Eastern Front, which had encouraged feelings of deep suspicion and unease – not only towards the direct environment but also towards their own – had culminated in thousands of executions, and now returned with these men onto German soil. Since it was ordinary Germans who were caught up in the executions of 1945, the next section examines to what extent the arrival of the military in Königsberg impacted the way law was interpreted in the fortress.

Upholding Military Law in Königsberg

On 28 January 1945, General Lasch accepted the position as fortress commander and the men he used to make up his fortress staff were veterans hardened by years of fighting on the Eastern Front. Establishing his authority, especially with regard to the Party, was one

---

[38] Neitzel and Welzer, *Soldaten*, p. 329.
[39] Richard Evans, *Rituals of Retribution: Capital Punishment in Germany 1600–1987* (Oxford: Oxford University Press, 1996), pp. 651–737.

of the general's primary concerns during the first days of his appointment. This section will examine how Lasch cemented his position by establishing a 'Wehrmacht rule of law' in Königsberg. By pushing through martial law in the city before the Party could regroup itself, he presented it as a fait accompli.[40] This in turn enabled Lasch to pursue his own agenda more effectively. Moreover, the implementation of martial law impressed a military way of thinking on the city, thereby giving credence to the Wehrmacht as the ultimate authority.

Prior to Lasch's appointment as fortress commander, the commander of the 1st Infanterie-Division, General Hans Schittnig, had held that position. The staff of his division was the only one large enough to oversee the running of the fortress, and they withdrew into Königsberg mainly to fulfil that task.[41] When Lasch took over as fortress commander, he asked General Schittnig to hand these men over to build a proper fortress staff, with which the latter complied.[42] The type of character that was expected for these positions fitted something that Hitler himself had clearly communicated since the earliest beginnings of the fortress strategy. On 21 June 1944, he encouraged Generalleutnant Karl-Wilhelm von Schlieben, the commander of the encircled Festung Cherbourg, to 'put the toughest men in the fortress on your staff and root out every appearance of cowardice or timidity'.[43] This was also clearly the case in Königsberg, as war correspondent Günther Heysing noted in his diary two weeks later: 'About 100 officers, telephonists, radio operators, drivers, cartographers, writers, and orderlies came over. They walked ... through the streets and immediately grabbed every uniformed man who made a halfway decent impression.'[44] The 1st Infanterie-Division was mustered in East Prussia, and many of these officers came from the city itself, as Königsberg had served as the garrison city of some of its regiments for over 300 years.

The symbolic value of these men defending their home city was not lost on the editors of the *Preußische Zeitung*: 'The fortunes of war have willed that numerous sons of the East Prussian Heimat have become the defenders of their Gau-capital.'[45] Of course, it was not so much the 'fortunes of war', but

---

[40] Hannes Heer, 'Extreme Normalität. Generalmajor Gustav Freiherr von Mauchenheim gen. Bechtolsheim: Umfeld, Motive und Entschlussbildung eines Holocaust-Täters', *Zeitschrift für Geschichtswissenschaft* (51) 2003, pp. 752–3.

[41] BArch Ost-Dok. 10/888, p. 30: Dieckert; Werner Richter, *Die 1. (ostpreussische) Infanterie-Division*, p. 150. Much to the outrage of its troops, the rest of the division was (temporarily) attached to the 56th Infanterie-Division which fought just south of Königsberg.

[42] Lasch, *So fiel Königsberg*, p. 38.

[43] TNA HW 1/2992, p. 2: West Europe, 21 June 1944.

[44] BArch Ost-Dok. 8/591, p. 43: Heysing.

[45] Herbert Schellhammer, 'Unsere Verpflichtung!', *Festung Königsberg*, 2 February 1945.

Figure 6.1 A person hanged for looting during the first days of Königsberg's siege. *Source:* Archiv Stadt Königsberg

rather the deliberate choices of the OKH, which in August 1944 had transferred the division from Nord-Ukraine to East Prussia to bolster its defence.[46] After two weeks of continuous retreat, few of the division's men recognised themselves in the upbeat reading of events, if only because what they encountered upon return gave little reason for optimism. On 26 January 1945, the war diary of the 1st Infanterie-Division noted: 'It is almost unbearable here – the city that we once left so happy and confident for victory is in great commotion.'[47] That pessimist sentiment, however, did not mean that the division intended to let this state of affairs continue.

[46] Tessin, *Verbände und Truppen der deutschen Wehrmacht, vol. 2*, s.v. '1'.
[47] BArch RH 26–1/100, p. 83: KTB der I.ID (aufgezeichnet von Hptm. Albrecht Meier-Hartigshof) 1939–1945, 23. Januar–26. Januar 1945.

Immediately after his appointment, Lasch established a fortress court.[48] Theoretically, it was the task of the military police, the Feldgendarmerie, to bring in deserters to face judgement by this court. However, since the immediate defence of Königsberg and the restoration of order were of overriding importance, Feldgendarmerie and officer patrols, Streifen of the 1st Infanterie-Division, supported by different police units, were permitted to pass their own judgement and General Lasch, as the supreme legal authority in the fortress, allowed these men virtually unrestricted leeway.[49] The chief editor of the *Königsberger Allgemeine Zeitung*, Martin Wegener, closely observed their behaviour and illustrated that the distinction between soldiers and civilians seemed to disappear:

Officer patrols were sent through the basements to fetch the hiding soldiers who in some cases had already changed to the civilian clothing that was present in abundance in the abandoned houses. The vast majority of the soldiers willingly obeyed the command to return to their units at the front. There was also resistance of the most serious kind which required the strongest application of the laws of war. More common than among soldiers were the executions among the plunderers, thieves, and murderers from the ranks of Ostarbeiter, refugees and locals. The drumhead courts that were deployed for these culprits only knew one punishment, even for small thefts: death through hanging. One of the assessors, an Ortsgruppenleiter (local leader) of the Nazi Party who normally oversaw the administration of a large hospital, otherwise known as an unusually good-natured man, in answer to the question of whether he could justify such judgements for his conscience, said: "It's what's best for them and us, and that is what determined my decision". Incidentally, headquarters demanded the speedy removal of the bodies of the hanged, among whom were women.[50]

The fortress command readily invoked the threat of summary execution. Werner Terpitz, a young forced recruit of the 561st Volksgrenadier-Division remembered: 'On big yellow posters on the hoardings it stated: All sixteen- to sixty-year olds have until 3 February to enrol in the Volkssturm or the Wehrmacht. Failure to comply is punishable by death.'[51] From a military point of view the patrols were highly successful, as they ensured that over 20,000 men, mostly stragglers, were returned to the front line, initially as 100-man emergency units which could later be incorporated into divisions

---

[48] Lasch, *So fiel Königsberg*, p. 129; BArch Ost-Dok. 10/890, p. 127: Dieckert. Presiding judge: Oberfeldrichter Walter von Zeddelmann, Assessor: Oberstleutnant d.R. Wilhelm Strüvy.

[49] Lasch, *So fiel Königsberg*, pp. 57–9; Wette and Vogel, *Das letzte Tabu*, pp. 24–5.

[50] AKO 22034–4: Wegener, *Der Untergang von Königsberg*, p. 1. The presence of Party officials in this procedure will be discussed later in the chapter.

[51] Werner Terpitz, 'Das letzte Aufgebot: Mit sechzehn Jahren als Soldat im untergehenden Königsberg', *Frankfurter Allgemeine Zeitung*, 16 March 1985, sec. Ereignisse und Gestalten.

when the front had stabilised.[52] The process of becoming part of these emergency units is best described by Guy Sajer, a veteran of the Grossdeutschland division:

> Our group was gone over with a fine-toothed comb by the Kommandos responsible for sending men back to their original units. As they didn't know where most of these units were, the best they could do was to form the strays into new groups, which everyone wished to avoid. These new units, with no official affiliation or assignments, simply sapped the actual strength of the army as recorded by military registration and on the maps at headquarters. The men assigned to these varied and unmeasurable groups could not be fitted into any logical organisation. Already classified as missing or dead by their original units, they were officially considered dead, and used as unexpected reinforcements whom there was no reason to spare.[53]

With the introduction of martial law, everyone in Königsberg could be measured by the same yardstick – the ability to contribute to the city's defence. Those who could not were a burden, a liability, or even a threat. The mention of women among those executed stresses to what extent fear and suspicion dominated the mindset of those conducting summary executions. These men had 'learned' to distinguish between the virtuous woman (the sister, the mother, and the nurse), and the so-called 'prole-tarian' or 'red' woman, who was morally promiscuous, threatening, and unnerving, and as such one of the defining elements of unrest.[54] Many troops that reached Königsberg had experience with these unnerving 'proletarian' women, having encountered them in the Soviet Union both as partisans and among the ranks of the Red Army. Within this sentiment, every civilian could be a potential threat, which allowed the army to justify the hard line it took as necessary. During the first week of the siege, the Streifen showed a complete disregard for the physical and mental state of those they encountered, and cracked down on any perceived threat, of which – in their eyes – desertion was the most obvious manifestation. Men were not allowed to leave the city anymore while doctors were forbidden to put anyone on sick leave.[55] Anyone who refused to go to the front was effectively deemed a deserter.

---

[52] Lasch, *So fiel Königsberg*, p. 58; BArch RH 26–1/112, p. 155 Hans-Joachim Schröder: Die letzten Monate des Div. Füs. Batl. 1; Barch Ost-Dok. 8/586, 2: Werbke. Werbke adds that the number was close to 10,000 within four days.

[53] Sajer, *The Forgotten Soldier*, pp. 140–1. This account stems from late 1942 but the process had not changed in the years that followed.

[54] Klaus Theweleit, *Männerphantasien, 1. Band* (Frankfurt a.M.: Verlag Roter Stern, 1979), pp. 88–105; Jones, *Founding Weimar*, pp. 22, 24.

[55] BArch Ost-Dok. 8/602, p. 5: Makowka; GAKO 'Nemetski Fondi', H54, No 48, Opis 1, Delo 11.1.9: Abschrift Wehrmachtkommandantur Königsberg (Pr) Abt. IIa, den 10.2.1945, Standort-Befehl.

The quality of the men the Streifen picked up appeared to be of the least importance. Lothar Finke, an Eastern Front veteran who arrived in the city in late January, recalled that the searches by these Heldengreifkommandos – 'hero-snatcher commandos' – were not limited solely to soldiers, but also focused on 'old, recovering and partly disabled men' and was an 'unpleasant and unfriendly activity'.[56] Despite his young age, even Hans-Burkhardt Sumowski noted civilians' fear and resentment of the military police.[57] Adolf Klein, who was sent with his Volkssturm unit to Königsberg, remembered how his men desperately tried to avoid being picked up by Streifen. When they were eventually rounded up, he felt treated like 'herded cattle, which would be brought to the slaughter in the coming hours'.[58] Volkssturm men disproportionally fell victim to summary courts since their units were most likely to disintegrate. Even though they had been incorporated into the military command structure, their battalions were often only to be deployed in the defence of their home towns. When this failed – which it usually did in the first weeks of the East Prussian offensive – Volkssturm units were likely to retreat in disorderly fashion. Many of these men had been called up to serve in the defence of East Prussia only after the offensive had already commenced and unlike other units they had never experienced a retreat before.[59] Poorly supplied, poorly armed, poorly clothed, and often in poor health, the men were soldiers only in name, which, moreover, most felt they were.[60]

Even though the officers of the 1st Infanterie-Division were ordered to crack down on people originating from their immediate peace time surroundings, they did not consider their assignment to conflict with their conscience. 'The first task is to establish order', wrote Hauptmann Gottfried Lenz, an adjutant in the staff of the 1st Infanterie-Division, after the war. 'With the help of the wounded officers of the division, stragglers are picked up, collected, and placed in emergency units and quickly thrown [into battle] at threatened parts of the front.'[61] In their

---

[56] Lothar Finke, *Eine silberne Uhr in Königsberg* (Frankfurt a.M: Fischer Verlag, 1993), pp. 35–7.

[57] Sumowski, *'Jetzt war ich ganz allein auf der Welt'*, p. 59.

[58] BArch Ost-Dok. 8/598, pp. 44–7: Klein.

[59] BArch RH 2/331b, p. 74: Fernschreiben gez. Guderian, Generaloberst und Chef des Generalstabes des Heeres. OKH/ GenStdH/ Op Abt/ Abt Lds Bef Nr. 539/45 g.Kdos. 14.1.45

[60] Shortly after the war, the psychologists Shils and Janowitz pointed out that Volkssturm men had 'not broken their family ties to the slightest extent. They still remained members of a primary group which did not fuse into the military primary group'. See: Shils and Janowitz, 'Cohesion and Disintegration in the Wehrmacht', p. 288.

[61] BArch Msg 2 / 240, p. 35: Militärische Berichte über den Kampf in Ostpreußen 1944–1945: Kampf um Ostpreußen 1945 von Hauptmann d. R. Lenz, Adj. Beim Stab der 1. Inf. Div. Frühjahr 1956

efforts to search for deserters the officers of the 1st Infanterie-Division showed no leniency and seemed proud of their behaviour, as the war diary of the division attests: 'With an iron broom the streets are "swept"', an officer of the 1st Infanterie-Division noted in the divisional war diary in late January 1945. 'We succeed to restore the order everywhere in a few days. . . . Saboteurs and shirkers are bore down on – nasty rumour-mongers will quickly be put a stop to.'[62] On 2 February, Generaloberst Rendulic passed down a circular to his subordinates to clarify how they should proceed upon encountering stragglers: 'From 3 February onwards, all soldiers of all branches of the Wehrmacht that are encountered away from their unit, in streets, towns, or refugee columns, or at field dressing stations without being wounded, and declare to be stragglers seeking their unit, are to be summarily shot! Flying courts-martial are immediately employed to this end.'[63] In the post-war years, Rendulic's order to deploy these highly mobile, 'flying', courts-martial has caused him to be viewed as a dyed-in-the-wool Nazi, but the order was eventually copied by all commanders in Germany including more moderate men such as Field Marshal Gerd von Rundstedt, the commander in chief in the West. Rather than a testimony of loyalty towards the Nazi regime, it is more likely that men like Rendulic saw the orders as a continuation of military law.[64]

On 10 February, just over a week after the encirclement of Königsberg, *The Times* reported on the measures taken by General Lasch: 'Königsberg is now in a desperate plight, though the garrison commander has repeated his orders to fight to the last and rounded up some 1,500 deserters for punishment duties on the front line.'[65] In the post-war years Lasch downplayed the scope of his actions and the reach of the Streifen. He had one of his former subordinates, Oberstleutnant Dr Sauvant, write down his recollections, rather than presenting his own. 'In the interest of maintaining discipline it was impossible to avoid, in special cases of blatant cowardice and desertion, the enforcement of courts-martial death sentences by shooting.' Sauvant subsequently stated that for Lasch, as the commander with the final responsibility, this was tough, but nonetheless considered an 'overriding requirement of duty'.[66] The Wehrmacht's duty those days was keeping the city out of the hands of the Soviets, something that was actively conveyed to the civilian population. After the summary

[62] BArch RH 26–1/100, p. 84: KTB der I.ID (aufgezeichnet von Hptm. Albrecht Meier-Hartigshof) 1939–1945, 29. Januar–15. Februar 1945.
[63] Heinz Schön, *Flucht aus Ostpreußen 1945, Die Menschenjagd der Roten Armee* (Kiel: Arndt-Verlag, 2001), pp. 25–6.
[64] Bessel, *Germany 1945*, p. 18.
[65] Our Special Correspondent, 'On Main Road to Stargard', *The Times*, 10 February 1945, p. 4. This information almost certainly reached the *Times* via Soviet military sources.
[66] Lasch, *So fiel Königsberg*, p. 59.

execution of two soldiers at the Nordbahnhof on the afternoon of 1 February, Major Ipsen, the NSFO of Festung Königsberg, gave a speech to those present which was printed the next day in the *Festung Königsberg* newspaper: 'With the enemy at the gates of the city', noted Ipsen, 'it is important that every one of us, soldier and Volkssturm man, woman and Hitler Youth, keeps their nerve in these critical hours, and is firm and determined to persevere and to fight.' He continued that 'it must and will succeed that Königsberg's brave battle community not only withstands these hours of crisis ..., but also decisively contributes to the imminent turning point!'[67] Passers-by often witnessed people being executed near the Nordbahnhof and the Hauptbahnhof during the last days of January in Königsberg. These were not only soldiers strung up for desertion, but also civilians executed for looting. Many of these executions were obligatory for soldiers to visit to deter them from deserting, and bodies were often left for days with placards attached to their chest indicating both their 'crime' and, in the case of soldiers, their former unit.[68] By the end of January order had returned in Königsberg, and the Streifen and military police had played an important role in achieving this. In some cases civilians had personally asked them to drive away plunderers, showing that they became almost immediately recognised as figures of authority.[69]

The visible presence of the Streifen and the harsh line they took were the clearest manifestations that a change of power had occurred in Königsberg. Also during the first years of the Weimar Republic authorities of the newly formed German state used this kind of 'pedagogical violence' to 'found its authority and prove its will to rule': this section shows that similar motivations were at play in Königsberg in 1945.[70] The readiness to crack down on perceived stragglers, saboteurs, and shirkers – including civilians – distinguished the Wehrmacht from the Party.[71] There should be no doubt that violence and authority were intrinsically linked in Königsberg, and that, after serving on the Eastern Front, many commanders had considerably more expertise in this regard. This made the army the major stakeholder in the public violence against the local community. Yet authority could not rest on violence alone. The next section will examine what efforts the fortress command made to accommodate the population of Königsberg and assess how these shaped the understanding between civilians and the former.

---

[67] 'Feiglinge werden erschossen', *Festung Königsberg*, 2 February 1945.
[68] BArch Ost-Dok. 8/602, p. 5: Makowka; Sumowski, *'Jetzt war ich ganz allein auf der Welt'*, p. 61; Clappier, *Festung Königsberg*, p. 93; Guido Knopp, *Der Sturm*, p. 81; Boree, *Ein Abschied*, pp. 38–9.
[69] Lehndorff, *Ostpreussisches Tagebuch*, pp. 28–9.   [70] Jones, *Founding Weimar*, p. 4.
[71] BArch RH 24–9/212, p. 7: Generalkommando IX. A.K. Abt. IIa/IIb Nr.3762/44, K.Gef. Stand, den 29.10.44, Korps-Tagesbefehl Nr.10. 'Strafsachen sind stets Eilsachen!'

Figure 6.2 A guard on the Grüne Brücke, early February 1945.
Source: Bundesarchiv, Bild 183-H26401, Wilhelm Engels

Königsberg under Siege

Two seemingly contradicting trends are clearly distinguishable in
Königsberg. As we will see in the subsequent sections, the fortress
command continued to crack down on any sign of disintegration. At
the same time, both Party and Wehrmacht invested much energy in
maintaining a sense of normality in the fortress.[72] To explain this
paradoxical behaviour, this section consists of two parts. Firstly, it
provides an overview of the efforts that were made to accommodate
the civilian population. We will then turn to the reservations and
concerns the fortress command connected to these efforts. The

---

[72] On the shifting of the concept of normality, see: Heer, 'Extreme Normalität'.

conclusion of this section will establish how this behaviour related to the broader German context in order to eventually determine how it tied into the radicalisation that took place in 1945.

During Königsberg's siege, the fortress command mainly seemed to have operated with two principles regarding civilians: assuring their basic needs – most importantly food and housing – and keeping track of their movement. In the first weeks of the encirclement, in early February, the provisioning of the civilian population was well organised. As a document concerning the provisioning of 'fortresses of which their inclusion at least has to be reckoned with', dated 25 February 1945, shows, food supply for fortress cities was assured well in advance of their encirclement.[73] Moreover, as Königsberg had been a major supply hub for the Eastern Front, it housed many warehouses that contained food stocks and the fortress could rely on the plentiful cattle that had been brought in from the east of the province.[74] Table 6.1 indicates that in a number of aspects the weekly rations in Königsberg fell below the national level during the siege. But contrary to the statistics, most civilians remember the fortress era as a time when food was well distributed, and few complained about food shortages.[75]

Furthermore, pregnant and breastfeeding women received extra rations of nutrients, butter, and milk, and babies received extra fats. In addition, diabetics received extra meat and nutrients while the gastrointestinal ill also received extra fats.[76] Meanwhile, the matter of housing was also tackled with relative ease. In the wake of the bombing of Königsberg many people had fled the city, and in early January another wave of civilians had departed. *Blockwarte* (block wardens) assessed which buildings were unoccupied and the homeless received the keys of the houses they had been allocated.[77] There continued to be running water and the local Siemens plant supplied energy.[78]

In a wider sense, the fortress command actively worked to assure an atmosphere of normality. On 19 February certificates for household

---

[73] BArch RW 4/710 Betr. Verpflegungsbevorratung der Festungen und Verteidigungsbereiche. F.H.Qu., 25.2.1945. This document does not discuss Königsberg, but does discuss a number of other 'Eastern Fortresses', such as Gotenhafen, Danzig, Kolberg, Breslau, Olmütz, and Pressburg.

[74] BArch NS 19/2068, p. 19: An Reichsführer-SS Betrifft: Meldungen aus den Ostraum, Königsberg, 21.2.45.; Grunberger, *A Social History of the Third Reich*, p. 205; Tooze, *Wages of Destruction*, p. 477.

[75] Richard Overy, *Historical Atlas of the Third Reich* (Harmondsworth: Penguin 1996), pp. 94–5; Noakes (ed.), *Nazism 1919/1945 Volume 4*, pp. 513–15.

[76] 'Der Bevollmächtigte Kommissar des Gauleiters gibt bekannt', *Preußische Zeitung*, 20 February 1945; 'Der Bevollmächtigte Kommissar des Gauleiters gibt bekannt', *Preußische Zeitung*, 23 February 1945.

[77] Sumowski, *'Jetzt war ich ganz allein auf der Welt'*, p. 61.

[78] AKO 22034–4: Lemke: *Die letzten Tage von Königsberg*; Lasch, *So fiel Königsberg*, p. 65.

Table 6.1 *Weekly rations in Königsberg during the siege, February 1945*

	National weekly ration 5 February to 4 March.[79]	Weekly ration Königsberg 5 to 11 February.[80]	Weekly ration Königsberg 12 to 18 February.[81]
Bread	2,225 grams	2,500 grams	2,500 grams
Fat	156,25 grams	150 grams	125 grams
Meat	362,5 grams	375 grams	250 grams
Sugar	312,5 grams	200 grams	125 grams
Spreads	-	187.5 grams	125 grams
Cereals	225 grams	150 grams	125 grams
Legumes	-	-	125 grams
Coffee subst.	31,25 grams	62.5 grams	62.5 grams
Cheese	15,63 grams	-	-
Potatoes	2,500 grams	Unknown*	Unknown
Fish	62,5 grams	-	-

* On 23 February, the *Preußische Zeitung* recorded: 'maximum 2 kg potatoes per person per week'.

goods were distributed which could be used in six different stores throughout the city. A seventh store for household goods opened on 23 February together with another for textiles and a store for footwear.[82] By order of Kreisleiter Wagner, all stores were to open their doors on Sunday as well. Three cinemas played a total of forty-two films per week.[83] And even though the Albertus University had officially been closed, some lectures continued albeit on a much smaller scale.[84] On top of the nine banks that already ensured that salaries and pensions were paid to labourers, employees, officials, and teachers, the giro-office was reopened for three hours a day.[85] Following Operation Westwind, there were even limited possibilities for civilians to send letters out of the city to relatives in the rest of Germany, although military mail was still

[79] Numbers are from monthly rations of February 1945 as cited in: Noakes (ed.), *Nazism 1919/1945 Volume 4*, p. 515, divided by four.
[80] Numbers were printed in the *Preußische Zeitung* of 3 February 1945.
[81] Numbers were printed in the *Preußische Zeitung* of 8 February 1945.
[82] 'Der Bevollmächtigte Kommissar des Gauleiters gibt bekannt', 19 February 1945; 'Der Bevollmächtigte Kommissar des Gauleiters gibt bekannt', 23 February 1945.
[83] 'Der Bevollmächtigte Kommissar des Gauleiters gibt bekannt', *Preußische Zeitung*, 20 February 1945; Clappier, *Festung Königsberg*, p. 121.
[84] Gause, *Die Geschichte der Stadt Königsberg*, p. 164.
[85] 'Der Bevollmächtigte Kommissar des Gauleiters gibt bekannt', 21 February 1945; 'Der Bevollmächtigte Kommissar des Gauleiters gibt bekannt', 22 February 1945; von Lehndorff, *Ostpreußisches Tagebuch*, p. 50.

prioritised.[86] These efforts were appreciated by the population and gave rise to a 'timid optimism'.[87] Different police authorities also continued to function. Feldwebel Mathias Nölke, for example, visited both the Gestapo headquarters and the Polizeipräsidium (police headquarters) in early March, trying to get clarification about his father-in-law who was missing.[88] Although the police apparatus in 1945 is often merely viewed through the lens of radicalisation, documents in Königsberg show a string of mundane tasks that were still being carried out by local police authorities. In mid-February, for instance, police patrols were sent through the streets to check up on blackout measures.[89] Whenever Volkssturm men were wounded during training, it was the task of the police to compile a report on it, which was done with great attention to detail.[90] People could still officially get married in March.[91] These efforts were in stark contrast to the minimal care that was provided in the refugee camps on the Samland and made the decision to remain in a besieged city appear sensible rather than life-threatening.

This did not mean that people in Königsberg were oblivious to the danger the city was in; it would be fairer to consider their attitude as 'resigned'. Like other Germans, many of those who remained considered Germany's defeat inevitable and preferred to suffer its total defeat in an environment that was at least familiar, rather than expose themselves to further risks.[92] Many parishes continued to operate as priests did not want to abandon their 'flock'.[93] During the siege, church services remained particularly well attended and peaked at Easter, just days before the final storming.[94] However, the accommodating stance of the fortress command towards civilians did not come about without hesitation or

---

[86] Erwin Lemke, 'Die Post kam bis zuletzt: Das Postwesen in Ostpreußen 1945/46', *Das Ostpreußenblatt*, 6 April 1968, p. 13.

[87] von Lehndorff, *Ostpreußisches Tagebuch*, p. 50; Clappier, *Festung Königsberg*, p. 121.

[88] Manfred Backhausen, 'Von Düsseldorf über Königsberg und Riga nach Gruiten: Bürgermeister Mathias Nölke (1912–1962)'. www.mjb-verlag.de/media/5f98fe0ac2 c541beffff800ffffffff1.pdf

[89] GAKO 'Nemetski Fondi', Fond H-54, No 48, Opis 1, Delo 11, 1. 9: Abschrift. Wehrmachtkommandantur Königsberg (Pr) den 10.2.1945 Standort-Befehl; GAKO 'Nemetski Fondi', Fond H-54, No 49, Opis 1, Delo 11, 1. 71: Der Polizeipräsident, Kommando der Schutzpolizei. Königsberg (Pr), den 20.2.1945. Befehlsstand Mündlich an Frau, Fräulein Margarete Horch hier Rudauerweg 28.

[90] GAKO 'Nemetski Fondi', Fond H-54, No 55, Opis 1, Delo 11, 1.486: Abschrift. Der Kommandeur der Schutzpolizei Königsberg, den 16.3.45 Befehlsstelle. Fernspruch von Abschn.Kdo. Süd (Oberltn. Fischer) 16.3.45, 11.30 Uhr.

[91] Gause, *Die Geschichte der Stadt Königsberg*, p. 166.   [92] Werner, *'Bleib übrig!'*, p. 351.

[93] Linck, *Königsberg 1945–1948*, pp. 10–11.

[94] von Lehndorff, *Ostpreussisches Tagebuch*, p. 56; Martin Wegener, 'Ostern 1945 in Königsberg, Ein Tag trügerischer Ruhe vor der Katastrophe', *Das Ostpreußenblatt*, 5 April 1950, p. 7; Jill Stephenson, 'War and Society: Germany in World War II', *German History* (3) 1986, p. 17.

concern. As indicated, military commanders had always tried to remove civilians from the area of operations, not only to allow for unrestricted movement but also to quell potential partisan activity. It was relatively easy to drop agents behind the lines on the Samland peninsula, who could then make their way into Königsberg.[95] The Soviets actively played on these fears by dropping leaflets into the fortress which encouraged civilians to stop working and hide deserters until Soviet troops arrived.[96] The fear increased as the siege went on, and on 19 March a 'Grossrazzia' was conducted by the police to search for enemy agents. Of the 2,560 people who were checked, twenty-three were detained by the authorities.[97] The *Preußische Zeitung* also devoted attention to the topic of fear in Königsberg. On 8 February, a week after the city's encirclement, it was announced: 'Anyone can be afraid. When it is dealt with, everything is clear. [However,] those who, out of fear, become cowards, throw in the towel and become criminals.'[98]

Civilians were not to be trusted, a notion that was repeatedly impressed on the troops. The 'Guidelines for the Preparation and Conduct of Defence of Cities' of November 1944 encouraged guards of defensive positions, especially in fortresses, to 'constantly observe ... surroundings and passers-by with the most intense attention', since 'a successful defence depends in the first place on the strongest distrust of the environment'.[99] Given their proximity it was nevertheless nearly impossible for military information to remain completely secret, especially in the crowded basements of the inner city. Günter Braunschweig, the commander of a detachment of self-propelled guns recalled that 'keeping our actions a secret is impossible, we are sitting, squatting, and lying almost on top of each other, rather than next to each other'.[100] During the fortress era, a stream of articles in the *Preußische Zeitung* sought to encourage the inhabitants to keep to themselves. Discretion was presented as a Prussian virtue.[101] Everyone was made aware that there were saboteurs and spies in the fortress. In a fictitious story, presented

---

[95] BArch NS 19/2068, p. 62. An Reichsführer-SS Feldkommandostelle, Betrifft: Meldungen aus dem Ostraum Königsberg, 22.3.45.

[96] BArch NS 19/2068, p. 65. An Reichsführer-SS Feldkommandostelle, Betrifft: Meldungen aus dem Ostraum Königsberg, 15.3.45.

[97] Ibid., p. 65.

[98] 'Partei-Ortsgruppen helfen mit Rat und Tat!', *Preußische Zeitung*, 8 February 1945.

[99] Russisch-deutsches Projekt zur Digitalisierung deutscher Dokumente in den Archiven der Russischen Föderation 'Akte 34: Verteidigungstaktik des Gegners – Übersetzungen von deutschen, ungarischen, rumänischen und italienischen Beutedokumenten zu taktischen Fragen', http://wwii.germandocsinrussia.org/de/nodes/1833#page/1/mode/grid/zoom/1

[100] Braunschweig, 'Untergangstage in Königsberg', p. 183.

[101] 'Preußische Anekdoten', *Preußische Zeitung*, 21 February 1945.

as if had actually occurred, a front-page article, 'The Secret', explained 'what garrulous women brought about'. The gossip of one of them included a story about German soldiers who walked through her garden at night. This was overheard by a spy. A few days later, a German patrol was ambushed in her garden.[102] The official advice to avoid such betrayals was stern and simple: *Mund halten* – shut up.[103] The efforts certainly paid off, as an SS report of early March illustrated: 'Among the population and the armed forces there is outrage over a broadcast message ... that a liqueurs and soap factory in Königsberg is now producing ammunition. This is considered as a breach of military secrets.'[104] The treatment of the refugees on the Samland, which we discussed in the previous chapter, makes clear that the well-being of the population was not the fortress command's prime concern. Nevertheless, from a military point of view, keeping a large civilian population in the city made sense, mainly because allowing civilians to stay in Königsberg assured that they continued to contribute to the local war effort.

At first sight, the efforts to maintain the living conditions in Königsberg, and the wave of violence that swept over the city, seem unrelated. To connect these two processes, we might turn to the concept of 'moral licencing', a theory that examines 'the internal balancing of moral self-worth and the cost inherent in altruistic behaviour'. This research suggests 'that affirming a moral identity leads people to act immorally'.[105] We have already seen that moral authority was of great importance in the establishment of the fortress command. The creation of 'normality' in Königsberg tied into the same tendency, as it provided a justification for the way the fortress command behaved towards the city's population. The authority of General Lasch and his staff was assured through draconian measures but – from a moral standpoint – this was justified in order to assure public order. It was unmistakable that the military in late January had restored order in Königsberg. Subsequently, a disciplined populace, controlled by the fortress command, had against the odds increased the liveability in the city. For Lasch, the balance sheet of his rule was therefore positive. This, in turn, meant that the fortress staff felt empowered to take further far-reaching measures to assure the continuation of this community. Any hesitation to deploy civilians in the

---

[102] R. Dahlmann, 'Das Geheimnis', *Preußische Zeitung*, 21 February 1945.
[103] Editorial, *Preußische Zeitung*, 7 February 1945; AKO 22034-4: Aufzeichnungen des Hauptschriftleiters der *KAZ* Wegener, p. 3.
[104] BArch NS 19/2068, p. 47. An Reichsführer-SS Feldkommandostelle, Betrifft: Meldungen aus dem Ostraum Königsberg, 5.3.45.
[105] Sonya Sachdeva, Rumen Iliev, and Douglas Medin, 'Sinning Saints and Saintly Sinners. The Paradox of Moral Self-Regulation', *Psychological Science* (20) 2009, pp. 523–8.

defence of the city fell away. As we will see in the coming sections, these measures were extensively used, becoming a vital element in the battle community – the Kampfgemeinschaft – the fortress command sought to create.

Festungsdienst in Königsberg

In his memoirs, General Lasch claimed to have transformed Königsberg into a Kampfgemeinschaft thanks to the willingness of the population to assist in its defence.[106] This narrative was developing during the siege itself as from early February onwards the *Preußische Zeitung* spoke of Königsberg as a *Festungsgemeinschaft*, a 'fortress community'.[107] Establishing how this community came to replace the Volksgemeinschaft, which had sufficed up to then, and what the new community encompassed, will help to explain the role of German civilians during the final months of war.

On 9 February, the fortress command took its final step towards Total War when it proclaimed *Festungsdienst* - fortress service. Explanatory pamphlets, meant for all Königsbergers – 'Men, women and children!' – were distributed among the population. The content of the pamphlets originated from Kreisleiter Wagner who nevertheless stressed that they had been agreed by Lasch. A martial tone, borrowed from the army, dominated the pamphlets. It was clear from the wording that the civilians who were still in Königsberg were to prove themselves worthy of being defended, and in a way 'earn' that right: 'Not only weapons and machines offer us protection, but above all the strong hearts. Danger and distress separate the wheat from the chaff. Sweat saves blood! Everyone pitches in!' The Kreisleiter went on:

> The Bolshevik stands before the gates of our city. Shoulder to shoulder with the Wehrmacht and the men of the Volkssturm we will defend our city. We will build out Königsberg into an impenetrable fortress and hold it until the Bolshevik hordes are annihilated by the armies of the Reich.
>
> Therefore, I order, in agreement with the battle commander, for every Königsberger, fortress service for four hours per day.[108]

On 11 February, on the front page of the *Preußische Zeitung*, the call to service was repeated and the scope of the call more closely defined. It was stressed that only 'mothers of infants and pregnant women' were to be

---

[106] Lasch, *So fiel Königsberg*, 64, p. 139.
[107] Untitled editorial, *Preußische Zeitung*, 11 February 1945.
[108] AKO 22034-4: Pamphlet: 9 February 1945: Aufruf! Packt alle an! Note that Wagner incorrectly speaks of a battle commander rather than a fortress commander.

Figure 6.3 Lasch in conversation with officers of Königsberg's fortress staff, February-March 1945. *Source:* Lasch, *So fiel Königsberg* (1958)

excluded from fortress service.[109] As most of the men were at the front, fortress service was thus mainly intended for older children, the elderly, and women who would serve for four hours per day. Failure to report for fortress service meant that one would not be eligible for ration cards.[110] Hans-Burkhardt Sumowski, who was only eight years old at the time of Königsberg's siege, remembers how he was asked to haul grenades with his sled, pass artillery coordinates, and help mine a bridge. Meanwhile, his grandmother was ordered to sew ammunition pouches while his grandfather was deployed in a tank repair depot.[111] The prevalence of older people was so clear that among German troops Königsberg was referred to as 'Festung der Greise': the fortress of the elderly.[112] Much fortress service consisted of constructing defensive positions, sometimes under Soviet artillery fire. During the first days of its implementation supervisors therefore showed

[109] Ernst Wagner, 'Aufruf zum Festungsdienst!', *Preußische Zeitung*, 11 February 1945.
[110] Starlinger, *Grenzen der Sowjetmacht*, pp. 36, 41–2.
[111] Sumowski, *'Jetzt war ich ganz allein auf der Welt'*, pp. 64–5, 68.
[112] AKO 22034-4: Schäfer, *Der Fall Königsbergs*, pp. 1–2.

up with carbines to ensure order, but armed guards were immediately forbidden by General Lasch due to the outrage their sight caused.[113]

A central role in the fortress service was allocated to the NS-Frauenschaft (NSF), or National Socialist Women's League, the women's wing of the Nazi Party. Since the SS, SA, and the Hitler Youth were already incorporated into the military command structure, the NSF remained the only noteworthy National Socialist organisation that could theoretically boast some independence from the Wehrmacht.[114] Although there are some sources that show that women were trained for combat roles in East Prussia from late-1944 onwards (known as *Fraueneinsatz*), nothing suggests that German women were deployed as soldiers in and around Festung Königsberg.[115] Rather, the fortress service was reminiscent of the *Kriegshilfsdienst*, or Auxiliary War Service, which was implemented in July 1941 with the purpose of drafting women into clerical work for the military or local administration, or into armaments.[116] The notable difference, of course, was that the Auxiliary War Service was not in an immediately threatened area.

In the last months of the war the regime came to rely more and more on women, who were increasingly recognised for their role in Germany's defence.[117] Within the defence of Königsberg they occupied a particular place: propaganda stressed both their submissiveness to the fighting men as well as their empowerment as a result of their behaviour during the fortress era. As an article devoted to the NSF put it, women did not merely find themselves 'between courage and hope', but also 'between seeking help and giving help'.[118] Giving credence to the assertiveness of

---

[113] GAKO 'Nemetski Fondi', Fond H-54, No 48 Opis 1 Delo 11,1,9: Abschrift Wehrmachtkommandantur Königsberg (Pr) Abt. IIa, den 10.2.1945, Standort-Befehl.

[114] The considerably smaller Nationalsozialistischer Deutscher Studentenbund (NSDStB) and the Nationalsozialistisches Kraftfahrerkorps (NSKK), the two other Nazi organisations, played no role of importance in Königsberg in 1945. For the German considerations about the deployment of German women in combat and support roles, see particularly: Perry Biddiscombe, 'Into the Maelstrom: German Women in Combat, 1944–45', *War & Society* (30) 2011, pp. 61–89 and D'Ann Campbell, 'Women in Combat: the World War II Experience in the United States, Great Britain, Germany, and the Soviet Union', *The Journal of Military History* (57) 1993, pp. 313–18.

[115] Evans, *The Third Reich at War*, p. 678; Biddiscombe, 'Into the Maelstrom', p. 69.

[116] Jill Stephenson, 'Women's Labor Service in Nazi Germany', *Central European History* (15) 1982, pp. 260–3.

[117] Eugen Geisler, 'Das Heldenmädchen von Lutterbach', *Preußische Zeitung*, 19 February 1945; Stiftung Topographie des Terrors, *Deutschland 1945 – Die letzten Kriegsmonate / Germany 1945 – The Last Months Of The War* (Berlin: Stiftung Topographie des Terrors, 2014), pp. 56–7.

[118] Wilke, 'Bewährte Kräfte der NS-Frauenschaft im Einsatz', *Preußische Zeitung*, 21 February 1945. Lower stresses that no social tradition exists 'that encourages women to tell war stories about the violence they saw, experienced, or perpetrated. In contrast, German women could speak about their hardships and victimisation on the home front'.

women during this period means redefining what has come to be known as 'the hour of the women'.[119] Their 'hour' did not only come after the capitulation of Germany in the rubble of a destroyed country; women filled the voids left by men from the moment this was required of them, either by their own decision or because they were ordered to do so by authorities.[120] Although women were not to take part in the actual fighting, their presence near the battlefield was nevertheless deemed of importance. It was considered that the female admiration for soldierly masculinity, and the spoken or unspoken appeal of women to the men to remain firm discouraged desertion since 'women and girls punish cowards with contempt'.[121] Moreover, for wounded soldiers, 'the mere sight of a nicely dressed woman makes a man's heart beat faster – even before you consider the cakes she brought'.[122]

As part of fortress service, the NSF was ordered, for example, to 'set up a sewing room for every Volkssturm battalion, where the men of the battalion can constantly have their laundry and socks fixed'.[123] More importantly, most of the care for refugees, bombed-out families, and mothers with small children was left to the NSF.[124] Together with the German Red Cross, the NSF ran all hospitals in the fortress, a role that was repeatedly emphasised in the propaganda: 'We visited these women in the hospitals and found all professions among them. On top of their chores and the care for their children and families, they worked in the sewing rooms, the catering, in the Ortsgruppen and so on, only to return a few hours per day to look after "their" wounded.'[125] The Party thus placed itself completely at the disposal of the Wehrmacht and although

See: Wendy Lower, *Hitler's Furies: German Women in the Nazi Killing Fields* (London: Vintage Books, 2014), pp. 97–8.

[119] Christian Graf von Krockow, *Die Stunde der Frauen: Bericht aus Pommern 1944 bis 1947* (Munich: dtv, 1992).

[120] Nicole Kramer, 'Von der "Volksgenossin" zur "Trümmerfrau"? – Deutungen von Frauen nach 1945', in Schmiechen-Ackermann (ed.), *Volksgemeinschaft'*, pp. 303–17; Jill Stephenson, *Women in Nazi Germany* (Harlow: Longman, 2001), pp. 106–8.

[121] Kühne, *Kameradschaft*, pp. 154–5; Die NSDAP Ostpreußen, 'Hier spricht die Partei', *Festung Königsberg*, 2 February 1945.

[122] Wilke, 'Bewährte Kräfte der NS-Frauenschaft im Einsatz', *Preußische Zeitung*, 21 February 1945.

[123] Ernst Wagner, 'Die Bevollmächtigte Kommissar des Gauleiters gibt bekannt', *Preußische Zeitung*, 11 February 1945.

[124] Die NSDAP Ostpreußen, 'Hier spricht die Partei', *Festung Königsberg*, 2 February 1945; 'Partei-Ortsgruppen helfen mit Rat und Tat!', *Preußische Zeitung*, 8 February 1945; 'Wo ein Wille, da ist ein Weg', *Preußische Zeitung*, 22 February 1945. On Volksopfer, see: Reichsgesetzblatt Teil I, Nr.2: 11 January 1945. 'Verordnung des Führers zum Schutz der Sammlung von Kleidung und Ausrüstungsgegenständen für die Wehrmacht und den Deutschen Volkssturm', p. 5.

[125] Wilke, 'Bewährte Kräfte der NS-Frauenschaft im Einsatz', *Preußische Zeitung*, 21 February 1945.

the NSF remained recognisable as a Party-controlled body, its National Socialist values took a back seat during the siege.

The way fortress service impacted daily life in besieged Königsberg tells us much about Germany's transition from a Volksgemeinschaft to a Kampfgemeinschaft. When the war turned against Germany, many, if not most Germans considered the Volksgemeinschaft as a purely utilitarian concept, an 'apathetic emergency organisation that had only one goal: surviving the war'.[126] The idea of a Kampfgemeinschaft, which emerged out of the Volksgemeinschaft, better reflected the wartime sentiments of the German population. *Kampf* was initially defined as 'struggle', in which the war itself represented a 'struggle for self-defence and survival of a threatened and beleaguered racial community'.[127] As the war reached the borders of Germany, the concept rid itself of its metaphysical baggage and *Kampf* was interpreted in military terms as 'battle'. Whereas the Volksgemeinschaft ideally consisted of a people with a shared vision, Königsberg's 'battle community' simply consisted of combatants and those who helped to prolong the defence. The introduction of the all-encompassing fortress service made inclusion in this community obligatory and was a clear way to determine who contributed to that community and who did not. For some civilians, this even meant taking their place on the front line.

The Volkssturm in Königsberg

In a series of meetings in late December 1944 and early January 1945 the army pushed for Volkssturm battalions to be used as an active part of Königsberg's security garrison.[128] Although arguments over their exact size and deployment continued in the weeks that followed, by the time the first Soviet troops approached the city there were indeed a number of battalions that could be deployed in its defence.[129] When on 26 January Soviet troops undertook a surprise attack (*coup de main*) east of the city at Palmburg, it was the Volkssturm, rather than the army, who fought them off. In Mandeln, in the same area, they even held the line while Luftwaffe units fled through their lines. The Bäckerberg, a hill overlooking Königsberg in the north, was similarly held by the Volkssturm during the first days of the attack on the city, and the earliest Soviet attack on

---

[126] Clemens Vollnhals, 'Disillusionment, Pragmatism, Indifference, German Society After the "Catastrophe"', in Kettenacker and Riotte (eds.), *The Legacies of Two World Wars*, p. 186.

[127] Browning, 'The Holocaust: Basis and Objective of the Volksgemeinschaft?', p. 223.

[128] BArch RH 2/331b, pp. 158–61: Op Abt/ Abt Lds Bef 252/45 geh. 5.1.1945. Vortragsnotiz Betr. Begriffsbestimmung der 'Festung Königsberg'.

[129] BArch RH 2/317, p. 103: Fernschreiben mit Anschriftenübermittlung, OKH/ GenStdH/Op.Abt/Abt.Lds.Bef. Nr 13079/44 g.K. 14.12.1944 gez. v. Bonin

Neuhausen was fended off by Volkssturm units led by Kreisleiter Wagner.[130] To bolster Königsberg's defence, in late January the Gestapo even released 'decent' criminals from prison and immediately sent them to Volkssturm units at the front where they joined the astonished defenders.[131] More than the city's inhabitants might have known, and certainly more than they were given credit for, Volkssturm troops held large parts of the city's eastern sector for two days, virtually on their own, against 'sustained attacks' from a Soviet corps, unaware whether reinforcements would arrive or what was happening around them.[132]

From the moment the Volkssturm was established by the Party in late 1944, the central complaint many field commanders consistently put forward concerned the militia's fighting capability as an independent unit. 'We lack manpower for our infantry regiments but they form the Volkssturm. It is absolute madness', an officer told the war correspondent Günter Heysing: 'Alone they are only cannon fodder.'[133] During the last months of 1944, Wehrmacht commanders continued to complain about the poor performance as a result of the restricted cooperation. On 27 January 1945, Hitler finally heeded their complaints and ordered that the Volkssturm be fully embedded into the army's command structure: 'The experience in the East shows that Volkssturm, emergency and *Ersatz* units, when relying on their own resources, have only slight fighting value and are quickly smashed. The fighting value of these units, for the most part numerically strong but inadequately armed for modern combat, is incomparably higher in the framework of troops of the field army.'[134] In effect, the order signalled that from then on the army would get the final say over the deployment of Volkssturm units, but also implicitly admitted that the Party had been unable to effectively lead these units. When the front around Königsberg stabilised in the first week of February, the Volkssturm men were duly incorporated into the fortress's military command structure.

In practice, this meant that Königsberg's Volkssturm contingent was slowly cannibalised. Some 10,000 Volkssturm members served in ten to

[130] Kissel, *Der Deutsche Volkssturm 1944/1945*, p. 63; AKO 22034: Aufzeichnungen des Hauptschriftleiters der *KAZ* Wegener, p. 3; AKO 22034-4: Magunia, *Abschrift*, pp. 4–5; BArch Ost-Dok. 8/588, p. 2: Dr. Will; BArch Ost-Dok. 10/890, p. 60: Dieckert.

[131] Yelton, *Hitler's Volkssturm*, p. 27; Tilitzki, *Alltag in Ostpreußen*, p. 308; BArch Ost-Dok. 8/598, p. 61: Klein. This release was in line with orders passed down by the Reich ministry of Justice in late 1944. See: Wachsmann, *Hitler's Prisons*, p. 331.

[132] Boiko, *S dumoj o Rodine*, p. 256; Lasch, *So fiel Königsberg*, p. 45; Willems, 'Defiant Breakwaters or Desperate Blunders?', pp. 362–4, 370–1.

[133] Noble, 'The People's Levy', pp. 174–5.

[134] BArch RH 2/331a, p. 57: Fernschreiben mit Anschriftenübermittlung. Abschrift von Führerbefehl: Betr.: Einsatz des Volkssturms, OKW/WFSt Op/Org-Nr. 00937/45 g. Kdos. vom 27.1.1945. This translation is taken from a British intelligence report. See: TNA HW1/3510, p. 3: BONIFACE report, 6 February 1945.

twelve battalions in late January, of which 5,000 remained by early April, days before the final storming.[135] Throughout February and March, many of the older and less able-bodied Volkssturm men were deployed to rear-area work that was often less demanding.[136] On the other hand, almost immediately, most young boys were taken from their Volkssturm units and drafted into the 1st Infanterie-Division, the 5th Panzer-Division, or the 548th or 561st Volksgrenadier-divisions.[137] Hauptmann Lenz remembered that

The division strives – just like the 5th Panzer-Division which is also present in the fortress – to again form units out of wounded and new recruits. The representative of Reich Defence Commissioner Gauleiter Koch, Kreisleiter Wagner (himself a reserve officer in the division), provides the division with young recruits subordinated to him, particularly several hundred Hitler Youth members.[138]

Sometimes their young age stunned the division's veterans. Hauptmann Hans-Joachim Schröder, the commander of Füsilier battalion 1, part of the 1st Infanterie-Division, recalled that

The battalion received 60 to 80 Hitlerjungen between age 14 and 15 as recruits for training in early February. With some shock, we accepted these half-kids. The swearing in took place in a dignified and festive form at the tennis court. With great and unparalleled zeal, these boys dove into their training. The majority could not be supplied with steel helmets as they were too large and fell over their eyes during firing. A solution was only partly found. Because of their youth, they received special rations, not alcohol or cigarettes, but bonbons and chocolate instead.[139]

These accounts were not exceptions. Volkssturm battalion 25/141 'Lützow' consisted entirely of sixteen and seventeen-year-old boys and after first being used as auxiliaries, they were deployed alongside an infantry battalion.[140]

In addition, the Volkssturm units that consisted exclusively of older men also had to give up their 'youngest'. The adjutant of Volkssturm

---

[135] Kissel, *Der Deutsche Volkssturm*, p. 63; BArch Ost-Dok.8/580, p. 4: Zerahn; BArch RH 2/335, pp. 175–6: Op.Abt/ I N/LdS Bef. Vortragsnotiz Betr.: Festung Königsberg, 6.4.1945.

[136] Yelton, *Hitler's Volkssturm*, pp. 119–20; AKO 22032: Magunia, p. 1; BArch Ost-Dok. 8/602, p. 6: Makowka; BArch Ost-Dok. 10/890, p. 127: Dieckert; Kissel, *Der Deutsche Volkssturm 1944/1945*, p. 54.

[137] BArch Ost-Dok.8/579, pp. 9, 13: Wendlandt.

[138] BArch Msg 2/240, p. 37 Kampf um Ostpreußen 1945 von Hauptmann d. R. Lenz, Adj. Beim Stab der 1. Inf. Div. Frühjahr 1956.

[139] BArch RH 26-1/112, p. 1. Inf. Div. Kampf um Ostpreußen und um Königsberg, 157; BArch RH 26-1/100, 84; Dieckert and Großmann, *Der Kampf um Ostpreussen*, p. 158.

[140] Springenschmid, *Raus aus Königsberg*, pp. 24–5, 30–5. On the mythisation of Lützow, see: Mosse, *Fallen Soldiers*, p. 24.

battalion 25/235, Leutnant Bruno Just wrote in his diary on 6 March 1945: 'We had to turn over all the men born in 1901 and younger to the Wehrmacht. After this the youngest is 44 years old.'[141] Even disabled men were drafted into the Volksstum. For example, Heinz Kroll, who had a prosthetic leg, was, after six medical examinations by the Wehrmacht, deemed suitable to serve in the Volkssturm and was sent back from Pillau to Königsberg.[142] That this behaviour was widespread can best be seen by a headline of the *Preußische Zeitung*: 'Despite prosthetic leg at the fore-front of a battalion reserve against the enemy', which not only showed that these severely disabled men were used for rear area work but were also deployed at the front line.[143]

The training of Volkssturm men intensified with special attention paid to the Panzerfaust, a single-shot recoilless anti-tank weapon, which – despite its incredible deadly potential – was one of the easiest weapons to master.[144] Nevertheless, accidents happened fairly fre-quently during weapons training.[145] Reading between the lines, the focus on the Panzerfaust revealed that the instructors did not fully trust Volkssturm men as part of their units since the weapon was especially suited to individual men or a twosome, rather than groups.[146] This, in turn, had an impact on the Volkssturm's reputation among Soviet troops, who regarded Volkssturm men with Panzerfausts as fanatics willing to continue to fight on their own. Moses Gorelik, a Jewish partisan from Belorussia who eventually fought in Königsberg, remembered they were referred to as *Faustnikov*. The men of his unit 'killed Faustnikov on the spot because no one looked at their age [and] they burned many of our tanks!'[147] Moreover, dressing these men remained a problem. As army uniforms were scarce, many were sup-plied with Party uniforms. Wearing a Party uniform was like a red rag to

[141] BArch Ost-Dok 8/600, p. 25: Just.

[142] BArch Msg 2/240, pp. 81, 83: Bericht des Herrn Heinz Kroll, früher Wehlau, jetzt Braunschweig.

[143] 'Trotz Beinprothese an der Spitze der Bataillonsreserve gegen den Feind', *Preußische Zeitung*, 21 Februar 1945.

[144] Newsreel 'Panzerfaustschiessen in einer deutschen Stadt', *Die Deutsche Wochenschau*, 22 March 1945: 'Even women can operate this weapon with ease'.

[145] GAKO 'Nemetski Fondi', Fond H-54, No 55, Opis 1, Delo 11, 1.486: Abschrift. Der Kommandeur der Schutzpolizei Königsberg, den 16.3.45 Befehlsstelle. Fernspruch von Abschn.Kdo. Süd (Oberltn. Fischer) 16.3.45, 11.30 Uhr; BArch Ost-Dok. 8/510, p. 26: Dieckert; BArch Ost-Dok. 8/567, p. 4: Elkes; Yelton, *Hitler's Volkssturm*, p. 123.

[146] BArch RH 2/334, p. 132: Der Generalinspekteur der Panzertruppen H.Qu.OKH, 19. März 1945. Nr. 178/45 g.Kdos Betrifft: Panzernahkampf; Yelton, *Hitler's Volkssturm*, p. 105.

[147] G. Koyfman, 'Gorelik Moisey Khaimovich', http://iremember.ru/memoirs/partizani/g orelik-moisey-khaimovich/

Soviets troops, and, as Waldemar Magunia stressed, had an adverse effect on Volkssturm morale.[148]

The Volkssturm was used as a kind of pool of manpower and the way its recruits were deployed seems to have been motivated by the intention to keep the 'hard core' seasoned veterans of the different Wehrmacht divisions intact, which allowed their staying power to remain at a relatively high level.[149] The young boys were separated from the older conscripts and their motivation seems to have been an important factor in that decision. Karl Springensmid, the commander of Volkssturm battalion 25/141 'Lützow', remembered that

These boys were convinced that everything that this war asked of them they would do better than the 'old', a designation in which they even included their fathers. What the 'old' had ruined, they, the 'young', had to put right, indeed, they were certain that they, in this almost lost war, could bring about a decisive turn.[150]

These youngsters were assigned to Kampfgruppe 1.I.D – battle group 1st Infanterie-Division – which consisted of two small regiments. During Operation Westwind they were put in the first line of attack. Like most officers of the 1st Infanterie-Division, Hauptmann Lenz felt that during the offensive to restore the link between Königsberg and Pillau they 'proved themselves worthy of the grand tradition of the division'.[151] After the first pioneers had removed mines, the young Hitler Youth stormed into the no-man's-land towards the first objective, the hamlet of Metgethen. An officer remarked: 'This day is a glorious chapter of the German youth, similar to Langemarck.'[152] 'Like madmen!', another told a war correspondent. 'They ran away from me. Just ran off to the front. They pulled the barbed wire apart with their hands, as if there are no mines in between. And then straight into the foxholes of Ivan to wreak

[148] AKO 22034-4: Magunia: *Der Volkssturm in Ostpreußen*, p. 2.

[149] Bartov, *Hitler's Army*, pp. 29–58; Shils and Janowitz, 'Cohesion and Disintegration in the Wehrmacht', pp. 286–7.

[150] Springenschmid, *Raus aus Königsberg*, p. 30. See also: Kunz, *Wehrmacht und Niederlage*, p. 233: On 27 March 1945 Reichsjugendführer Artur Axmann asked of the Hitlerjugend to 'be boundless in the love to your people, and just as boundless in your hate against the enemy. It is your duty to guard, when others get tired; to stand, when others yield'.

[151] BArch RH 26-1/112, pp. 125–7: 1. Inf. Div. Kampf um Ostpreußen und um Königsberg (Sammlung von Erlebnisberichten) 1945; BArch Msg 2/ 240, p. 37: Kampf um Ostpreußen 1945 (Frühjahr 1956).

[152] BArch Ost-Dok. 10/888, p. 83: Dieckert. According to the bulletin of the *Oberste Heeresleitung*, on 11 November 1914, 'West of Langemarck, young regiments, while singing "Deutschland, Deutschland über alles" attacked the first line of enemy positions and conquered them'. It marked the beginning of the 'Myth of the heroic youth'. See: Baird, *To Die for Germany*, ch. 1; Mosse, *Fallen Soldiers*, pp. 70–1.

havoc!'[153] It led, however, to high casualties amongst these boys, many of whom had only served for a mere two weeks. The fanatical Hauptmann Hans-Joachim Schröder recalled that 'the attack squadrons suffered nearly 50 per cent dead and wounded. In the next few days, squadron leaders had to inform many a Königsberg mother about the heroic death of her son'.[154] The young boys, as a whole, were repeatedly hailed in the aftermath of Operation Westwind while the older age group did not receive similar praise.[155]

In contrast, the older militiamen were mainly used in the defence of the city. Their service in the Volkssturm was much less driven by fanatic élan but rather by 'traditional values of patriotism and duty, a long-standing distrust of and distaste for their Slavic neighbours, and the desire to protect family and possessions against the feared Bolsheviks'.[156] They were thus placed in less hard-pressed areas of the front. In turn, the Soviets were well aware that they had older men in front of them and tried to demoralise them, blasting 'old grandfathers, go home!' from loudspeaker cars in the sectors where Volkssturm units lay.[157] Days before the final storming they dropped leaflets aimed specifically at the Volkssturm, reiterating that 'the Nazi chiefs delay the fighting, throw you peaceful citizens of East Prussia in the battle and try to convince you, that you should "save" your Heimat'. But, it was stressed: 'You know yourself, what kind of "fighters" you are.'[158] The Soviets were correct in their assessment. There should be no doubt that these older Volkssturm men were considered expendable: in the defence plans of Königsberg, the priority was placed on the north of the river Pregel where the city connected to the adjacent Samland peninsula.[159] Most of the Volkssturm units, however, were assigned to positions south of the river with little chance of escape, while the more effective units were placed to the north.[160] The Hitler Youth boys had much better chances to survive: Volkssturm battalion 25/141 'Lützow', consisting solely of young boys,

---

[153] BArch Ost-Dok. 8/591, p. 48: Heysing.
[154] BArch RH 26-1/112, p. 1. Inf. Div. Kampf um Ostpreußen und um Königsberg (Sammlung von Erlebnisberichten) 1945, pp. 127, 157.
[155] 'Heroischer Angriff Königsberger Hitler-Jungen', Preußische Zeitung, 23 February 1945.
[156] Yelton, Hitler's Volkssturm, p. 133.
[157] AKO 22034-4: Aufzeichnungen des Hauptschriftleiters der KAZ Wegener, p. 4.
[158] Bastiaan Willems, 'Pamphlet: Volkssturmmänner!', www.bpvwillems.com/documents/the-siege-of-festung-koenigsberg/
[159] BArch RH 2/ 328, p. 240: OKH/GenStdH/Op Abt (roem 1a) Nr. 450 137/45 g.Kdos. Chefs 21.2.1945 gez. Guderian. Yelton found that of the Volkssturm men that fought on the Eastern Front, almost three-quarters of those missing in action were forty-five years or over. Yelton, Hitler's Volkssturm, p. 133.
[160] Lasch, So fiel Königsberg, p. 83.

was even ordered to stay out of the fighting entirely and managed to escape the city in order to be deployed in Berlin.[161]

There is no doubt that the Volkssturm suffered heavily in the fighting. The manner of their death was often brutal and especially those given brown attire (which the Red Army troops saw as Party uniforms) met with horrible fates when captured.[162] In all, the Volkssturm suffered much heavier losses than the regular Wehrmacht: of the roughly 10,000 men of Königsberg's original contingent, 2,400 – a quarter – were listed as dead or missing in action after the war.[163] That many of these men – young boys, invalids, elderly – should have been properly evacuated out of the city as civilians was hardly considered at all. Instead, they were subject to ever more military coercion.

Radicalisation Through the Pretext of Law

The intensive efforts to transform Königsberg into a battle community were accompanied by the increasing violence of the summary courts. Intra-ethnic violence in the final months of the war is generally traced back to Party legislation, particularly to the 'Decree on the Establishment of Summary Courts' implemented on 15 February 1945 by Reich Minister of Justice Otto Thierack. The decree called for the formation of summary courts in areas that were immediately threatened.[164] It is tempting to view the violence as a continuation of the National Socialist violence that started in 1932–3.[165] There is a strong case for this argument since up to then, at a local level, Kreisleiter had often presided over 'kangaroo-courts' in their cities, while Ortsgruppenleiter had long led the charge against subversive elements in their respective districts.[166]

Yet this line of reasoning has a number of limitations. Throughout the war there had been a steady militarisation of home-front law, and Germany's juridical apparatus explicitly expressed the intention to fashion it to correspond better with the military ethos. Already in September

---

[161] Springenschmid, *Raus aus Königsberg*, pp. 47–8. The full title of this book ('Get Out of Königsberg! How 420 East Prussian Boys Were Rescued in 1945 from Combat and Deployment') is misleading since these boys were not 'rescued', but ordered by the OKH to be transported to assist in the defence of Berlin. See: BArch RH 2/335, pp. 102–3, Op Abt I N/K Nr. 4116/45 g.Kdos 3. April 1945 Abschrift von FS H. Gr. Nord an 2. Und 4. Armee; BArch RH 2/335, pp. 106–7 Fernschreiben Betr. Abtransport aus Ostpreußen, OKH/GenStdH / Op Abt röm. 1a Nr. 4167/45 g. 4.4.45

[162] Seidler, *'Deutscher Volkssturm'*, pp. 247–8.   [163] Ibid., p. 374.

[164] Reichsgesetzblatt Teil I, Nr. 6: 20 February 1945. 'Verordnung über die Errichtung von Standgerichten', p. 30.

[165] See: Keller, 'Volksgemeinschaft and Violence'.

[166] Kater, *The Nazi Party*, pp. 223–4. Merrion Webster s.v. 'kangaroo court': a mock court in which the principles of law and justice are disregarded or perverted.

1939, Reich Justice Minister Franz Gürtner opened the periodical *Deutsches Strafrecht* by stating: 'During war time we demand that soldiers ruthlessly and without hesitation commit life and limb to the defence of their people. Also in the Heimat, the personal fortune has to be ruthlessly subordinated to the idea of the defence of our people.'[167] The more the war's ferocity touched Germans as the war progressed, the more they were inclined to accept that in order to settle it, measures of ever greater severity had to be considered. It meant that after six years of war, violence was perceived completely differently. Death – by 'terror-bombing' or on the front line – had become a part of everyday life with which every family was forced to deal. Whereas in 1932 and 1933 acts of Party violence in Königsberg caused an outrage worthy of international headlines, by 1945 violence had become normalised and considered part of the overall consequence of Total War.[168] More importantly, by portraying violence merely as an inherent part of Nazi society and by consistently linking the German intra-ethnic violence in 1945 back to the 'dyed-in-the-wool National Socialists', the dialogue between the different actors that took place at the time is underplayed, as such failing to appreciate the different faces of this kind of violence.[169] Certainly, not all Party dignitaries were in favour of an increase in the use of summary courts. For example, Gauleiter Joachim Eggeling of Halle-Merseburg asked whether it was 'politically acceptable ... to summarily try' Party officials after they had failed to do their job and then to subsequently report on this failure in newspapers: 'How are political leaders to be trusted by the population, if such derailments are cried out every day? ... Among the Wehrmacht such incidents are kept secret, in order not to damage the nimbus of leadership.'[170] Moreover, the radicalising nature of this fragmentation of law was also recognised and its implications were discussed between the highest representatives of Party and Wehrmacht. 'As always with heavy setbacks, the present stage of the war is marked by a tendency to search for those responsible for – or guilty of – it', a draft proposing a more careful approach towards summary courts read. Wehrmacht officers blamed Party officials for the defeats while Party officials tried to pin the responsibility on the military commanders. 'On both sides there are quitters and deserters', the draft continued:

---

[167] Süß, *Tod aus der Luft*, pp. 153–4. See also: Evans, *Rituals of Retribution*, p. 689.

[168] On 1932 see for example: Our own correspondent, 'Nazi Terrorist Outbreak'. *The Times*, 2 August 1932, p. 10; Our own correspondent, 'The Königsberg Outrages', *The Times*, 3 August 1932; p. 9.

[169] Keller, 'Volksgemeinschaft and Violence', p. 233; Bessel, *Germany 1945*, p. 60; Kershaw, *The End*, pp. 224–5.

[170] IfZArch Akten der Partei-Kanzlei der NSDAP: 13202379. Beleg Nr. 5, 10. Febr. 1945 An die Partei-Kanzlei z. Hd. Herrn Reichsleiter M. Bormann. gez. Eggeling Gauleiter.

The Party and the Wehrmacht now only have the duty to stand together, fight together, and eradicate parasites from their ranks. So, when the execution of the holder of a Golden Party Badge is announced, this is no reason for the Wehrmacht to take position against the Party; vice versa, for the Party there is no cause for *Schadenfreude* when officers are sentenced to death for desertion or dereliction of duty.[171]

As a reappraisal of the summary court practices, the draft came much too late in the day in mid-March 1945, and never made it into law: by then, the direction taken was irreversible.

Those Party members who favoured tougher punishment for those men and women who evaded their duty left little doubt as to where they got their inspiration. Thierack's Decree on the Establishment of Summary Courts adopted a martial tone but totalling a mere 250 words certainly did not break much new ground. Indeed, in a circular to the Gauleiter, which Reichsleiter Bormann distributed on 9 March 1945, he stressed that it was the example of Generaloberst Rendulic's treatment of 'so-called stragglers' in the area of his Army Group, and his use of highly mobile, 'flying', courts-martial, that had served as inspiration.[172] That same week Goebbels, who had 'anxiously awaited'[173] Thierack's decree, also praised the efforts of Rendulic in his diary: 'In East Prussia Rendulic has restored order again. In one of his reports I read that when he took over the Army Group, he counted some 16,000 soldiers that had "lost their unit". He reduced that number in no time to 400, using most rigorous means. ... Rendulic seems to have the ambition to be among the first of our modern army leaders.'[174] Goebbels expressed similar praise for Generaloberst (later Field Marshal) Ferdinand Schörner, who

spends most time alongside the fighting troops, with whom he has admittedly a harsh but yet also a trusting relationship. He especially targets the so-called "trained stragglers". With that he means soldiers who time and again see the chance to detach themselves from the troops in critical situations and make off to the hinterland under some pretext. He is rather brutal to those characters in that he has them strung up on the first possible tree with a sign that reads: "I am a deserter and I have refused to protect German women and children." That surely

---

[171] IfZArch Akten der Partei-Kanzlei der NSDAP: 13201916: Entwurf für ein gemeinsames Rundschreiben des Leiters der Partei-Kanzlei und des Chefs des Oberkommandos der Wehrmacht, 21 March 1945.

[172] BArch NS6/354, p. 88: Der Leiter der Partei-Kanzlei, Führerhauptquartier, den 9.3.1945. Rundschreiben 123/45 g. Betrifft: Maßnahmen zur Stärkung der Front durch Erfassung Versprengter. Rendulic's order concerning flying courts-martial was cited in full in this circular.

[173] Kershaw, *The End*, p. 224.

[174] Goebbels, *Tagebücher 1945*, p. 161; Kershaw, *The End*, p. 224.

exerts a very deterrent effect on the other deserters or on those who consider deserting.[175]

With Party members expressing admiration for the military's widespread use of summary courts-martial, and lauding its successes, Thierack's decree to establish summary courts seems fairly redundant. What Thierack did, however, was to restore agency to the Party in 'areas threatened by the enemy'; areas which were likely to be under martial law. By elevating the responsibilities of the Party in these areas, the decree represented an inroad into martial law but one that could hardly be challenged without raising the suspicion of harbouring a wavering attitude. The decree made clear that a *Standgericht* was no longer strictly a military affair. It was not merely a court- martial anymore, but rather a summary court that 'had jurisdiction over all criminal acts that threaten the German fighting strength and determination to fight'.[176] It was the final step along a course that detached the legal process from the judiciary.

In Königsberg, this led to a diverse set of 'law enforcers'. In a report, written one year after the city's siege, Walter Kemsies, a German intelligence officer present in Königsberg at the time, mentions that checks were conducted by police units Feldgendarmerie, Jagd-Kommandos of the SS and SD, and regular army officers and the Gestapo: 'These measures caused numerous soldiers and civilians without proper papers to be imprisoned, yes, even executed. Often, this was unjust and illogical.'[177] A few days after Thierack's decree, Gauleiter Koch despatched six special SS squads, each consisting of twelve men, into the city to carry out these duties: 'The SS guard of Königsberg has to carry out raids and patrols in all accommodations and flats of war wives [i.e. wives whose husbands are serving at the front] and prostitutes and summarily shoot all encountered conscripted men without a valid leave pass.'[178] The plethora of law enforcers has given rise to many sweeping assumptions regarding their motives. Some of these men might have been 'settling old scores', and might have had a 'private lust for power, [and] pathological bloodthirst', but in Königsberg some executioners even seemed to have struggled with their task.[179] After two Party officials had conducted a public execution of two soldiers who, during the final storming, had deserted and changed into civilian clothing, they immediately fled to the

---

[175] Ibid., p. 165.
[176] Reichsgesetzblatt Teil I, Nr. 6: 20 February 1945. 'Verordnung über die Errichtung von Standgerichten', p. 30.
[177] AKO 22034: Kemsies: *Stimmungsbilder aus Königsberg*, p. 10.
[178] Armin Fuhrer and Heinz Schön, *Erich Koch, Hitlers brauner Zar: Gauleiter von Ostpreussen und Reichskommissar der Ukraine* (Munich: Olzog, 2010), p. 178.
[179] Klaus-Dietmar Henke, *Die amerikanische Besetzung Deutschlands* (Munich: R. Oldenbourg Verlag, 1996), p. 847.

Figure 6.4 A summary court convened at the village of Kahlberg on the Frische Nehrung, late February 1945. *Source:* bpk / Vinzenz Engel, Image-No.30016534

hinterland, only to be caught and executed the following day themselves.[180] Nevertheless, the randomness of the checks and the executions created a climate of fear in the city. The French prisoner of war Clappier remembered that 'a minimum of terror was enough to strike fear and apathy into the population. ... The Streifen of the military police combed the cellars and bunkers, hunting for deserters, people without papers, and suspicious foreigners.' In addition to the Nordbahnhof and Hauptbahnhof, in February and March the Königsberg zoo was also used as a place of execution.[181] This visible violence, under the guise of the rule of law, ensured that civilians continued to cooperate and were easier to control.

Thanks to the focus on the summary courts, we tend to forget that in Königsberg, an area of operations under martial law, other courts also continued to operate. Both the fortress court, which General Lasch established, as well as the SS- und Polizeigericht XXVII, which handled police cases in Königsberg, continued to pass sentences.[182] Yet unlike the summary courts, when these courts passed death sentences, it did not always result in immediate execution. Instead, up to the final storming some soldiers who were sentenced to death were sent to a penal battalion, Polizei Battalion Elias. They were temporarily pardoned and had to fight as probation soldiers (*Bewährungsschützen*). In all likelihood, this battalion was deployed in the south of Königsberg and completely wiped out.[183] Yet the main difference between the summary courts and these courts was that although these courts could often be just as harsh, accused soldiers were sometimes able to argue their case, and occasionally walked away with minor sentences such as extra guard duty.[184] Civilians could also be tried by these courts but being

---

[180] Fuhrer and Schön, *Erich Koch, Hitlers brauner Zar*, p. 179.

[181] Clappier, *Festung Königsberg*, p. 121; On the importance of the use of public places to conduct violence, see: Pamela Swett, 'Political Violence, Gesinnung, and the Courts in Late Weimar Berlin', in Biess, Roseman, and Schissler (eds.), *Conflict, Catastrophe and Continuity*, pp. 104–16.

[182] GAKO 'Nemetski Fondi' Fond H-54, No. 36, Opis 1, Delo 1, 1. 476: SS-und Polizeigericht XXVII Königsberg (Pr.), den 26.2.45. An den Befehlshaber der Ordnungspolizei Königsberg (Pr); 'Feiglinge wurden erschossen', *Festung Königsberg*, 2 February 1945.

[183] GAKO 'Nemetski Fondi' Fond H-54, No. 35, Opis 1, Delo 1, 1. 470: Der Befehlshaber der Ordnungspolizei Königsberg. Königsberg (pr.), den 20.3.1945 Betr. Strafsache gegen den ehem. SS-Sturmmann Günter Neumann – hier Abordnung zum Pol.Btl. Elias; GAKO 'Nemetski Fondi' Fond H-54, No. 34, Opis 1, Delo 1, 1. 468: 8. Pol. Komp. Königsberg (Pr), den 30.3.45. An das Kommando der Schutzpolizei; BArch NS 6/135, 62: Betr: Einsatz von zum Tode verurteilten Soldaten. 24 December 1944.

[184] GAKO 'Nemetski Fondi' Fond H-54, No. 43, Opis 1, Delo 1, 1. 492: Königsberg (Pr), den 20.3.1945 Vernemung! Adolf Plügge. GAKO 'Nemetski Fondi' Fond H-494, No. 45, Opis 1, Delo 1, 1. 494: 8. Kompanie Königsberg Pr. den 20. März 1945 An das Kommando der Schutzpolizei.

tried under the martial law meant that they inevitably fell short and would thus face harsh punishment. Moreover, 'accused' civilians in the area of operations would often not even reach the courtroom but instead be tried by the summary courts.

Whether regular courts or summary courts, the rationale for their judgements were fairly similar. Most condemned were judged in the light of a continuous struggle for Germany and by their willingness to fend off 'un-German' influences rather than merely within the framework of the National Socialist cause. The case of 51-year old Rottwachtmeister der Schutzpolizei der Reserve Alois M., which was brought before the SS- und Polizeigericht XXVII in late February 1945, is an example. Fearing he was about to be overrun by the Soviet advance, M. deserted his unit on 29 January, changed into civilian clothing and hid in different houses and basements. On 7 February he was found by the Streifen and handed over to the SS court. His death sentence was read out to police troops in the fortress:

The court has indeed recognised as mitigation that the accused has done his duty in the [First] World War and had been awarded with the Iron Cross Second Class. Also taken into account is that the defendant was judged to be satisfactory so far. But due to the severity of the deed, these mitigating circumstances cannot preserve the defendant from receiving the harshest punishment. He who in this decisive phase of the war tiptoes around the fulfilment of service and as such not only breaks his oath to the Führer, but also betrays the German Volksgemeinschaft, must be eradicated according to the harshness of war. He who out of cowardice wants to avoid deployment has to lose under all circumstances the life that he so cowardly tried to save. That is the expectation of every decent and well-behaved soldier, who, in loyal fulfilment of duty during heavy fighting, every day bravely puts his life on the line. The famous principle, based on the front-line experience of the Führer, that the brave soldier can indeed fall, but that the weaklings have to fall under all circumstances, is unrelentingly carried out by the court.[185]

That this sentence, passed in late February by the 'regular' SS- und Polizeigericht XXVII, was to be made public draws attention to another dimension of the summary courts. The summary courts emulated the ceremonial aspect of regular courts and courts-martial, as much of their legitimacy rested precisely on linking their judgements to the larger German (military) legal tradition – something particularly important since summary courts tended to consist of men with little

[185] GAKO 'Nemetski Fondi' Fond H-54, No. 36, Opis 1, Delo 1, l. 476: SS-und Polizeigericht XXVII Königsberg (Pr.), den 26.2.45. An den Befehlshaber der Ordnungspolizei Königsberg (Pr); GAKO 'Nemetski Fondi' Fond H-54, No. 37, Opis 1, Delo 1, l. 477: Der Befehlshaber der Ordungspolizei Königsberg. Königsberg, (Pr.), den 27.2.1945.

legal background. The ritualistic element of the summary courts, attaching a sign around the necks of the victims or gathering a crowd to witness an execution, was a vital part of the process.[186] The French prisoner of war Clappier recalled that when he walked beside improvised gallows, the five condemned soldiers all 'had rectangular plates fixed to the chests. Inscriptions on the signs in large black letters: "I hang here because I'm a coward", or "I did not want to protect Germany".'[187] Onlookers also played an important role in the executions. Sometimes crowds of over 1,000 people were gathered together to view these executions on the central square, the Adolf-Hitler-Platz.[188] On occasion the church was also used to legitimise the process. As part of a public execution of twenty-four soldiers in March, a pastor told the condemned men: 'You have to fight for your relatives at home and you cannot let them down.'[189]

Executions of military personnel, Party members, and civilians continued right up to the surrender of the city. While walking past the Nordbahnhof in early March, a labourer, Karl Danisch, counted no less than seventy-two bodies – some in uniform, others in civilian clothing – with an accompanying sign stating: 'A soldier can die, a coward must die.'[190] On 6 April 1945, the final Soviet storming of Königsberg started, and although it was immediately clear that resistance would be futile, the executions continued as before. Despite constant artillery and aerial bombardment, civilians were still repeatedly forced to attend them.[191] Michael Wieck recalled walking past the Nordbahnhof during these days: 'There I saw hanged soldiers, who had wanted to do the only sensible thing: stop this pointless war. They did what the army commanders – with Hitler at the top – were too cowardly to do. Instead a plate was attached to their chests: I had to die, because I am a coward.'[192] The summary courts brought the regime's criminality right out into the open, and rank among the clearest examples of 'violence as a means of communication'.[193] The ceremonial aspect of these courts is therefore of vital importance to understand their practice as it unambiguously communicated the line to which authorities expected the population to adhere.[194]

[186] Wildt, *Hitler's Volksgemeinschaft*, pp. 155–8.
[187] Clappier, *Festung Königsberg*, pp. 120–1.
[188] Guido Knopp, *Der Sturm, Kriegsende im Osten* (Berlin: Econ, 2004), p. 81; AKO 22034-4: Twiehaus, *Die letzte Tage von Königsberg*, p. 1.
[189] Fuhrer and Schön, *Erich Koch, Hitlers brauner Zar*, p. 178.   [190] Ibid.
[191] Ibid., p. 179.
[192] Wieck, *Königsberg, Zeugnis vom Untergang einer Stadt*, pp. 183–4.
[193] Keller, *Volksgemeinschaft am Ende*, pp. 406–17, 422.
[194] This is reminiscent of Michael Wildt's findings concerning the empowerment of the Volksgemeinschaft. See: Wildt, *Hitler's Volksgemeinschaft and the Dynamics of Racial Exclusion*.

The extent of the killing is difficult to judge. After the war, in a article in the expellee newspaper *Ostpreussen-Warte*, a commentator claimed that there were 'hardly any lampposts left in Königsberg to hang the condemned'.[195] A member of one of the six SS-guard commando squads who had been despatched by Gauleiter Koch claimed to have participated in over 200 executions.[196] The Volkssturm man Adolf Klein remembered that the summary courts were dreaded among the civilian population, as 'every day [they] executed men, women and children for minor offences, primarily in public'.[197] He estimated that, in March alone, between thirty to forty people were executed every day.[198] The names of these people were announced on large posters shortly afterwards.[199] If these numbers are correct, at least 1,500 people would have died throughout the fortress era as a result of the different summary courts.

The Soviet besiegers seemed to confirm such numbers, with the Red Army newspaper *Krasnaya Zvezda* claiming that 'in the fortress dozens of deserters were shot each day'.[200] Upon entering the city, Major K. Melnikov found that many deserters 'had been shot and then hung upside down and not removed for a few days. In each edition, the newspaper *Königsberger Zeitung* had printed the lists of the soldiers executed for desertion. Platoon commanders were ordered to read the lists to their soldiers'.[201] Although the exact number of executions is impossible to reconstruct, if we accept the number of 1,500 during the two month fortress era, this translates into the execution of almost 1 per cent of all people present (civilians and soldiers), or almost 3 per cent of the garrison of 50,000. Comparing these numbers to the 27,000 people who were executed by courts-martial until late-1944, we find that the arrival on home soil marked a sharp increase in the practice. The case study of Königsberg shows that extreme intra-ethnic violence was not necessarily born out of a tendency to maintain order in an alien or hostile environment abroad – it was dependent on local factors and actors and largely determined by those actors' preparedness to act on perceived threats.

---

[195] 'Kurt Knuth: 'Iwan, der Schreckliche', *Ostpreussen-Warte*, February 1954, p. 2. See also: Lucas-Busemann, *So fielen Königsberg und Breslau*, p. 59.
[196] Lucas-Busemann, *So fielen Königsberg und Breslau*, p. 169.
[197] BArch Ost-Dok. 8/598, p. 98: Klein.   [198] Ibid.
[199] Hensel, *Medizin in und aus Ostpreußen*, pp. 71–2.
[200] 'Blestyashhaya Pobeda' [Brilliant victory], *Krasnaya Zvezda*, 10 April 1945.
[201] K. Melnikov, 'Sturm Kenigsberga' [The storming of Königsberg], *Krasnaya Zvezda*, 10 April 1945.

Conclusion

In the summer of 1944, the German Wehrmacht fell back on East Prussian territory. Since the area of operations around the province's borders was cleared of its population, the contact between soldiers and civilians was initially limited. The first time that German troops in East Prussia came into contact with large numbers of German civilians was in January 1945, as the Soviet offensives pushed westwards. By the end of that month, German soldiers and civilians were trapped in and around Königsberg. Of the 200,000 civilians who were present in the city when it was first encircled, around 100,000 still remained by early April despite the existence of a corridor to the port city of Pillau. The majority of these people were fully deployed in the defence of the city, either as part of the Volkssturm or because they had to perform Festungsdienst, with women and youths being allocated a more active role than before. The fortress command's efforts to transform Königsberg into a Kampfgemeinschaft offer clear insight into how the concept of Total War could shape a local community. Those who were considered part of this community were not judged according to their loyalty to the *Volk*, but to their willingness to contribute to the local war effort.

This chapter has demonstrated the role the Wehrmacht played in the regulation and enforcement of the rule of law in Königsberg, particularly highlighting its preparedness to resort to extreme means of coercion. It traces this behaviour back to its stay on the Eastern Front, where – driven by 'criminal orders' – hostility between civilians and troops was actively fuelled. The connection between the Weltanschauungskrieg and the German army's behaviour abroad has been the focus of sustained research, yet this research has not been expanded to include military violence towards its own citizens. Although the defining characteristic of earlier Wehrmacht violence against civilians – its racial component – lost its importance as troops moved back into Germany, other factors such as alienation, panic, stress, and trauma, increased as the war continued. Moreover, as we saw earlier in Chapter 2, both the sense of military camaraderie and the fear of a repetition of '1918' helped sustain the view, held particularly by the more hard-line segments in the army, that even German civilians should be treated with a certain scepticism.

In the Soviet Union, members of the Wehrmacht had adhered to a completely different set of laws that met the demands of the barbarous nature of the Eastern Front, and even though the laws on the German home front had also considerably hardened during the war years, military law was more stringent. This difference clearly manifested itself in Königsberg, where the remaining civilians were expected to adapt –

virtually overnight – to the 'extreme normality' of the front. The impossibility of this demand became evident in the first week of military rule in the city, when officer patrols struck in force against 'dissenters', rounding up men who had gone into hiding, or executing people caught entering the abandoned houses of neighbours who had fled. The population did not challenge this behaviour but accepted it with a resigned attitude.

These developments were recognised by the Party. It feared that these emergency legal measures in German territory would weaken its authority and would lead to a further decline in support for the regime. Thus, heavily influenced by military law, in February and March 1945 it implemented regulations concerning summary courts along similar lines to the military. Yet due to the fragmented state of Germany, the proclamation of these laws did not automatically lead to their implementation. Local actors would have a significant impact on the practice of these courts as their evaluation of the situation determined the immediacy of setting an example, while their personal convictions remained of importance in individual cases. In respect to Königsberg, the two-month long proximity to the front line meant that the Party and the army used the full panoply of the law at their disposal in the most ruthless fashion. This process represented the final step in their cumulative radicalisation under the pretext of law, and eventually pushed many communities to progress towards previously unknown levels of violence.

Conclusion

The year 1945 will ultimately be considered as one of the most violent in German history. For the East Prussian capital of Königsberg it was its final year, since on 4 July 1946 the city was rechristened Kaliningrad after the recently deceased Soviet President Mikhail Kalinin, who, as the political scientist Richard Krickus somewhat sarcastically noted, 'never visited the place'.[1] Königsberg was in a death struggle for its status as a German city, a battle it would ultimately lose. Four years later, all German citizens had been expelled and in the years that followed the new Russian authorities sought to erase all signs of what they considered to be 'Prussian militarism', culminating in the destruction of the ruins of the Königsberger Schloss in 1968.[2] During the siege, few people envisioned themselves as part of a German future for Königsberg. This study highlights that the concerns of the principal actors did not centre on their role in the Third Reich; rather, it reveals how strongly people clung to their immediate local environment and how this impacted behavioural patterns.

Every major group of actors, be it the East Prussian civilians, the Wehrmacht, or the Party, nevertheless perceived their direct environment differently and that perception shaped their behavioural patterns. East Prussians, who lived in an idyllic land of dark forests, crystal lakes, and Prussian estates, in a province out of reach of Royal Air Force bombers and less affected by rationing than the rest of the country, experienced a different war than their compatriots. These unique factors provided a convenient pretext for its population to distance themselves from the rest of the country which they increasingly started doing as soon as the fortunes of war turned against Germany. Other Germans did not care

---

[1] Richard Krickus, *The Kaliningrad Question* (Lanham, MD: Rowman & Littlefield, 2002), p. 39.

[2] Robert Albinus, *Lexicon der Stadt Königsberg Pr. und Umgebung* (Leer: Verlag Gerhardt Rautenberg, 1985), s.v. 'Königsberger Schloß'.

much for East Prussians' attempts to distance themselves from the regime, as a joke dating from the early post-war era testifies:

Two painters meet in the west and compare their prospects. One of them is doing very well, the other less so. The poorer one asks his colleague the reason for his success, whereupon he is invited to visit the other's studio. Here he finds the place full of portraits of the late Adolf Hitler. 'How on earth can you sell such rubbish.' he asks. 'I sell them to refugees from East Prussia – they've never heard of Adolf Hitler!'[3]

In reality, the province fitted particularly well within the regime's vision. Its academics willingly catered their research to the regime's vision of racial domination of 'the East', while East Prussia's agriculture – encouraged by Germany's desire to become an autarkic state, and, once the war was underway, stimulated by an inexhaustible pool of cheap forced labour – also benefited tremendously. The regime also repurposed the province's martial narrative. Königsberg, the capital of East Prussia, had long been presented as the easternmost bulwark of Germandom and defences around the city had consistently been strengthened in fear of 'the East'. This *Grenzland*-narrative was also adhered to under National Socialism, although this never translated into a population that was significantly more resolute than their compatriots in other parts of Germany. Nevertheless, from the summer of 1944 onwards, large parts of the East Prussian population were deployed in the construction of defensive positions along the province's border while that autumn its men were called up to serve in the Volkssturm. The two efforts – the first two Total War drives in the province – showed that, on a local level, Party and Wehrmacht were willing and able to cooperate and that, as a sense of urgency set in, they both proved fully prepared to deploy civilians in defensive efforts.

As a result, during the final months of 1944 the personal changes for the province's inhabitants were massive and caused a considerable drop in morale. Large parts of the East Prussian population definitively broke with the idea of a larger German Volksgemeinschaft, feeling that the National Socialist regime had proved unable to meet its promises. Contributing to this notion was the realisation that the province was about to become a battlefield: while the increasing presence of front-line troops, supply-train units, and military staffs on East Prussia territory kindled the first anxieties, the atrocity propaganda that followed in the wake of the Gumbinnen Operation fuelled the primordial fear of 'the East' even further. In January 1945, this fear became a reality as a result of

[3] Fritz Hillenbrand, *Underground Humour in Nazi Germany 1933–1945* (London: Routledge, 1995), p. 208.

the Red Army's East Prussian offensive, and by the end of the month most of the province was in Soviet hands and Königsberg was surrounded. Four tattered divisions, which were tasked to defend Königsberg at all costs, managed to reach the city before its encirclement.

It soon became clear, however, that German soldiers had a completely different mindset and prioritised different matters than the civilians they were to protect. Most of the men defending East Prussia had previously fought in the Soviet Union and the actions of the troops who fell back on German territory reveal that their frame of reference had been shaped – barbarised – by the years of war on the Eastern Front. Their conduct was the result of an attitude towards warfare that had come to dominate the German High Command, in which the concept of 'grand strategy' had steadily been pushed to the background. Instead, the German art of war had come to rely heavily on operational success which resulted in the 'mission' being put at the heart of German warfare. This development moved the responsibility of operational success away from the commander-in-chief, instead placing it with the individual field commander. The pressure that was subsequently put on commanders to complete their missions ensured that they would seek to accomplish them with a ruthlessness so far unknown. The set of 'criminal orders' gave these men a mandate to act with a complete disregard for their immediate environment, and as long as their objective could at all be regarded as pragmatic or a military necessity, they showed little reluctance to carry out even the most inhumane orders. Moreover, they were encouraged to spur on their men to fight with increasing disregard for their own lives. The rallying call became *Durchhalten* – persevere – until the tide turned; a slogan that expected unconditional trust in the leadership but promised nothing in return. The average German soldier was hardly able to reflect on the radicalisation of the army nor his own role in it; when he thought about these matters at all, he often did not consider the newly emerging behavioural patterns to result from the concerted efforts of the regime but rather as the outcome of the changing demands of warfare.

The wider implications of this calloused outlook towards what constituted normality at times of war, the 'lowered resting heart rate of the Wehrmacht soldier', becomes clear upon examining the troops' return to Germany. With the war's call for the annihilation of 'sub-humans', most orders on the Eastern Front had encompassed civilians and it was thus the soldiers' perception of civilians that had undergone the largest perversion. During the fighting in the Soviet Union, the line between civilians and combatants had been deliberately blurred, not only as a result of the scope of the Wehrmacht's orders but also because the Soviet defenders readily deployed them in militias or as a labour force. In contrast, German civilians – who 'merely' contributed to the war indirectly – could not claim that same determination. It did not take long for comparisons with the First World War to be made, when the wavering attitude of the home front – so soldiers were taught – had cost Germany its victory. The bugbear of the home front's 'stab in the back' of 1918, combined with the notion that the Soviets *had* in fact managed to turn the tide between 1941 and 1944 through the uncompromising use of their civilians, removed many of the reservations to deploy their own population in the defence.

What finally contributed to this sentiment was that, for both commanders and the rank-and-file, the approach towards fighting did not necessarily have to change much as it moved onto home soil. The realisation that they were now fighting on German territory did not prompt these men to substantially change their behaviour. As the battles continued to rage, soldiers' attitudes towards the enemy they faced changed little (if anything, these hardened further), while also the military structures remained unaltered. Notions of strategy, tactical considerations, or operational choices all continued to be drawn from the exact same sources as before, and the question of what constituted 'military necessity' was therefore approached as it had always been. With the army's radicalised attitude on one hand, and the desire of men like Gauleiter Koch to profess their commitment on the other hand, the idea that the state of the war would necessitate civilians to contribute to Germany's defence was readily accepted in East Prussia.

In Festung Königsberg the mindset that underpinned these behavioural patterns was on full display. When German troops moved into the city, they brought with them their experiences of the Eastern Front. Not only had cities proven costly to conquer in the Soviet Union, the subsequent rule had been marked by distrust towards an unfamiliar population, whose hostility repeatedly led to unrest or even open rebellion. Cities remained unpopular as battlegrounds, and especially in defeat commanders preferred to avoid tying their troops to them. Nevertheless, on 8 March 1944 Hitler issued War Directive 53, which gave birth to the fortress strategy. The strategy called for the garrisons of cities designated as 'fortresses' to allow themselves to be surrounded, as such pinning down large numbers of Soviet troops and disrupting their advance. The Soviet summer offensive, Operation Bagration, proved the fallacy of the strategy, as these *Festungen* were often bypassed by the first echelon and captured by second-tier units. Tens of thousands of German soldiers were captured or killed in the ensuing encirclements and by the end of the year the principles that underpinned the strategy had lost all credibility.

As the battles moved onto German soil, a new string of cities – roughly following the pre-war Polish–German border – were nevertheless designated as fortresses. Their garrisons were, for the last time, lulled into a false sense of safety, as these fortress cities were consciously being built to better serve their function, were better stocked, and were incorporated in larger defensive systems. Consequently, Königsberg stayed in German hands in late January 1945, and would remain so for over two more months. During this period, the final authority came to rest with a staff consisting of military personnel, led by Königsberg's fortress commander, General Otto Lasch, and Party officials, led by Kreisleiter Ernst Wagner. These men would determine the policies in the city and actively sought to direct the behavioural patterns of civilians, soldiers, and officials alike.

The two men had a good working relationship which, to a large extent, rested upon the willingness of Kreisleiter Wagner to subordinate himself to General Lasch. Wagner did so because, besides legal authority, the Wehrmacht also had moral authority over the Party. There was no doubt that few of East Prussia's other Party members truly cared whether Königsberg would hold or not, since most of them, Gauleiter Koch included, had left the city shortly before the Soviet encirclement. This action ranged the remaining Party members against the absent Party elite, rather than against the Wehrmacht, not least because the army had stayed put, fighting off the Soviet attack at the city's borders. There was nevertheless considerable friction between the two 'factions', largely caused by the inroads made into each other's traditional power structures. Whereas the Party allocated itself more martial tasks, the Wehrmacht took over large parts of local administration. On different occasions, they would seek to outdo each other, often at the expense of the civilian population, creating a deadly dynamic that was virtually unparalleled in Germany.

This was aggravated by the personal history of these men themselves. General Lasch, who framed his entire life as a battle against the encroachment of 'the East' (having fought on the Eastern Front in the First World War, serving in a *Freikorps* during the immediate post-war era and again serving on the Eastern Front in the Second World War), had long accepted violence as a viable tool in shaping a community. Kreisleiter Wagner, in turn, was staunchly loyal to the National Socialist promise, and as a former officer of the 1st Infanterie-Division would have been aware – and most likely also had first-hand knowledge – of the indiscriminate violence perpetrated by the Wehrmacht. As a result, a martial agenda came to dominate the fortress staff – one that, if need be, could be stringently enforced. Loyalties aside, by this stage of the war the fight against Slavic Bolshevism was for both men their *raison d'être*, and the community the fortress command sought to create to fulfil that immediate purpose – the Kampfgemeinschaft – did not have to comprise more than Festung Königsberg.

The efforts of the fortress's propagandists reveal the motivations to continue fighting. The themes these men chose reveal that a utilitarian approach dominated the way they sought to interact with their audience. From the first day of the siege, sustained efforts were made to forge a Kampfgemeinschaft, based on Königsberg's 'battle', rather than on Germany's 'struggle'. What eventually emerged was a reaction to the population's more outspoken disaffection with the regime, while the propaganda simultaneously served to raise the mood of the troops and countered the announcements of the NKFD coming from the other side of the front line. Rather than paying attention to developments on a national or international level, propagandists instead devoted most of their energy to addressing local issues. The 'fortress identity' came to rely heavily on what was at hand: instead of linking the defence of the city to the defence of National Socialist principles, propagandists invoked an image of Königsberg as a centuries-long embattled bulwark of Germandom. As part of this effort, the population and garrison of Königsberg were 'spurred on' by the heroes of Königsberg's history, such as General Ludwig Yorck von Wartenburg and the philosopher Immanuel Kant. In the East Prussian Volkssturm Knight's Cross recipient, Ernst Tiburzy, propagandists found a tangible example of defiance, who they repeatedly used to replace the grandiose boasts of the different Nazi figureheads.

This local approach is also reflected in the set of rumours that the fortress command sought to introduce. Their focus on local issues meant that there was little need to inform people about matters beyond their immediate horizon, while the rumours' rapid spread attests to the willingness of significant parts of the population to continue to consider the information that reached them as plausible. The fortress command's persistence in seeking to shape popular opinion in the city can be clearly observed in the wake of the discovery of Soviet atrocities in the Metgethen suburb, west of Königsberg. The orchestrated release of the initially embargoed news, which combined coverage in the official Party outlet, the *Preußische Zeitung*, with a rumour campaign spearheaded by soldiers of the divisions deployed during the suburb's recapture, reveals the lengths propagandists were still willing to go to by this stage of the war. Given the continuous destruction of the city, these men also had the vital task of upholding the idea that Königsberg was still worth defending. The reluctance of the population to leave the city, even as a corridor was created between Königsberg and Pillau, is a sombre testament to the success propagandists had in downplaying the dangers that the population was exposed to.

Such behaviour seemingly conflicts with what is regarded as one of the core tasks of an army: the safeguarding of its civilians. Even though the evacuation of civilians was not considered the army's core task, as the Wehrmacht moved into East Prussia it assumed a role in their evacuation – but this was hardly out of selflessness. The organisation of the evacuation of civilians rested with local Party officials, but with large parts of the province placed under martial law due to the proximity of the front and the immediacy of a main Soviet attack, they were ordered to cooperate with military commanders. Although at times the collaboration was strained, by and large Party and Wehrmacht reached agreement with relative ease. The demands of the military centred on the removal of local populations from the area of operations, and as such, the concerns for civilians – or better the lack thereof – were virtually identical to those earlier on the Eastern Front. There, these men had been taught to disregard civilian property, and this behaviour continued once back on East Prussian soil. Complaints about the poor behaviour of troops spread almost as soon as the Wehrmacht entered Germany, and turned into outrage as their stay in the province continued. The wanton destruction and the plunder of German property worried commanders but, despite the introduction of strict orders to counter soldiers' behaviour, remained an unresolved problem until the end of the war. In the light of a continuous retreat, the soldiers' actions are understandable, especially since the decision-making processes that underpinned evacuation measures in East Prussia essentially differed little from those during the earlier years of retreat, and thus did not require the average soldier to rethink his behaviour. In this period, the impetus behind 'evacuation' was not the preservation of property. Instead, extensive orders were passed down to assure that military and civilian materiel was either broken down, evacuated, paralysed, or destroyed; a policy whose effects would be felt well into the post-war years. Troops were also to adhere to this policy once back in Germany which, as reports of numerous local officials indicated, they did readily and without question or consideration.

Once the Soviet offensives commenced in January 1945, military concerns immediately gained the upper hand, and concern for civilians was no longer a priority. Most damning about the behaviour of the military was that, even though a humanitarian drama – the like which German history had not seen since the Thirty Years' War – unfolded in front of commanders' very eyes, military orders almost completely ignored it. Although individual Landser often professed a sincere desire to protect their compatriots, the compartmentalisation of higher commands ensured that the army would continue to act in a criminally detached manner. Trains and ships were prioritised for the transport of ammunition and the wounded while roads were cleared of refugees to allow the army unrestricted movement. It is in this regard that 'cumulative radicalisation' manifested itself. The Wehrmacht's radical stance towards civilians found consensus among its ranks, as it allowed commanders to present themselves as determined defenders of Germany. With the defence of Germany as the overriding concern, the Party elite also accepted this course or even tried to outdo the Wehrmacht. The pervasiveness of this attitude, however, meant that civilian interests were routinely ignored.

This becomes particularly clear during Operation Westwind, the operation that sought to connect Königsberg to the port of Pillau. By allocating three of the garrison's five divisions to it, and by positioning the strongest remaining division in such a way that it would be able to head west at short notice as well, General Lasch left the population dangerously exposed in the case of a Soviet attack. In this critical chapter of Königsberg's siege, Lasch's loyalty lay with his troops. Meanwhile, the care for the population was at best of minor importance. In the period following the successful breakout, the evacuation of civilians was still not actively pursued despite the existence of a corridor to Pillau. In the newly established 'refugee camps' on the Samland, care for evacuees remained low with famine and diseases rampant. Unsurprisingly, civilians were often reluctant to be evacuated from Königsberg, and by mid-March the evacuation of Königsberg was halted. From then on, the population of Königsberg even increased since refugees from around the city flooded back to the city in search of proper food and shelter. It meant that about 100,000 civilians found themselves in Königsberg as the final Soviet storming commenced. Although there is no doubt that the fortress command was aware of these numbers, it undertook no attempts to pursue alternatives to prevent a high civilian death toll. Multiple Soviet calls for surrender, both immediately prior to and during the final storming, or the idea of declaring Königsberg an open city, were dismissed out of hand. With surrender closely linked to dishonour, the defence of the city continued for over three days, by which time Soviet troops had advanced deep into the city centre and were closing in on General Lasch's command post. Perhaps the most damning evidence of the German army's disregard for its population are the terms of Königsberg's capitulation: no stipulations were included to assure their subsequent safety and no efforts were made to protect their status as civilians.

This hard line can also be distinguished in the way the military sought to ensure Königsberg's Kampfgemeinschaft. The army's arrival led to a sharp increase in intra-ethnic violence in the city. During the previous years on the Eastern Front, German troops had actively supported the regime's various genocidal policies and criminal orders and fought with increasing ruthlessness against a much dreaded, visible or invisible, enemy. This resulted in a 'barbarised' mindset with which they returned to East Prussia. Their arrival on German soil did not necessarily alleviate feelings of fear and anxiety, if only because on a day-to-day basis nothing changed for the troops: they still faced the same enemy and they were still part of close-knit military structures that were held together by a sense of Kameradschaft. The constant rotation of troops caused by the large military losses increased a sense of mistrust among the men, while they were now also confronted with the civilians' defeatist attitude. Parallels could be drawn to the 'stab in the back' of 1918 and the following collapse of order and rule of law, especially as the Party was seen giving in to civilian demands.

To quell any potential unrest, General Lasch sought to establish a 'Wehrmacht rule of law' immediately after his arrival in the city. Officer patrols, Streifen, were to restore order in Königsberg and bring deserters to the front, and in this capacity were given considerable leeway to determine what constituted 'disorder' or who exactly qualified as a 'deserter'. During the first week of Königsberg's siege, in late January 1945, they executed men and women for minor infractions, signalling an abrupt departure of an already stringent home front regime. Other officers even acted on their own initiative and executed those they considered 'cowards', fully exploiting the authority that the late-war military regulations provided them with. From a military standpoint, this approach was highly successful: not only did Königsberg stay in German hands; the army was also immediately recognised as the final authority in the city. It marked the beginning of an era during which the extreme normalities of military life became the norm. In the midst of artillery shelling and aerial bombardment, the fortress command provided food, shelter, water, and electricity for the population, and also assured that stores, banks, and cinemas remained open for the people who were willing to contribute to the envisioned Kampfgemeinschaft. But this willingness was – of course – relative: the decision to stay in Königsberg was above all shaped by a reluctance to flee, or was rooted in the consideration that living out the war in a familiar environment would be the best chance of surviving it.

For a significant group, moreover, leaving Königsberg was strictly forbidden: as many as 10,000 Volkssturm militia men were deployed during the defence of Königsberg and these men were fully integrated in the fortress's command structure. The fortress command even differentiated between the different age groups: young boys were used in the first wave of attack during the assault on Metgethen whereas the older men were given defensive tasks on poorly held sectors of the front. Moreover, in early February, the fortress command proclaimed Festungsdienst, or fortress service, which called for the complete integration of the civilian population in the fortress's defensive efforts. With all men of military age already at the front, Festungsdienst encompassed older children, the elderly, and women, who were all to contribute to the fortress's defence for four hours per day. The decision signalled the final step towards Total War and was justified by pointing to the safety the city provided despite being immediately threatened by Soviet forces. Subsequently, the willingness to contribute to the defence became the unofficial measuring rod of the civilians' relation to the Kampfgemeinschaft.

The continuing reliance on the strict military mindset ensured that – even though they were now fighting on German territory – army commanders continued to consider the defence of an area as their primary goal. There should be no doubt that the Party elite looked at the army's stringent emergency measures and its ruthless use of civilians with both admiration and concern. On the one hand, the Wehrmacht's means of coercion were seen as highly effective in ensuring the involvement of the population; on the other, set against the existing legislation, their severity and increasing grip on civilians' lives corroded the traditional rule of law. Still following the pattern of 'cumulative radicalisation', throughout February and March laws were enacted that also gave the Party the authority to summarily execute people. This led to an increasing and diverse set of perpetrators, in turn resulting in an explosive increase in the number of victims. Personal motivations might have played a role in the severity of the summary courts, but impotence in the face of the dire situation and misdirected panic nevertheless seem to have been of overarching importance.

It is nearly impossible to determine to what extent this final intra-ethnic violence was perceived as extraordinary since violence and National Socialism had always had a symbiotic relationship. Violence was born out of National Socialism, just as National Socialism was born out of violence. Already during the Weimar regime, clashes between SA and communists had been framed as a Hobbesian struggle of 'every man against every man', while also a few years later home-front support for the war effort certainly partially rested on the ability to 'bring distant terrors near' by exposing 'the aggressive intentions of Jewish

Bolshevism'.[4] Those distant terrors were infinitely nearer on the Eastern Front, where the lives of German troops were indeed, in Hobbes's words, 'nasty, brutish and short'.[5] The behavioural patterns of the Wehrmacht in East Prussia highlight an aspect which within the research into its relationship to the Nazi regime remains underappreciated: the Wehrmacht was not merely violent because it was part of the National Socialist apparatus – it was also an instrument of violence itself. Eventually, violence migrated together with the Wehrmacht, and in the end indeed brought the terrors of the Eastern Front to the streets of Königsberg.

What needs to be stressed, however, is that Königsberg was part of a crumbling mosaic: the regime's ideology had not permeated all strata of society, and of what had been accomplished, the war ensured that dissolution set in well before Allied troops neared Germany's borders. These chapters elaborate on the violence and brutality experienced by East Prussian civilians, violence which was ubiquitous across Germany during the final year of the war; nevertheless, it is equally important to emphasise that, because of the considerable influence of local factors and actors, the situation in another location, however near or distant, could be very different. For every town where a local dignitary was hanged for defeatism in the face of the enemy, another town's commanders and Party officials allowed the front line to roll over them, having offered only symbolic resistance or none at all. Many Germans were carefully looking beyond the war, but since the suppression of dissonant voices was sustained until the final moments of the regime's existence, it was hard to gauge whether one's 'defeatist' conviction reflected that of the rest of the local community. As a result, views on the transition 'from war to peace', or 'from German rule to foreign subjugation', could even within different German communities differ sharply.

In Königsberg moderate voices can certainly be distinguished but there should be no doubt that the city's military and Party authorities were gearing all means towards the city's defence. As such, the city fits well within the traditional 'fighting to the last bullet' narrative of Germany 1945. Königsberg's bitter defence, however, was fairly unique even within East Prussia, as certainly not every house in the province became a bunker, nor every city a fortress. Looking at the East Prussian offensive, we see that the vast majority of the province's cities and towns were defended in a fairly traditional manner, as part of a larger and often brittle front line, which meant that fighting there only took place for one or two

---

[4] Dietrich, 'National Renewal, Anti-Semitism, and Political Continuity', p. 395; Jürgen Förster, 'Ludendorff and Hitler in Perspective: the Battle for the German Soldier's Mind, 1917–1944', *War In History* (10) 2003, p. 333.
[5] Hansen, 'War, Suffering and Modern German History', p. 368.

days, or even mere hours. A closer examination of some of East Prussia's 'larger' cities shows that they all underwent the final stage of the war in different ways. Often, these cities were defended by rearguard units that merely sought to slow down the Soviet advance rather than bring it to a halt. On the road to Königsberg, Gumbinnen, and Insterburg are examples of this defensive practice. Red Army troops reached Gumbinnen's eastern suburbs by 19 January 1945 and captured the city the next day, while Insterburg, twenty miles to the west, was reached on 21 January and in Soviet hands by the evening of 22 January. This is not to say that these cities survived the war intact. In both cases Red Army troops expected heavy opposition (precisely because of boasts to defend cities to the last bullet) and subjected them to heavy artillery shelling and bombing. Moreover, since Gumbinnen and Insterburg were among the first major German cities to fall in Soviet hands, they also suffered from the wrath of the attackers, who set hundreds of buildings ablaze. The same held true for Allenstein, in the south of the province, whose destruction at the hand of Red Army troops has been documented by both Lev Kopelev and Alexander Solzhenitzyn.[6]

The cities Lötzen, Memel, and Tilsit tell a completely different story. Lötzen and Memel had been steadily built up as Festungen in the months leading up to the final Soviet offensive, but both were left undefended when the time came. In the case of Memel, this was because Hitler on 26 January ordered the evacuation of its garrison so that it could bolster the defence of the Samland and Festung Königsberg (again highlighting that Hitler's 'stand firm' orders were not as rigid as often assumed). The fortress system around Lötzen, on the other hand, was abandoned without Hitler's consent. Lötzen lay within the area that was to be defended by the Fourth Army, but during the first two weeks of the offensive Red Army units hardly engaged the formation. Instead, they pushed past the Army both on its north and south, attempting a pincer operation. Fearing encirclement, Fourth Army's commander General Friedrich Hossbach decided to fall back westwards without informing the High Command, attempting to take up positions along the Vistula river which separated East Prussia from West Prussia. When on 29 January his intentions became clear in Berlin, Hossbach was sacked for insubordination but by that time Lötzen was already in Soviet hands.[7] Something similar happened in the north of the province, in Tilsit, which lay at the south bank of the Memel river. Its garrison, the 551st Volksgrenadier-Division, had

---

[6] Kopelev, *No Jail for Thought*, pp. 46–7; Alexander Solzhenitsyn, *Prussian Nights, a Narrative Poem* (London: Collins and Harvill, 1977).

[7] Willems, 'Defiant Breakwaters or Desperate Blunders?', p. 359.

been expecting Soviet troops to attempt a cross-river attack with infantry from the north, but instead, on the evening of 19 January came to realise that strong motorised units were coming from the east. This realisation prompted the decision to abandon the city by cover of darkness and by the next morning the city was in Soviet hands, still largely intact.

The only city in East Prussia to suffer more from the fighting for the province than Königsberg was Braunsberg, situated on the Frische Haff. The city, however, was not declared a Festung but was reduced to rubble because for two months it lay in the centre of the Heiligenbeil Pocket, the last stand of the Fourth Army, and it was incessantly bombed and shelled as a result. Other cities that suffered heavily during the province's defence were Elbing and Marienburg. Soviet spearheads entered Elbing on 24 January during the initial push to the Frische Haff, after which it was defended for three weeks, before it fell on 10 February. Marienburg, with its beautiful castle, was reached on 25 January and fell on 9 March 1945. Red Army commanders had hoped to rush the two cities, a *coup de main*, but in both cities a motley force of Volkssturm men and regular troops managed to fight them off, after which the Soviet troops changed the focus and direction of their attacks. Indeed, it is important to note that by 1945 the Red Army was superior to the Wehrmacht in virtually every respect and could somewhat 'choose' their battle grounds, either by deciding to engage the opposing force or by avoiding immediate confrontation. Contrary to Germans perceptions, Soviet reserves were certainly not inexhaustible, and by the last year of the war both the Soviet High Command and Red Army field commanders were considerably more cautious than during the previous years.

Every East Prussian city tells a different story, with human suffering the only communality. Nevertheless, the decision to base the defence of Germany around its cities was the most tangible step towards Total War, and especially since most refugees fled towards them, brought the majority of the German population into close contact with combatants. Subsequently, the proximity of civilians' defeatist sentiments to soldiers' negative emotions of fear and suspicion had the potential to turn cities into pressure cookers.[8]

Finally, let us return to Königsberg. What would eventually determine how a city and its inhabitants underwent the last months of the war were local dynamics, attitudes, and loyalties. In Königsberg, members of the Wehrmacht vastly outnumbered Party and state officials which ensured

---

[8] The range of emotions surfacing within a city faced with severe adversity is beautifully examined in Albert Camus's 1947 novel *La Peste*.

that military behaviour would often determine the day-to-day decision-making processes. Most troops that defended Königsberg had previously fought in the Soviet Union where they had subscribed to the notion of 'military utilitarianism' which, within the superstructure of the Wehrmacht, had been steadily hollowed out to mean 'conduct without considering the consequences'. This was a long and extended process which, once taught, was hard to 'unlearn'. It is, however, important to stress that this behaviour had had many 'fathers'; practices had been theorised and exercised in the pre-1918 *Kaiserheer* and the interwar *Reichswehr* long before the Nazi assumption of power. Men like General Lasch were just as much products of the years prior to 1933 as of the years of National Socialism. The motivations of the actors in East Prussia in 1944–5 should therefore not be sought exclusively in the experiences of the Eastern Front immediately prior to the fighting in the province, but also in more general and long-standing notions of the use and misuse of the immediate environment.

How perverted these ideas of 'military necessity' had become over the previous years can best be gauged by the harsh stance of the officers of the 1st (Ostpreussische) Infanterie-Division, who, although primarily recruited in Königsberg, did not hesitate to carry out executions of their former city neighbours to cement martial law. Their actions highlight the complexity of military behavioural patterns, immediately underlining the impracticality of reconstructing 'the' Wehrmacht soldier during the final year of the war. Nevertheless, we can draw some conclusions. Firstly, there are clear limits to the well-worn idea of the Wehrmacht as an obstacle for radicalisation in German society: in Königsberg, it can even be considered as a 'stakeholder of violence', since by readily resorting to it, the fortress command was able to establish its authority virtually overnight. During a time of omnipresent confusion, executions could communicate a simple message – either you assist in Königsberg's defence, or you die. Although less explicit, this was also the line that was adhered to during East Prussia's evacuation, as those unable to contribute to the province's defence were virtually left to fend for themselves. Secondly, the Wehrmacht contributed significantly to the destruction of East Prussia's infrastructure, turning on the same society it had protected for years. Indeed, in its purpose, the March 1945 'Nero Decree', so often portrayed as an outburst of a Führer disillusioned by his own people, differed little from an already widely accepted military practice. Lastly, the troops' constantly expanding image of the enemy during Nazi Germany's Weltanschauungskrieg also included civilians, and in that respect their brutalised behaviour towards their own population above all attests to deep-seated group imperatives. Once the Wehrmacht returned to East Prussian soil, the totality of the war ensured that the preconceptions of the troops of the civilian as 'other' inevitably came into conflict with their duties as protectors. It was this tension that set the stage for the widespread violence of the war's final months.

Appendices

Appendix 1: Strength of Königsberg's Garrison, 6 April 1945

Division	Battalions	Attached artillery	Armoured support	Anti-tank guns	Total Strength
561st VGD	8 'middle-strong'	60 light guns 43 heavy guns	9 Sturmgeschütze	43	5,588 men
548th VGD	6 'middle-strong'	31 light guns 21 heavy guns	no armoured support	21	3,776 men
367th Inf. Div. *	9 'middle-strong'	43 light guns 48 heavy guns	7 Sturmgeschütze	48	7,123 men.
69th Inf. Div	10 'average'	41 light guns 48 heavy guns	no armoured support	48	7,430 men

* Attached were Sich. Rgt 75 and Fest. Inf. Btl. 1441

Further present in Königsberg:	Volkssturm	5,000 men
	Fest. Pak Verband I	800 men
	Festungspioniere	900 men
	Police battalion	500 men

49 foreign guns ranging from 7.62 cm to 15.2 cm.

Total manpower:

'Kampfstärke', ('battle strength'),   28,617 men.

'Tagestärke', (daily-/maximum strength) 47,800 + 5,000 Volkssturm

Source: RH 2/335, pp. 175–6: Op. Abt/ I N/ LdS Bef. Vortragsnotiz Betr.: Festung Königsberg, 6.4.1945.

In the days between 31 March 1945 and 6 April 1945 the staff of the 61st Infantry division and the decimated 'Kampfgruppe Hannibal' also arrived in Königsberg.

The final daily strength, therefore, must have been around 55,000.

Appendix 2: The Capitulation of Königsberg

Commander of Fortress   10.4.45
    Königsberg.

Order Concerning Marching-Off of the Remnants of the Troops

1. The officers keep their sidearms (but blade weapons only)

2. Every officer can bring along a personal orderly

3. The officers can bring along their kit (as long as it can be carried personally or by the orderly)

4. Troops gather in companies or columns under the guidance of a responsible officer or non-commissioned officer

5. They bring with them their weapons with ammunition until they encounter Russian troops. There they will then lay down their weapons and ammunition

6. Until Russian lines are reached, a white flag is to be carried at the head of every column

7. March route: Leave the city by crossing the railway bridge and the pontoon bridge constructed westerly thereof near the Nasser Garten

8. Russian troops shall not fire at German troops lined up in order

9. Eliminating remaining strongholds is the task of the Russian army

10. The above measures are to be executed immediately.

   The Commander: For the commander
                                   The Chief of General Staff

    LASCH   SÜSSKIND-SCHWENDI
General der Infanterie   Oberst i.G.

Source: Museum Lasch-Bunker Kaliningrad

Bibliography

Archival Sources

Archiv Kulturzentrum Ostpreußen, Ellingen (AKO)

22032: Königsberg 1939–45

22032–2: Werner Strahl: *Erlebnisse Januar bis Mai 1945*

22032–2: 'Die Sturmglocke', März 1945

22032–3: Pamphlet: *Haß unsere Pflicht, Rache unsere Tugend* (late January 1945)

22034: Königsberg 1945–8

22034–3: Aus der Rundfunksprache von Professor Baumgarten

22034–4: Oberleutnant Eberhard Knieper (O 3 der Festung): *Bericht über meine Erlebnisse in Königsberg in der Zeit von Mitte Februar bis Anfang April 1945* (undated)

22034–4: Hauptmann Banneitz, Ic der Festung: *Erlebnisbericht über meine Tage in der Festung Koenigsberg* (undated)

22034–4: Hptm. d. R. Lemke: *Die letzten Tage von Königsberg* (undated)

22034–4: Major i.G. a.D. Dr. Hans Schäfer, Ia der Festung: *Der Fall Königsbergs* (1.12.56)

22034–4: Dr. Eugen Sauvant: *Die letzten Tage von Königsberg 27. Januar bis 10. April 1945* (undated)

22034–4: Generalleutnant O.v. Natzmer: *Einsatz der 4. Armee ab Februar 1945* (undated)

22034–4: Oberst i.G. Von Süsskind-Schwendi: *Gespräch mit Herrn General d. Inf. Lasch um Ostern 1945* (undated)

22034–4: Friedrich Dorfmüller, Oberstabsinterdant der Reserve: *Zusammenstoß mit dem stellv. Gauleiter Großherr* (undated)

22034–4: Hauptmann d. Res. Sommer: *Vermerk* (undated)

22034–4: Friedrich Dorfmüller: *Vernichtung des Führerbefehls „Verbrannte Erde"* (undated)

22034–4: Pamphlet: 9 February 1945: *Aufruf! Packt alle an!*

22034–4: Walter Kemsies: *Stimmungsbilder aus Königsberg i. Pr. 1945 (Die Festungszeit der ostpr. Hauptstadt)* (Verfaßt um 1946)

22034–4: Friedrich Dorfmüller, Oberstabsinterdant der Reserve: *Ferngespräch des Kreisleiter Wagner mit Gauleiter Koch am 7.4.1945* (undated)

22034–4: Obergefreiter Sinzig: *Meine Erinnerungen an die letzte Stunden in Königsberg* (4.12.56)

22034–4: Aufzeichnungen des Hauptschriftleiters der Königsberger Allgemeine Zeitung Wegener über seine Erlebnisse in Königsberg Januar/März 1945 (undated)

22034–4: Wegener, *Der Untergang von Königsberg* (undated)

22034–4: Waldemar Magunia: *Der Volkssturm in Ostpreußen 1944/45* (10 April 1955)

22034–4: Waldemar Magunia: *Abschrift* (12.2.1955)

Archiwum Museum Stutthof, Sztutowo (AMS)

Sygn. I-IB-3: Kommandanturbefehl 1944–1945

Bundesarchiv – Lastenausgleichsarchiv, Bayreuth (BArch)

Ost-Dok. 8: Berichte von Angehörigen der Politischen Führungsschicht aus den ostdeutschen Vertreibungsgebieten zum Zeitgeschehen von 1939–1945

Ost-Dok. 8/507: Kurt Jacobi, Ministerialdirigent im Reichsministerium des Innern: Räumung der Provinz Ostpreußen 1944–1945. (6.3.1953)

Ost-Dok. 8/508: Karl Friedrich, Beauftragter des Reichsverteidigungs-kommissars Ostpreußen: instead of. „Bericht über Flüchtlingsab-transporte in Pillau im Jahre 1945'. (23.3.1956)

Ost-Dok. 8/510: Kurt Dieckert, Verbindungsoffizier zwischen Zivilverwaltung und 3. Panzerarmee (April 1948)

Ost-Dok. 8/519: Oberst d. Gendarmerie Hans Leberecht von Bredow: 'Partisanenbekämpfung in Ostpreußen' 1944–1945 (ohne Datum)

Ost-Dok. 8/531: Klaus von der Groeben, Landrat des Kreises Samland: 'Das Ende in Ostpreußen. Den Ablauf der Geschehnisse in Samland' 1944–1945 (1.10.1952)

Ost-Dok. 8/536: Dr. Paul Hoffmann, Regierungspräsident beim Oberpräsidium Königsberg, stellv. Oberpräsident: Räumungsplan für Ostpreußen 1944 (11.3.1955)

Ost-Dok. 8/557: Generalmajor Burkhart Müller-Hillebrand, Chef des Generalstabes des Panzer-Armeeoberkommandos 3: Die Kämpfe der 3. Panzerarmee in Ostpreußen 1944–1945 (18.12.1952)

Ost-Dok. 8/560: Walter Marquardt, Oberregierungsrat beim Oberpräsidium in Königsberg: Die Aufstellung eines Räumungsplanes für Ostpreußen 1943–1945 (24.6.1952)

Ost-Dok. 8/561: Heinrich Lindner, Regierungsrat, Unterabteilungsleiter beim RVK: Bau von Befestigungen in Ostpreußen 1944–1945 (10.12.1952)

Ost-Dok. 8/565: Oberst Schaefer: Vorbereitung und Durchführung der Räumung in Ostpreußen 1944–1945 (ohne Datum)

Ost-Dok. 8/579: Oberstleutnant Hans-Heinrich Wendtlandt, Kommandeur des Grenadierregiments 1094: 'Der Endkampf' (ohne Datum)

Ost-Dok. 8/580: Erich Zerahn, Oberfinanzpräsident in Königsberg: 'Erste Belagerung Königsberg vom 30.1.-22.2.1945' (14.10.1953)

Ost-Dok. 8/584: Wenzel, Oberregierungsrat, Referent beim Reichsverteidigungskommissar: Die Einstellung des Gauleiters Koch zum ostwallbau und zur Räumung Ostpreußens (10.12.1952)

Ost-Dok. 8/586: Dr. Victor Werbke, Stabsoffizier beim Festungs-kommandanten von Königsberg: Aufstellung neuer Truppenteile in Königsberg, Verhältnis zwischen Stab Lasch (General d. Inf. Und Kommandant der Festung Königsberg) und Parteidienststelle (4.6.1953)

Ost-Dok. 8/588: Dr. Hellmuth Will, Oberbürgermeister der Stadt Königsberg: Die Kämpfe um die Stadt Königsberg, Räumung der Stadt 1945 (19.2.1955)

Ost-Dok. 8/591: Oberleutnant Günther Heysing, Kriegsberichter: 'Von Leningrad bis Königsberg' Ostpreußische Erinnerungsblätter eines Kriegsberichters (Dezember 1953)

Ost-Dok. 8/593: Waldemar Magunia, Präsident der Handwerkskammer Königsberg: Der Ostwall, seine Entstehung, sein Verlauf und seine Bewährung mit Kartenskizzen (10.4.1955)

Ost-Dok. 8/594: Waldemar Magunia: Gauleiter Erich Koch und die Räumung Ostpreußen (10.4.1955)

Ost-Dok. 8/598: Adolf Klein, Angestellter beim Oberforstamt Elchwald in Pfeil: Einsatz des Volkssturms in Königsberg 1945 (29.3.1952)

Ost-Dok. 8/600: Bruno Just, Bataillons-Adjutant (11.6.1952)

Ost-Dok. 8/602: Gustav Makowka, Bürgermeister a.D.: 'Aufzeichnungen über die Ereignisse in den letzten 3 Monate in Königsberg/PR.' 1945 (Januar 1946)

Ost-Dok. 10: Berichte über Verwaltung und Wirtschaft in Ostpreußen, Pommern, Ostbrandenburg und Niederschlesien, 1930–1945

Ost-Dok. 10/888: Major der Reserve Kurt Dieckert: Einsatz der 1. Ostpreußischen Infanteriedivision (1956)

Ost-Dok. 10/889: Major der Reserve Kurt Dieckert: Einsatz von weiteren Einheiten des Heeres, der Waffen SS, der Marine und Luftwaffe (1956)

Ost-Dok. 10/890: Major der Reserve Kurt Dieckert: Die Einschließung und Belagerung von Königsberg (1956)

Bundesarchiv – Berlin Lichtefelde (BArch)

NS 1: Reichssschatzmeister der NSDAP
NS 1/544: SD Berichte, 1944

NS 6: Partei-Kanzlei

NS 6/ 135: Meldungen, Erfahrungs– und Stimmungsberichte über die Haltung der Wehrmacht und der Bevölkerung angesichts der Verschlechterung der Kriegslage

NS 6/ 348: Bd. 39: Rundschreiben, Anordnungen, Verfügungen, Bekanntgaben des Stellvertreters des Führers bzw. der Partei-Kanzlei

NS 6/ 354: Befehlsführung bei abgeschnittenen Truppenteilen und Bestimmungen über Festungen, Verteidigungsbereiche usw

NS 19: Persönlicher Stab Reichsführer-SS

NS 19/813: SA-Sturmführer Herbert Nerger, Panzer-Grenadier

NS 19/2068: 'Meldungen aus dem Ostraum'

NS 19/2606: Berichterstattungen über Auflösungserscheinungen an der deutschen Ostfront

NS 19/2721: Befehle der Heeresgruppe Weichsel, insbes. zur Stärkung des Kampfgeistes

NS 19/3118: Verhalten von Offizieren und Männern, sowie speziell von Festungs– und Kampfkommandanten in aussichtsloser Lage

NS 19/3814: Bevorratung und ARLZ-Maßnahmen auf zivilem Sektor im Bereich der Ostfestungen

R 55: Reichsministerium für Volksaufklärung und Propaganda

R 55/317: Deutsche Ostmesse Königsberg, 1936–1941

R 55/464: Bd. 2: Berichte der Reichspropagandaämter Linz, Königsberg, Salzburg, 1941–1942

R 55/602: Bd. 21: Einzelne Propagandaaktionen, 1942–1945

R 55/608: Propagandaparolen. Anfragen einzelner RPÄ über ihre Behandlung, 1942–1945

R 55/616: Umquartierung der Zivilbevölkerung aus feindbedrohten Gebieten, 1944–1945

R 58: Reichssicherheitshauptamt

R 58/976: Sicherheitspolizei und SD Sonderkommando 7b, Dezember 1944

R 59: Volksdeutsche Mittelstelle

R 59/65: Organisation und Geschäftsbetrieb, Ansiedlung und Einsatz von Rußlanddeutschen, Truppenbetreuung, 1943–1945

Bundesarchiv – Mitlitärarchiv, Freiburg (BArch)

RH 2: Oberkommando des Heeres / Generalstab des Heeres

RH 2/316: Bd. 2/1 – 1. – 30. Nov. 1944

RH 2/317: Bd. 2/2 – 1. – 31. Dez. 1944
RH 2/328: Bd. 1/2 – 11. Jan. – 7. März 1945
RH 2/331a: Bd. 2/3 – 1. – 31. Jan. 1945
RH 2/331b: Bd. 2/3 – 1. – 31. Jan. 1945
RH 2/332: Bd. 2/4 – 1. – 28. Feb. 1945
RH 2/333: Bd. 2/5 – 1. – 26. März 1945
RH 2/334: Bd. 2/6 – 25. – 31. März 1945
RH 2/335: Bd. 2/7 – 1. – 8. Apr. 1945
RH 2/2026: Armee-Abt. Samland und Festung Königsberg 1. März – 9.
  Apr. 1945

RH 10: OKH / Generalinspekteur der Panzertruppen
RH 10/144: Gliederung, Zustand (materielle und personelle Lage) und
  dgl. der Panzerdivisionen. – 5. Pz. Div.

RH 12–20: Inspektion der Festungen des Heeres (In Fest)
RH 12–20/46: Ausbau und Armierung der Oststellungen
RH 12–20/50: Geschütze und Munition für Festungsbereich Ost, Dez.
  1944–Apr. 1945

RH 24: Korps
RH 24–9/137: Kriegstagebuch Nr. 13 des IX. AK Ia Anlage II, Teil 3
  (Nov.) 1944
RH 24–9/138: Kriegstagebuch Nr. 13 des IX. AK Ia Anlage II, Teil 4
  (Dez.) 1944
RH 24–9/212: Korpstagesbefehle, 6. Sept.–31. Dez. 1944
RH 24–9/291: Kriegstagebuch Nr. 11 1. Sept.–31. Dez. 1944
RH 24–9/293: Verschiedene Quartiermeisterangelegenheiten, 1. Sept.–
  30. Dez. 1944
RH 24–9/294: Tätigkeitsberichte der Abteilungen, 1944
RH 24–28/106: Tagesbefehl des Gen. d. Inf. Gollnick, 1. März 1945

RH 26: Infanteriedivisionen
RH 26–1/100: KTB der I.ID, 1939–1945
RH 26–1/112: 1. Inf. Div. Kampf um Ostpreußen und um Königsberg
RH 26–561/1: 561. Infanterie Grenadier Division

RH 53–1: Wehrkreiskommando I
RH 53–1/27: Wehrkreisarzt I Bericht!

RW 4: Oberkommando der Wehrmacht / Wehrmachtführungsstab
RW 4/702: Vorbereitungen für die Verteidigung des Reiches
RW 4/704: Vorbereitungen der Verteidigungsfähigkeit der Ostfestungen

RW 4/705: Operationen im östlichen Reichsgebiet
RW 4/710: Versorgung im allgemeinen, Versorgung und Bevorratung von Festungen

RW 62: Nationalsozialistischer Führungsstab des OKW
RW/62–1: 'Der politische Soldat', 1944–1945

PERS 6: Personalakten ranghoher Offiziere
PERS 6/251: Heeres-Personalamt. Personalakten für Lasch, Otto
PERS 6/300107: Lasch, Bernhard Otto
PERS 6/282148: Personalakten Frhr. von Süskind-Schwendi, Hugo

Militärgeschichtliche Sammlung (MSg 2)
MSg 2 /240: Militärische Berichte über den Kampf in Ostpreußen 1944–1945

Gosudarstvennyi Arkhiv Kaliningradskoi Oblasti, Kaliningrad (GAKO)

Nemetski Fondi
F.21, 1942–1944 gg., Die Deutsche Arbeitsfront. Gau Ostpreußen
F.54, 1922–1945 gg., Polizeipräsidium Königsberg

Institut für Zeitgeschichte, Munich (IfZArch)

Zeugenschrifttum
ZS/A-2/ 02–96: Bericht von Herrn Dr. Gerhardt
ZS/A-2/ 04–140: Gerhardt Kretschmer, Nuernberg-Zabo, d. 11.4.49
ZS/A-2/ 04–34: Bruno Kerwin, Herford/ Westfalen, Bruchstrasse 6, den 9. April 1949

Akten der Partei-Kanzlei der NSDAP
10700993: Führerhauptquartier, den 1. März 1945 Bo/Lch. Herrn Reichsführer-SS Himmler Betrifft: Beobachtungen im Heimatkriegsgebiet
10700994: Geheime Kommandosache, Abschrift von SSD-Fernschreiben Chef des Genstb. Ob. West/ NSFO Nr. 75/45 g. Kdos. von 28.II.45 an Chef OKW
13201458: Komm.Leiter Pro Ref. MR. Imhoff. Dem Herrn Staatssekretär. Berlin, den 21. Februar 1945. Betr.: Lage der Evakuierung
13201916: Entwurf für ein gemeinsames Rundschreiben des Leiters der Partei-Kanzlei und des Chefs des Oberkommandos der Wehrmacht, 21 March 1945

13202379: Beleg Nr. 5, 10. Febr. 1945 An die Partei-Kanzlei z. Hd. Herrn Reichsleiter M. Bormann. gez. Eggeling Gauleiter

Nationalsozialistische Deutsche Arbeiterpartei (NSDAP), Hauptarchiv

MA 736: NSDAP Hauptarchiv Gau Ostpreussen, Königsberg Pr., den 2 Dezember 1944. Aufstellung A. Ostwallbau (K. Aktion)

MA 736: NSDAP Hauptarchiv Gau Ostpreussen: Semesterbericht der Studentenführung Ostpreußen für die Monate Juli, August und September

MA 757: Persönlicher Stab Reichsführer-SS, Schriftverwaltung Akt.Nr. Geh./ 353. H.Qu., den 23. Februar 1945. Oberkommando der Heeresgruppe Weichsel, Via/ NSF: Richtlinien für die Arbeit des NSFO

The National Archives, Kew (TNA)

HW 1: Government Code and Cypher School

HW 1/2992: West Europe, 21 June 1944

HW 1/3301A: West Europe, 31 October 1944

HW 1/3341: Germany: Morale of Armies in East Prussia, 22 November 1944

HW 1/3479: Western Europe, 25 January 1945

HW 1/3495: BONIFACE report, 30 January 1945

HW 1/3510: BONIFACE report, 6 February 1945

HH 1/3520: Mr Bromley BONIFACE summaries, 13 February 1945

HW 1/3523: Boniface report, 15 February 1945

FO 371: Foreign Office, Political Departments, General Correspondence from 1906–1966

FO 371/ 46859: Press reports and articles on the situation in Germany and in Russian-occupied zone

Imperial War Museum, London (IWM)

IWM Sound Archive, Catalogue No. 12287, Sigrun Johanna Wilhelmiene Strooband, Reel 2

Ostpreußisches Landesmuseum, Lüneburg (OL)

Kleine Werke

OL XC Königs3 c Mat: Hermann Matzkowski: Bericht über die Vorkommnisse und Zustände in Königsberg/Pr. seit der Einnahme durch die Sowjettruppen im April 1945 (2 May 1946)

IV M 4 DIE, 4: Erich Diester, Zur Tagung der Kulturwarte am 6. u. 7. März 1965 in München: Verjagt – beraubt – geschändet – erschlagen!

Yad Vashem Archives, Jerusalem

O.33: Testimonies, Diaries and Memoirs Collection
O.33/8569: Memoirs of Sheva (Levi) Kopolovitz

Photo Archives
1603/2: Riga, Latvia. A festive parade of German soldiers on the anniversary of the city's occupation

Newspapers

The Argus (1945)
Berliner Morgenpost (1945)
Front und Heimat, Soldatenzeitung d. Gaues Schwaben (1944)
Jewish Telegraph Agency (1929)
Königsberger Allgemeine Zeitung (1945)
Krasnaya Zvezda (1944–1945)
Pravda (1945)
Preußische Zeitung (1945)
Das Schwarze Korps (1941)
Soldat im Ordensland Preußen (1941–1942)
Soviet War News (1944–1945)
The Times (1932, 1941, 1945)
Völkischer Beobachter (1944–1945)

Published Primary Sources

Absolon, Rudolf (ed.), *Das Wehrmachtstrafrecht im 2. Weltkrieg – Sammlung der grundlegenden Gesetze, Verordnungen und Erlasse* (Kornelimünster: Bundesarchiv, Abt. Zentralnachweisstelle, 1958).

Beckherrn, Eberhard and Alexei Dubatov, *Die Königsberg Papiere, Schicksal einer deutschen Stadt, Neue Dokumente aus russischen Archiven* (Munich: Langen Mueller, 1994).

Boberach, Heinz (ed.), *Meldungen aus dem Reich: Die geheimen Lageberichte des Sicherheitsdienstes der SS 1938–1945, Band 7* (Herrsching: Pawlak Verlag, 1984).

Meldungen aus dem Reich: Die geheimen Lageberichte des Sicherheitsdienstes der SS 1938–1945, Band 17 (Herrsching: Pawlak Verlag, 1984).

Bytwerk, Randall (ed.), *Landmark Speeches of National Socialism* (College Station: Texas A&M University Press: 2008).

Deutschen Institut für Außenpolitische Forschung, *Europa, Handbuch der politischen, wirtschaftlichen und kulturellen Entwicklung des neuen Europa* (Leipzig: Helingsche Verlagsanstalt, 1943).

Die Deutsche Bibliothek, *Einwohnerbuch Königsberg (Pr.) 1941* (Hildesheim: Georg Olms Verlag, 1996).

Domarus, Max (ed.), *Hitler Reden und Proklamationen 1932–1945 I. Band Triumph (1932–1938)* (Neusstadt a.d. Aisch: Verlagsdruckerei Schmidt, 1962).

Hitler: Reden und Proklamationen, 1932–1945. II. Band: Untergang (1939–1945) (Neusstadt a.d. Aisch: Verlagsdruckerei Schmidt, 1963).

Foertsch, Hermann, *Der Offizier der deutschen Wehrmacht: Eine Pflichtenlehre* (Berlin: Verlag E. Eisenschmidt, 1942).

Heiber, Helmut and David Glantz (eds.), *Hitler and His Generals, Military Conferences 1942–1945: the First Complete Stenographic Record of the Military Situation Conferences, from Stalingrad to Berlin* (London: Greenhill, 2002).

Hensel, Joachim (ed.), *Medizin in und aus Ostpreußen, Nachdrucke aus den Rundbriefen der „Ostpreußischen Arztfamilie' 1945–1995* (Starnberg, Druckerei Josef Jägerhuber, 1996.

Hirschfeld, Gerhard and Lothar Kettenacker (eds.), *The 'Führer State': Myth and Reality, Studies on the Structure and Politics of the Third Reich* (Stuttgart: Klett-Cotta, 1981)

Hubatsch, Walther, *Hitlers Weisungen für die Kriegsführung 1939–1945* (Utting: Dörfler, 2000).

Internationaler Militär Gerichtshof Nürnberg, *Der Prozess gegen die Hauptkriegsverbrecher vor dem Internationalen Militärgerichtshof Nürnberg 14. November 1945 – 1. Oktober 1946, Band XI, Amtlicher Text in deutscher Sprache* Verhandlungsniederschriften *8. April 1946–17. April 1946* (Nürnberg: Reichenbach Verlag/ Obersten Kontrollrat, 1947).

Kuby, Erich (ed.), *Das Ende des Schreckens, Januar bis Mai 1945* (Munich: dtv, 1986).

Ludendorff, Erich, *Der Totale Krieg* (Munich: Ludendorff Verlag, 1935).

Mehner, Kurt (ed.), *Die geheimen Tagesberichte der deutschen Wehrmachtführung im Zweiten Weltkrieg 1939–1945, Band 11: 1. September–31. Dezember 1944* (Osnabrück: Biblio Verlag, 1984).

Die geheimen Tagesberichte der deutschen Wehrmachtführung im Zweiten Weltkrieg 1939–1945, Band 12: 1. Januar 1945–9. Mai 1945 (Osnabrück: Biblio Verlag, 1984).

Moll, Martin (ed.), *Führer-Erlasse 1939–1945* (Hamburg: Nikol Verlag, 2011).

Müller, Norbert (ed.), *Okkupation, Raub, Vernichtung, Dokumente zur Besatzungspolitik der faschistischen Wehrmacht auf Sowjetischem Territorium 1941 bis 1944*, (Berlin, Militärverlag der Deutschen Demokratischen Republik, 1980).

Die faschistische Okkupationspolitik in den zeitweilig besetzten Gebieten der Sowjetunion (1941–1944) (Berlin, Deutscher Verlag der Wissenschaften, 1991).

Müller, Rolf-Dieter (ed.), *Die deutsche Wirtschaftspolitik in den besetzten sowjetischen Gebieten 1941 – 1943: Der Abschlußbericht des Wirtschaftsstabes Ost und Aufzeichnungen eines Angehörigen des Wirtschaftskommandos Kiew* (Boppard am Rhein: Harald Boldt Verlag, 1991).

Noakes, Jeremy (ed.), *Nazism 1919–1945, Volume 4: The German Home Front in World War II, A Documentary Reader* (Exeter: University of Exeter Press, 1998).

Der Oberbefehlshaber des Heeres, *H.Dv. 130/2a Ausbildungsvorschrift für die Infanterie (A.V.I.) Heft 2a: Die Schützenkompanie* (Berlin: Offene Worte, 1941).

Rahm, Werner and Gerhard Schreiber (eds.), *Kriegstagebuch der Seekriegsleitung 1939–1945 Teil A, Band 59/I: 1. bis 15. Juli 1944* (Berlin: E.S. Mittler & Sohn, 1995).

Kriegstagebuch der Seekriegsleitung 1939–1945 Teil A, Band 59/II: 16. bis 31. Juli 1944 (Berlin: E.S. Mittler & Sohn, 1995).

Kriegstagebuch der Seekriegsleitung 1939–1945 Teil A, Band 60/I: 1. bis 15. August 1944 (Berlin: E.S. Mittler & Sohn, 1995).

Kriegstagebuch der Seekriegsleitung 1939–1945 Teil A, Band 65: Januar 1945 (Berlin: E.S. Mittler & Sohn, 1996).

Kriegstagebuch der Seekriegsleitung 1939–1945 Teil A, Band 67: März 1945 (Berlin: E.S. Mittler & Sohn, 1997).

Reichsgesetzblatt Teil I, Nr. 158, 2 September 1939. 'Verordnung über die Bestellung von Reichsverteidigungskommissaren', p. 1565.

Reichsgesetzblatt Teil I, Nr. 218, 4 November 1939. 'Erste Verordnung zur Ergänzung der Kriegssonderstrafrechtsverordnung', p. 2131.

Reichsgesetzblatt Teil I, Nr. 2: 11 January 1945. 'Verordnung des Führers zum Schutz der Sammlung von Kleidung und Ausrüstungsgegenständen für die Wehrmacht und den Deutschen Volkssturm', p. 5.

Reichsgesetzblatt Teil I, Nr. 3: 22 January 1945. 'Elfte Verordnung zur Durchführung und Ergänzung, Verordnung über das militärische Strafverfahren im Kriege und bei besonderem Einsatz', p. 13.

Reichsgesetzblatt Teil I, Nr. 6: 20 February 1945. 'Verordnung über die Errichtung von Standgerichte', p. 30.

Scherstjanoi, Elke (ed.), *Rotarmisten schreiben aus Deutschland: Briefe von der Front (1945) und historische Analysen* (Munich: K.G. Saur, 2004).

Schieder, Theodor (ed.), *Dokumentation der Vertreibung der Deutschen aus Ost-Mitteleuropa, Die Vertreibung der deutschen Bevölkerung aus den Gebieten östlich der Oder-Neisse, Band I* (Munich: Deutschen Taschenbuch Verlag, 1984).

Schramm, Percy, *Kriegstagebuch des OKW, Band IV: 1. Januar 1944–22. Mai 1945* (Frankfurt am Main: Bernard & Graefe, 1961).

Stirk, Samuel, *The Prussian Spirit: a Survey of German Literature and Politics 1914–1940* (London: Faber and Faber, 1941).

Trevor-Roper, Hugh, *The Bormann Letters: the Private Correspondence Between Martin Bormann and His Wife from 1943 to April 1945* (London: Weidenfeld and Nicolson, 1954).

(ed.), *Hitler's War Directives 1939–1945* (London, Sidgwick and Jackson, 1964).

United States Army Center for Military History, *Handbook on German Military Forces* (Washington, DC: US War Department, 1945).

Wagner, Gerhard (ed.), *Lagevorträge des Oberbefehlshabers der Kriegsmarine vor Hitler 1939–1945* (Munich: J.F. Lehmanns, 1972).

Wehrkreiskommando I, *Schlachtfelder in Ostpreußen* (Königsberg, Königsberger Allgemeine Zeitung Volz & Co., 1932).

Diaries and Memoirs

Alexander, Christine and Mason Kunze (eds.), *Eastern Inferno: the Journals of a German Panzerjäger on the Eastern Front, 1941–1943* (Philadelphia, PA: Casemate, 2010).

Bagramyan, Ivan, *Tak shli my k pobede* [Thus We Achieved Victory] (Moscow: Voenizdat, 1977).

'The Storming of Königsberg', in Erickson (ed.), *Main Front*, pp. 221–44.

Baltuttis, Günter, *Auf verlorenem Posten* (Würzburg: Verlagshaus Würzburg, 2006).

Belobodorov, Afanasii, *Vsegda v boju* [Always in the Fray] (Moscow: Voenizdat, 1978).

Bjelfvenstam, Dorothea, *Man nannte uns Hitlermädchen: Kinderlandverschickung von Königsberg nach Sachsen* (Föritz: Amicus-Verlag, 2012).

Blankenhorn, Fritz, *... und fahr'n wir ohne Wiederkehr. Von Ostpreußen nach Siberien 1944–1949* (Hamburg: Rowohlt Taschenbuch Verlag, 2006).

Boiko, Vasili, *S dumoj o Rodine* [With a Thought of the Motherland] (Moscow: Voenizdat, 1982).

Boree, Karl-Friedrich, *Ein Abschied* (Wiesbaden: Verlag der Greif, 1951).

Bragin, Mikhail, *Ot Moskvy do Berlina: Stat'i i ocherki voyennogo korrespondenta* [From Moscow to Berlin: Articles and Essays of a War Correspondent] (Moscow, Politizdat, 1947).

Braun, Magnus von, *Weg durch vier Zeitepochen: Vom ostpreußischen Gutsleben der Väter bis zur Weltraumforschung des Sohnes* (Limburg a.d. Lahn: C. A. Starke Verlag, 1965).

Braunschweig, Günter, 'Untergangstage in Königsberg', *Jahrbuch der Albertus-Universität zu Königsberg, Pr.* (3) 1953, pp. 182–220.

Brooke, Alan, Alex Danchev, and Daniel Todman (eds.), *War Diaries 1939–1945: Field Marshal Lord Alanbrooke* (London: Weidenfeld & Nicolson, 2001).

Cheeseman, Ursula, *Unter der Zeitbrücke: Aufzeichnungen einer Ostpreußin* (Germany: Books on Demand, 2000).

Deichelmann, Hans, *Ich sah Königsberg sterben* (Schnellbach: Verlag S. Bublies, 2000).

Dönitz, Karl, *Zehn Jahre und Zwanzig Tage* (Bonn: Athenäum-Verlag, 1958).

Fröhlich, Elke (ed.), *Die Tagebücher von Joseph Goebbels, Teil II Diktate 1941–1945, Band 14: Oktober bis Dezember 1944* (Munich: K. G. Saur, 1996).

Die Tagebücher von Joseph Goebbels, Teil I Aufzeichnungen 1923–1941, Band 4: März – November 1937 (Munich: K. G. Saur, 2000).

Galitsky, Kuzma, *V boyakh za Vostochnuyu Prussiyu: Zapiski komanduyushchego 11-y gvardeyskoy armiyey* [In the Battles for East Prussia: Notes of the Commander of the 11th Guards Army] (Moscow: Naika, 1970).

Gerhardi, Helga, *Helga: the True Story of a Young Woman's Flight As a Refugee and How She Re-united Her War-Scattered Family* (Aylesbury: Virona Publishing, 1994).

Goebbels, Joseph, *Tagebücher 1945: Die letzten Aufzeichnungen* (Hamburg: Hoffmann und Campe, 1977).

Guderian, Heinz, *Panzer Leader* (London: Penguin, 2009).

Halder, Franz, *War Journal of Franz Halder* (Fort Leavensworth, KS: Archives Section, 1950).

Hoßbach, Friedrich, *Die Schlacht um Ostpreußen: Aus den Kämpfen der deutschen 4. Armee um Ostpreussen in der Zeit vom 19.7.1944 – 30. 1.1945*(Überlingen: Otto Dikreiter Verlag, 1951).

Just, Bruno, Wolfgang Rothe, and Horst Rehagen (eds.), *Hitler's Last Levy in East Prussia: Volkssturm Einsatz Bataillon Goldap (25/235)* (Solihull: Helion, 2015).

Kalusche, Elfriede (ed.), *Unter dem Sowjetstern: Erlebnisse eine Königsbergerin in Nordostpreußen 1945–1947* (Munich: Schild Verlag, 1981).

Keitel, Wilhelm and Walter Gorlitz (eds.), *The Memoirs of Field Marshal Keitel* (London: William Kimber, 1965).

Khlebnikov, Nikolai, *Pod grohot soten batarej* [Under the Thunder of Hundred Batteries] (Moscow: Voenizdat, 1974).

Kleine, Bodo, *Bevor die Erinnerung verblaßt, Infanterist an der Ostfront: zwischen Woronesch und Königsberg – Kriegsgefangenschaft in Rußland 1942/1948* (Aachen: Helios, 2004).

Kopolev, Lev, *No Jail for Thought* (London: Secker & Warburg, 1977).

Krockow, Christian von, *Die Stunde der Frauen: Bericht aus Pommern 1944 bis 1947* (Munich: dtv, 2001).

Lasch, Otto, *So fiel Königsberg: Kampf und Untergang von Ostpreußens Hauptstadt* (Munich: Gräfe und Unzer Verlag, 1958).

Zuckerbrot und Peitsche: Ein Bericht aus russischer Kriegsgefangenschaft – 20 Jahre danach (Ilm: Ilmgau Verlag, 1965).

Lehndorff, Hans von, *Ostpreußisches Tagebuch: Aufzeichnungen eines Arztes aus den Jahren 1945–1947* (Munich: dtv, 1961).

East Prussian Diary: a Journal of Faith 1945–1947 (London: Oswald Wolff, 1963).

Linck, Hugo, *Königsberg 1945–1948* (Leer: Verlag Rautenberg & Moeckel, 1952).

Marinov, Alexander, *Komsomol v soldatskoj shineli* [Komsomol in a Soldier's Overcoat] (Moscow, Voenizdat, 1988).

Oppel, Christian von and Hartmut Mathieu (eds.), *Im Rücken des Feindes: Erinnerungen von Edgar Burger 1925–1945* (Norderstedt: Books on Demand, 2004).

Padover, Saul, *Lügendetektor: Vernehmungen im besiegten Deutschland 1944/45* (Frankfurt a.M.: Eichborn Verlag, 1999).

Petershagen, Rudolf, *Gewissen in Aufruhr* (Berlin: Verlag der Nation, 1957).

Raus, Erhard and Steven Newton, *Panzer Operations* (London: Da Capo Press, 2003).

Reese, Willy, *Mir selber seltsam fremd: die Unmenschlichkeit des Krieges, Russland 1941–44* (Berlin: List Taschenbuch, 2004).

Rendulic, Lothar, *Gekämpft, gesiegt, geschlagen* (Wels-Heidelberg: Welsermühl, 1952).

Ronge, Paul, *Im Namen der Gerechtigkeit, Erinnerungen eines Strafverteidigers* (Munich, Mindler Verlag, 1963).

Sajer, Guy, *The Forgotten Soldier* (London: Sphere Books, 1977).

Simat, Heinz, *Blutiger Abschied, Tatsachenbericht über die verzweifelten Abwehrkämpfe der 349. Volksgrenadier-Division in Ostpreußen von Januar bis April 1945* (Stade: Self-Published, 1986).

Speer, Albert, *Erinnerungen* (Berlin: Propyläen Verlag, 1969).

Springenschmid, Karl, *Raus aus Königsberg! Wie 420 ostpreußische Jungen 1945 aus Kampf und Einsatz gerettet wurden* (Kiel: Arndt, 1993).

Starlinger, Wilhelm, *Grenzen der Sowjetmacht* (Würzburg, Holzner-Verlag, 1955).

Sumowski, Hans-Burkhard, *'Jetzt war ich ganz allein auf die Welt', Erinnerungen an eine Kindheit in Königsberg 1944–1947* (Munich: btb-Verlag, 2009).

Süßkind-Schwendi, Hugo Freiherr von, 'Aus meinem Soldatenleben – Teil V', *Deutsches Soldatenjahrbuch* (41) 1993, pp. 347–52.

'Kurze Ruckschau auf die militärischen Ereignisse in Königsberg (Pr.)', in Kalusche (ed.), *Unter dem Sowjetstern*, pp. 221–27.

Terpitz, Werner, *Wege aus dem Osten. Flucht und Vertreibung einer ostpreußischen Pfarrersfamilie* (Munich: Oldenbourg Wissenschaftsverlag, 1997).

Vasilevsky, Alexander, *Delo vsej zhizni* [The Matter of My Whole Life] (Moscow: Politizdat, 1978).

Warlimont, Walter, *Im Hauptquartier der deutschen Wehrmacht 1939 bis 1945* (Koblenz: Weltbild Verlag, 1990).

Werth, Alexander, *Russia at War 1941–1945* (London: Barrie and Rockliff, 1964).

Wieck, Michael, *Königsberg, Zeugnis vom Untergang einer Stadt* (Augsburg: Bechtermünz Verlag, 1998).

Secondary Sources

Absolon, Rudolf, *Die Wehrmacht im Dritten Reich, Bd. 6. 19. Dezember 1941 bis 9. Mai 1945* (Boppard am Rhein: Harald Boldt Verlag, 1995).

Addison, Paul and Angus Calder (eds.), *Time to Kill: the Soldier's Experience of War in the West, 1939–1945* (London: Pimlico, 1997).

Addison, Paul and Jeremy Crang (eds.), *Firestorm: the Bombing of Dresden 1945* (London: Pimlico, 2006).

Ahonen, Pertti, 'Domestic Constraints on West German Ostpolitik: the Role of the Expellee Organizations in the Adenauer Era', *Central European History* (31) 1998, pp. 31–63.

Albinus, Robert, *Lexicon der Stadt Königsberg Pr. und Umgebung* (Leer: Verlag Gerhardt Rautenberg, 1985).

Aly, Götz, *Hitlers Volksstaat: Raub, Rassenkrieg und nationaler Sozialismus* (Bonn: Bundeszentrale für politische Bildung, 2014).

Angrick, Andrej and Peter Klein, *The 'Final Solution' in Riga: Exploration and Annihilation, 1941–1944* (Oxford: Berghahn Books, 2012).

Applegate, Celia, *A Nation of Provincials: the German Idea of Heimat* (Berkeley: University of California Press, 1990).

Arendes, Cord, Edgar Wolfrun, and Jörg Zedler (eds.), *Terror nach Innen: Verbrechen am Ende des Zweiten Weltkrieges* (Göttingen: Wallstein Verlag, 2006).

Ashworth, Gregory, *War and the City* (London: Routledge, 1991).

Author Collective, *Sovetskiye Voyenno-vozdushnyye sily v Velikoy Otechestvennoy voyne 1941–1945 gg* [The Soviet Air Force in the Great Patriotic War of 1941–1945] (Moscow: Voenizdat, 1968).

Baird, Jay, *To Die for Germany: Heroes in the Nazi Pantheon* (Bloomington: Indiana University Press, 1990).

Balfour, Michael, *Propaganda in War 1939–1945: Organisations, Policies and Publics in Britain and Germany* (London: Routledge & Kegan Paul, 1979).

Bankier, David, *The Germans and the Final Solution: Public Opinion under Nazism* (Oxford: Blackwell, 1992).

Barber, John and Mark Harrison, *The Soviet Home Front: a Social and Economic History of the USSR in World War II* (London: Longman, 1991).

Barnouw, Dagmar, *Germany 1945: Views of War and Violence* (Bloomington: Indiana University Press, 1996).

Bartov, Omer, *The Eastern Front 1941–45: German Troops and the Barbarisation of Warfare* (London: Macmillan / St Antony's College Oxford, 1985).

'The Missing Years: German Workers, German Soldiers', *German History* (8) 1990, pp. 46–65.

Hitler's Army: Soldiers, Nazis, and War in the Third Reich (Oxford: Oxford University Press, 1992).

'The Conduct of War: Soldiers and the Barbarization of Warfare', *The Journal of Modern History* (64) 1992, pp. 32–45.

'Trauma and Absence: France and Germany, 1914–1945', in Addison and Calder (eds.), *Time to Kill*, pp. 347–58.

Bartov, Omer and Eric Weitz (eds.), *Shatterzones of Empire: Coexistence and Violence in the German, Habsburg, Russian, and Ottoman Borderlands* (Bloomington: Indiana University Press, 2013).

Baumann, Ulrich and Magnus Koch, *'Was damals Recht war ... ' Soldaten und Zivilisten vor Gerichten der Wehrmacht* (Berlin: Be.Bra verlag, 2008).

Baumer, Robert, *Aachen: the U.S. Army's Battle for Charlemagne's City in World War II* (Mechanicsburg, PA: Stackpole Books, 2015).

Beer, Mathias, 'Im Spannungsfeld von Politik und Zeitgeschichte. Das Großforschungsprojekt ‚Dokumentation der Vertreibung der Deutschen aus Ost-Mitteleuropa", *VfZ* (46) 1998, pp. 345–90.

Beevor, Antony, *The Fall of Berlin* (Penguin: New York, 2002).

Beorn, Waitman, *Marching into Darkness: the Wehrmacht and the Holocaust in Belarus* (Cambridge, MA., Harvard University Press, 2014).

Bessel, Richard, *Political Violence and the Rise of Nazism: the Storm Troopers in Eastern Germany 1925–1934* (New Haven, CT: Yale University Press, 1984).

Nazism and War (Modern Library: New York, 2006).

Germany 1945, From War to Peace (New York: Pocket Books, 2010).

'Eine "Volksgemeinschaft" der Gewalt', in Schmiechen-Ackermann (ed.), *'Volksgemeinschaft'*, pp. 357–60.

'The War to End All Wars: the Shock of Violence in 1945 and Its Aftermath in Germany', in Lüdtke and Weisbrod (eds.), *No Man's Land of Violence*, pp. 71–99.

Besson, Waldemar, 'Zur Geschichte des nationalsozialistischen Führungsoffiziers (NSFO)', *VfZ* (9) 1961, pp. 76–116.

Biddiscombe Perry, *Werwolf!: the History of the National Socialist Guerilla Movement, 1944–1946* (Toronto: University of Toronto Press, 1998).

"Freies Deutschland' Guerrilla Warfare in East Prussia, 1944–1945: a Contribution to the History of the German Resistance' *German Studies Association* (27) 2004, pp. 45–62.

Biess, Frank, Mark Roseman, and Hanna Schissler (eds.), *Conflict, Catastrophe and Continuity: Essays on Modern German History* (Oxford: Berghahn Books, 2007).

Billig, Michael, *Banal Nationalism* (London: Sage, 1995).

Blatman, Daniel, *The Death Marches, the Final Phase of Nazi Genocide* (London: Belknap Press of Harvard University Press, 2011).

Borkowski, Helmut, *Die Kämpfe um Ostpreußen und das Samland 1944–1945* (Lengerich: Self-published, 1994).

Bradley, Dermot, Markus Rövekamp, and Ernes Henriot, *Deutschlands Generale und Admirale: Teil IV/ Band 7: Die Generale des Heeres 1921–1945. Knabe – Luz* (Osnabrück: Biblio-Verlag, 2004).

Brighton, Terry, *Masters of Battle: Monty, Patton and Rommel at War* (London: Penguin, 2009).

Broszat, Martin, *The Hitler State: the Foundation and Development of the Internal Structure of the Third Reich* (London: Longman, 1981).

Broszat, Martin, Klaus-Dietmar Henke, and Hans Woller (eds.), *Von Stalingrad zur Währungsreform: Zur Sozialgeschichte des Umbruchs in Deutschland* (Munich: R. Oldenbourg Verlag, 1988).

Browning, Christopher, *Ordinary Men: Reserve Battalion 101 and the Final Solution in Poland* (London: Penguin, 1998).

'The Holocaust: Basis and Objective of the Volksgemeinschaft?', in Steber and Gotto (eds.), *Visions of Community in Nazi Germany*, pp. 217–25.

Burleigh, Michael, *The Third Reich: A New History* (London: MacMillan, 2000).

Germany Turns Eastwards: a Study of Ostforschung in the Third Reich (London: Pan, 2001).

Buruma, Ian, *Year Zero: a History of 1945* (London: Atlantic Books, 2013).

Chickering, Roger and Stig Förster (eds.), *Great War, Total War* (Cambridge: Cambridge University Press, 2000).

'Are We There Yet? World War II and the Theory of Total War', in Chickering, Förster, and Greiner (eds.), *A World at Total War*, pp. 1–16.

Chickering Roger, Stig Förster, and Bernd Greiner (eds.) *A World at Total War: Global Conflict and the Politics of Destruction, 1937–1945* (Cambridge: Cambridge University Press, 2005).

Christoffel, Edgar, *Krieg am Westwall 1944/45, Das Grenzland im Westen zwischen Aachen und Saarbrücken in den letzten Kriegsmonaten* (Trier: Verlag der Akademischen Buchhandlung Interbook, 1989).

Citino, Robert, *The German Way of War: From the Thirty Years' War to the Third Reich* (Lawrence: University Press of Kansas, 2005).

Clappier, Louis, *Festung Königsberg* (Cologne: Kiepenheuer & Witsch, 1952).

Clarck, Christopher, *Iron Kingdom: the Rise and Downfall of Prussia 1600–1947* (London: Penguin, 2007).

Clausewitz, Carl von, *On War* (Princeton, NJ: Princeton University Press, 1976).

Clough, Patricia, *In Langer Reihe über das Haff: Die Flucht der Trakehner aus Ostpreußen* (Munich: Deutsche Verlags-Anstalt, 2005).

Cocks, Geoffrey, *Psychotherapy in the Third Reich: the Göring Institute* (New Brunswick: Transaction, 1997).

Collins, Randall, *Violence: a Micro-Sociological Theory* (Princeton, NJ: Princeton University Press, 2008).

Connelly, John, 'The Uses of Volksgemeinschaft: Letters to the NSDAP Kreisleitung Eisenach, 1939–1940', in Fitzpatrick and Gellately (eds.), *Accusatory Practices*, pp. 153–84.

Craig, Gordon, *The Politics of the Prussian Army 1640–1945* (London: Oxford University Press, 1964).

Crefeld, Martin van, *Command in War* (Cambridge, MA: Harvard University Press, 1985).

The Culture of War (New York: Spellmount, 2009).

Dallin, Alexander, *German Rule in Russia 1941–1945: a Study of Occupation Policies* (London: Macmillan, 1981).

Davies, Norman and Roger Moorhouse, *Microcosm: a Portrait of a Central European City* (London: Pimlico, 2003).

Dennis, Peter and Jeffrey Grey (eds.), *Victory or Defeat: Armies in the Aftermath of Conflict* (Canberra: Big Sky Publishing, 2010).

Denny, Isabel, *The Fall of Hitler's Fortress City: the Battle for Königsberg 1945* (London: Greenhill Books, 2007).

Deist, Wilhelm, 'Die Aufrüstung der Wehrmacht', in Militargeschichtlichen Forschunsamt (ed.), *Das Deutsche Reich und der Zweite Weltkrieg, Band 1*, pp. 371–532.

Deist, Wilhelm (ed.), *Das Deutsche Reich und der Zweite Weltkrieg, Band 1: Ursache und Voraussetzungen der deutschen Kriegspolitik* (Stuttgart: Deutsche Verlags-Anstalt, 1979).

Dieckert, Kurt and Horst Großman, *Der Kampf um Ostpreussen. Der umfassende Dokumentarbericht* (Stuttgart: Motorbuch Verlag, 1998).

Dietrich, Donald, 'National Renewal, Anti-Semitism, and Political Continuity: a Psychological Assessment', *Political Psychology* (9) 1988, pp. 385–411.

DiNardo, R. L. and Austin Bay, 'Horse-Drawn Transport in the German Army', *Journal of Contemporary History* (23) 1988, pp. 129–42.

Doob, Leonard, 'Goebbels' Principles of Propaganda', *The Public Opinion Quarterly* (14) 1950, pp. 419–42.

Dröll, Hajo, 'Die Zusammenbruchskrise des faschistischen Systems in Deutschland', in Niethammer, Borsdorf, and Brandt (eds.), *Arbeiterinitiative 1945*, pp. 130–74.

Drywa, Danuta, *The Extermination of Jews in Stutthof Concentration Camp* (Gdańsk: Stutthof Museum in Sztutowo, 2004).

Duffy, Christopher, *Red Storm on the Reich: the Soviet March on Germany, 1945* (New York: Da Capo Press, 1991).

Dumas, Alexandre, *Twenty Years After* (Oxford: Oxford University Press, 2008).

Echternkamp, Jörg, *Soldaten im Nachkrieg: Historische Deutungskonflikte und west-deutsche Demokratisierung 1945–1955* (Munich: Oldenbourg, 2014).

Echternkamp, Jörg (ed.), *Das Deutsche Reich und der Zweite Weltkrieg 9/2: Die Deutsche Kriegsgesellschaft 1939 bis 1945* (Munich: Deutsche Verlagsanstalt, 2005).

Ehrhardt, Traugott, *Die Geschichte der Festung Königsberg/Pr. 1257–1945* (Würzburg: Holzner Verlag, 1960).

Erickson, John, *The Road to Berlin* (London: Cassell, 2008).

Evans, Richard, *Rituals of Retribution: Capital Punishment in Germany 1600–1987* (Oxford: Oxford University Press, 1996).

The Third Reich in Power, 1933–1939: How the Nazis Won Over the Hearts and Minds of a Nation (London: Penguin, 2006).

The Third Reich at War, How the Nazis Led Germany from Conquest to Disaster (London: Penguin, 2009).

Fahlbusch Michael and Ingo Haar (eds.), *German Scholars and Ethnic Cleansing, 1919–1945* (Oxford: Berghahn Books, 2007).

Fait, Barbara, 'Die Kreisleiter der NSDAP – nach 1945', in Broszat, Henke, and Woller (eds.), *Von Stalingrad zur Währungsreform*, pp. 213–300.

Ferguson, Niall, 'Prisoner Taking and Prisoner Killing in the Age of Total War: Towards a Political Economy of Military Defeat', *War In History* (11) 2004, pp. 148–92.

Fisch, Bernhard, *Nemmersdorf, Oktober 1944: Was in Ostpreußen tatsächlich geschah* (Berlin: edition ost, 1997).

'Nemmersdorf 1944: ein bisher unbekanntes zeitnahes Zeugnis', *Zeitschrift für Ostmitteleuropa-Forschung* (56) 2007, pp. 105–14.

Fisher, Conan and Alan Sharp (eds.), *After the Versailles Treaty: Enforcement, Compliance, Contested Identities* (London: Routledge, 2008).

Fitzpatrick, Sheila and Robert Gellately (eds.), *Accusatory Practices: Denunciation in Modern European History, 1789–1989* (Chicago: University of Chicago Press, 1997).

Fleming, Peter, *Invasion 1940: an Account of the German Preparations and the British Counter-measures* (London: Rupert Hart-Davis, 1957).

Foerster, Roland (ed.), *Seelower Höhen 1945* (Hamburg: Verlag E.S. Mittler & Sohn, 1998).

Förster, Gerhard and Richard Lakowski, *1945: Das Jahr der endgultigen Niederlage der faschistischen Wehrmacht* (Berlin: Deutscher Militärverlag, 1985).

Förster, Jürgen, 'Ludendorff and Hitler in Perspective: the Battle for the German Soldier's Mind, 1917–1944', *War In History* (10) 2003, pp. 321–34.

Die Wehrmacht im NS-Staat: Eine Strukturgeschichtliche Analyse (Munich: R. Oldenbourg Verlag, 2007).

'Motivation and Indoctrination in the Wehrmacht, 1933–45', in Addison and Calder, *Time to Kill*, pp. 263–73.

'Die Niederlage der Wehrmacht: Das Ende des "Dritten Reiches"', in Foerster (ed.), *Seelower Höhen 1945*, pp. 1–14.

'From "Blitzkrieg" to "Total War", Germany's War in Europe', in Chickering, Förster, and Greiner (eds.), *A World at Total War*, pp. 89–107.

Fotion, Nicholas, *War and Ethics: a New Just War Theory* (London: Continuum, 2007).

Fox, Aimeé, *Learning to Fight: Military Innovation and Change in the British Army, 1914–1918* (Cambridge: Cambridge University Press, 2018).

Fricke, Gert, *'Fester Platz' Tarnopol 1944* (Freiburg: Verlag Rombach, 1986).

Friedlander, Saul, *The Years of Extermination: Nazi Germany and the Jews 1939–1945* (London: Weidenfeld & Nicolson, 2007).

Frieser, Karl-Heinz, 'Die Rückzugsoperationen der Heeresgruppe Süd in der Ukraine', in Frieser (ed.), *Das Deutsche Reich und der Zweiten Weltkrieg 8*, pp. 339–450.

'Irrtümer und Illusionen: Die Fehleinschätzungen der deutschen Führung', in Frieser (ed.), *Das Deutsche Reich und der Zweiten Weltkrieg 8*, pp. 493–525.

'Der Zusammenbruch der Heeresgruppe Mitte', in Frieser (ed.), *Das Deutsche Reich und der Zweiten Weltkrieg 8*, pp. 526–603.

'Die Rückzugskämpfe der Heeresgruppe Nord bis Kurland', in Frieser (ed.), *Das Deutsche Reich und der Zweiten Weltkrieg 8*, pp. 623–78.

Frieser, Karl-Heinz (ed.), *Das Deutsche Reich und der Zweiten Weltkrieg 8: Die Ostfront 1943/44. Der Krieg im Osten und an den Nebenfronten* (Munich: Deutsche Verlags-Anstalt, 2007).

Fritz, Stephen, *Frontsoldaten: the German Soldier in World War II* (Lexington: The University Press of Kentucky, 1995).

Endkampf: Soldiers, Civilians, and the Death of the Third Reich (Lexington: University Press of Kentucky, 2004).

Fritzsche, Peter, *Life and Death in the Third Reich* (Cambridge, MA: The Belknap Press of Harvard University Press, 2008).

Fuhrer, Armin and Heinz Schön, *Erich Koch, Hitlers brauner Zar: Gauleiter von Ostpreussen und Reichskommissar der Ukraine* (Munich: Olzog, 2010).

Gause, Fritz, *Die Geschichte der Stadt Königsberg in Preußen, III. Band, Vom Ersten Weltkrieg bis zum Untergang Königsbergs* (Cologne: Böhlau, 1971).

Gellately, Robert and Nathan Stoltzfus, *Social Outsiders in Nazi Germany* (Princeton, NJ: Princeton University Press, 2001).

Gerlach, Christian, *Kalkulierte Morde: Die deutsche Wirtschaftsund Vernichtungspolitik in Weißrußland 1941 bis 1944* (Hamburg: Hamburger Edition, 1999).

Geyer, Michael, 'Insurrectionary Warfare: the German Debate about a *Levée en Masse* in October 1918', *The Journal of Modern History* (73) 2001, pp. 459–527.

'German Strategy in the Age of Machine Warfare, 1914–1945', in Paret (ed.), *Makers of Modern Strategy: From Machiavelli to the Nuclear Age*, pp. 527–97.

'Endkampf 1918 and 1945: German Nationalism, Annihilation, and Self-Destruction', in Lüdtke and Weisbrod (eds.), *No Man's Land of Violence*, pp. 35–68.

Geyer, Michael and Adam Tooze (eds.), *The Cambridge History of the Second World War, Volume III, Total War: Economy, Society and Culture* (Cambridge: Cambridge University Press, 2015).

Gillespie, Alexander, *A History of the Laws of War: Volume 2. The Customs and Laws of War with Regards to Civilians in Times of Conflict* (Oxford: Hart Publishing, 2011).

Glantz, David and Jonathan House, *When Titans Clashed: How the Red Army Stopped Hitler* (Edinburgh: Birlinn, 2000).

Goebel, Stefan, *The Great War and Medieval Memory: War, Remembrance and Medievalism in Britain and Germany, 1914–1940* (Cambridge: Cambridge University Press, 2007).

Goebel, Stefan and Derek Keene, 'Towards a Metropolitan History of Total War: an Introduction', in Goebel and Keene (eds.), *Cities into Battlefields*, pp. 1–46.

Goebel, Stefan and Derek Keene (eds.), *Cities into Battlefields: Metropolitan Scenarios, Experiences and Commemorations Of Total War* (Farnham: Ashgate, 2011).

Goeschel, Christian, *Suicide in Nazi Germany* (Oxford: Oxford University Press, 2015).

Goltermann, Svenja, *Die Gesellschaft der Überlebenden: Deutsche Kriegsheimkehrer und ihre Gewalterfahrungen im Zweiten Weltkrieg* (Munich: Deutsche Verlagsanstalt, 2009).

Görtemaker, Manfred, *Geschichte der Bundesrepublik Deutschland, Von der Gründung bis zur Gegenwart* (Munich: C. H. Beck, 1999).

Gottwaldt, Alfred, 'Die Deportation der Juden aus Ostpreußen 1942/43', in Neumärker and Kossert (eds.), *'Das war mal unsere Heimat . . . '*, pp. 125–35.

Grayling, A. C., *Among the Dead Cities: Was the Allied Bombing of Civilians in WWII a Necessity or a Crime?* (London: Bloomsbury, 2006).

Gregor, Niall, 'A Schicksalsgemeinschaft? Allied Bombing, Civilian Morale, and Social Dissolution in Nuremberg, 1942–1945', *The Historical Journal* (43) 2000, pp. 1051–70.

Grier, Howard, *Hitler, Dönitz and the Baltic Sea: the Third Reich's Last Hope, 1944–1945* (Annapolis, MD: Naval Institute Press, 2007).

Grosse, Walther, 'Königsberg (Pr.) als Garnisonsund Festungsstadt', *Deutsches Soldatenjahrbuch* (15) 1967, pp. 227–35.

Grossmann, Atina, *Jews, Germans, and Allies: Close Encounters in Occupied Germany* (Princeton, NJ: Princeton University Press, 2007).

Grunberger, Richard, *A Social History of the Third Reich* (London: Weidenfeld and Nicolson, 1971).

Gruner, Wolf and Jörg Osterloh (eds.), *Das 'Großdeutsche Reich' und die Juden. Nationalsozialistische Verfolgung in den 'angegliederten' Gebieten* (Frankfurt a.M.: Campus Verlag, 2010).

Haar, Ingo, 'German Ostforschung and Anti-Semitism', in Fahlbusch and Haar (eds.), *German Scholars and Ethnic Cleansing, 1919–1945*, pp. 1–27.

Hahn, Hans Henning and Eva Hahn, *Die Vertreibung im deutschen Erinnern: Legenden, Mythos, Geschichte* (Paderborn: Ferdinant Schöningh, 2010).

Hamburg Institute for Social Research, *Crimes of the German Wehrmacht: Dimensions of a War of Annihilation 1941–1944. An Outline of the Exhibition* (Hamburg: Hamburger Edition, 2004).

Hamilton, Richard, *Who Voted for Hitler?* (Princeton, NJ: Princeton University Press, 1982).

Hancock, Eleanor, *The National Socialist Leadership and Total War, 1941–5* (New York: St Martin's Press, 1991).

Hansen, Randall, 'War, Suffering and Modern German History', *German History* (29) 2011, pp. 365–79.

Hanson, Joanna, *The Civilian Population and the Warsaw Uprising of 1944* (Cambridge: Cambridge University Press, 1982).

Hartmann, Christian, *Wehrmacht im Ostkrieg: Front und militärisches Hinterland 1941/42* (Munich: R. Oldenbourg Verlag, 2009).

Operation Barbarossa: Nazi Germany's War in the East, 1941–1945 (Oxford: Oxford University Press, 2013).

Hartmann, Christian, Johannes Hürter and Ulrike Jureit (eds.), *Verbrechen der Wehrmacht: Bilanz einer Debatte* (Munich: C. H. Beck, 2014).

Hartmann, Rüdiger, 'The War of the Cities: Industrial Labouring Forces, in Geyer and Tooze (eds.), *The Cambridge History of the Second World War, Volume III*, pp. 298–328.

Hastings, Max, *Armageddon: the Battle for Germany, 1944–45* (London: Macmillan, 2004).

Haupt, Werner, *Königsberg – Breslau – Wien – Berlin: Der Bildbericht vom Ende der Ostfront* (Friedberg: Podzun-Pallas Verlag, 1978).

Als die Rote Armee nach Deutschland kam (Friedberg: Podzun-Pallas-Verlag, 1981).

Hébert, Valerie, *Hitler's Generals on Trial: the Last War Crimes Tribunal at Nuremberg* (Lawrence: University Press of Kansas, 2010).

Heer, Hannes, 'Extreme Normalität. Generalmajor Gustav Freiherr von Mauchenheim gen. Bechtolsheim: Umfeld, Motive und Entschlussbildung eines Holocaust-Täters', *Zeitschrift für Geschichtswissenschaft* (51) 2003, pp. 729–53.

Vom Verschwinden der Täter: der Vernichtungskrieg fand statt, aber keiner war dabei (Berlin: Aufbau-Verlag 2004)

'How Amorality Became Normality: Reflections on the Mentality of German Soldiers on the Eastern Front', in Heer and Naumann (eds.), *War of Extermination*, pp. 329–44.

Heer, Hannes and Klaus Naumann (eds.), *War of Extermination: the German Military in World War II 1941–1944* (New York: Berghahn, 2006).

Hellbeck, Jochen, 'Battles for Morale: an Entangled History of Total War in Europe', in Geyer and Tooze (eds.), *The Cambridge History of the Second World War, Volume III*, pp. 329–62.

Henke, Klaus-Dietmar, *Die amerikanische Besetzung Deutschlands* (Munich, R. Oldenbourg Verlag, 1996).

Hertz-Eichenrode, Dieter, *Politik und Landwirtschaft in Ostpreußen 1919–1930: Untersuchung eines Strukturproblems in der Weimarer Republik* (Cologne: Westdeutscher Verlag, 1969).

Hill, Alexander, *The Red Army and the Second World War* (Cambridge: Cambridge University Press, 2017).

Hillenbrand, Fritz, *Underground Humour in Nazi Germany 1933–1945* (London: Routledge, 1995).

Hillgruber, Andreas, *Zweierlei Untergang. Die Zerschlagung des Deutschen Reiches und das Ende des europäischen Judentums* (Berlin: Siedler, 1986).

Hillmann, Jörg and John Zimmermann (eds.), *Kriegsende 1945 in Deutschland* (Munich: Oldenbourg Wissenschaftsverlag, 2002).

Hinze, Rolf, *Das Ostfrontdrama 1944: Rückzugkämpfe Heeresgruppe Mitte* (Stuttgart: Motorbuch-Verlag, 1987).

Höffkes, Karl, *Hitlers politische Generale: Die Gauleiter des Dritten Reiches. Ein Biographisches Nachschlagwerk* (Tübingen: Grabert-Verlag, 1997).

Holub, Robert, 'Reception Theory: School of Constance', in Selden (ed.), *The Cambridge History of Literary Criticism, Vol. 8*, pp. 319–46.

Honig, Jan Willem, 'The Idea of Total War: From Clausewitz to Ludendorff', in National Institute for Defence Studies (ed.), *The Pacific War as Total War*, pp. 29–41.

Hubatsch, Walther, *Die 61. Infanterie-Division: 1939–1945* (Eggolsheim: Dörfler, 2004).

Huber, Florian, *Kind, versprich mir, dass du dich erschießt: Der Untergang der kleinen Leute 1945* (Berlin: Berlin Verlag, 2015).

Hull, Isabel, *Absolute Destruction: Military Culture and the Practices of War in Imperial Germany* (Ithaca: Cornell University Press, 2004).

Humburg, Martin, '"Ich glaube, daß meine Zeit bald gezählt sein dürfte": Feldpostbriefe am Ende des Krieges: Zwei Beispiele', in Hillmann and Zimmermann (eds.), *Kriegsende 1945 in Deutschland*, pp. 239–62.

Hund, Wulf, Christian Koller, and Moshe Zimmermann (eds.), *Racisms Made in Germany* (Münster: LIT Verlag, 2011).

Hunt Tooley, T., 'German Political Violence and the Border Plebiscite in Upper Silesia, 1919–1921', *Central European History* (21) 1988, pp. 56–98.

Hürter, Johannes, 'Auf dem Weg zur Militäropposition. Tresckow, Gersdorff, der Vernichtungskrieg und der Judenmord. Neue Dokumente über das Verhältnis der Heeresgruppe Mitte zur Einsatzgruppe B im Jahr 1941', *VfZ* (52) 2004, pp. 527–62.

Hitlers Heerführer: Die deutschen Oberbefehlshaber im Krieg gegen die Sowjetunion 1941/42 (Munich: R. Oldenbourg Verlag, 2006).

'The Military Elite and the Volksgemeinschaft', in Steber and Gotto (eds.), *Visions of Community in Nazi Germany*, pp. 257–69.

Hürter, Johannes and Felix Römer, 'Alte und neue Geschichtsbilder von Widerstand und Ostkrieg', *VfZ* (54) 2006, pp. 301–22.

Hüttenberger, Peter, *Die Gauleiter, Studie zum Wandel des Machtsgefüges in der NSDAP* (Stuttgart: Deutsche Verlags-Anstalt, 1969).

International Military Tribunal, *The Trial of German Major War Criminals: Proceedings of the International Military Tribunal Sitting at Nuremberg, Germany, Part 17* (London: HMSO, 1948).

Jähnig, Bernhart and Silke Spieler (eds.), *Das Königsberger Gebiet im Schnittpunkt deutscher Geschichte und in seinen europäischen Bezügen* (Bonn: Kulturstiftung der deutschen Vertriebenen, 1993).

Jones, Edgar and Simon Wessely, *Shell Shock to PTSD: Military Psychiatry from 1900 to the Gulf War* (Hove: Psychology Press, 2005).

Jones, Mark, *Founding Weimar: Violence and the German Revolution of 1918–1919* (Cambridge: Cambridge University Press, 2016).

Kabath, Rudolf and Friedrich Forstmeier, 'Die Rolle der Seebrückenköpfe beim Kampf um Ostpreussen', in Meier-Welcker (ed.), *Abwehrkämpfe am Nordflügel der Ostfront 1944 – 1945*, pp. 217–451.

Kallis, Aristotle, 'Die Niedergang der Deutungsmacht. Nationalsozialistische Propaganda im Kriegsverlauf', in Echternkamp (ed.), *Das Deutsche Reich und der Zweite Weltkrieg 9/2*, pp. 203–50.

Kalmbach, Peter Lutz, 'Polizeiliche Ermittlungsorgane der Wehrmachtjustiz', *Kriminalistik*, February 2013, p. 118–22.

'Feldjäger, Sicherheitsdienst, Sonderkommandos Polizeiorgane und Standgerichtsbarkeit in der Endphase des Zweiten Weltkriegs', *Kriminalistik*, July 2014, p. 454–58.

'"Das neue Recht ermöglicht energisches Vorgehen"', *Deutsche Richterzeitung* (93) 2016, pp. 26–31.

Kater, Michael, *The Nazi Party: a Social Profile of Members and Leaders, 1919–1945* (Oxford: Blackwell, 1983).

Hitler Youth (Cambridge, MA: Harvard University Press, 2004).

Kay, Alex, Jeff Rutherford, and David Stahel (eds.), *Nazi Policy on the Eastern Front, 1941: Total War, Genocide, and Radicalisation* (Rochester, NY: University of Rochester Press, 2012).

Keller, Sven, *Volksgemeinschaft am Ende: Gesellschaft und Gewalt 1944/45* (Munich: Oldenbourg Verlag, 2013).

'Volksgemeinschaft and Violence: Some Reflections on Interdependencies', in Steber and Gotto (eds.), *Visions of Community in Nazi Germany*, pp. 226–39.

Kershaw, Ian, 'Working Towards the Führer.' Reflections on the Nature of the Hitler Dictatorship', *Contemporary European History* (2) 1993, pp. 103–18.

The End, Hitler's Germany, 1944–45 (London: Allen Lane 2011).

Hitler 1936–45: Nemesis (London: Penguin, 2001).

The 'Hitler Myth': Image and Reality in the Third Reich (Oxford: Oxford University Press, 2001).

Kettenacker, Lothar and Torsten Riotte (eds.), *The Legacies of Two World Wars: European Societies in the Twentieth Century* (Oxford: Berghahn Books, 2011).

Kibelka, Ruth, *Ostpreußens Schicksaljahre 1944–1948* (Berlin: Aufbau-Verlag, 2000).

Kilian, Jürgen, 'Wehrmacht, Partisanenkrieg und Rückzugsverbrechen an der nördlichen Ostfront im Herbst und Winter 1943', *VfZ* (61) 2013, pp. 173–99.

Kissel, Hans, *Der Deutsche Volkssturm 1944/1945: Eine territoriale Miliz im Rahmen der Landesverteidigung* (Berlin: Verlag E.S. Mittler, 1962).

Kitchen, Martin, *Nazi Germany at War* (London: Longman, 1995).

Kittel, Manfred, 'Preußens Osten in der Zeitgeschichte. Mehr als nur eine landeshistorische Forschungslücke', *VfZ* (50) 2002, pp. 435–65.

Kitterman, David, 'Those Who Said "No!": Germans Who Refused to Execute Civilians during World War II', *German Studies Review* (11) 1988, pp. 241–54.

Klemperer, Victor, *To the Bitter End: the Diaries of Victor Klemperer 1942–45* (London: Phoenix, 1999).

The Language of the Third Reich: LTI – Lingua Tertii Imperii, A Philologist's Notebook (London: Continuum, 2000).

Knopp, Guido, *Der Sturm, Kriegsende im Osten* (Berlin: Econ, 2004).

Koch, Hannsjoachim, *A History of Prussia* (London: Longman, 1978).

Koller, Christian, 'Racisms Made in Germany: Without "Sonderweg" to a "Rupture in Civilisation"', in Hund, Koller, and Zimmermann (eds.), *Racisms Made in Germany*, pp. 9–40.

Koolhaas, Elisabeth, "'Aus einem Haus, aus dem eine weiße Fahne erscheint, sind alle männliche Personen zu erschießen": Durchhalteterror und Gewalt gegen Zivilisten am Kriegsende 1945', in Arendes, Wolfrun, and Zedler (eds.), *Terror nach Innen*, pp. 51–79.

Kossert, Andreas, "'Grenzlandpolitik" und Ostforschung an der Peripherie des Reiches. Das ostpreußische Masuren 1919–1945', *VfZ* (51) 2003, pp. 117–46.

Ostpreußen, Geschichte und Mythos (Munich: Siedler, 2005).

Damals in Ostpreussen, Der Untergang einer deutschen Provinz (Munich: Pantheon Verlag, 2008).

Kalte Heimat: Der Geschichte der deutsche Vertriebenen nach 1945 (Bonn: Bundeszentrale für politische Bildung, 2008).

Kramer, Nicole, 'Von der "Volksgenossin" zur "Trümmerfrau"? – Deutungen von Frauen nach 1945', in Schmiechen-Ackermann (ed.), *'Volksgemeinschaft'*, pp. 303–17.

Krausnick, Helmut, 'Kommissarbefehl und "Gerichtsbarkeitserlaß Barbarossa" in neuer Sicht', *VfZ* (25) 1977, pp. 682–738.

Kreisgemeinschaft Wehlau, *Heimatbuch des Kreises Wehlau Alle-Pregel-Deime-Gebiet, I. Band* (Leer: Verlag Gerhard Rauterberg, 1975).

Kretinin, Gennadii, 'Shturm Konigsberga v 1945 g.: chislennost' i poteri protivostoyashchikh storon i grazhdanskogo naseleniya' [The Storming of Königsberg in 1945: the Strength and Losses of the Opposing Parties and the Civilian Population], *Problemy Nacional'noi Strategii* (11) 2012), pp. 138–54.

'Implitsitnaya pamyat', ili Vnov' o nemetskom naselenii Konigsberga vo vremya osady kreposti v fevrale–aprele 1945 goda' [Implicit Memory, or Once Again on German Civilians in Königsberg During the Fortress' Siege in February–April 1945], *Vestnik Baltiyskevo Federal'nevo Universiteta im. I. Kanta* (12) 2016, pp. 16–22.

Krickus, Richard, *The Kaliningrad Question* (Lanham: MD, Rowman & Littlefield Publishers, 2002).

Kroener, Bernhard, "'Frontochsen" und "Etappenbullen". Zur Ideologisierung militärischen Organisationsstrukturen im Zweiten Weltkrieg', in Müller and Volkmann (eds.), *Die Wehrmacht: Mythos und Realität*, pp. 371–84.

Kühne, Thomas, *Kameradschaft: Die Soldaten des nationalsozialistischen Krieges und das 20. Jahrhundert, Kritische Studien zur Geschichtswissenschaft* (Göttingen: Vanderhoeck & Ruprecht, 2006).

Kulturstiftung der deutschen Vertriebenen, *Frauen in Königsberg 1945–1948* (Bonn: Kulturstiftung der Dt. Vertriebenen 1999).

Kunz, Andreas, *Wehrmacht und Niederlage: Die bewaffnete Macht in der Endphase der nationalsozialistischen Herrschaft 1944 bis 1945* (Munich: R. Oldenbourg Verlag, 2005).

'Die Wehrmacht in der Agonie der nationalsozialistischen Herrschaft 1944/45. Eine Gedankenskizze', in Hillmann and Zimmermann (eds.), *Kriegsende 1945 in Deutschland*, pp. 9–34.

Kurlander, Eric, *Hitler's Monsters: a Supernatural History of the Third Reich* (New Haven: Yale University Press, 2017).

Lakowski, Richard, *Ostpreußen 1944/45: Krieg im Nordosten des Deutschen Reiches* (Paderborn: Ferdinand Schöningh, 2016).

'Der Zusammenbruch der deutschen Verteidigung zwischen Ostsee und Karpaten', in Müller (ed.), *Das Deutsche Reich und der Zweiten Weltkrieg 10/ 1*, pp. 491–680.

Lang, Jochen von, *Bormann, The Man Who Manipulated Hitler* (London: Book Club Associates, 1979).

Lass, Edgar, *Die Flucht, Ostpreussen 1944/45* (Bad Neuheim: Podzun-Verlag, 1964).

Lehmann, Peter, *Geachtet – Geleugnet – Geehrt. Oberst Gustav Petri, Retter von Wernigerode* (Berlin: Lukas-Verlag, 2013).

Lehnstaedt, Stephan, *Okkupation im Osten: Besatzeralltag in Warschau und Minsk 1939–1944* (Munich: Oldenbourg, 2010).

Lewy, Guenter, *The Nazi Persecution of the Gypsies* (Oxford: Oxford University Press, 2000).

Lieb, Peter, *Konventioneller Krieg oder NS-Weltanschauungskrieg? Kriegsführung und Partisanenbekämpfung in Frankreich 1943/44* (Munich: R. Oldenbourg Verlag, 2007).

'Der deutsche Krieg im Osten von 1914 bis 1919: Ein Vorläufer des Vernichtungskriegs?', *VfZ* (65) 2017, pp. 465–506.

Lindeiner-Stráský, Karina von, 'Indoctrinated, but Not Incurable? Klaus Mann's Interrogation of German Prisoners of War in 1944', *German Life and Letters* (64) 2011, pp. 217–34.

Link, Fabian, *Burgen und Burgenforschung im Nationalsozialismus: Wissenschaft und Weltanschauung 1933–1945* (Cologne: Böhlau Verlag, 2014).

Liulevicius, Vejas, *War Land on the Eastern Front: Culture, National Identity, and German Occupation in World War I* (Cambridge: Cambridge University Press, 2001).

Loeffel, Robert, 'Soldiers and Terror: Re-evaluating the Complicity of the *Wehrmacht* in Nazi Germany', *German History* (27) 2009, pp. 514–30.

Family Punishment in Nazi Germany: Sippenhaft, Terror and Myth (Basingstoke: Palgrave MacMillan, 2012).

Lölhöffel, Hedwig von, *Landleben in Ostpreußen* (Hamburg: Landmannschaft Ostpreußen, 1976).

Longerich, Peter, *Heinrich Himmler* (Oxford, Oxford University Press, 2012).

Goebbels: a Biography (London: Bodley Head, 2015).

Lorenz, Hilke, *Kriegskinder: Das Schicksal einer Generation* (Munich: List, 2003).

Lowe, Keith, *Savage Continent: Europe in the Aftermath of World War II* (London: Penguin, 2012).

Lower, Wendy, *Nazi Empire-Building and the Holocaust in Ukraine* (Chapel Hill: University of North Carolina Press, 2005).

Hitler's Furies: German Women in the Nazi Killing Fields (London: Vintage Books, 2014).

Lucas, James, *The Last Year of the German Army, May 1944–May 1945* (London: Arms and Armour, 1994).

Lucas-Busemann, Erhard, *So fielen Königsberg und Breslau* (Berlin: Aufbau Taschenbuch Verlag, 1994).

Lüdecke, Alexander, *Waffentechnik im Zweiten Weltkrieg* (Bath: Parragon, 2007).

Lüdtke, Alf and Bernd Weisbrod (eds.), *No Man's Land of Violence: Extreme Wars in the Twentieth Century* (Göttingen: Wallstein Verlag, 2006).

Majer, Diemut, *"Non-Germans" under the Third Reich: the Nazi Judicial and Administrative System in Germany and Occupied Eastern Europe, with Special Regard to Occupied Poland, 1939–1945* (New York: Johns Hopkins University Press, 2003).

Malešević, Siniša, *Identity As Ideology: Understanding Ethnicity and Nationalism* (Basingstoke: Palgrave MacMillan, 2006).

Malinowski, Stephan, *Von König zum Führer: Sozialer Niedergang und politische Radikalisierung im deutschen Adel zwischen Kaiserreich und NS-Staat* (Berlin: Akademie Verlag, 2003).

Malter, Rudolf, *'Denken wir uns aber als verpflichtet . . . ' Königsberger Kant-Ansprachen 1804–1945* (Erlangen: H. Fischer, 1992).

Manthey, Jürgen, *Königsberg, Geschichte einer Weltbürgerrepublik* (Munich: Carl Hanser Verlag, 2005).

Maslov, Alexander, *Fallen Soviet Generals: Soviet General Officers Killed in Battle, 1941–1945* (London: Frank Cass, 1998).

Mason, Timothy, *Social Policy in the Third Reich: the Working Class and the 'National Community'* (Oxford: Berg, 1993).

Mawdsley, Evan, *Thunder in the East: The Nazi-Soviet War 1941–1945* (New York: Hodder Arnold, 2007).

Medvedev, Konstantin (ed.), *Sturm Kenigsberga, K 40Letniyu Pobedy* (Kaliningrad: Kaliningradskoe Knizhnoe Izdatel'stvo, 1985).

Megargee, Geoffrey, *Inside Hitler's High Command* (Lawrence: University Press of Kansas, 2000).

'The German Army after the Great War: a Case Study in Selective Self-Deception', in Dennis and Grey (eds.), *Victory or Defeat*, pp. 104–17.

Megargee, Geoffrey (ed.), *The United States Holocaust Memorial Museum Encyclopedia of Camps and Ghettos, 1933–1945, Volume I: Early Camps, and Concentration Camps and Subcamps under the SS-Business Administration Main Officer (WVHA) Part B* (Bloomington: Indiana University Press, 2009).

Meier-Welcker, Hans (ed.), *Abwehrkämpfe am Nordflügel der Ostfront 1944–1945* (Stuttgart: Deutsche Verlags-Anstalt, 1963).

Meindl, Ralf, *Ostpreußens Gauleiter Erich Koch – eine politische Biographie* (Osnabrück: fibre Verlag, 2007).

Mellenthin, Friedrich von, *Panzer Battles 1939–1945: a Study of the Employment of Armour in the Second World War* (London: Cassell, 1955).

Merridale, Catherine, *Iwans krieg. Die Rote Armee 1939 bis 1945* (Frankfurt am Main: Fischer Taschenbuch Verlag, 2008).

Messerschmidt, Manfred, *Die Wehrmachtjustiz 1933–1945* (Paderborn: Ferdinand Schöningh, 2005).

Messerschmidt, Manfred and Fritz Wüllner, *Die Wehrmachtjustiz im Dienste des Nationalsozialismus. Zerstörung einer Legende* (Baden-Baden: Nomos Verlagsgesellschaft, 1987).

Moll, Albert, *Der Deutsche Festungsbau von der Memel zum Atlantik 1900–1945* (Utting: Dörfler, 2002).

Mommsen, Hans, 'Der Nationalsozialismus. Kumulative Radikalisierung und Selbstzerstörung des Regimes', in *Meyers Enzyklopädisches Lexikon, Band 16* (Munich: Lexicon Verlag, 1976), pp. 785–90.

'The Dissolution of the Third Reich: Crisis Management and Collapse, 1943–1945', *Bulletin of the German Historical Institute* (27) 2000, pp. 9–23.

'The Indian Summer and the Collapse of the Third Reich: The Last Act', in Mommsen (ed.), *The Third Reich Between Vision and Reality*, pp. 109–27.

Mommsen, Hans (ed.), *The Third Reich Between Vision and Reality: New Perspectives on German History 1918–1945* (Oxford: Berg, 2001).

Moorhouse, Roger, ' 'The Sore That Would Never Heal': the Genesis of the Polish Corridor', in Fisher and Sharp (eds.), *After the Versailles Treaty*, pp. 185–95.

Mosse, George, *The Crisis of German Ideology: Intellectual Origins of the Third Reich* (New York: Grosset & Dunlap, 1964).

Fallen Soldiers: Reshaping the Memory of the World Wars (Oxford: Oxford University Press, 1990).

Motadel, David, 'Islam and Germany's War in the Soviet Borderlands, 1941–5', *Journal of Contemporary History* (48), 2013, pp. 784–820.

Mühlenfeld, Daniel, 'Between State and Party. Position and Function of the Gau Propaganda Leader in National Socialist Leadership', *German History* (28) 2010, pp. 167–92.

Müller, Rolf-Dieter, *Reinhard Gehlen: Geheimdienstchef im Hintergrund der Bonner Republik, Die Biografie. Teil 1: 1902–1950* (Berlin: Ch. Links Verlag, 2017)

Müller, Rolf-Dieter and Hans-Erich Volkmann (eds.), *Die Wehrmacht: Mythos und Realität* (Munich: Oldenbourg, 1999).

Müller, Rolf-Dieter (ed.), *Das Deutsche Reich und der Zweiten Weltkrieg 10/1: Der Zusammenbruch des Deutschen Reiches 1945. Die militärische Niederwerfung der Wehrmacht* (Munich: Deutsche Verlags-Anstalt, 2007).

Müller, Sven, *Deutsche Soldaten und ihre Feinde, Nationalismus an Front und Heimatfront im Zweiten Weltkrieg* (Frankfurt a.M.: S. Fischer, 2007).

'Nationalismus in der deutschen Kriegsgesellschaft 1939 bis 1945', in Echternkamp (ed.), *Das Deutsche Reich und der Zweite Weltkrieg 9/2*, pp. 9–92.

Müller-Hillebrand, Burkhart, *Horses in the German Army (1941–1945)* (Washington DC: Historical Division, 1952).

Mulligan, Timothy, *The Politics of Illusion and Empire: German Occupation Policy in the Soviet Union, 1942–1943* (New York: Praeger, 1988).

Münch, Ingo von, *'Frau, komm!': Die Massenvergewaltigungen deutscher Frauen und Mädchen 1944/45* (Graz: Ares Verlag, 2009).

M. V. Frunze Military Academy, *Durchbruch der Schützenverbände durch eine vorbereitete Verteidigung* (Berlin: Ministerium für Nationale Verteidigung, 1959).

Naimark, Norman, *The Russians in Germany: a history of the Soviet Zone of Occupation, 1945–1949* (Cambridge, MA: The Belknap Press of Harvard University Press, 1995).

National Institute for Defence Studies (ed.), *The Pacific War as Total War: Proceedings of the 2011 International Forum on War History* (Tokyo: National Institute for Defence Studies, 2012).

Neitzel, Sönke, 'Der Kampf um die deutsche Atlantikund Kanalfestungen und sein Einfluß auf den alliierten Nachschub während der Befreiung Frankreichs 1944/45', *Militärgeschichtliche Mitteilungen* (55) 1996, pp. 381–430.

Abgehört: Deutsche Generäle in britischer Kriegsgefangenschaft 1942–1945 (Berlin: Propyläen, 2005).

'The City under Attack', in Addison and Crang (eds.), *Firestorm: the Bombing of Dresden 1945*, pp. 62–77.

Neitzel, Sönke and Harald Welzer, *Soldaten, On Fighting, Killing and Dying: the Secret World War II Transcripts of German POWs* (New York: Alfred A. Knopf, 2012).

Neumärker, Uwe and Andreas Kossert (eds.), *'Das war mal unsere Heimat . . .': Jüdische Geschichte im preußischen Osten* (Berlin: Die Stiftungen Flucht, Vertreibung, Versöhnung und Denkmal für die ermordeten Juden Europas, 2013).

Nielsen, Holger and Richard Landwehr, *Nordic Warriors: SS-Panzergrenadier-Regiment 24 Danmark, Eastern Front, 1943–45* (Coventry: Shelf Books, 1999).

Niethammer Lutz, Ulrich Borsdorf, and Peter Brandt (eds.), *Arbeiterinitiative 1945: Antifaschistische Ausschüsse und Reorganisation der Arbeiterbewegung in Deutschland* (Wuppertal: Peter Hammer Verlag, 1976).

Niven, Bill (ed.), *Germans As Victims Remembering the Past in Contemporary Germany* (Basingstoke: Palgrave Macmillan, 2006).

Noakes, Jeremy, 'Oberbürgermeister and Gauleiter. City Government Between Party and State', in Hirschfeld and Kettenacker (eds.), *The 'Führer State'*, pp. 194–227.

Noble, Alastair, 'The People's Levy: the Volkssturm and Popular Mobilisation in Eastern Germany 1944–45', *Journal of Strategic Studies* (24) 2001, pp. 165–87.

'The Phantom Barrier: Ostwallbau 1944–1945', *War In History* (8) 2001, pp. 442–67.

'A Most Distant Target: The Bombing of Königsberg, August 1944', *War & Society* (25) 2006, pp. 55–75.

Nazi Rule and the Soviet Offensive in Eastern Germany, 1944–1945: the Darkest Hour (Eastbourne: Sussex Academic Press, 2010).

Orlow, Dietrich, *The History of the Nazi Party: Volume II 1933–1945* (Newton Abbot: David & Charles, 1973).

Overmans, Rüdiger, *Deutsche militärische Verluste im Zweiten Weltkrieg* (Munich: R. Oldenburg Verlag, 1999).

Overy, Richard, *War and Economy in the Third Reich* (Oxford: Clarendon Press, 1994).

Historical Atlas of the Third Reich (Harmondsworth: Penguin, 1996).

Why the Allies Won (London: Pimlico, 2006).

The Bombing War: Europe 1939–1945 (London: Penguin, 2014).

Padfield, Peter, *Dönitz, The Last Führer* (London: Panther, 1985).

Padover, Saul, *Lügendetektor: Vernehmungen im besiegten Deutschland 1944/45* (Frankfurt a.M., Eichborn Verlag, 1999).

Paret, Peter (ed.), *Makers of Modern Strategy: From Machiavelli to the Nuclear Age* (Princeton, NJ, Princeton University Press, 1986).

Paul, Gerhard, '"Diese Erschießungen haben mich innerlich gar nicht mehr berührt": Die Kriegsendphasenverbrechen der Gestapo 1944/45', in Paul and Mallmann (eds.), *Die Gestapo im Zweiten Weltkrieg*, pp. 543–68.

Paul, Gerhard and Klaus-Michael Mallmann (eds.), *Die Gestapo im Zweiten Weltkrieg: 'Heimatfront' und besetztes Europa* (Darmstadt: Primus Verlag, 2000).

Peifer, Douglas, 'Selfless Saviours or Diehard Fanatics? West and East German Memories of the *Kriegsmarine* and the Baltic Evacuation', *War & Society* (26) 2007, pp. 99–120.

Persico, Joseph, *Roosevelt's Centurions: FDR and the Commanders He Led to Victory in World War II* (New York: Random House, 2013).

Peukert, Detlev, *Volksgenossen und Gemeinschaftsfremde, Anpassung, Ausmerze und Aufbegehren unter dem Nationalsozialismus* (Cologne: Bund-Verlag, 1982).

Plato, Anton Detlev von, *Die Geschichte der 5. Panzerdivision: 1938 bis 1945* (Lüchow, Gemeinschaft d. Angehörigen d. Ehem. 5. Panzerdivision, 1978).

Pohl, Dieter, *Die Herrschaft der Wehrmacht: Deutsche Militärbesatzung und einheimische Bevölkerung in der Sowjetunion 1941–1944* (Munich: R. Oldenbourg Verlag, 2008).

Pölking, Hermann, *Ostpreußen: Biographie einer Provinz* (Berlin: be.bra Verlag, 2011).

Pyta, Wolfram, *Hitler: Der Künstler als Politiker und Feldherr: Eine Herrschafsanalyse* (Munich: Siedler, 2015).

Raschke, Helga, *'Damit Gotha leben kann, muss ich sterben', Ein Grazer Offizier: Josef Ritter von Gadolla und die letzten Kriegstage in Gotha* (Raschke: Gotha, 2007).

Rass, Christoph, 'Verbrecheriche Kriegsführung an der Front: Eine Infanteriedivision und ihre Soldaten', in Hartmann, Hürter, and Jureit (eds.), *Verbrechen der Wehrmacht*, pp. 80–90.

Rautenberg, Hans-Werner, 'Der Zusammenbruch der deutschen Stellung im Osten und das Ende Königsbergs. Flucht und Vertreibung als Europäisches Problem', in Jähnig and Spieler (eds.), *Das Königsberger Gebiet im Schnittpunkt deutscher Geschichte*, pp. 107–22.

Ready, J. Lee, *The Forgotten Axis: Germany's Partners and Foreign Volunteers in World War II* (London: McFarland, 1987).

Reibel, Carl-Wilhelm, *Das Fundament der Diktatur: Die NSDAP-Ortsgruppen 1932–1945* (Paderborn: Ferdinand Schöningh, 2002).

Reitlinger, Gerald, *The House Built on Sand: the Conflicts of German Policy in Russia 1939–1945* (London: Weidenfeld and Nicolson, 1960)

Richter, Werner, *Die 1. (ostpreussische) Infanterie-Division* (Munich: Schildbuchdienst-Verlag, 1975).

Römer, Felix, '"Im alten Deutschland wäre solcher Befehl nicht möglich gewesen": Rezeption, Adaption und Umsetzung des Kriegsgerichtsbarkeitserlass im Ostheer 1941/42', *VfZ* (56) 2008, pp. 53–99.

Kameraden: Die Wehrmacht von innen (Munich: Piper, 2014).

'Volksgemeinschaft in der Wehrmacht? Milieus, Mentalitäten und militärische Moral in den Streitkräften des NS-Staates', in Welzer, Neitzel and Gudehus (eds.), *Der Führer war viel zu human, viel zu gefühlvoll'*, pp. 55–94.

'The Wehrmacht in the War of Ideologies: the Army and Hitler's Criminal Orders on the Eastern Front', in Kay, Rutherford, and Stahel (eds.), *Nazi Policy on the Eastern Front, 1941*, pp. 73–100.

Rosnow, Ralph, 'Psychology of Rumor Reconsidered', *Psychological Bulletin* (89) 1980, pp. 578–91.

Rusinek, Bernd-A. (ed.), *Kriegsende 1945: Verbrechen, Katastrophen, Befreiungen in nationaler und internationaler Perspektive* (Göttingen: Wallstein Verlag, 2004).

Rutherford, Jeff, *Combat and Genocide on the Eastern Front: the German Infantry's War, 1941–1944* (Cambridge: Cambridge University Press, 2014).

Ryan, Cornelius, *The Last Battle* (New York: Simon & Schuster, 1966).

Sachdeva, Sonya, Rumen Iliev, and Douglas Medin, 'Sinning Saints and Saintly Sinners: the Paradox of Moral Self-Regulation', *Psychological Science* (20) 2009, pp. 523–28.

Sait, Bryce, *The Indoctrination of the Wehrmacht: Nazi Ideology and the War Crimes of the German Military* (Oxford: Berghahn, 2019).

Salewski, Michael, *Die deutsche Seekriegsleitung 1935–1945, Band II: 1942–1945* (Munich: Bernard & Graefe Verlag für Wehrwesen, 1975).

Sammartino, Annemarie, *The Impossible Border: Germany and the East, 1914–1922* (Ithaca, NY: Cornell University Press, 2011).

Schivelbusch, Wolfgang, *The Culture of Defeat: On National Trauma, Mourning, and Recovery* (London: Granta, 2003).

Three New Deals: Reflections on Roosevelt's America, Mussolini's Italy, and Hitler's Germany, 1933–1939 (New York: Picador, 2007).

Schmidtke, Martin, *Rettungsaktion Ostsee 1944/1945: eine Großtat der Menschlichkeit, Zusammenfassende Dokumentation einschließlich der beteiligten Schiffe und Boote von Handelsflotte, Kriegsmarine, Luftwaffe und Heer* (Bonn: Bernard & Graefe Verlag, 2006).

Schmiechen-Ackermann, Detlef (ed.), *'Volksgemeinschaft': Mythos, wirkungsmächtige soziale Verheißung oder soziale Realität im ,Dritten Reich'?* (Paderborn: Ferdinand Schöningh, 2012).

Schneider, Wolfgang, *Alltag unter Hitler* (Berlin: Rowohlt, 2000).

Schön, Heinz, *Die letzten Kriegstage: Ostseehäfen 1945* (Stuttgart: Motorbuch-Verlag, 1995).

Flucht aus Ostpreußen 1945: Die Menschenjagd der Roten Armee (Kiel: Arndt-Verlag, 2001).

Schreckenberg, Heinz, *Ideologie und Alltag im Dritten Reich* (Frankfurt: Peter Lang, 2003).

Schröder, Hans, '"Ich hänge hier, weil ich getürmt bin": Terror und Verfall im deutschen Militär bei Kriegsende 1945', in Wette (ed.), *Der Krieg des Kleinen Mannes*, pp. 279–94.

Schüler-Springorum, Stefanie, *Die jüdische Minderheit in Königsberg, Preussen: 1871 – 1945* (Göttingen: Vandenhoeck & Ruprecht, 1996).

Schulte, Theo, *The German Army and Nazi Policies in Occupied Russia* (Oxford: Berg, 1989).

Schumann, Dirk, *Political Violence in the Weimar Republic 1918–1933: Fight for the Streets and Fear of Civil War* (Oxford: Berghahn Books, 2012).

Schumann, Wolfgang and Olaf Groehler (eds.) *Deutschland im Zweiten Weltkrieg 6: Die Zerschlagung des Hitlerfaschismus und die Befreiung des deutschen Volkes (Juni 1944 bis zum 8. Mai 1945)* (Berlin: Akademie-Verlag, 1985).

Schwendemann, Heinrich, 'Tod zwischen den Fronten', *Spiegel Special*, June 2002, pp. 42–47.

'Inferno und Befreiung: "Schickt Schiffe!"', *Die Zeit*, 13 January 2005, p. 84.

'Strategie der Selbstvernichtung: Die Wehrmachtführung im "Endkampf" um das 'Dritte Reich', in Müller and Volkmann (eds.), *Die Wehrmacht: Mythos und Realität*, pp. 224–44.

'"Deutsche Menschen vor der Vernichtung durch den Bolschewismus zu retten": Das Programm der Regierung Dönitz und der Beginn einer Legendenbildung', in Hillmann and Zimmermann (eds.), *Kriegsende 1945 in Deutschland*, pp. 9–34.

'Der deutsche Zusammenbruch im Osten 1944/45', in Rusinek (ed.), *Kriegsende 1945*, pp. 125–50.

Seidler, Franz, *'Deutscher Volkssturm': Das letzte Aufgebot 1944/45* (Munich: Herbig, 1989).

Selden, Raman (ed.), *The Cambridge History of Literary Criticism, Vol. 8: From Formalism to Poststructuralism* (Cambridge: Cambridge University Press, 1995).

Sella, Amnon, *The Value of Human Life in Soviet Warfare* (London: Routledge, 1992).

Semelin, Jaques *Purify and Destroy: the Political Uses of Massacre and Genocide* (London, Hurst, 2007).

Shepherd, Ben, *War in the Wild East: the German Army and Soviet Partisans* (Cambridge, MA Harvard University Press, 2004).

Hitler's Soldiers: the German Army in the Third Reich (London: Yale University Press, 2017).

Shils, Edward and Morris Janowitz, 'Cohesion and Disintegration in the Wehrmacht in World War II', *The Public Opinion Quarterly* (12) 1948, pp. 280–315.

Sigg, Marco, *Der Unterführer als Feldherr im Taschenformat: Theorie und Praxis der Auftragstaktik im deutschen Heer 1869 bis 1945* (Paderborn: Schöningh, 2014).

Simpson, Brooks D. and Jean V. Berlin (eds.), *Sherman's Civil War: Selected Correspondence of William T. Sherman, 1860–1865* (Chapel Hill, NC: University of North Carolina Press, 1999).

Slepyan, Kenneth, 'The People's Avengers: the Partisan Movement', in Stone (ed.), *The Soviet Union at War*, pp. 154–81.

Smith Serrano, Andrew, *German Propaganda in Military Decline 1943–1945* (Edinburgh: Pentland Press, 1999).

Solzhenitsyn, Alexander, *Prussian Nights, a Narrative Poem* (London: Collins and Harvill, 1977).

Spieler, Silke (ed.), *Vertreibung und Vertreibungsverbrechen, 1945–1948: Bericht des Bundesarchivs vom 28. Mai 1974, Archivalien und ausgewählte Erlebnisberichte* (Bonn: Kulturstiftung der Deutschen Vertriebenen, 1989).

Stackelberg, Roderick, *Idealism Debased: From Völkisch Ideology to National Socialism* (Kent, OH.: Kent State University Press, 1981).

Stahel, David, 'The Wehrmacht and National Socialist Military Thinking', *War in History* (24) 2017, pp. 336–61.

Stargardt, Nicholas, 'The Troubled Patriot: German Innerlichkeit in World War II', *German History* (28) 2010, pp. 326–42.

The German War: a Nation under Arms, 1939–1945 (London:Bodley Head, 2015).

Steber, Martina and Bernhard Gotto (eds.), *Visions of Community in Nazi Germany: Social Engineering and Private Lives* (New York: Oxford University Press, 2014).

Steinert, Marlis, *Hitler's War and the Germans: Public Mood and Attitude During the Second World War* (Athens, OH: Ohio University Press, 1984).

Stephenson, David, *1914–1918: The History of the First World War* (London: Allen Lane, 2004).

Stephenson, Jill, 'Women's Labor Service in Nazi Germany', *Central European History* (15) 1982, pp. 241–65.

'War and Society: Germany in World War II', *German History* (3) 1986, pp. 15–23.

Hitler's Home Front, Württemberg under the Nazis (London: Hambledon Continuum, 2006).

'The Volksgemeinschaft and the Problems of Permeability: the Persistence of Traditional Attitudes in Württemberg Villages', *German History* (34) 2016, pp. 49–69.

Stiftung Topographie des Terrors, *Deutschland 1945: Die letzten Kriegsmonate – Germany 1945: The Last Months of the War* (Berlin: Stiftung Topographie des Terrors, 2014).

Stoltzfus Nathan, *Hitler's Compromises: Coercion and Consensus in Nazi Germany* (New Haven, CT: Yale University Press, 2016).

Stone, David (ed.), *The Soviet Union at War, 1941–1945* (Barnsley: Pen & Sword, 2010).

Strachan, Hew, 'Training, Morale and Modern War', *Journal of Contemporary History* (41) 2006, pp. 211–27.

'From Cabinet War to Total War: The Perspective of Military Doctrine, 1861–1918', in Chickering and Förster (eds.), *Great War, Total War*, pp. 19–34.

Streit, Christian, *Keine Kameraden: Die Wehrmacht und die sowjetischen Kriegsgefangenen 1941–1945* (Stuttgart: Deutsche Verlags-Anstalt, 1978).

Strohn, Matthias, *The German Army and the Defence of the Reich: Military Doctrine and the Conduct of the Defensive Battle 1918–1939* (Cambridge: Cambridge University Press, 2011).

Süß, Dietmar, *Tod aus der Luft: Kriegsgesellschaft und Luftkrieg in Deutschland und England* (Bonn: Bundeszentrale für politische Bildung, 2011).

Swett, Pamela, 'Political Violence, Gesinnung, and the Courts in Late Weimar Berlin', in Biess, Roseman, and Schissler (eds.), *Conflict, Catastrophe and Continuity*, pp. 104–16.

Theweleit, Klaus, *Männerphantasien, 1. Band* (Frankfurt a.M.: Verlag Roter Stern, 1979).

Thomas, Nigel, *Hitler's Russian & Cossack Allies 1941–45* (Oxford: Osprey, 2015).

Thorwald, Jürgen, *Es begann an der Weichsel. Flucht und Vertreibung der Deutschen aus dem Osten* (Stuttgart: Steingrüben 1949).

Das Ende an der Elbe. Die letzten Monate des Zweiten Weltkriegs im Osten (Stuttgart: Steingrüben 1950).

Die Ungeklärten Fälle (Stuttgart: Steingrüben, 1950).

Thum, Gregor, 'Megalomania and Angst: the Nineteenth-Century Mythization of Germany's Eastern Borderlands', in Bartov and Weitz (eds.), *Shatterzones of Empire*, pp. 42–60.

Tilitzki, Christian, *Alltag in Ostpreußen 1940–45. Die geheimen Lageberichte der Königsberger Justiz* (Würzburg: Flechsig, 2003).

Tooze, Adam, *The Wages of Destruction: the Making and Breaking of the Nazi Economy* (London: Allen Lane, 2006).

Torrie, Julia, *'For Their Own Good': Civilian Evacuations in Germany and France, 1939–1945* (London: Berghahn Books, 2010).

Tversky, Amos and Daniel Kahneman, 'Judgment under Uncertainty: Heuristics and Biases', Science (185) 1974, pp. 1124–31.

Ueberschär, Gerd (ed.), *Das Nationalkomitee "Freies Deutschland" und der Bund Deutscher Offiziere* (Frankfurt a.M.: Fischer Verlag, 1996).

Vareikis, Vygantas, 'Klaipėda (Memel) in der Nachkriegszeit 1945–1953', *Annaberger Annalen* (3) 1995, pp. 52–66.

Vollnhals, Clemens, 'Disillusionment, Pragmatism, Indifference: German Society after the "Catastrophe"', in Kettenacker and Riotte (eds.), *The Legacies of Two World Wars*, pp. 185–203.

Wachsmann, Nikolaus, *Hitler's Prisons: Legal Terror in Nazi Germany* (London: Yale University Press, 2004).

Wagner Ruth and Hans-Ulrich Stamm, *Die Letzten Stunden daheim: Ostpreussens Schicksal in schwerer Zeit* (Cologne: Staatsund Wirtschaftspolitische Gesellschaft, 1972).

Walzer, Michael, *Just and Unjust Wars: a Moral Argument with Historical Illustrations* (New York: Basic Books, 2000).

Watson, Alexander, *Ring of Steel: Germany and Austria–Hungary at War, 1914–1918* (London: Allen Lane, 2014).

Weber, Max, *The City* (New York: The Free Press, 1966).

The Essential Weber: a Reader, ed. Sam Whimster (London: Routledge, 2004).

Webster, Charles and Noble Frankland, *The Strategic Air Offensive Against Germany 1939–1945, Volume IV: Annexes and Appendices* (London: HMSO, 1961).

Wegner, Bernd, 'Hitler, der Zweite Weltkrieg und die Choreographie des Untergangs', *Geschichte und Gesellschaft* (26) 2000, pp. 493–518.

'Abkehr von Osten? Die "Festung Europa" und das Dilemma des vernetzten Krieges', in Frieser (ed.), *Das Deutsche Reich und der Zweite Weltkrieg 8*, pp. 246–74.

'Die Kriegsführung des "als ob": Deutschlands strategische Lage seit Frühjahr 1944', in Frieser (ed.), *Das Deutsche Reich und der Zweite Weltkrieg 8*, pp. 1165–91.

Wehler, Hans-Ulrich, *Deutsche Gesellschaftsgeschichte: Bd. 4: Vom Beginn des Ersten Weltkrieges bis zur Gründung der beiden deutschen Staaten 1914–1949* (Munich: C. H. Beck, 2003).

Weinberg, Gerhard, 'Adolf Hitler und der NS-Führungsoffizier (NSFO)' *VfZ* (12) 1964, pp. 443–56.

Germany, Hitler, and World War II (Cambridge: Cambridge University Press, 1995).

Welch, David, *Propaganda and the German Cinema 1933–1945* (Oxford: Clarendon Press, 1983).

Welch, Steven, ' 'Harsh but Just'? German Military Justice in the Second World War: a Comparative Study of the Court-Martialling of German and US Deserters', *German History* (17) 1999, pp. 369–99.

Welzer, Harald, *Täter: Wie aus ganz normale Menschen Massenmörder werden* (Frankfurt a.M.: Fischer Verlag, 2005).

Welzer, Harald, Sönke Neitzel, and Christian Gudehus (eds.), *'Der Führer war viel zu human, viel zu gefühlvoll': Der Zweite Weltkrieg aus der Sicht deutscher und italienischer Soldaten* (Frankfurt am Main: Fischer Taschenbuch Verlag, 2011).

Werner, Wolfgang, *'Bleib übrig!': Deutsche Arbeiter in der nationalsozialistischen Kriegswirtschaft* (Düsseldorf: Schwann, 1983).

Wette, Wolfram, *Die Wehrmacht: Feindbilde, Vernichtungskrieg, Legende* (Frankfurt a.M.: S. Fischer Verlag, 2002).

Das letzte Tabu: NS-Militärjustiz und »Kriegsverrat« (Bonn: Bundeszentrale für politische Bildung, 2007).

Wette, Wolfram (ed.), *Der Krieg des kleinen Mannes: Eine Militärgeschichte von unten* (Munich: Piper, 1992).

Wette, Wolfram, Ricarda Bremer, and Detlev Vögel (eds.), *Das letzte halbe Jahr, Stimmungsberichte der Wehrmachtpropaganda 1944/45* (Essen: Klartext Verlag, 2001).

Wettstein, Adrian, *Die Wehrmacht im Stadtkampf 1939–1942* (Paderborn: Ferdinand Schöningh, 2014).

'Urban Warfare Doctrine on the Eastern Front', in Kay, Rutherford, and Stahel (eds.) *Nazi Policy on the Eastern Front*, pp. 45–72.

Whiting, Charles, *Bloody Aachen* (Staplehurst: Spellmount, 2000).

Wildt, Michael, *Hitler's Volksgemeinschaft and the Dynamics of Racial Exclusion. Violence against Jews in Provincial Germany, 1919–1939* (Oxford: Berghahn Books, 2012).

'Volksgemeinschaft: A Modern Perspective on National Socialist Society', in Steber and Gotto (eds.) *Visions of Community in Nazi Germany*, pp. 43–59.

Willems, Bastiaan, 'Defiant Breakwaters or Desperate Blunders? A Revision of the German Late-War Fortress Strategy', *The Journal of Slavic Military Studies* (28) 2015, pp. 353–78.

'Mezhdu souchastnikom i zhertvoy: opyt grazhdanskogo naseleniya pri osade kreposti Konigsberg v 1945 godu' [Between Accomplice and Victim: Civilians During the Siege of Königsberg in 1945], *Vestnik Baltiyskevo Federal'nevo Universiteta im. I. Kanta* (12) 2015, pp. 43–51.

'Krepost' Konigsberg v 1945 godu: garnizon i naseleniye. Otvet na zame-chaniya G.V. Kretinina' [Festung Königsberg in 1945: the Garrison and Its Population. A Reply to G.V. Kretinin's Remarks], *Vestnik Baltiyskevo Federal'nevo Universiteta im. I. Kanta* (12) 2016, pp. 23–31.

'Nachbeben des Totalen Kriegs: Der Rückzug der Wehrmacht durch Ostpreußen und seine Folgen', *VfZ* (66), 2018, pp. 403–33.

Willems, Bastiaan and Joe Schuldt, 'The "European Boundaries" of the East Prussian Expellees in West-Germany, 1948–1955', *Novoe Proshloe/The New Past* (3) 2018, pp. 28–47.

Williamson, Gordon, *German Military Police Units 1939–45* (London: Osprey, 1989).

Wirsching, Andreas, 'Volksgemeinschaft and the Illusion of "Normality" from the 1920s to the 1940s', in Steber and Gotto (eds.), *Visions of Community in Nazi Germany*, pp. 149–56.

Yelton, David, *Hitler's Volkssturm: the Nazi Militia and the Fall of Germany 1944–1945* (Lawrence: University Press of Kansas, 2002).

de Zayas, Alfred-Maurice, *Anmerkungen zur Vertreibung der Deutschen aus dem Osten* (Stuttgart: Verlag W. Kohlhammer, 1986).

'The Wehrmacht Bureau on War Crimes', *The Historical Journal* (34) 1992, pp. 383–99.

Zeidler, Manfred, 'Die Rote Armee auf deutschem Boden', in Müller (ed.), *Das Deutsche Reich und der Zweiten Weltkrieg 10/1*, pp. 681–776.

'Der Zusammenbruch des NS-Staates', in Giordano (ed.), *Kriegsende in Deutschland*, pp. 42–9.

Ziemke, Earl, *Stalingrad to Berlin: the German Defeat in the East* (New York: Dorset Press, 1986).

Zierenberg, Malte, *Berlin's Black Market: 1939–1950* (Basingstoke: Palgrave MacMillan, 2015).

Zimmermann, John, 'Die Eroberung und Besetzung des Deutschen Reiches', in Müller (ed.), *Das Deutsche Reich und der Zweiten Weltkrieg 10/1*, pp. 277–408.

Newspapers Articles (Post-war, Chronological)

Das Ostpreußenblatt

Wegener, Martin, 'Ostern 1945 in Königsberg, Ein Tag trügerischer Ruhe vor der Katastrophe', *Das Ostpreußenblatt*, 5 April 1950.

Unknown, 'Wilhelm Strüvy siebzig Jahre', *Das Ostpreußenblatt*, 10 March 1956.

Dikreiter, Otto, ' Das letzte Kapitel, 10000 Milchkarten für Säuglinge', *Das Ostpreußenblatt*, 22 July 1967.

Lemke, Erwin, 'Die Post kam bis zuletzt: Das Postwesen in Ostpreußen 1945/46', *Das Ostpreußenblatt*, 6 April 1968.

F.G., 'Abschied von General a.D. Lasch', *Das Ostpreußenblatt*, 15 May 1971.

Kerwin, Bruno, 'Dokument der Geschichte, Königsberg im April 1945', *Das Ostpreußenblatt*, 14 July 1979.

Hung, Johannes, 'Die letzten Kriegsmonate in Ostpreußen', *Das Ostpreußenblatt*, 17 January 1987.

Weber, Reinhold, 'Zuerst lagen dort Schwarze Husaren', *Das Ostpreußenblatt*, 20 August 1988.

Tillitzki, Christian, 'Wie ein versunkenes Vineta, Albertina 1944–1945', *Das Ostpreußenblatt*, 25 September 1999.

Geede, Ruth, 'Die Vergangenheit ist noch längst nicht vergangen', *Das Ostpreußenblatt*, 29 January 2000.

Ostpreussen-Warte

Seeling, August, 'Duisburg übernimmt Patenschaft für Königsberg', *Ostpreussen-Warte*, January 1952.

Unknown, 'Kurt Knuth: „Iwan, der Schreckliche"', *Ostpreussen-Warte*, February 1954.

Naujok, Rudolf, 'Das Mädchen von Königsberg', *Ostpreussen-Warte*, June 1958.

Wir Ostpreußen

Bieske, Erich, 'Von 1945 bis 1948 in Königsberg', *Wir Ostpreußen*, 1 August 1949.

Unknown, 'Die Gauleitung erklärte ...', *Wir Ostpreußen*, 15 September 1949.

Websites

Deutsch-Russisches Projekt zur Digitalisierung deutscher Dokumente in Archiven der Russischen Föderation, 'Verschiedene Materialien (Funksprüche, Fernschreiben, Befehle, Anordnungen) über die Kapitulation der Armee 'Ostpreußen' für die Zeit vom 7. bis 11. Mai 1945', http://wwii.germandocsinrussia.org/de/nodes/2390#page/1/mode/grid/zoom/1

Deutsch-Russisches Projekt zur Digitalisierung deutscher Dokumente in Archiven der Russischen Föderation, 'Verbände des AOK Ostpreußen, Stand 7. 5.45', http://wwii.germandocsinrussia.org/de/nodes/2377-akte-241-angaben-des-oberkommandos-der-wehrmacht-ber-bestand-und-st-rke-der-deutsche-truppen#page/1/mode/grid/zoom/1

Deutsch-Russisches Projekt zur Digitalisierung deutscher Dokumente in Archiven der Russischen Föderation, 'Verteidigungstaktik des Gegners – Übersetzungen von deutschen, ungarischen, rumänischen und italienischen Beutedokumenten zu taktischen Fragen', http://wwii.germandocsinrussia.org/de/nodes/1833#page/1/mode/grid/zoom/1.

G. Koyfman, 'Gorelik Moisey Khaimovich', http://iremember.ru/memoirs/partizani/gorelik-moisey-khaimovich/

Jörg Wurdack, 'Propagandatruppen des Heeres', www.lexikon-der-wehrmacht.de/Gliederungen/Propaganda/Propaganda-R.htm

Library of Congress, 'Bildbericht über von den Bolschewisten ermordete und geschandete Deutsche in Metgethen', www.loc.gov/pictures/item/2005675708/

Library of Congress, 'Die NSDAP sichert die Volksgemeinschaft: Volksgenossen braucht Ihr Rat und Hilfe so wendet Euch an die Ortsgruppe',www.loc.gov /pictures/item/2004680176/

Manfred Backhausen, 'Von Düsseldorf über Königsberg und Riga nach Gruiten: Bürgermeister Mathias Nölke (1912 – 1962).' www.mjb-verlag.de/media/5 f98fe0ac2c541beffff800ffffffff1.pdf

Office of the Historian, 'The Chairman of the Council of People's Commissar of the Soviet Union (Stalin) to President Roosevelt', https://history.state.gov/ historicaldocuments/frus1945v03/d538

The Avalon Project – Documents in Law, History and Diplomacy, 'Laws of War: Laws and Customs of War on Land (Hague IV); October 18, 1907', http:// avalon.law.yale.edu/20th_century/hague04.asp

Bastiaan Willems, 'Pamphlet: Volkssturmmänner!', www.bpvwillems.com/docu ments/the-siege-of-festung-koenigsberg/

Index

Printed in the USA
CPSIA information can be obtained
at www.ICGtesting.com
CBHW071747200824
13480CB00005B/227